The Constitution and the New Deal

Also by G. Edward White

The Eastern Establishment and the Western Experience (1968)

The American Judicial Tradition (1976, 2d ed. 1988)

Patterns of American Legal Thought (1978)

Tort Law in America: An Intellectual History (1980)

Earl Warren: A Public Life (1982)

The Marshall Court and Cultural Change (1988, 2d ed. 1991)

Justice Oliver Wendell Holmes: Law and the Inner Self (1993)

Intervention and Detachment: Essays in Legal History and Jurisprudence (1994)

Creating the National Pastime: Baseball Transforms Itself, 1903–1953 (1996)

The Constitution
and the New Deal

G. Edward White

Harvard University Press

Cambridge, Massachusetts, and London, England

Library of Congress Cataloging-in-Publication Data

White, G. Edward
    The Constitution and the New Deal / G. Edward White.
        p. cm.
    Includes bibliographical references and index.
    ISBN 0-674-00341-1 (cloth : alk. paper)
    1. Constitutional history—United States.   2. United States—Economic
policy—1933–1945.   3. New Deal, 1933–1939. I. Title.
    KF4541 .W48 2000
    342.73′029—dc21   00-033545

Second printing, 2001

For Alexandra Valre White

Contents

Preface

I have been indebted in producing this book not only to the kindness of people who have read and commented on earlier drafts but to a number of scholars, whose work is identified in the notes, who have been engaged in revisionist work on topics in late nineteenth- and early twentieth-century American constitutional history.

In acknowledging the contributions of others to this book I want to start with a group of my colleagues at the University of Virginia School of Law, who for several years have had a common interest in undertaking revisionist forays into late nineteenth- and twentieth-century constitutional history. The contributions of Charles W. McCurdy to that enterprise go back to the 1970s, when he began revising conventional wisdom in his studies of the jurisprudential context of Justice Stephen Field's decisions. Barry Cushman, John C. Harrison, and Michael J. Klarman have each been involved in revisionist projects of their own, some of which have had a direct connection to this book. All of those persons have set high standards of scholarly originality and collegiality, and it has been a pleasure to be in their company.

The next group of contributors I want to single out are a group of twentieth-century political historians who read earlier drafts of the book. I expected those individuals to resist my interpretive conclusions, but I felt their reactions might improve the end product. My first expectation was met, and I hope those readers will find some accommodations to their criticisms in this version. It was a pleasure to be able to exchange views with John Morton Blum, one of my mentors in graduate school; David Kennedy, one of my graduate school contemporaries; and Laura Kalman, whose regular comments on my work have always been helpful. If they subsequently regret missing an opportunity to jump on the revisionist bandwagon, I can at least feel that I offered them that chance.

In addition to the above persons I am grateful to Barry Friedman, Alfred S. Konefsky, L. A. Powe, Eric Segall, and William M. Wiecek for their comments on earlier drafts of the book, and to Reuel Schiller for his comments on Chapter 4 and Howard Gillman for his comments on Chapter 7. Thanks also to the two anonymous readers for Harvard University Press, who made helpful suggestions for revision, and to Cathleen Curran, Anna Riggle, Dean Romhilt, and Wendy Wrosch, who provided valuable research assistance. Aïda Donald of Harvard University Press and Richard Audet have been a pleasure to work with in the editorial and production process. Portions of the book were delivered as the 1995 Rosenthal Lectures at Northwestern University Law School and as the 1997 inaugural Jerome B. Hall Lecture at the Hastings College of Law, University of California. Research for the book was supported by the University of Virginia Law Foundation and by the E. James Kelly and Class of 1963 Research Professorships of Law at the University of Virginia School of Law. Thanks to the reference staff at the University of Virginia Law Library, who assiduously unearthed the location of some obscure historical sources.

Portions of chapters in the book were previously published as "The Canonization of Holmes and Brandeis," 70 *New York University Law Review* 576 (1995); "The First Amendment Comes of Age," 95 *Michigan Law Review* 299 (1996); "The American Law Institute and the Triumph of Modernist Jurisprudence," 15 *Law and History Review* 1 (1997); "Revisiting Substantive Due Process and Holmes's *Lochner* Dissent," 63 *Brooklyn Law Review* 87 (1997); "The Constitutional Revolution as a Crisis in Adaptivity," 48 *Hastings Law Journal* 867 (1997); and "The Transformation of the Constitutional Regime of Foreign Relations," 85 *Virginia Law Review* 1 (1999). These articles contain considerably more documentation than the chapters on which they have been based, so specialists might prefer to consult them. Portions of the book were presented in faculty workshops at Brooklyn Law School, the University of Chicago, New York University Law School, Texas Law School, and the University of Virginia School of Law.

This book is dedicated to my elder daughter, Alexandra Valre White, who has always had the special gift of making others feel appreciated. I hope that the dedication will be one of a continuing series of gestures of reciprocal appreciation to Alexandra. I also hope that my younger daughter, Elisabeth McCafferty Davis White, will be able to make the kind of painless transition from college to the working world that she has made from one sport to another. As for Susan Davis White, I hope she stays just as she is.

A final retrospective thanks to Frances McCafferty White. She had the pleasure of knowing that her son had eventually settled down to doing things he found consistently fun and fulfilling and that were neither illegal nor unremunerated. I am hard-pressed to think of a better aspirational example.

The Constitution and the New Deal

Introduction

This book has two related purposes. One is to complicate what I am calling the conventional account of early twentieth-century constitutional history, a collection of narratives about constitutional law and jurisprudence in the first three decades of the twentieth century that invariably culminate in a "constitutional revolution," inspired by the New Deal and precipitated by the Roosevelt administration's 1937 effort to "pack" the Supreme Court.[1] The other is to historicize that account: to show that its durability has been a function of the shared starting premises of its narrators rather than the historical accuracy of its conclusions.

The primary themes of the book evolved in a slow and roundabout fashion. In the mid-1980s I concluded that the role of legal elites in the New Deal was ripe for reexamination, and that two characteristics of elite legal policymakers in the 1930s appeared to have significant cultural ramifications. One was their shared sense of operating in a new world of governance in which they were no longer bound by the policies or theories of their predecessors. They saw themselves as a new generation of "modern" policymakers, engaging in hitherto untried experiments in government—writing laws on a clean slate. I wondered why the generation of New Deal lawyers had approached their policymaking tasks with this distinctive attitude and where the grounds for that attitude had originated.

The other characteristic of legal elites in the New Deal period that I found suggestive was a common tendency, in at least some of their members, to treat their experiences as governmental policymakers in the 1930s as a particularly heady set of adventures in the exercise of power, experiences that gave them a feeling of being an especially fortunate, perhaps gifted, group of persons. This tendency surfaced in two quite different ways in the later careers of New Deal lawyers. Some, such as Thomas Corcoran, Abe Fortas, Alger Hiss, James Landis, and Edward Pritchard, found themselves in legal or ethical

1

difficulties. Their predicaments could fairly be traced to their common belief that either ordinary legal rules did not apply to them, or their great skills as government lawyers and policymakers would enable them to avoid legal or ethical censure. Other New Deal lawyers, such as many of the subjects interviewed by Katie Louchheim in her 1984 collection, *The Making of the New Deal: The Insiders Speak*,[2] emphasized the excitement they had felt as pioneers in modern governance, as participants in the drafting and administration of government programs that were destined to make fundamental changes in the state of American society.

After publishing some essays on New Deal lawyers that began a historical exploration of those tendencies,[3] I put aside that project to write two other books. When I returned to the New Deal period, the context of my inquiry had changed. In the early 1980s developments in American politics, symbolized by the election of Ronald Reagan to the presidency, had suggested that the model of expanding government initiated by the New Deal had passed from unquestioned orthodoxy to a more contested status. By the mid-1990s politicians in the center of both of the major political parties had disassociated themselves from the reflexive invocation of government as a basis for solving social and economic problems. The New Deal model of government had seemingly evolved from instructive example to historical phenomenon.

At the same time I became aware of two scholarly developments in the fields of twentieth-century constitutional law and constitutional history that seemed to bear on my New Deal project. One was that despite the altered memory of the New Deal in the 1990s, a line of commentary on early twentieth-century constitutional law continued to ascribe a particularly significant status to the New Deal period as a moment in which a "constitutional revolution" initiated by the Supreme Court had laid the groundwork for an expansive, regulatory, modern state. Further, this group of commentators conveyed an implicit excitement about the "revolutionary" constitutional character of the New Deal years. Their sense of being energized, even inspired, by an exposure to New Deal constitutional history seemed comparable to the explicit excitement that had been conveyed in the reminiscences of New Deal lawyers.

The other development that I observed was the beginning of a line of scholarship in late nineteenth- and early twentieth-century constitutional history that revised conventional characterizations of some of the dominant doctrinal tendencies of those periods. A common message of the revisionist studies was that mid and late twentieth-century scholars had imposed anachronistic analytical categories on early twentieth-century constitutional opinions and commentary, and their anachronistic readings had served to prevent an adequate understanding of the world of late nineteenth- and early twentieth-century constitutional jurisprudence.

I hypothesized that the anachronistic readings of early twentieth-century constitutional jurisprudence that revisionist scholarship had exposed were related to the sense of excitement late twentieth-century scholars had found in the New Deal as the source of a constitutional revolution. I decided to reassess the meaning of that "revolution" through a series of studies of topics in early twentieth-century constitutional law. I first included the standard areas singled out by commentators: the jurisprudence of due process, Contracts Clause, Commerce Clause, and free speech cases, as well as those raising issues related to the constitutional status of federal administrative agencies. Eventually I added areas that I found to be more closely connected to the relationship of the Constitution to the New Deal than I had first thought, such as the jurisprudence of constitutional foreign affairs cases and the jurisprudential debate over the nature and interpretation of common law sources precipitated by the American Law Institute's 1923 commissioning of "Restatements" of legal subjects.

As this work began to take shape, I realized that although revisionist work had made significant inroads into conventional narratives in some areas, the durability of these conventional approaches, despite their frequently inaccurate and anachronistic portraits of early twentieth-century constitutional history, was extraordinary.[4] It became clear to me that the influence of the conventional approaches came from their interpretive resonance. Their characterizations of early twentieth-century constitutional cases and commentary, however oversimplified or distorted, were still seen as instinctively sound. I concluded that one could not engage in a full-scale reassessment of the relationship of the New Deal to early twentieth-century constitutional law without exploring the meaning of this resonance. At that point my study became an exercise in mid and late twentieth-century historiography as well as in early twentieth-century constitutional history.

The conventional account of early twentieth-century constitutional history begins by identifying the New Deal as the source of a new era of constitutional law and constitutional interpretation, in which the Constitution was adapted to facilitate a new realm of American governance. That realm featured an affirmative role for the states, and especially for the federal government, as regulators of the economy and distributors of economic benefits throughout the population. It also featured a phalanx of federal administrative agencies as mechanisms of affirmative, regulatory government. It posited as well an aggressive, creative role for the executive branch in the formation of foreign policy, with little congressional, Senatorial, or judicial scrutiny of discretionary executive decisions.

Finally, the new realm of American governance anticipated an altered role for judges as constitutional interpreters, one in which judges would assume a scrutiny of the decisions of other branches of government that was, depending on the issues raised in a case, either deferential or aggressive. On the one hand, judges would conclude that the Constitution permitted a great deal of legislative and administrative authority to regulate the economy and redistribute economic benefits, and a great deal of discretionary power in the executive branch to make foreign policy. They would defer to Congress, the states, and the executive when laws or policies affecting those areas were challenged on constitutional grounds. On the other hand, judges would insist that the Constitution required significant judicial scrutiny of laws or policies infringing on certain specified civil rights and liberties, those deemed foundational to a modern democratic society.

In performing those dual functions judges abandoned their traditional posture in constitutional interpretation as guardians and appliers of a realm of prepolitical, essentialist constitutional principles. Instead of serving as general overseers of the constitutional line between permissible public regulations and impermissible encroachments into the private sphere of life, judges separated laws and policies they reviewed on constitutional grounds into two groups, one requiring only a relaxed scrutiny and the other demanding heightened scrutiny. (I will be representing the traditional posture and that which replaced it by the terms *guardian review* and *bifurcated review*.) This general change in judicial attitudes toward constitutional review helped facilitate transformations in specific areas of constitutional law, producing a "constitutional revolution."

None of the conventional account's conclusions withstand close historical analysis. Doctrinal changes in constitutional law did occur over the course of the twentieth century, but their causal relationship to the New Deal was far more complicated, and attenuated, than existing scholarship has suggested. In some areas changes were well under way before the New Deal was launched. In other areas doctrinal developments have been given anachronistic and misleading labels that serve to overemphasize their novelty. In still others the time sequence of change has been framed too narrowly, lending too much causal weight to political events in the late 1930s. Nor did a change in the Supreme Court's constitutional review posture occur as dramatically, or over as short a time span, as the conventional account suggests. The continuing authoritativeness of the conventional account in the face of its deficiencies presents an interesting historiographical problem.

I have concluded that the continued resonance of the conventional account has been intimately related to a general perception of the New Deal as a symbolic historical episode. Commentators have taken the New Deal to have been an inevitable and archetypal response to a crisis of governance in modern America and have invested in that response. From that starting point it has been easy to see changes in constitutional law as satellites of the New

Deal's formative gravitational pull. I have sought to understand why the New Deal as a symbol of twentieth-century governance has had this powerful and distorting historiographical effect.

In the course of probing the New Deal's powerful cultural resonance I have asked two general questions. Why has the immediate social context of the New Deal—as distinguished, say, from that of the 1920s or 1950s—been seen as so fundamental and transformative by twentieth-century constitutional historians? And why has the New Deal's vast, if selective, expansion of the regulatory and redistributive powers of government been taken by those scholars as both historically inevitable and normatively unproblematic? Those questions have invited me to investigate the intellectual process by which twentieth-century Americans have sought to make sense of their immediate past. In that investigation two terms employed by intellectual historians have been useful. The terms are *modernity* and *modernism*.

The fundamental cultural problem for twentieth-century Americans, whether they have been actors in the area of constitutional governance or elsewhere, has been confronting and making sense of modernity. I am using the term modernity, following Dorothy Ross and others, to mean the actual world brought about by a combination of advanced industrial capitalism, increased participatory democracy, the weakening of a hierarchical class-based social order, and the emergence of science as an authoritative method of intellectual inquiry. Modernity, in its American version, was only partially established by the opening of the twentieth century; its full flowering would take place in the next four decades.

The emergence of modernity in the twentieth century contributed to the formation of a distinctive consciousness that has shaped the responses of Americans to their encounters with modern life. This consciousness has manifested itself in an attitude that elevates human agency, as distinguished from potent external forces, to a position of causal primacy in the universe, and thus takes for granted that humans are capable of controlling their environment and shaping their collective destinies. I am calling that consciousness modernist and will occasionally use that term, or the term modernism, to characterize the attitudes of judges, legal scholars, or historians exhibiting it.[5]

My limited definition of modernism and my chronological location of both modernity and a modernist consciousness are at variance with a number of other scholarly formulations[6] and thus require some justification at this point.

This work can be seen as connected to a historiographical tradition, most prominently identified with the work of J. G. A. Pocock and Dorothy Ross, which has emphasized connections between republican theory and distinctively American conceptions of governance and law, but stops short of equating eighteenth-century American republicanism with modernism. It also emphasizes the dominance, in late eighteenth- and nineteenth-century America, of distinctive conceptions of the course of ideas and institutions over time and across space. In this tradition "premodern" and "prehistoricist" conceptions of cultural change and of causal agency so decisively affected the democratization of American constitutional jurisprudence in the nineteenth century as to strip the term "democratization" of much value as a historical construct applied to that time frame.[7]

In this work, which focuses primarily on twentieth-century developments, I stress the delayed impact of both modernity and modernist theories of causal agency in America, at least with respect to the areas of constitutional law and jurisprudence. I have, however, made some modifications that neither Pocock nor Ross might accept. First, I have not employed the labels historicist and prehistoricist to describe the attitudes of constitutional commentators and judges, preferring to proceed on ground more familiar to them, that of theories of constitutional interpretation. For me the label modernist presupposes a historicist theory of change over time, which is itself closely related to a human-centered theory of causal agency. Second, I have pushed the chronological origins of modernism, as an orthodoxy in American constitutional jurisprudence, back further in time than Ross might accept, to the late 1930s and early 1940s. I recognize that both these modifications may be regarded as controversial. Indeed, Pocock and Ross, on discovering my stated affinity with their work, may want to get out of town or start a more exclusive tradition.

The New Deal can be seen as twentieth-century America's first effort in governance where policy responses to cultural tensions accentuated by modernity were unqualifiedly modernist in their assumptions about the power of humans as causal agents. As a cultural symbol, it serves as a testament to the belief that Americans can themselves alter the course of their future by changing the shape of their government and changing the meaning of their Constitution. The New Deal can also be seen as America's first twentieth-century effort to respond definitively to some parallel and long-standing crises in social relations, politics, economics, and intellectual inquiry that stretched from at least the 1880s through the 1930s.

The focus of this book is on constitutional law and jurisprudence, so I will be treating those crises only as backdrops to the issues that are its central concern. But a brief overview of the impact of modernity on America seems warranted at this point. The period between the 1880s and the 1940s witnessed the replacement of one dominant model of social relations, politics, economics, and intellectual inquiry with another. At the outset of that period the dominant model of social relations was class; that of politics republican democracy, by which I mean the theory and practice of popular sovereignty channeled through elite representation; that of economics hierarchical industrial freedom, personified by self-regulating industrial capitalism; and that of intellectual inquiry natural science.[8]

During this period a large influx of European immigrants and the introduction into America of collectivist models of social organization helped initiate a process that would result in the emergence of an alternative model of social relations to that of class. By the 1940s a class-based model of American social relations was being threatened by a model that stressed the importance of group identities and "interests" as the most salient badges of social identity.[9]

In the realm of political theory and practice, the Progressive movement of the early twentieth century can be seen as simultaneously preserving an elite-directed model of political reform and contributing to the broadening of popular participation. By the 1928 election elite reformers had been displaced by nonpartisan "experts," and coalition politics, emphasizing bloc voting by groups with defined interests or identities, was in competition with electioneering managed by traditional elites. Harry S. Truman's defeat of Thomas E. Dewey in 1948 confirmed the reconfiguration of republican democracy along lines emphasizing wider appeals to the diverse groups that composed the American electorate.[10]

Accentuating the early twentieth-century crisis of participatory governance in modern America was the perceived failure of a self-regulating model of the American economy, emphasizing the power and autonomy of elite capitalist enterprises. Late nineteenth-century economists had suggested that modern, self-regulating industrial economies tended to spawn economic interdependence and massive inequalities of wealth; by the early twentieth century experiments with expanded state intervention to regulate the conduct of private economic actors and to redistribute economic benefits had begun to be implemented on a modest scale. Initially these experiments were lightning rods of controversy, but by the early 1930s a self-regulating, hierarchical model of political economy, featuring a modernized version of late nineteenth-century industrial capitalism, seemed on the verge of collapse. The New Deal, in contrast, appeared to be an experiment with comparatively massive federal intervention in the service of a government-managed, welfare-oriented model.[11] Of all the crises of this time period, that in political economy was perceived by contemporaries as the most charged, the most divisive, and the most fundamental. But that crisis was related to the others. Political economy, the theory and practice of republican democracy, and changing models of social relations had become indissolubly linked in the early twentieth century. They were each features of a process of coming to terms with, and making sense of, modernity in America.

By the advent of the 1940s the process of understanding and responding to the challenges of modern life was increasingly filtered through government. Laws and policies began to be predicated on the newer models of social relations, politics, and economics. Politicians cultivated groups identified by their ethnic or racial identity or by their economic interests, rather than by their social class. Regulation of modern industrial capitalism and alternatives to the market distribution of economic benefits were undertaken by governmental institutions. The growth of participatory democracy was furthered by government-sponsored literacy programs, increased public funding for education, and mandatory school attendance legislation.

Each of these developments was accentuated and abetted by the expansion of techniques of higher learning that increasingly associated scientific inquiry with the social rather than the natural sciences. The field of political economy was separated into political science and economics, each employing its specialized techniques of empirical inquiry and analysis. The disciplines of psychology, sociology, and anthropology employed comparable techniques to advance generalizations about the behavior of individuals, groups, or cultures. As twentieth-century government grew, it was increasingly staffed by persons whose training in the social sciences enabled them to be called experts.

In the timing of those parallel crises and in the New Deal's hitherto unprecedented response to them lie important clues to the durability of the conventional account of early twentieth-century American constitutional history. By the close of the Second World War each of those crises could be understood as having been resolved. New models of social relations, republican democracy, political economy, and scientific inquiry appeared to be in place, and expansive government seemed to be a permanent feature of American life. A sociology in which identity and interest replaced class as the salient characteristics of American social relations had become mainstream; a theory and practice of republican democracy with broader and more diverse definitions of popular sovereignty had become entrenched; a welfare state model of political economy had gained legitimacy; and the social sciences had become established, influential fields of learning.

In the last four decades of the twentieth century the provisional responses to the crises of modernity that we have found in place by the 1940s have acquired the status of deeply entrenched features of modern American culture. A common cognitive thread has linked the acceptance of those provisional resolutions. Each of the models of social relations, republican democracy, political economy, and intellectual inquiry that were displaced had given prominence to externalist forces, such as class, the natural laws of political economy, or the inevitable competition among members of the human species for a limited supply of resources, which constrained and sometimes overwhelmed the capacity of humans to shape the course of their experience. Each of the models that displaced them was erected on the premise that humans could understand and master their environment, in the process breaking the constraints of class, relaxing the grip of natural laws, and adjusting their forms of government to fit the changing conditions of modern life. In short, the apparent entrenchment of the new models, in the decades after the Second World War, has seemed to confirm the capacity of humans to control their destinies in the face of modernity.

Since the New Deal was the period in which provisional resolutions of modernity's parallel crises had first been attempted, and in which government had first been employed on a massive scale to facilitate those resolutions, the apparent entrenchment of the models after 1945 has had another effect. It has served to identify the New Deal as the formative period of modernist governance in America, as a period whose special cultural significance was not unlike that encompassing the Declaration of Independence, the Revolutionary War, and the framing of the Constitution. For Americans to invest in New Deal governance over the succeeding decades has meant confirming the capacity of humans to master, through creative uses of government, the problems of modernity. To be characterized as a twentieth-century historical actor who resisted New Deal resolutions, and the governmental institutions that helped facilitate them, is to be identified as trapped in an older age that subscribed to more limited views of human potential.

This tacit identification of the New Deal as the formative period of modernist governance, with all the above implications, can be regarded as the deepest source of both the durability and the distorted quality of the conventional account of early twentieth-century constitutional history. At the levels of historical narrative and causal explanation, the special role assigned to the New Deal by modernist commentators has encouraged them to make it the epicenter of early twentieth-century constitutional change, resulting in the telescoping and distorting of developments in some doctrinal areas and the ignoring of developments in others. And at the level of historiographic empathy, the identification of the New Deal as the primary force producing a "revolution" in twentieth-century constitutional jurisprudence has seemed indubitably sound to modernist readers.

I will be seeking to dislodge the conventional account from this position of indubitable soundness. I will be employing three strategies in that effort, which are reflected in the separate parts of the book.

Part One investigates a series of doctrinal decisions and accompanying commentary that cannot be made to bear a meaningful causal connection to the events conventionally identified as forging a constitutional revolution, such as the 1936 presidential election or the introduction of the Court-packing plan in February 1937.

Part Two takes up areas of constitutional law at the very center of the conventional account—lines of cases in the realm of political economy from the 1920s through the early 1940s—in order to advance an alternative explanation for "revolutionary" changes in the Supreme Court's interpretation of constitutional provisions affecting the economy in that period. That explanation associates those changes with a jurisprudential crisis regarding the nature and meaning of authoritative sources of law, including interpretations of the Constitution by judges. The crisis was eventually resolved through the formulation and implementation of modernist theories of the Constitution's capacity to adapt to change and the judiciary's capacity to create new meanings for constitutional provisions. Those theories of constitutional adaptivity permitted "revolutionary" judge-created changes in constitutional law.

With this explanation in place, and some inadequacies in the conventional account exposed, Part Three provides case studies of the conventional account's formation, emphasizing the way in which generations of mid and late twentieth-century commentators have contributed to the creation of triumphalist narratives of early twentieth-century constitutional history. In those narratives the constitutional supporters of the New Deal are vindicated, and the obsolescent approaches of its constitutional opponents revealed, in the service of modernist theories of governance and modernist conceptions of judicial behavior.

Cumulatively, the strategies are designed to detach our understanding of early twentieth-century American constitutional history from the special concerns of commentators who have invested in the New Deal as a symbolic historical episode, and ultimately to gain a fuller picture of the world of constitutional law jurisprudence that has been obscured by their collective investment.

I

Complicating the Conventional Account

This part initiates a critique of the conventional account of early twentieth-century constitutional history. Chapter 1 sets forth that account, as it has evolved in successive versions from the 1930s to the present, sketching its core thesis—the precipitation of a "constitutional revolution" by the "Court-packing crisis" of 1937—and emphasizing its starting assumptions about the nature of constitutional decisionmaking by judges and the role of the New Deal as a symbolic episode in twentieth-century American governance.

The next four chapters take up areas of early twentieth-century constitutional jurisprudence that have received comparatively little attention in the conventional narrative's coverage or that have been overshadowed by the narrative's central themes.

In most versions of the conventional account changes in the early twentieth-century constitutional law of foreign affairs are not even mentioned, but that area witnessed one of the most radical jurisprudential transformations of the early twentieth century, some of which took place before the New Deal came into existence, and almost all of which had been anticipated before the Court-packing crisis surfaced.

In many versions of the account the growth of federal administrative agencies and the emergence of administrative law as an academic subject and field of legal practice are identified as among the side effects of the New Deal, and the eventual acceptance of federal agencies as constitutionally legitimate forms of government is loosely associated with the constitutional revolution. But descriptions of agency growth have, on the whole, not paid close attention to the constitutional dimensions of the agency form of government as it evolved, and such a focus reveals that the establishment of agencies as governmental units only produced an incremental modification of orthodox separation of powers jurisprudence. Administrative law remained a subject with an important constitutional component, and that component incorporated traditional constitutional objections to agency government as well as extra-constitutional arguments on behalf of agency autonomy.

The emergence of enhanced constitutional protection for free speech has been widely described as a central theme of early twentieth-century constitutional law and has commonly been associated with the constitutional revolution. But that association has been at a very high level of generality, and closer analysis suggests that causal connections between the appearance of the New Deal, or the Court-packing crisis, and increased judicial solicitude for speech claims are difficult to establish.

I have chosen to begin my effort to complicate the conventional story of constitutional change in early twentieth-century America with these areas, all of which may be said to lie somewhere on the periphery of the conventional narrative's focus, before addressing the changes that have traditionally been at the center of the conventional narrative. I have started on the periphery because the conventional account, in its most ambitious versions, has tended to posit a constitutional revolution that swept through all areas of constitutional law in the wake of the New Deal and the Court-packing crisis. By demonstrating that early twentieth-century changes in three areas of constitutional law either bore almost no connection to the New Deal or the Court-packing crisis, or were far more gradualist than revolutionary in character, I hope to engender an attitude of skepticism toward the conventional account's treatment of its central areas of concern.

The Conventional Account

For the last sixty years a particular account of the history of early twentieth-century constitutional jurisprudence has been accepted as conventional wisdom. My purpose in this chapter is to sketch that account in its evolving versions and to begin to suggest why it has continued to be accepted despite its descriptive and analytical difficulties. There have been three versions of the account in the years of its dominance, which I am calling the original, mainstream, and reconstructed versions. The versions differ in their chronological time frames and their methodological emphases, but they nonetheless exhibit striking descriptive and normative similarities. Those similarities have fostered an appearance of continuity, so that the versions have tended to blend into one another, reinforcing the authoritativeness of the account.

At the core of the conventional narrative is a group of events, taking place within a relatively short time span, which have been invested with causal prominence and whose ramifications have been assumed to extend backward and forward over a considerable range of time. The events, taken in chronological succession, begin with the election of 1932, in which the Democratic Party, representing a more diverse configuration of voters than those that had provided it with election victories in 1912 and 1916, assumed control of the presidency and both houses of Congress. Next come the experiments with nationally directed economic regulation, personified by federal agencies such as the National Recovery Administration and the Agricultural Adjustment Administration, in the first years of the Roosevelt administration. These developments are followed by the Supreme Court's initial response in its 1934 and 1935 Terms to those experiments and to additional federal and state legislation attempting to regulate various industries, the cumulative effect of which was to invalidate most of the legislation on constitutional grounds.[1]

At this point the narrative's central theme—that of a confrontation between the governmental experiments of the New Deal and the Supreme

Court's response to those experiments—is in place. The remaining events of the narrative amplify that theme. Next is the presidential election of 1936, in which Roosevelt wins an overwhelming popular mandate. Next is the introduction, in February 1937, of a proposal by the Roosevelt administration to expand the composition of the Supreme Court to as many as twelve justices should sitting justices remain on the Court after the age of seventy. Although the "Court-packing" plan was immediately unpopular with the public and was eventually buried in the Senate Judiciary Committee, it is treated in the narrative, along with the election of 1936, as chastening the Court and facilitating its accommodation to New Deal legislation. That accommodation, featuring cases decided between 1937 and 1942,[2] completes the core of the narrative.

The narrative thus features apparently dramatic constitutional change occurring in a short time frame, in which the popularity of New Deal legislative programs was confirmed by an electoral mandate, and in which a recalcitrant Supreme Court was directly threatened by a proposal to change its composition. The obvious inference is that the Court's validation, after 1937, of many New Deal legislative programs it had previously declared unconstitutional was a pragmatic, self-preservationist response to the Roosevelt administration's 1936 electoral mandate and to the Court-packing plan itself. A great many works on early twentieth-century constitutional history, stretching from 1938 to the mid-1990s, have drawn that inference.

The ramifications of the conventional account's core narrative extend beyond its description and explanation of a series of changes in constitutional jurisprudence in the 1930s. They have served to identify the New Deal period as the locus of a "constitutional revolution" that ushered in a different role for the Supreme Court in modern American society. The association of the New Deal with this constitutional revolution has had three significant historiographical consequences. First, it has identified a series of constitutional phenomena loosely identified with that revolution—expanded power in Congress, the executive, and the states to regulate the economy, the emergence of federal administrative agencies as agents in the regulatory process, increased protection for free speech and other designated civil rights and liberties, the hegemony of the federal government, and especially the federal executive, in foreign affairs, and the replacement of the judicial stance of guardian review with that of bifurcated review in constitutional interpretation—as orthodox characteristics of the modern twentieth-century constitutional order. The New Deal is seen as the period in which that order first took shape.

Second, constitutional issues that surfaced in the first three decades of the twentieth century are seen from the perspective of their purported resolution in the New Deal constitutional revolution. This has had the effect of making some positions taken on those issues appear to be jurisprudentially "obsoles-cent" or "reactionary," and other positions appear "modern" or "progres-sive," and to have resulted in comparable labels for the judges or commenta-tors who advanced the positions.

Third, the altered conception of the role of the Supreme Court justice that accompanied the shift from guardian to bifurcated review has been taken to be grounded on an accurate description of the nature of constitutional inter-pretation by Supreme Court justices. Justices are seen not as apolitical savants discerning the essentialist principles of the Constitution but as political actors with their own ideological agendas, distinguished from other governmental officials primarily by their lack of electoral accountability. As political actors they, and their decisions, are capable of being given conventional ideological labels, such as "liberal" or "conservative," and their performances are capable of being evaluated from an ideological perspective. This legacy of the New Deal constitutional revolution has had the effect of transforming early twen-tieth-century developments in constitutional jurisprudence, not only during the conventional time frame of that revolution but during decades preceding it, into episodes in political history.

I will be suggesting throughout this book that all of the historiographic consequences that have followed from the conventional association of the New Deal with a constitutional revolution serve to reinforce the symbolic status of the New Deal as the formative era of modernist-inspired governance in America. The changes in constitutional jurisprudence identified with the New Deal can each be seen as doctrinal developments logically entailed by the recognition that the American constitutional order was a creation of the policy judgments of human constitutional interpreters rather than the re-flection of essentialist external forces governing the universe. The projection of evaluative labels developed from the 1930s onto constitutional debates that occurred prior to that decade amounted to a tacit judgment that those who failed to grasp the implications of that recognition could have their posi-tions dismissed as outmoded or reactionary. And the emergence of a new stance for Supreme Court justices as constitutional interpreters itself followed from the modernist insights that humans had the power to use government to control their destinies, but that in a democratic society the wielding of such power by unelected judges who held their positions for life needed to be curtailed.

In the evolution of the conventional account its central historiographic consequences have been expressed in discernibly different modes, enabling the works that have associated the New Deal with a constitutional revolution to be grouped into three different stages. In the first stage, the account's original version, the consequences are expressed as historical arguments, often in polemical form, that seek to displace previous orthodoxies about the role of Supreme Court justices, the Court's relationship to politics, and the nature of constitutional change. In the second, or mainstream version of the narrative, those historical arguments are themselves treated as orthodoxy, and contributors to the account implicitly define their task as adding details to an interpretation of constitutional change already in place. In the third stage, those subscribing to the conventional association of the New Deal with a constitutional revolution recognize that association to be vulnerable in places, especially in the breadth of its causal claims, but continue to find congenial the conventional account's starting assumptions about constitutional interpretation, the relationship of judging to politics, and the nature of constitutional change. Accordingly, they undertake to produce a reconstructed version of the narrative.

I now turn to the versions of the account themselves. Version One, the original version, emerged from contemporaneous commentary on a cluster of constitutional issues that came to be perceived as especially pressing and contentious in the mid-1930s and early 1940s. Some commentators began to suggest that the Court's jurisprudence had significantly changed with respect to some of those issues and to identify the changes with external political events associated with the New Deal. I have previously identified the principal contested issues, each of which is taken up in detail in this study: judicial invalidation of regulatory and redistributive legislation on constitutional grounds; congressional and judicial resistance to federal administrative agencies; legislative and judicial opposition to extensive executive discretion in the conduct of foreign policy; legislative efforts to restrict speech; and the appropriate stance of judges seeking to interpret the meaning of constitutional provisions in the context of changing external conditions.

In the late 1930s a series of works attempted to intervene in the most visible constitutional debates of that time by suggesting that the debates represented a potentially historic watershed in American constitutional jurisprudence. That suggestion followed from a characterization of the Supreme Court's orthodox interpretations of the Constitution's arrangement of governmental powers as being incompatible with the New Deal's proposed agenda of governance. As this theme of incompatibility between a majority of the Court's understanding of the Constitution and New Deal legislation was played out in the years between the mid-1930s and the early 1940s, it appeared, to this set of commentators, that the Court was altering the cast of its constitutional jurisprudence to validate New Deal programs. The collective decisions in which alterations could be identified amounted to a "constitutional revolution."

Having identified this "revolution," the commentators set out to explain it. Their explanation emphasized sudden alterations in the Court's stance between the mid-1930s and the early 1940s; the impressive popular mandate of the Roosevelt administrations in that period; and the role of the Court-packing plan as both a confirmation of the "old," obsolescent constitutional jurisprudence of the Court that had resisted the New Deal and the acquiescence of Supreme Court justices to popular pressures. There were several lessons about constitutional law, judicial decisionmaking, and the relationship of the Court to external political events to be drawn from that explanation. The works of these commentators can be seen as sharing an implicit common agenda, that of the creation of a historical pedigree for a set of modernist-inspired jurisprudential goals in the realm of constitutional law. In the course of that pedigree's being fashioned, the conventional narrative of early American constitutional history was launched.

Any list of the works that first sought to reorient early twentieth-century constitutional history around the emergence of the New Deal, the Supreme Court's initial resistance to and then eventual accommodation of New Deal legislation (the "constitutional revolution"), and the significant role of the Court-packing plan in that process would need to start with Edward Corwin's contemporary accounts of constitutional jurisprudence in the "watershed" years: *The Twilight of the Supreme Court* (1934), *Commerce Power versus States Rights* (1936), *Court over Constitution* (1938), and *Constitutional Revolution, Ltd.* (1942). In these sequential works the powers of one of the ablest American scholars of the twentieth century, himself a strong New Deal partisan, were enlisted in the formation of the main themes of the conventional narrative. Corwin, who played a role in the formation of the Court-packing plan itself[3] and who is generally thought to have coined the phrase encapsulating the Court's accommodation to political pressures from the Roosevelt administration, "the switch in time that saved nine,"[4] clearly had a personal investment in the normative lessons of his narrative. But other works appearing in the same time frame raised themes similar to Corwin's.

Drew Pearson and Robert S. Allen's *The Nine Old Men* (1936) and Joseph Alsop and Turner Catledge's *The 168 Days* (1938) emphasized the incompatibility of orthodox early twentieth-century constitutional jurisprudence with the experiments in expanded regulatory government associated with the New Deal. So did Robert H. Jackson's *The Struggle for Judicial Supremacy* (1941), Benjamin F. Wright's *The Growth of American Constitutional Law* (1942), and Carl B. Swisher's *American Constitutional Development* (1943). In Alsop and Catledge's discussions of changes in the Court's constitutional jurisprudence, and that of Wright, changes were directly traced to the appearance of the Court-packing plan.[5] In Corwin's *Court over Constitution* and *Constitutional Revolution, Ltd.* the plan was seen as a substantial factor precipitating change.[6] All the above sources approached debates about issues in constitutional jurisprudence as if they were debates about contemporary politics.

It is important to grasp the dual character of the original versions of the conventional narrative. They served both as fashioners of the skeleton of a general account of early twentieth-century constitutional change and vivid, polemical examples of a modernist critique of orthodox attitudes about constitutional law and judging. Their conceptualizations of constitutional issues in political terms, and their portraits of Court majorities resisting or supporting New Deal legislation as political blocs, were devices through which they communicated a view of constitutional decisionmaking by judges as another exercise in policymaking by humans occupying positions of governmental power. They took this view to be unorthodox, even heretical, and thus they emphasized the apparent suddenness of the Court's accommodation to New Deal policies after the introduction of the Court-packing plan as strong evidence that judges were influenced by external political pressures.

By the early 1960s the dual character of the original narratives had largely been lost as the polemical goals of the first wave of narrators had been achieved. Changes in constitutional jurisprudence were widely assumed to be responses to external political events; the approaches of judges to questions of constitutional law were widely regarded as affected by political ideology. Explanations of constitutional decisions were sought in their political context and in the orientation of the judges who decided them. As the normative lessons of the original versions of the conventional account came to be internalized, the account assumed authoritative status. The Court-packing plan and its relationship to the constitutional revolution were located at the very center of a dominant narrative of early twentieth-century constitutional history. Both were symbols of the essentially ideological nature of Supreme Court judging and the inevitable effect on the Court of external political developments.

As mainstream versions of the conventional narrative appeared, a tendency to broaden the scope of the "constitutional revolution" surfaced. Some works continued to emphasize the core cases of the "revolution," those involving legislative and administrative regulation of sectors of the economy. Corwin's second edition of *Court over Constitution* (1950) was an example. But others identified the watershed of the late 1930s as having additional ramifications for twentieth-century constitutional jurisprudence. In Robert McCloskey's *The American Supreme Court* (1960) the Court's eventual capitulation to New Deal political ideology was described as fostering a nascent awareness of the importance of free speech and other civil rights. In Louis Henkin's articles in the 1950s the successive diminution of constitutional checks on the growth of federal power in foreign affairs was emphasized.[7] Meanwhile, Kenneth Culp Davis's *Administrative Law* (1958) deemphasized the controversiality of federal administrative agencies and treated their discretionary autonomy as one of the legacies of the New Deal.

Mainstream versions of the conventional account featured, above all, two themes. One was the tacit or explicit elevation of the Court-packing tale, with its culmination in a constitutional revolution, to historical truth. The other was the ascription of stereotyped political labels to early twentieth-century Supreme Court justices, including those who had resisted the New Deal and those whose jurisprudential views were thought consistent with the eventual changes associated with broadened definitions of the constitutional revolution, even though in some cases they had not even been on the Court during the New Deal period.[8] Justices Oliver Wendell Holmes and Louis Brandeis, consistently labeled "progressive" or "liberal" judges, were examples of the latter category: Brandeis had voted to invalidate several New Deal statutes, and Holmes had left the Court in the early months of 1932. Justices Willis Van Devanter, James McReynolds, George Sutherland, and Pierce Butler, consistently described as judicial "conservatives" or "reactionaries" and ultimately grouped as "The Four Horsemen," were examples of the former.

Studies such as Alpheus Thomas Mason, *Harlan Fiske Stone: Pillar of the Law* (1956), Bernard Schwartz, *The Supreme Court: Constitutional Revolution in Retrospect* (1957), and Mario Einaudi, *The Roosevelt Revolution* (1959) introduced the Court-packing tale and attendant "revolution" to a variety of audiences, including political scientists, lawyers, and historians. In each of these works conventional descriptions of Holmes, Brandeis, and the "Four Horsemen" appeared, the label "Four Horsemen" first being applied to the four "reactionary" justices in Fred Rodell's *Nine Men* (1955), which argued that because Supreme Court justices were "powerful, irresponsible, and human," constitutional law amounted to their ideological whims. Rodell's book may not have been regarded as a serious scholarly effort—he identified his fourteen-year-old son as his research assistant—but its underlying messages about the human and political dimensions of judging had become entrenched.

By the appearance of William Leuchtenburg's *Franklin D. Roosevelt and the New Deal* (1963), early twentieth-century developments in constitutional jurisprudence had come to be seen as episodes in political history. The Court-packing tale figured prominently in Leuchtenburg's narrative, signifying his tendency to subsume legal events to political themes. The obvious inferences to be drawn from Leuchtenburg's synthesis were that Supreme Court justices were a species of political actors, constitutional jurisprudence evolved in response to political events, and attitudes toward constitutional interpretation could be represented by conventional political labels. Between 1963 and the 1980s the central illustrative episodes of the conventional account, with their apparent historiographic and normative lessons, became even more entrenched, finding their way into law school and undergraduate constitutional law casebooks and textbooks. Meanwhile, additional monographic studies added details to the account and reinforced its conclusions.

Richard Cortner's *The Wagner Act Cases* (1964) and *The Jones & Laughlin Case* (1970) portrayed the Court's labor relations decisions as accommodations to the changing social realities of industrial labor in modern America. Alpheus Mason popularized the Court-packing and constitutional revolution tales, as well as the labeling of justices, in two general political science texts, *The Supreme Court: Palladium of Freedom* (1963) and *The Supreme Court in a Free Society* (1968). Walter Murphy emphasized the role of the Supreme Court as an ongoing political presence in the American system of government in *Congress and the Court* (1962). Paul Murphy's *The Constitution in Crisis Times, 1918–1969* (1972) brought the conventional narrative to the attention of American historians and their students. Leo Pfeffer's *This Honorable Court* (1965) signaled that the Court-packing/constitutional revolution episode was now taken to be the center of any popularized description of early twentieth-century constitutional history. William Swindler's two-volume history of constitutional law in the twentieth century was organized around the concepts of "old" and "new" legal orders, with the dividing line coming in 1932.[9] And in the midst of these efforts Leuchtenburg began his long-term, detailed account of the Court-packing plan and the constitutional revolution, publishing an offshoot of that project as a 1995 collection of essays, *The Supreme Court Reborn*.[10]

The extent of Leuchtenburg's commitment to the production of a definitive account of the Court-packing tale, a commitment that has stretched from the 1960s through the 1990s, itself testifies to the durability of the once polemical account of changes in early twentieth-century constitutional jurisprudence fashioned by Corwin and his contemporaries. One of the standard arguments on behalf of the conventional account's durability, advanced by Leuchtenburg himself, is that its emphasis on the centrality of the New Deal and the Court-packing episode in facilitating an early twentieth-century "constitutional revolution" is obviously and necessarily correct.[11]

Nonetheless, since the late 1980s, signs that the mainstream version of the conventional account might need some buttressing and reconfiguring have appeared. One set of signs appeared in the literature of constitutional history itself. In that genre some earlier work, notably that of Michael Parrish, had begun to exhibit a certain distance from the conventional account. In "The Hughes Court, the Great Depression, and the Historians" (1978)[12] and "The Great Depression, the New Deal, and the American Legal Order" (1984),[13] Parrish showed an awareness of the unreflective investment by subsequent historians in the Roosevelt administrations's policy goals. But at the same time Parrish's work, despite its sophistication, employed the categories, and rested on the same selective database, as the conventional account.

Meanwhile, a series of articles in the 1970s and 1980s that reconfigured the starting analytical premises of late nineteenth-century constitutional jurisprudence began to suggest that the conventional account's characterizations of early twentieth-century constitutional orthodoxy might be oversimple. Essays by Charles McCurdy, such as "Justice Field and the Jurisprudence of Government-Business Relations: Some Parameters of Laissez-Faire Constitutionalism, 1863–1897" (1975),[14] "The *Knight* Sugar Decision of 1895 and the Modernization of American Corporation Law, 1869–1903" (1979),[15] and "The Roots of 'Liberty of Contract' Reconsidered: Major Premises in the Law of Employment" (1984),[16] were particularly important. McCurdy's abandonment of the conventional categories of political history in his characterizations of nineteenth-century constitutional jurisprudence was followed by Michael Les Benedict in "Laissez- Faire and Liberty: A Re-Evaluation of the Meaning and Origins of Laissez-Faire Constitutionalism" (1985)[17] and William Forbath in "The Ambiguities of Free Labor: Labor and Law in the Gilded Age" (1985).[18] Meanwhile, Melvin Urofsky's "Myth and Reality: The Supreme Court and Protective Legislation in the Progressive Era" (1983)[19] showed an awareness of the relevance of McCurdy's reconfigurations for early twentieth-century constitutional jurisprudence. Although the principal impact of this literature was to abandon the usefulness of the politically derived category of "laissez-faire constitutionalism" as a meaningful description of orthodox late nineteenth-century jurisprudence, by the 1990s studies such as Howard Gillman's *The Constitution Besieged* (1991), Morton Horwitz's *The Transformation of American Law 1870–1960* (1992), and Owen Fiss's *Troubled Beginnings of the Modern State, 1888–1910* (1993) recognized that orthodox late nineteenth-century police power categories were still controlling the analysis of constitutional cases in the realm of political economy for the first three decades of the twentieth century.

In the same time period Barry Cushman and Richard Friedman began their reexaminations of constitutional jurisprudence between the two World

Wars, attempting to view constitutional decisions as exercises in extending or modifying currently authoritative doctrinal propositions rather than through the established political categories of the conventional account. By adopting this approach Cushman, whose earlier articles culminated in *Rethinking the New Deal Court* (1998), and Friedman, whose initial assessment of constitutional developments in the 1930s appeared in a 1994 article, "Switching Time and Other Thought Experiments: The Hughes Court and Constitutional Transformation,"[20] found that causal connections between the introduction of the Court-packing plan and a dramatic shift in the Court's constitutional jurisprudence were attenuated, and that constitutional change over the first three decades of the twentieth century had been imperfectly described by the conventional account.

The other set of signals that the mainstream version of the conventional account was losing its resonance could be found in the tendency of a new generation of twentieth-century political historians to regard its preoccupation with "the voices of peak political actors," such as presidents, their advisers, members of Congress, or justices of the Supreme Court, as producing a historical narrative resting on a limited, and not particularly fruitful, database. In a recent survey of political histories of the New Deal period that appeared in the 1970s, '80s, and '90s, Colin Gordon finds general agreement that the conventional account, in its mainstream versions, served to "condense . . . a lengthy, and in many respects quite limited, pattern of legal and political changes into a brief and shining moment bounded by the Court's challenge to the New Deal in 1935 and its capitulation two years later." Although the tale of the Court-packing plan and the subsequent constitutional revolution is "a good story," Gordon suggests, "[i]t ignores patterns of economic power and influence, . . . misses much of the politics of social protest, . . . is largely indifferent to the oft-noted constraints of American party politics, and views elections as genuinely historical moments in which voters are able to make substantive and programmatic choices."[21] For most contemporary political historians, Gordon suggests, the New Deal was a much more complicated, and broad-gauged, historical episode than the emphasis of the conventional mainstream account might suggest.

This evidence that revisionist work in constitutional jurisprudence and the disaffection of current political historians with mainstream versions of the conventional account were beginning to threaten the account's central tale of constitutional change and to reduce the apparent usefulness of its descriptive categories has prompted some defensive reactions from mainstream proponents of that account.[22] It also contributed, however, to the appearance of a reconstructed version of the conventional narrative, in which the signposts of "New Deal" constitutional jurisprudence have been recast in 1990s terms.

The context in which this reconstructed version has appeared is dramatically different from those in which the first two versions of the conventional account were produced. In the late 1970s the momentum of governmental policies modeled on New Deal experiments with expansive regulatory and redistributive government began to slow. A recoil on the part of the American electorate from reflexive support for extensions of the regulatory and bureaucratic authority of the federal government resulted in Jimmy Carter's "outsider" status being an asset rather than a liability in the 1976 election, and helped catapult Ronald Reagan to a two-term presidency four years later. During the Reagan administrations a theory of constitutional interpretation, known as "originalism," was revived, in which adherence to the "original intent" of the Constitution's framers was posited as the touchstone for constitutional analysis. Although the 1980s versions of originalism tended to be oversimplified and anachronistic,[23] originalist analysis revealed the stark gap between the arrangement of constitutional powers fashioned by decisions of the Supreme Court in the late 1930s and 1940s and the arrangement contemplated by the framers of the Constitution. Its thrust was to identify the New Deal model of governance, and the Court's accommodations to that model, as unusual and controversial departures from traditional understandings rather than natural responses to the onset of modernity.

At the same time the normative implications of the conventional account, stressing the role of the New Deal and the constitutional revolution as formative episodes in the triumph of a modernist-inspired approach to governance in twentieth-century America, remained a source of inspiration to many members of the academic community in the 1990s. The conventional narrative's portrayal of the inevitable triumph of a constitutional jurisprudence sympathetic to governmental regulation, and at the same time protective of certain civil rights and liberties, remained a beacon to those who felt that 1980s versions of originalism were being enlisted as part of a campaign to undermine that triumph. But the revisionist scholarship of the early 1990s suggested that, at best, the conventional account needed some updating. The originalist challenge suggested that the historical authority of the New Deal might be tarnished. And the increasing inability of the central tale of the conventional account to excite new generations of twentieth-century political historians threatened to call into question that account's implicit claim that the heart of the New Deal's legacy lay in its formation of a new constitutional order. To those who continued to see the New Deal as the formative episode of modernist governance in America, some refurbishing of the account seemed necessary.

In response to this implicit challenge three prominent scholars, Cass Sunstein, Bruce Ackerman, and Laura Kalman, have attempted to fashion versions of a reconstructed conventional narrative. Despite the quite different approaches to their historical materials employed by these scholars, their projects can be said to share a common grounding. Each, in the course of a reconfiguration of the symbolic meaning of New Deal constitutional jurisprudence, seeks to retain the analytical categories and to reemphasize the normative implications of the conventional account. Each continues to characterize changes in constitutional jurisprudence in the terms and labels of political history. By doing so each, implicitly or explicitly, accepts the conventional account's modernist conception of Supreme Court constitutional law decisions as responses to external political events made by human participants in the arena of national politics.

The technique employed by Sunstein has been a sophisticated form of history as special pleading, in which historical data are selectively employed for the purposes of supporting contemporary legal arguments. Sunstein's forays into early twentieth-century constitutional jurisprudence start from the premise that the primary consequences of one of the defining characteristics of that jurisprudence, the shift from guardian to bifurcated review, are desirable. He then seeks to reframe the meaning of early twentieth-century constitutional decisions supporting deferential review in the realm of political economy and aggressive review in certain civil rights and liberties cases. In the process Sunstein discards some of the oversimple characterizations of those decisions common to the original and mainstream versions of the conventional account but at the same time introduces his own anachronistic characterizations.

The first set of cases that has occupied Sunstein's attention consists of those in which "laissez-faire" constitutional jurisprudence was criticized and eventually abandoned in a line of due process decisions. The decisions stretched from *Lochner v. New York* (1905)[24] to the Court's purportedly dramatic shift from *Morehead v. New York ex rel. Tipaldo* (1936),[25] reaffirming *Lochner*, to *West Coast Hotel v. Parrish* (1937),[26] abandoning guardian review of wages and hours legislation under the Due Process Clauses. In a series of articles in the 1980s Sunstein discarded the original and mainstream accounts' portrayal of *Lochner* as a paean to "laissez-faire," suggesting that the controversy between supporters and opponents of *Lochner* was one about the appropriate baselines to be employed in cases involving the redistribution of benefits from one class to another. This strategy, pursued by Sunstein in "Naked Preferences and the Constitution" (1984)[27] and "Interest Groups in American Public Law" (1985),[28] accepted the recharacterization of early twentieth-century constitutional political economy decisions posited by revisionists, but at the same time employed the terms of late twentieth-century public choice theory to revitalize the critique of *Lochner*. In 1987 Sunstein made the normative implications of his "baseline" analysis of the *Lochner* line of cases explicit in "*Lochner*'s Legacy."[29]

Having restated and endorsed the rationale for the deferential prong of bifurcated review, Sunstein next sought to reframe the aggressive prong by underscoring what he took to be the primary basis of heightened scrutiny of legislation restricting speech. Whereas Sunstein's agenda in offering a reconstructed version of the critique of *Lochner* was to safeguard it against efforts to revive aggressive review of regulatory or redistributive legislation affecting economic "liberties,"[30] his goal in reframing New Deal speech cases was to prevent heightened scrutiny being extended to legislation restricting forms of expression he judged to be particularly undeserving of protection, such as pornography or hate speech. His technique was to suggest, in "Free Speech Now"[31] and *Democracy and the Problem of Free Speech* (1993), that the governing theory of early twentieth-century decisions extending constitutional protection for speech was the furtherment of the American ideal of "deliberative democracy," and that therefore there was little historical support for the protection of speech unrelated to the processes of democratic government. Sunstein's "New Deal" for free speech was actually an effort to restore what he presented as mainstream free speech jurisprudence in the late 1930s and forties. Thus although Sunstein's constitutional law casebook continues to describe early American constitutional history in the terms of the conventional narrative,[32] he has made a sustained effort to refashion that narrative so as to make it appear directly relevant to contemporary legal issues.

Sunstein's reconstructed version of the conventional account has had comparatively little detailed historical grounding. Although recognizing that history, in the form of foundational constitutional commitments, must play a role in efforts to apply the Constitution to contemporary legal disputes, Sunstein has also frankly described his version of historical research as predicated on searches for "a useable past," that is, attempts to enlist history as a weapon for progressive change.[33] His reframed versions of changes in early twentieth-century due process and free speech jurisprudence thus mainly serve as efforts to keep the inspirational dimensions of the conventional account alive at the close of the twentieth century. In contrast, Bruce Ackerman's efforts at reconstructing the conventional account include a detailed reinterpretation of early twentieth-century constitutional jurisprudence itself. Ackerman's work has also brought him into closer touch than Sunstein with the revisionist treatments of early twentieth-century constitutional jurisprudence that have appeared in the 1990s, but he has chosen to deflect, rather than to incorporate or engage with, that literature.

Ackerman's historical reinterpretation, first put forth in book form in *We the People: Foundations* (1991) and reiterated in *We the People: Transforma-*

tions (1998), pivots on a distinction between what he calls ordinary politics and constitutional politics. At particular "constitutional moments," he argues, the American people suspend ordinary politics to effectuate transformative change.[34] Three episodes in American constitutional history qualify as "special" moments: the Founding itself, encompassing the Declaration of Independence and the Constitution; the Civil War and Reconstruction, culminating in the Thirteenth, Fourteenth, and Fifteenth Amendments; and the "legitimation of activist national government during and after the Great Depression."[35] The last constitutional moment, the New Deal moment, is unique, however, in that transformative change was not effectuated by formal amendments to the Constitution but by the equivalent of such amendments, a jurisprudential revolution in constitutional law. That revolution was initiated by the executive in partnership with Congress during the New Deal, ratified by the American people in the form of electoral mandates between 1932 and 1948, and ultimately ratified as well by the Supreme Court.[36]

Ackerman's conception of America as a "dualist democracy" with two tracks of lawmaking, ordinary and "higher," is intended to help him explain the periods of apparently radical constitutional change embedded in longer periods of apparent gradualism. In the transformative periods "higher" lawmaking, featuring a conscious intervention on the part of the American people as a whole in support of dramatic constitutional change, is in the ascendancy. In the other periods ordinary politics controls. Since almost no one would deny that the Founding, Reconstruction, and New Deal periods were marked by highly contested, divisive legal issues and provisional resolutions of those issues, their choice as "constitutional moments" appears to convey a commonsensical quality to Ackerman's account. But the choice serves another purpose as well.

Ackerman has a normative investment in the provisional resolutions of each of his constitutional moments. Most contemporary Americans would share his investments in the first two moments: there are not many Tories, or anti-Federalists, in today's world, let alone unreconstructed advocates of slavery and white supremacy. By equating the New Deal's provisional constitutional resolutions with those of the Founding and Reconstruction Ackerman invests them with the status of bedrock American principles. But "the legitimation of activist national government" is hardly as unproblematic a proposition as the legitimation of a constitutional republic itself or the legitimation of a Constitution dedicated to the abolition of slavery. Thus, Ackerman's initial strategy in equating the New Deal moment with the others is to elevate it to a period where Americans cohered around transformative constitutional change in the name of foundational American values. That strategy can be seen as a response to the originalist literature of the 1980s, which served to strip New Deal constitutional jurisprudence of its foundational character.

Ackerman's account of the transformation of constitutional jurisprudence that he identifies with the New Deal emphasizes the election of 1936, the Court-packing plan, "transformative" judicial appointments by Roosevelt, and "transformative" judicial decisions, especially in the late 1930s and early 1940s. Each development signals the American public's intervention to legitimate the New Deal and transform the Constitution without the necessity of resorting to a formal amendment. Although the account cleverly integrates Ackerman's data with his "dualist democracy" theme and with his claim that the New Deal period witnessed a special "constitutional moment," it does not depart very far, in its research base or in its historical analysis, from the original or mainstream versions of the conventional account. Ackerman retains the Court-packing tale as a central event in his narrative, gives the same attenuated picture of the established jurisprudential world confronted by New Dealers as did the original polemicist narrators, and structures his causal claims around the theme of governmental actors reacting to external events by modifying traditional interpretations of the Constitution.[37]

Ultimately Ackerman lets his normative and schematic goals overwhelm his historical narrative. The result is an ingenious but overdetermined portrait of constitutional jurisprudence at the time of the New Deal, and a remarkably sparse and derivative portrait of the years that preceded Ackerman's transformative moment in the 1930s. This sparseness is itself helpful to Ackerman's goals, since a radical discontinuity between the decades that preceded the New Deal and the New Deal itself helps highlight the New Deal's transformative character. In the end Ackerman's narrative of early twentieth-century constitutional jurisprudence remains in the service of his effort to create a historical pedigree for the formative years of modernist-inspired, activist government.

In both Sunstein's and Ackerman's reconstructed versions of the conventional narrative the historical evidence they present never detaches itself from the analytical and normative framework in which it is presented. The result is that their accounts appear less as efforts to present more complete or accurate portraits of early twentieth-century constitutional jurisprudence than attempts to underscore the continued relevance of the New Deal, as a transformative event, to constitutional governance in the 1990s. But although the anachronistic features of their narratives may undermine their credibility as historical descriptions, those features actually serve to enhance the vitality of the conventional account. After Sunstein and Ackerman it is clear that the shift from guardian to bifurcated review and the legitimation of the modern activist state that accompanied it have now taken on the stature of foundational constitutional principles for one set of influential scholars at the close of the twentieth century.

Thus, it is possible to trace a normative progression in the successive versions of the conventional account and to associate the descriptive and analytical continuities of that account with that progression. In all of the versions of the account constitutional change is associated with the response of human political actors, including Supreme Court justices, to external events. Much of the polemical power of original versions of the account was generated from this association. The "old" Court's initial resistance to New Deal legislation demonstrated the reactionary ideology of its justices and their lack of awareness of the changed conditions of modern America. The "new" Court's accommodation to the New Deal demonstrated that political actors had responded to political pressures.

For the first generation of contributors to the conventional account, this behavioralist view of judging and constitutional change was itself controversial. It was important to them that the "old" Court be seen as reactionary and out of touch lest its decisions be regarded simply as the apolitical application of established constitutional principles. For the next generation of authors, the ideas that judges were political actors and constitutional law decisions a species of political responses to external events were taken as common wisdom, and the context of the Court's continued participation in the shift from bifurcated to guardian review, and in the constitutional legitimation of an expanded activist state, was seen as underscoring the formative character of the New Deal years, with their evocative Court-packing episode.

For Sunstein and Ackerman, a potential threat to the activist state and the uneasy coexistence of bifurcated review with originalist theories of constitutional interpretation provide motivation for investing New Deal developments in constitutional jurisprudence with a foundational character. Those developments come to be seen, in Ackerman's history, as illustrating the way in which dramatic constitutional change inevitably takes place in America, that is, through the transformative responses of governmental officials, including those on the Court, to external crises involving the public at large. A modernist-inspired model of constitutional change as the creative use of government to control the scope and pace of external events becomes *the* model for the course of American constitutional history.

We can now appreciate the continued significance of the Court-packing/constitutional revolution tale for each generation of narrators. For the first generation the tale provides evidence for an argument emphasizing the ideological character of Supreme Court judging and the Court's susceptibility to external political pressures. For the mainstream narrators the Court-packing episode, taken in connection with the Court's continued sponsorship of bifurcated review and the growth of activist government in the decades following the Second World War, confirms the validity of a behavioralist approach to constitutional jurisprudence. For Ackerman the tale becomes incorporated into a larger model of constitutional change that reveals the ultimately democratic and progressive character of transformative episodes in American constitutional history.

But in the same time period that Ackerman's and Sunstein's versions of the conventional account were being produced, revisionist scholarship in late nineteenth- and early twentieth-century constitutional jurisprudence was suggesting that the use of conventional political labels derived from behavioralist models of judging served as a barrier to coming to grips with the intellectual assumptions of judges or commentators in those eras. At the same time the work of Cushman and Friedman argued that a close study of developments in constitutional jurisprudence around the time of the Court-packing crisis served to undermine behavioralist-inspired explanations of the constitutional revolution. Taken together, such work served to revive the possibility that Supreme Court decisions were significantly affected by the established jurisprudential categories in which individual cases were framed, and that those categories, despite being historically determined in a large sense, were not easily characterizable as direct responses to contemporary events. Further, this work suggested that the categorical framework in which a given judge decided a case might provide a more telling index of the judge's decisions than any ideological label.

The cumulative effect of this revisionist work has been to offer a less behavioralist, externally determined model of constitutional jurisprudence than that offered by the conventional account. It has cautioned against the indiscriminate association of changes in constitutional law with specific historical events, and revived the importance of authoritative legal doctrines as influences on the content and direction of constitutional change. It has also renewed "internalist" explanations for developments in constitutional jurisprudence.

The reaction of Laura Kalman to recent revisionist work on constitutional change in the New Deal period, and to Ackerman's version of similar events, suggests that the most fundamental challenge to the conventional account of American constitutional history may be one directed toward its modernist-inspired, behavioralist assumptions about constitutional law and judging. Kalman, a prominent scholar whose work has continually analyzed legal materials,[38] nonetheless regards herself primarily as a twentieth-century political historian. Her recent responses to the revisionists and Ackerman, which amount to another reconstructed version of the conventional account, pay much greater attention to historical evidence and to historiography than those of Sunstein or Ackerman. Kalman stays within her areas of keenest interest and concern, political history and historiography. Her mission is to contrast the externalist orientation of Ackerman's narrative with what she takes to be the internalist emphasis of the revisionists.

Kalman's concern is to engage the revisionist work directly and, through a strategy of confession and avoidance, to buttress the conventional account in the face of revisionist criticism. She began this effort with a long footnote in *The Strange Career of Legal Liberalism* (1996). In that note she sought to support Ackerman's earlier accounts of the relationship between the Constitution and the New Deal with some evidence culled from contemporary sources by mainstream narrators, primarily Leuchtenburg. She then suggested that she was unconvinced by Cushman's and Friedman's revisions of the Court-packing tale, admitted that she was "only guessing when I postulate that the Court switched under pressure and that 1937 might be considered a constitutional moment," and cited Ackerman for the proposition that "'considering its importance' the constitutional dimensions of the New Deal are 'incredibly underresearched.'" She remained "sympathetic to Ackerman's view of the New Deal."[39]

But work critical of the Court-packing centerpiece of the mainstream account, and skeptical of Ackerman's reconstructed version, has continued to appear, the most prominent example being Cushman's *Rethinking the New Deal Court* (1998). In the face of that work Kalman has produced another defense of a modified conventional account, her essay "Law, Politics, and the New Deal(s)," in a *Yale Law Journal* symposium commemorating the publication of Ackerman's *We the People: Transformations.*[40]

After reading Cushman, Kalman admitted, she "resolved to treat the internalists with greater respect." Nonetheless, she concluded, "as a political historian (and self-avowed liberal) I am . . . invested in the externalism explanation for the Court's shift."[41] The latter sentence was another way of signaling that she shared the behavioralist grounding of the conventional account. Ackerman had made a similar distinction, contrasting the "legalist" emphasis of revisionists with the "realist" orientation of conventional narrators, who took judges to be another species of political actors, but he had suggested that the "legalist"/"realist" debate was stale.[42] In contrast, that debate furnishes Kalman with a central distinction between the revisionists and herself. "Though old," she suggests, the debate "is neither tired nor unimportant": it "involves the legal academy's most enduring concern, . . . the relationship between law and politics."[43]

The revisionist scholars, for Kalman, are "internalists" and "legalists" in that they come close to denying that constitutional law can be treated as a species of constitutional politics. They appear to be constructing a brief for "those formalist turn-of-the-century Harvard law professors—or more probably, for their Legal Process successors who had to live in the post-realist, post–New Deal world."[44] By characterizing the revisionists as internalists and legalists, Kalman means to suggest that they are seeking to resurrect an older mythology of law as divorced from politics. In contrast, "externalist" and "realist" scholars have their feet firmly planted in the stuff of American life.

The contrast between a behavioralist, externally driven, "realistic" view of judging and the outmoded conception of the Supreme Court as a bastion of timeless constitutional principles has fueled the energies of the original narrators of the conventional account and has helped sustain that account in its subsequent versions. Kalman, being a self-described political historian, cannot give much credence to a theory of constitutional change that appears to minimize the deeply behavioral character of judging and the apparently inevitable tendency of constitutional law to become subsumed in politics. It is not merely that conventional politics always counts in making sense of constitutional change; it is that to emphasize the role of established legal ideas and doctrines as causative factors is to invite the revival of an older, unreflective caricature of judging as an apolitical process. In contrast, Ackerman's claim that in the New Deal period all segments and institutions of American society appear to be uniting behind some transformative agenda underscores the primacy of political behavior as a force causing qualitative constitutional change.

One thus can see how deeply modernist-inspired Kalman's reconstructed narrative remains. She cannot imagine the motivation of twentieth-century judges to be any different from that of other actors seeking to adapt constitutional government to the conditions of modern America. When she examines sources from the New Deal period, and when she assesses subsequent historical portraits of those sources, she draws conclusions consistent with her own investment in behavioralist models of judging and constitutional change. That is why, for her, the Court-packing tale remains evocative. The Court-packing plan is not so much the primary agent of constitutional change in the early twentieth century—she concedes that "portions of the shift [in constitutional jurisprudence] began before 1937"[45]—as it is a dual symbol of the obvious validity of behavioralist models. Not only did the Court change its jurisprudence after the plan was introduced, the very nature of the plan assumed that judging, at bottom, was ideological and politically inspired.

With Kalman's restatement of the conventional narrative as predicated on a more "realistic" theory of constitutional change than that she identifies with the revisionists, the stakes in the debate have been elevated. Two contrasting models from which the course of early twentieth-century constitutional history can be traced are being offered by conventional and revisionist work. In the first model judging is a species of politics, making the categories of political history appropriate for categorizing the performance of individual judges and courts and enabling external political events to be given causative weight in the process of constitutional change. In the revisionist model one cannot expect so close, or direct, a connection between external political events and changes in constitutional jurisprudence. This is because constitutional decisions are significantly affected by the existing universe of legal doctrines and categories and by prevailing conceptions of the role of judges as constitutional interpreters, which serve as analytical frameworks for those decisions.

If what might be called the jurisprudential setting of early twentieth-century constitutional decisions does have a significant effect on the scope and pace of constitutional change, one might expect an account of early twentieth-century constitutional history to be more complex, less easily characterizable in behavioralist labels, and less easily correlated with external developments than the narrative produced by the conventional account. One might expect an account in which different areas in the realm of constitutional jurisprudence evolved at different rates, reflecting their special doctrinal concerns. One might expect the ideological ramifications of positions taken by judges or courts to be affected by the juristic context in which those positions were advanced. And one might expect the relationship between the New Deal and early twentieth-century constitutional change to be far more attenuated, and complicated, than the conventional account has suggested.

But none of these suppositions can be tested without a thorough analysis of the world of early twentieth-century constitutional jurisprudence. The conventional account has not produced that analysis because its narrators have assumed that the juristic setting of constitutional cases pales in significance to the political context of those cases and to the ideological orientation of the judges deciding them. Consequently, a large hole exists in all of the versions of the conventional account, a hole that can only be filled by close analysis of the world of early twentieth-century constitutional doctrines, categories, and analogies that formed the setting for cases and commentary in that period. That analysis, moreover, needs to avoid being skewed by the modernist-inspired presuppositions of the conventional account, lest the force of jurisprudential positions once seriously entertained, and subsequently discarded in the course of the century, be unduly minimized.

I have tried to adopt both those guidelines in the analysis of several topics in early twentieth-century constitutional history that follows. My analysis will require that the reader indulge in some relatively technical discussions of constitutional issues that may no longer seem urgent or contested. I hope, however, that such analysis will enable me to demonstrate that the conventional narrative of early twentieth-century constitutional history cannot claim to furnish an accurate description of the relationship between the New Deal and constitutional change nor to rest on an accurate understanding of the relationship of Supreme Court constitutional decisions to their historical context.

2

The Transformation of the Constitutional Jurisprudence of Foreign Relations: The Orthodox Regime under Stress

In this chapter and the three chapters that follow, I will be pursuing two general inquiries. The first is whether the conventional characterizations of doctrinal changes in a particular area of early twentieth-century constitutional law are accurate. On the whole, that inquiry yields the conclusion that conventional accounts have caricatured or ignored a number of doctrinal propositions in early twentieth-century constitutional jurisprudence, and that the process of doctrinal change was more gradual, and irregular, than those accounts suggest.

The first inquiry thus engages us with the details of early twentieth-century constitutional law and commentary. But we cannot rest in those details because a second inquiry immediately surfaces: if a more accurate portrait of jurisprudential changes in an area of constitutional law can be assembled, what relationship existed between those changes and the New Deal? This inquiry is necessary because the conventional account has not only posited the existence of an early twentieth-century "constitutional revolution," it has explicitly linked that revolution to the emergence of New Deal governmental policies and the Supreme Court's eventual accommodation to those policies. I have chosen to begin my survey with an area of early twentieth-century constitutional jurisprudence that has received very little treatment from recent constitutional scholars and historians, the constitutional jurisprudence of foreign relations. A conventional description of the area exists, but the description has primarily been formulated by modern internationalist scholars who have not engaged in much detailed historical analysis, and who have had strong contemporary reasons for wanting to characterize developments in early twentieth-century constitutional foreign relations jurisprudence in a particular fashion.

The area of early twentieth-century constitutional foreign relations jurisprudence offers an especially promising place to begin my two general inquiries. Moreover, the early twentieth-century transformation of this jurisprudence provides a vivid example of the process by which once-dominant constitutional doctrines and attitudes can be lost from the view of subsequent generations. As we will observe, once a set of doctrinal propositions establishing the principle of virtually limitless federal executive discretion in foreign affairs policymaking was established, subsequent courts and commentators treated that principle as having always been in existence, losing sight of previously influential alternative formulations. Orthodox early twentieth-century constitutional foreign relations jurisprudence has become particularly inaccessible to late twentieth-century scholars, so the recovery of some of its principal doctrines may prove startling even to specialists.

In addition, doctrinal transformations in early twentieth-century foreign relations jurisprudence were noticeably widespread and dramatic. Within four decades the governing principles of the entire body of jurisprudence were altered, expanding the power of the national government, especially that of the national executive, at the expense of the powers of the states, both in Congress and in their own sovereign capacities. This expansion of national power was undertaken primarily in constitutional decisions of the Supreme Court of the United States, making foreign relations jurisprudence potentially one of the most visible examples of an early twentieth-century "constitutional revolution."

But the transformation in constitutional foreign relations jurisprudence cannot be easily related to the Court-packing crisis or even to the emergence of the New Deal in American political life. Its earliest stages took place decades before the New Deal came into existence. The Supreme Court's extensions of federal power in foreign affairs took place at the same time that a Court majority was resisting extensions of federal power in the domestic arena. The principal early twentieth-century intellectual architect of a rationale for extensive federal foreign relations power, Justice George Sutherland, has typically been described as an opponent of the New Deal and rejected several pieces of New Deal domestic legislation on constitutional grounds. The leading case establishing the plenary powers of the federal government in foreign affairs was decided before the Court-packing crisis surfaced.

In short, any account of early twentieth-century American constitutional history that seeks to associate a constitutional revolution with the New Deal, the Court-packing crisis, and judicial acquiescence in extended federal power needs to reckon with a major transformation in constitutional jurisprudence that cannot remotely be linked with the Court-packing tale and that serves to complicate the ideological labeling of a judge habitually described as a "reactionary" opponent of expanding national power. The example of early twentieth-century foreign affairs jurisprudence thus can serve us as an introductory corrective to inaccuracies and stereotypes in the conventional account.

The attenuated recent historiography of early twentieth-century constitutional foreign affairs jurisprudence has fostered a myth of continuity about the constitutional arrangement of powers in that area. It is widely assumed that because the Constitution singles out the president as engaging in certain foreign affairs functions, such as making treaties and receiving foreign ambassadors, and prohibits the states from making treaties, it has always been the case that "in respect of our foreign relations generally, state lines disappear."[1] Late twentieth-century commentators on the constitutional dimensions of foreign relations cases have tended to regard this assumption as not worth probing,[2] although some corrective scholarly investigations have recently been launched.[3]

To make sense of the history of early twentieth-century constitutional foreign relations jurisprudence, it is necessary to reject the myth of continuity and to recognize the radical doctrinal transformations that occurred in the area. This requires an excursion into the orthodox world of constitutional foreign relations law and into the perspectives of judges and commentators who sought to revise the constitutional orthodoxy of their time.

There were four principal governing assumptions of orthodox late nineteenth-century constitutional foreign relations jurisprudence. First, courts and commentators treated the exercise of foreign relations powers as a constitutional exercise, one controlled by the enumerated and reserved powers parceled out in the Constitution's text. Second, they assumed that the principal mechanism for entering into international obligations was the treaty-making process. A treaty-making power had been identified in the Constitution,[4] distributed between the president and the Senate[5] and forbidden to the states.[6] Treaties that had been made or were to be made "under the authority of the United States" had been given the status of supreme law, trumping any state law to the contrary.[7] Although the Constitution recognized the existence of "Agreement[s] or Compact[s] . . . with . . . foreign Power[s]," it forbade the states from entering into such without the consent of Congress,[8] and no state had attempted to do so since the framing.

These first two assumptions, taken together, produced what can be called a "treaty-centered" consciousness in the orthodox regime. Courts and commentators assumed that most international agreements would be treaties, that they would be entered into by the federal government, and that they were both part of the "supreme law of the land" and subject to the limitations of the Constitution. A corollary to this set of assumptions was that since most agreements between the United States and foreign powers would take the form of treaties, the Senate would participate in most exercises of foreign affairs powers. This meant that any other foreign relations agreements entered into by branches of the federal government were constitutionally irregular.

A third entrenched assumption of the orthodox regime of constitutional foreign relations jurisprudence was that despite the Constitution's having specifically conferred the treaty power on two of the branches of the federal government, and having specifically prohibited the states from entering into treaties, the exercise of any foreign relations powers by the federal government needed to be mindful of the reserved powers of the states under the structure of sovereignty created by the Constitution. Alongside the treaty consciousness of orthodox constitutional foreign relations jurisprudence was a reserved powers consciousness.

The idea of reserved constitutional powers was connected to a general theory that enumerated constitutional powers were carved out of a residuum of state power at the time of the Constitution's framing. According to that theory, the states had surrendered power to the federal government in the designated areas referred to in the Constitution's text but had retained power over all other areas that were the proper subject matter of republican governments. Thus, the exercise of federal power needed to be undertaken with an awareness that the prerogatives of the federal government had been specially conferred, and the residuum of state power could not be blithely invaded. If an exercise of power by the federal government was not the kind of exercise that could be squarely located under one of the enumerated federal powers, or easily analogized to one of them, its radiations into the sphere of reserved state powers were constitutionally inappropriate, and a boundary line needed to be drawn to preserve the integrity of the constitutional design.

In drawing lines between the spheres of federal and state autonomy, judges were not expected to treat foreign relations cases differently from domestic cases. There was a sphere of enumerated federal foreign relations powers and a residual sphere of state powers from which those enumerated powers had been extracted; there was a boundary between those spheres. Judges were expected to decide constitutional foreign relations cases, as they were expected to decide domestic cases, by pricking out boundaries between the respective spheres. Sometimes the cases involved separation of powers issues, sometimes issues of federalism, but the search in both cases was for the appropriate sphere of constitutional autonomy. Boundary pricking, which consisted of a process by which new cases were placed in one or another essentialist category, and consequently in one sphere of authority or another, was the essence of guardian judicial review in constitutional law.[9]

A fourth assumption of the orthodox regime that served to facilitate the process of categorization and boundary pricking was the doctrine of "political questions." This doctrine served to render certain issues that on their face had legal, even constitutional, dimensions (such as whether a "republican government" currently existed in one of the states in the Union) not susceptible to judicial resolution because they could only be determined by the "lawmaking" branches of government.[10] Since the boundaries between branches of government were taken to be essentialist and easily discernible, and the distinction between the judicial and lawmaking branches was treated as unproblematic, the category of political questions could be readily grasped.[11]

But in orthodox mid and late nineteenth-century jurisprudence the category was not a particularly large one. Examples from the realm of foreign affairs included the annexation of territory,[12] the recognition of new governments,[13] the termination of treaties,[14] or the determination that a state of insurgency,[15] belligerency,[16] or war[17] existed in or with a foreign nation. Where contested questions of private rights arose in an international setting, courts did not treat them as raising "political questions" even if a foreign government was involved. On the contrary, they treated the international setting as potentially providing additional legal principles that might be applied to the case because they assumed that principles of international law were among the sources of the common law laid down by domestic courts.[18]

Such were the governing constitutional foreign relations principles of late nineteenth-century American law, principles that followed from an essentialist conception of constitutional powers and were enforced by an assumption that judges could guard the integrity of the constitutional design by pricking boundaries and easily distinguishing legal from political questions. But by the 1890s the dominant separation of powers paradigm of the regime, in which the president initiated foreign relations policies by making treaties and the Senate implemented or thwarted those policies in its ratification process, was placed under strain when a new category of executive foreign policy initiatives began to surface.

The constitutionality of that new form of executive foreign affairs policymaking was considered by the Supreme Court in the 1892 case of *Field v. Clark*.[19] In that case Justice John Marshall Harlan, for a 7–2 majority of the Court, concluded that when Congress had authorized the president to implement a series of unratified reciprocal commercial agreements between the United States and foreign producers of sugar, tea, coffee, molasses, or hides, that action was constitutionally legitimate, even though the Senate had not approved it and even though it allowed the president to impose tariff duties on those products at his discretion.

The congressional legislation challenged in *Field v. Clark* consisted of a series of reciprocal free trade agreements made between President William Mc-Kinley and several countries that imported American products. The legislation, known as the McKinley Tariff Act, provided that the president would monitor the tariff policies of those nations, and if he concluded that a particular foreign nation producing sugar, tea, coffee, molasses, or hides was imposing duties on United States exports, he might suspend the free trade treatment of those products. Those provisions were challenged on the ground that they amounted to an unconstitutional delegation of lawmaking and treaty-making power to the president.[20]

Harlan's opinion for the Court, in upholding the constitutionality of the Act, rehearsed a number of previous instances in which "[C]ongress . . . conferred upon the president powers, with reference to trade and commerce, like those conferred by [the McKinley Tariff Act]."[21] But none of the precedents he cited, which ranged back to the "Non-Intercourse Acts" of 1809 and 1810,[22] amounted to the same sort of delegation from Congress to the executive that had taken place in the McKinley Tariff Act. In all of the previous examples Congress had instructed the president that if he found facts previously specified by Congress to exist, he could issue a proclamation and eventually implement the foreign policy measures Congress had spelled out. In the McKinley Tariff Act, the president had been given the power to "deem" when the actions of foreign nations supplying the specified products had been "reciprocally unequal and unreasonable." He had also been given the power to suspend the privileges of those nations to export the products free to the United States and to impose duties on the products, "for such time as he may deem just."[23]

The dissenting justices in *Field v. Clark* argued that the McKinley Tariff Act had done more than merely authorize the president to implement commercial foreign policy measures that had previously been legislated by Congress. It had given the president power to make commercial foreign policy decisions himself.[24] By the standards of the orthodox regime of constitutional foreign relations jurisprudence, they were correct. That regime assumed that to determine the permissible scope and allocation of foreign relations powers, one looked to the enumeration of those powers in the Constitution. Congress had been granted the power to regulate commerce with foreign nations (tariff legislation being an example), and the president had been granted the power to make treaties with the consent of two-thirds of the Senate. But the McKinley Tariff legislation had created reciprocal commercial agreements that were not treaties, and assumed that the president might impose tariff duties when he saw fit.

Between the 1890s and the First World War the reciprocal commercial agreement was to become included in a more general category, that of the "executive agreement," in which the president conducted foreign policy out-side of the treaty process. Those executive agreements, which a commentator cataloged in 1905 and distinguished from treaties,[25] lacked an overriding constitutional rationale. Some involved military agreements made pursuant to the president's powers as commander in chief of the armed services.[26] Oth-ers were placed in the category of modus vivendi, a "temporary or working arrangement, made in order to bridge over some difficulty, pending a perma-nent settlement," and were justified on the basis that the permanent settle-ment would involve formal Senate ratification of a treaty.[27] Still others in-volved postal treaties, a species of agreements that had apparently never been regarded as requiring Senate ratification.[28]

As the nineteenth century gave way to the twentieth, two additional types of executive agreements became increasingly common. The first type involved the settlement of pecuniary claims against foreign governments through arbitration or other means. Although such settlements were some-times made through treaties, they were also quite regularly made by the pres-ident, and the international law scholar John B. Moore asserted in 1905 that "no question as to [the president's] possession of such a power . . . appears ever to have been seriously raised."[29] Moore pointed out that presidents had repeatedly referred such claims to arbitration, and that even where no treaties specifically provided for that action, it was well settled that presidents could do so without Senate approval.[30] The obvious practical difficulties in involv-ing the Senate in the settlement of any claim by an American citizen against a foreign government, and the discrete implications of the claims themselves, contributed to the unproblematic status of executive hegemony. Nonethe-less, Moore cited the pecuniary claims settlement practice as evidence that "the position that the president can make no agreement with a foreign power, except in the form of a treaty approved by the Senate, cannot be maintained."[31]

A more contested type of executive agreement, and one more potentially threatening to the orthodox constitutional regime of foreign affairs, was the protocol. This was a generic category in which agreements related to both military conflicts and commercial activity were placed.[32] President McKin-ley's peace protocol with Spain creating a general armistice ending the Span-ish-American War was an uncontroversial example of what Moore called a "purely executive agreement," being "no doubt within the power of the commander-in-chief of the army in time of war." But the protocol also in-cluded a cession of Spanish territory in the Caribbean, including Puerto Rico and some West Indian islands, which had not been part of the theatre of the Spanish-American War. These provisions were not submitted to the Senate, an action that Moore described as "of far reaching importance." Equally "remarkable" in Moore's view was the protocol negotiated in 1901 between the McKinley administration, other western nations, and China, in which, after the unsuccessful Boxer Rebellion, China paid reparations to the western nations, agreed to the creation of extraterritorial space for foreign legations in Peking, prohibited itself from importing arms and ammunition, and agreed to make its rivers more navigable to foreign commerce.[33] Although the Spanish-American War armistice was eventually reflected in a treaty of peace, the Boxer protocol was never ratified by the Senate. Neither were protocols in which presidents made agreements with Japan and China between 1905 and 1917.[34]

Thus, by World War I deviations from the orthodox separation of powers paradigm had begun to emerge with some regularity. Commentators had begun to suggest that the constitutional legitimacy of particular exercises of the foreign relations power could not always be determined simply by asking whether the exercise was a tariff, a treaty, or something else. The increased use of the kind of executive agreement validated in *Field v. Clark* suggested that the bright-line separation of powers boundaries of the orthodox regime had become fuzzier.

Meanwhile, another series of developments served to place pressure on the orthodox regime's federalism paradigm. The meaning of "reserved powers" in the foreign relations area was clouded by a constitutional framework in which the states were expressly prohibited from making treaties and limited in their capacity to make any international agreements. This created a potential conflict between the specific language of constitutional provisions dealing with the treaty power and the general constitutional design in which those subscribing to orthodoxy situated those provisions. On the one hand, Article I, Section 10, Article II, Section 2, Article VI, Section 2, and the Tenth Amendment seemed to add up to the proposition that the treaty power might be not only plenary but exclusive in the national government. On the other hand, those who had sought to describe the treaty power treated it as comparable to any other enumerated national power in that it could not be exercised in a fashion inconsistent with a robust conception of residual state powers.

Thus, the federalism paradigm of orthodox constitutional foreign relations jurisprudence was far more responsive to state concerns than might first appear. One can see two sorts of evidence of this responsiveness. States, throughout the nineteenth century, engaged in a series of legislative efforts that were unmistakably in the realm of foreign affairs. These included the extradition of criminals to foreign governments,[35] the regulation of immigration,[36] and efforts to retaliate against foreign nations for restricting the efforts of state-based corporations to engage in business in those nations.[37]

These efforts were not challenged on the basis that foreign affairs powers were the exclusive province of the national government.[38] Such a challenge would have had to confront Article I, Section 10's assumption that states might be inclined to enter into "Agreement[s] or Compact[s] . . . with a Foreign Power."[39]

In addition, opinions of the Court during the same time period regularly intimated that there might be some powers so essential to the sovereignty of the states that the federal government could not abrogate them through exercise of the treaty power.[40] Although successive Supreme Court cases regularly sustained the treaty power when the provisions of a treaty conflicted with specific state laws,[41] the Court consistently considered the effect of treaties on state laws within a framework that suggested that the constitutional provisions giving plenary and exclusive treaty-making power to the federal government did not by any means end reserved power inquiries. While the Court's holdings tended to be limited to the construction of the treaties before it, the Court's broad pronouncements lent support both for the proposition that the federal treaty-making power was plenary and exclusive and for the proposition that it was subject to federalism limitations.

Nonetheless, two sets of cases surfaced in the late nineteenth century in which the Court hinted that in some contexts the federal government might be able to conduct foreign affairs policymaking relatively unencumbered by federalism concerns and possibly unencumbered by the text of the Constitution itself. The first set was the *Chinese Exclusion Cases*,[42] in which late nineteenth-century congressional statutes excluding Chinese laborers from the United States were challenged as inconsistent with an 1868 treaty in which the United States had granted Chinese residents the same privileges and immunities as would be enjoyed by American residents of China. In two of its eleven decisions on the question of Chinese exclusion between 1884 and 1900,[43] the Court suggested that although there was no enumerated power in the federal government to exclude aliens, that power, as Justice Harold Gray put it, was "an inherent and inalienable right of every sovereign and independent nation, essential to its safety, its independence, and its welfare."[44] The decisions, taken together with the Court's subsequent insistence in a domestic case that the federal government could only exercise enumerated powers,[45] caused commentators to speculate that some federal foreign relations powers might be grounded on the sovereignty of nations in an international community, and hence might have an extraconstitutional basis.[46]

The other set of cases suggesting that the federal government's exercise of foreign relations powers might not be limited to grants of enumerated power was the so-called *Insular Cases*, a series of constitutional challenges to the power of Congress to acquire and to govern territories.[47] Here again the enumerated basis of that power was attenuated, resting only in Article IV's statement that Congress "shall have power to dispose of and make all needful Rules and Regulations respecting the Territory . . . belonging to the United States."[48] The challenges advanced in the *Insular Cases,* most of which involved efforts on the part of Congress to impose tariffs on Puerto Rico and the Philippines that it could not have imposed on states of the Union, were based on the argument that since there were no explicit provisions of the Constitution granting Congress the power to acquire territory or distinguishing between its treatment of territories and states, all territories acquired by the United States through treaties had the constitutional status of prospective states.

In a series of closely divided decisions, a majority of the Supreme Court eventually concluded that Congress could decide for itself whether to incorporate acquired territories into the Union, and that before a decision to incorporate a territory was made, Congress was not bound to follow all of the Constitution's requirements in its treatment of that territory and its inhabitants. Thus if Congress wanted to impose lower tariffs on goods shipped from the territory of Puerto Rico to American states than on goods shipped to those states from foreign nations, the Uniformity Clause was not violated.[49] Nor did Congress have to conform to every particular of the Bill of Rights in drafting codes of criminal procedure for Hawaii[50] or the Philippines.[51] This finding that congressional management of newly acquired territories was not invariably subject to constitutional limitations was not easily harmonized with the framework of the orthodox regime, and one commentator described the Court majority's conclusions in the *Insular Cases* as a "radical" departure from existing constitutional principles and practices.[52]

Despite these pressures on the separation of powers and federalism paradigms of orthodox late nineteenth-century constitutional foreign relations jurisprudence, those paradigms remained relatively intact as late as the 1920s. At the same time, the emergence of constitutionally sanctioned executive agreements with foreign states, and the hints of "inherent" national foreign affairs powers in the *Chinese Exclusion Cases* and the *Insular Cases,* had resulted in a growing perception among commentators that American constitutional foreign relations jurisprudence had a dual character. On the one hand, it was "constitutional," governed by the same boundaries, categories, and judicial pricking out of enumerated and reserved powers that existed in the domestic arena. On the other hand, it was "international," concerned with the growing role of the United States as sovereign nation, participating in world affairs and operating within a body of international law. No work better captured the degree to which American constitutional foreign relations jurisprudence in the 1920s was thought of as a composite of constitutional and international principles and practices than Quincy Wright's 1922 treatise, *The Control of American Foreign Relations.*

By the appearance of Wright's treatise, two decades of scholarship had addressed the question of how executive agreements could be made to fit within the orthodox separation of powers paradigm, and Wright was able to offer a summary of that work as well as to take advantage of the efforts of his contemporaries.[53] He separated his discussion of the power to make international agreements into two components, that exercised by "the President acting alone" and that exercised by "the President acting with advice and consent of the Senate."[54] His treatment of those two exercises of the foreign relations power as separate yet comparable was itself a departure from the orthodox separation of powers paradigm.[55]

Wright reviewed the various categories of executive agreements that had emerged in the late nineteenth and early twentieth centuries. He covered military agreements, modi vivendi, protocols, and reciprocal commercial agreements, treating them as embodiments of the president's constitutional power to make international agreements without the approval of the Senate. This approach was consistent with the orthodox regime's assumption that the federal foreign relations powers were derived from enumerated constitutional provisions rather than from any extraconstitutional or contextual sources. Wright identified three sources of presidential power: those of the president as "head of the administration," as commander in chief, and as "the representative organ in international relations."[56] This typology allowed him to sweep the various species of executive agreements that had sprung up since 1890 into constitutional categories.[57]

Wright then turned to a lengthy discussion of the treaty power, in which he demonstrated that treaties were still the principal mechanism of foreign relations.[58] His analysis of the treaty power emphasized the settled principles and practices of a treaty-centered orthodoxy. When he came to summarize his chapter, however, he chose to characterize the topic of international agreements in a way that more reflected the developments that had placed the orthodox regime under stress than the principles that undergirded it. "We conclude," Wright wrote,

> that the power of making international agreements is largely vested in the President. The states' power in this respect is practically nil. Though the Senate has an absolute veto on treaties, and Congress may suggest the opening of negotiations, may authorize executive agreements and

may refuse to execute treaties, yet the real initiative, the negotiation and the final decision to ratify are all at the discretion of the President. Furthermore, many agreements of a temporary or purely executive or military character may be made by him without consulting the Senate at all.[59]

Wright's 1922 synthesis of the role of treaties and executive agreements indicated that a large potential space had developed in the interstices of nineteenth-century orthodoxy. That space had resulted from actions taken by the executive branch, in the context of a widening participation by the United States in international affairs, which had no precise nineteenth-century counterparts and thus were difficult to conceptualize in the terms of the orthodox constitutional jurisprudence of foreign affairs. Nonetheless, Wright's summary suggested that whenever the president entered into an international agreement other than a treaty, it was still something of a constitutional novelty, and the treaty-centeredness of the orthodox constitutional foreign relations jurisprudence created a certain amount of pressure for congressional or senatorial oversight.

Wright also discussed the category of international political questions. When his discussion is placed alongside his treatment of the relationship between treaties and executive agreements, one gets a sense of the transitional character of constitutional foreign relations jurisprudence in the 1920s. Wright had recognized that the emergence of the executive agreement had significant separation of powers implications in that it augured an expanded category of foreign affairs policymaking from which the Senate was excluded. If executive agreements were to have the same constitutional status as treaties, the ambit of executive discretion in foreign relations jurisprudence would be significantly expanded.

Wright did not, however, anticipate a parallel expansion of executive influence through a widening of the category of international political questions. Not only did he expect that both federal and state courts would continue to decide common law questions involving international plaintiffs or defendants, he believed that those courts' invocation of international law principles as part of their common law decisions would be a salutary development.

Wright remained mindful of the enumerated and reserved power framework of nineteenth and early twentieth-century constitutional jurisprudence. He devoted an entire section of his treatise, composed of four chapters, to constitutional limitations on the foreign relations power, and included in that section a relatively lengthy discussion of "states' rights" limitations upon the powers of the national government.[60] Nonetheless, he concluded that the presence of a residuum of state power did not have any overriding significance for foreign relations policymaking. As he put it,

[I]t has been alleged that all state powers are not merely residual but that some, for instance the police power, are "reserved" powers incapable of limitation by any exercise of its delegated powers by the national government. It will readily be seen that this notion is wholly incompatible with the principle of national supremacy and while it has great historic importance, it never commanded whole-hearted support from the courts and at present enjoys no legal recognition.[61]

Wright supported these generalizations with a detailed analysis of the role of reserved state powers in the foreign relations context. He distinguished between express limitations on the states enumerated in the Constitution and the reserved powers of the states. The former, which he called "genuine 'states' rights'" and characterized as "definite limitations on the exercise of national power," included guarantees of territorial integrity,[62] a republican form of government,[63] immunity of necessary state governmental organs from federal taxation,[64] and limitations on export taxes and discriminatory revenue regulations or tariffs.[65] The latter, he suggested, "if they restrict the exercise of national powers at all, do so simply by virtue of constitutional understandings."[66]

When unraveled, Quincy Wright's 1922 summary of the constitutional jurisprudence of foreign relations conveyed two sets of messages, one at the surface and another deeper and potentially subversive of his surface findings. The former set of messages suggested that the central paradigms of the orthodox regime were still intact. Executive agreements that were not treaties had proliferated in the first two decades of the twentieth century, but they still constituted exceptional rather than typical exercises of the foreign affairs power, and thus could be expected to elicit congressional and senatorial oversight. The mainstream view among courts and commentators was overwhelmingly that the reserved powers of the states could not prevail over competing exercises of the treaty-making power by the national government. But the Senate, peopled with representatives of the states, remained an important reserved power check on the treaty-making process, and its continuing involvement, plus the "understanding" among courts and commentators that treaties should be made with an idea toward preserving the residuum of state powers, indicated that reserved power consciousness was still a dominant element in the universe of twentieth-century constitutional foreign relations jurisprudence. Finally, the judicial treatment of international political questions suggested that judicial deference to executive policymaking remained confined to a few traditional areas.

But there were some potentially contradictory messages lying beneath the surface of Wright's analysis. The first such message was that there was no explicit constitutional limitation on the president's power to make international agreements without the consent of the Senate; the only limitation was on the president's power to make treaties. And there was abundant evidence that twentieth-century presidents were increasingly resorting to the executive agreement as a regular mechanism for conducting foreign policy. There was even evidence that they were making deliberate choices to use that mechanism as a way of avoiding senatorial scrutiny and involvement.

Moreover, Wright's survey indicated that the national government could constitutionally ignore the interests of the states in many of its exercises in foreign affairs policymaking. Only where the Constitution had expressly created "states' rights" in the foreign relations realm would such deference be necessary, and those instances had been very few and far between. The residuum of reserved state power could be seen, in Wright's analysis, as having very little constitutional significance in foreign affairs. It only came into play through an "understanding" that the Senate symbolically represented the states in the ratification of treaties. When one considered that there was no necessary Senate involvement in the executive agreement process, even that understanding had its limits.

Taken together, these findings of Wright were threatening to the orthodox regime. He suggested that if foreign relations policy were to be largely exercised in the form of executive agreements in the future, there would be little role for the Senate or the states in the conduct of foreign affairs. Moreover, if the national government entered into executive agreements with foreign countries that were regarded as interfering with the autonomy of the states or the prerogatives of the Senate, there was little, constitutionally, that those parties could do about it. Wright's belief in the efficacy of constitutional "understandings" in the foreign relations area did not mean that he was equating understandings and powers. His conclusion that understandings were vital in foreign relations policymaking was linked to the fact that he had not found very many limitations on the power of the federal government, personified by the president, to conduct foreign affairs. Thus, a treatise that may have been designed as a synthesis of the principles of the orthodox regime provided instead a revealing snapshot of that regime in a process of significant jurisprudential transition.

At approximately the same time that commentators were debating the relationship of "inherent" national foreign relations powers to the enumerated powers framework of orthodox constitutional jurisprudence, an alternative theory of the sources of national foreign relations powers surfaced. That theory, once established, began to extend its implications, eventually providing a justification for some transformative doctrinal changes in the constitutional regime of foreign relations in the period between the First and Second World Wars. These changes included not only the continued employment of executive agreements as principal mechanisms of foreign relations policymaking but also the virtual disappearance of consideration for the reserved powers of the states in constitutional foreign affairs jurisprudence and, perhaps most startlingly, the sharply reduced role of not only the states and the Senate, but of the courts, as significant overseers of executive foreign policy decisions.

Eventually the theory would buttress a revisionist orthodoxy for constitutional foreign relations jurisprudence whose central principle was that of expanded executive discretion. But in its early stages it was only implicitly concerned with bypassing the treaty power, eliminating the states as actors in foreign affairs policymaking, or reducing judicial oversight of executive foreign policy determinations. Its primary concern, in those stages, was to develop the argument that a number of foreign policy decisions did not require a close investigation of enumerated powers and responsibilities because they did not raise constitutional issues at all.

In 1909 George Sutherland, then a Republican senator from Utah,[67] issued a Senate document,[68] which he reprinted as an essay, "The Internal and External Powers of the National Government," in the March 1910 issue of the *North American Review.*[69] That essay was the first of a series of efforts on the part of Sutherland, which would stretch over the next twenty-seven years, to revise the cast of orthodoxy in the constitutional jurisprudence of foreign relations. Although Sutherland was not alone in his revisionist undertaking, he was a singularly influential force in the transformation of constitutional foreign relations jurisprudence. That fact may be all the more surprising because of Sutherland's image as an opponent of twentieth-century constitutional change and because of the relatively thin historical and jurisprudential groundings of his theory.

Sutherland's theory of the sources of federal foreign affairs powers ultimately found its way into two Supreme Court opinions that he authored, those in the 1936 case of *United States v. Curtiss-Wright Export Co.*[70] and the 1937 case of *United States v. Belmont.*[71] I will be discussing those cases and their historical and jurisprudential contexts in the next chapter. At this point I am interested in exploring the evolution of the theory from its 1909 origins to a more refined version Sutherland advanced in 1919 in a series of lectures at Columbia University. My emphasis here is on the contexts in which Sutherland presented the successive versions of his theory and his jurisprudential goals in developing it, bearing in mind Sutherland's regular opposition to New Deal legislation that sought to advance executive discretion in the domestic arena.[72]

Sutherland's 1910 essay attempted to stake out a position on the scope of the constitutional powers of the federal government, which lay "[b]etween those who . . . would put the government of the United States in a constitutional strait-jacket, and those who . . . would turn it adrift upon a boundless sea of unrestricted power." His position rested on what he claimed was a critical distinction. That distinction was "between our *internal* and our *external* relations— . . . the difference which, from the structure and character of the American dual political system, must of necessity exist between the Federal powers of the general government, which are exerted in its dealings with the several states and their people, and the national powers which are exerted in its dealings with the outside world."[73]

Throughout the remainder of his essay Sutherland made only two kinds of contemporary references. The first was to late nineteenth-century cases in which the Supreme Court seemed to have taken for granted that the United States possessed some inherent sovereign powers.[74] The second was to a proposed congressional statute barring from interstate commerce any articles manufactured by child labor.[75]

The importance of those references becomes clear when one explores the textual basis of Sutherland's distinction between "internal" and "external" federal powers. He derived that distinction from a maxim of constitutional interpretation that he took to be imperative in a Constitution whose powers were essentialist and ultimately derived from the sovereignty of the people. The maxim was that there must be an allocation of all the powers of the three sovereign entities identified in the Constitution—the general government, the states, and the people—throughout the entire corpus of the constitutional text. In support of this maxim Sutherland quoted his former law professor, Chief Justice James V. Campbell of the Michigan Supreme Court.[76] As Campbell had put it in a Michigan case,

> Under the Constitution of the United States all possible powers must be found in the Union or the States, or else they remain among those reserved rights which the people have retained as not essential to be vested in any government. That which is forbidden to the States is not necessarily in the Union, because it may be among the reserved powers. But if that which is essential to government is prohibited to one it must of necessity be found in the other, and the prohibition in such case on the one side is equivalent to a grant on the other.[77]

The maxim was useful to Sutherland's dual purposes in writing his 1910 essay. On the one hand, he wanted to advance an argument that unless Congress had been given specific powers with respect to domestic issues, those powers "essential to government" in internal affairs rested in the states. On the other hand, he wanted to demonstrate that since the Constitution had specifically prohibited the states from conducting foreign relations, and those powers obviously had to be vested in some governmental body, all powers related to the external affairs of the United States lay in the hands of the federal government.

The context of Sutherland's essay reinforces this interpretation of its purposes. Sutherland had been in Congress when the *Insular Cases* were decided, and in the Senate when the constitutional status of executive agreements had been debated in 1905 and 1906. In 1909 discussions took place in the Senate on tariff policy and on the possibility of prohibiting the interstate transportation of articles manufactured by convict labor.[78] Sutherland had strong views on both issues. He was concerned that if legislation using the Commerce Clause as a basis for prohibiting the interstate transportation of materials made by convict labor, or child labor, were approved, "there would seem to be no phase of the business of domestic manufacture which it could not in the same way control."[79] At the same time he supported aggressive, expansionist foreign policy initiatives, to which he felt some of his fellow senators might be a roadblock. A distinction between the constitutional domestic and foreign relations realms, based on a bright-line separation of "internal" from "external" powers of the national government, was helpful to him in pursuing these twin objectives.

Campbell's maxim had itself been a product of the orthodox constitutional jurisprudence of the nineteenth century, with its emphasis on essentialist constitutional powers, preordained constitutional spheres, and a guardian role for judges as constitutional interpreters. But that jurisprudential regime had also emphasized the importance of an enumerated textual basis for the exercise of the national government's powers. Early twentieth-century senatorial debates over the role of executive agreements in foreign policy, however, had demonstrated that the enumerated foreign relations powers of the federal government were quite rudimentary and did not furnish clear mandates for many of the commercial and diplomatic activities of the United States as an international power in the twentieth century. Further, the logic of Sutherland's constitutional textualism in domestic issues, which led toward a strict construction of enumerated national powers, could also be said to lead toward the maintenance of a reserved power consciousness in the foreign relations sphere.

Thus, it was to Sutherland's advantage to develop a theory of national foreign relations powers that was not strictly tied to the enumerated provisions of the Constitution. Consequently, he spent the great bulk of his 1910 essay developing justifications for the proposition that the foreign relations power of the federal government was "inherent" in the sovereignty of the nation and thus "extraconstitutional" but not unconstitutional.[80]

Sutherland asserted that some framers took the creation of a new federal government to render the states incompetent to perform certain functions, one of which was to conduct external affairs.[81] He also claimed that some framers associated the "United Colonies," or the United States, with "full Power to . . . do all Acts and Things which Independent States may of right do,"[82] so that "national sovereignty inhered in the United States" even before the Constitution came into being.[83] He then invoked Campbell's maxim to conclude that the framers "distributed *all* necessary authority over domestic affairs . . . either to the Nation by enumeration or to the States by non-enumeration" and "did not intend to provide less completely for foreign affairs."[84]

Sutherland thus took Campbell's maxim to mean that the foreign relations powers of the newly created United States government included not only its constitutionally enumerated powers but all of the inherent powers of "a fully sovereign nation, possessing and capable of exercising in the family of nations every sovereign power which any sovereign government possessed."[85] He then surveyed cases in which the Supreme Court of the United States had explicitly or implicitly recognized "inherent" powers in the national government. Although his sample was thin, and one of the cases did not even involve foreign affairs,[86] he was able to convey a sense that certain powers conceded to exist in the federal government, such as acquiring territory by discovery and occupation,[87] or excluding[88] or expelling[89] aliens, or governing continental territories,[90] could not easily be traced to enumerated powers. He admitted, however, that "some of the Justices have apparently repudiated the doctrine [that the power of the national government could be extraconstitutional], and have vigorously denied the possession by the general government of any inherent power."[91]

Nonetheless, Sutherland was prepared to suggest, in summary, that

[t]he American people, in whom all sovereign authority ultimately resides, have provided as the instrument for the practical expression of this authority a complete governmental system, consisting of the General government and the State governments, and in this system have vested every power necessary to accomplish the constitutionally declared ends of government. Because of the dual character of the agency which exercises the *domestic* sovereignty of the people the line between the State and the Federal powers has been carefully drawn and must be rigidly observed . . . Over *external* matters, however, no residuary powers do or can exist in the several States, and from the necessity of the case all necessary authority must be found in the National government, such authority being expressly conferred or implied from one or more of the express powers, or from all of them combined, or resulting from the very fact of nationality as inherently inseparable therefrom.[92]

Sutherland was given another opportunity to expound his views on the Constitution and foreign affairs in 1918, when Nicholas Murray Butler, the president of Columbia University, invited him to deliver the George Blumenthal Lectures.[93] Sutherland chose the topic of "Constitutional Power and World Affairs."

The shadow of America's experience in World War I hung prominently over Sutherland's lectures. They were delivered only a month after the Armistice, and four of Sutherland's seven chapters were explicitly devoted to the war, its aftermath, or the nature and extent of the war powers under the Constitution. The recent wartime experience served to underscore for Sutherland the dilemma that he had first identified in 1910. The United States was confronting a rapidly changing, increasingly demanding universe of international affairs with an apparently sketchy and rudimentary array of constitutionally enumerated foreign affairs powers.

In his Columbia lectures Sutherland refined his theory of the sources of broad federal powers in the realm of foreign affairs. He retained his claim that the exercise of foreign relations powers by the national government had a significant extraconstitutional basis, and proposed that in interpretations of the constitutional scope of foreign relations powers "a rule of constitutional construction radically more liberal than that which obtains in the case of the domestic powers" should be applied. The analytical justification for this "radically more liberal" interpretive posture was once again Campbell's maxim that all constitutional power was parceled out among the sovereign entities created by the Constitution.

In Sutherland's view the historical sources he had assembled in his 1910 essay demonstrated that at the framing of the Constitution the states did not possess any powers of external sovereignty, and thus could not have ceded any to the federal government. Thus, if one presumed, following Campbell's maxim, that the framers of the Constitution intended to make an entire distribution of the totality of power they identified, the principle that the federal government could exercise a full range of unenumerated powers in the realm of foreign affairs[94] did not simply "flow from a claim of inherent power." It was also the product of "a legitimate and logical rule of construction." In domestic affairs "the sovereign will of the Nation . . . is manifested by what [the Constitution] affirms," in foreign affairs "by what it fails to negative."[95]

The constitutional jurisprudence of foreign relations, Sutherland believed, should be governed by this "legitimate and logical," but "radically more liberal," rule of constitutional construction. In that regime, characterized by nonexistent state powers and rudimentary national powers, the federal government was free to exercise all "external" powers other than those explicitly prohibited to it by the Constitution, contrary to the Constitution's fundamental principles, or not "essential" to governance. Sutherland's rule was buttressed by his historical claim that the external powers of the federal government had originally been thought of as inherent and extraconstitutional. But it did not depend entirely on that proposition. It was also based on the states being prohibited from making treaties and on Campbell's maxim about the Constitution's distribution of sovereign powers.

Sutherland's rule of construction had obvious implications for all the central issues of orthodox constitutional foreign relations jurisprudence. First, it decisively resolved the issue Sutherland had debated in the Senate a decade earlier: whether executive agreements were constitutionally valid even without Senate ratification. Sutherland's rule easily led to the conclusion that the federal government's power "to make such international agreements as do not constitute treaties in the constitutional sense" existed "under and by warrant of the Constitution so construed."[96]

The "radically more liberal" rule of construction for the external powers of the federal government also resolved the effect of treaties on the reserved police powers of the states. If Campbell's maxim were followed, the Constitution parceled out enumerated powers to the federal government and reserved the remaining powers in the states or in the people. But such a parceling presupposed that the states and the people were capable of exercising powers that had been distributed. If, historically, the states had never exercised the treaty-making power, and if that power was an inherent attribute of sovereignty, then the enumeration of a treaty-making power in the national government did not suggest that the power had been carved out of the general residuum of state powers. It was obviously not a power that fell within the category of those not appropriately exercised by any government: it was, on the contrary, vital to a government's peaceful existence. Hence, unlike the case of many enumerated powers affecting domestic issues, there was no potential conflict between the treaty-making power and reserved Tenth Amendment powers with respect to the subject matter of a given treaty. The federal government's power to make rules affecting states and individual citizens through treaties was plenary and exclusive.

Thus, at approximately the same moment that Quincy Wright was identifying complexities and difficulties in each of the central areas of the orthodox regime of constitutional foreign relations jurisprudence, Sutherland was proposing a "radically more liberal" approach to the interpretation of federal foreign affairs powers designed to avoid the complexities and eliminate the difficulties. As Sutherland's approach, whose primary thrust was to disassociate the exercise of "external" powers from the essentialist structure of enumerated and reserved constitutional jurisprudence, was in gestation, that structure received another jolt. The Supreme Court, in an opinion by Justice Oliver Wendell Holmes, declared that the federal government could, pursuant to a treaty, pass legislation invading the residuum of state police powers to a degree that would have been constitutionally impermissible had no treaty supported the legislation being challenged.

"A striking example" of a conflict between the exercise of the treaty power and state police powers, Sutherland wrote in one of his Columbia lectures, was "afforded by the treaty recently concluded between ourselves and Great Britain for the protection of migratory birds."[97] In the absence of a treaty, he noted, it was "clear that the subject [of regulating the killing of migratory birds] is one beyond the powers of Congress, since wild game is not the property of the Nation but of the states in their public capacity for the common benefit of the people." "May a treaty lawfully stipulate," Sutherland concluded, "for rights and privileges which but for the treaty would confessedly be exclusively under the control of the state?"[98]

Sutherland had anticipated the central issue in *Missouri v. Holland,* in which the Supreme Court considered a challenge to the constitutionality of the migratory bird treaty he had mentioned. In *Missouri v. Holland,* the line of judicial language and commentary suggesting that the treaty power was based on the sovereignty of a nation in the international community—and thus, within its appropriate subject matter range, nearly unlimited—clashed with the line of judicial language and commentary suggesting that the treaty power was based on the Constitution and its scope limited by the constitutional framework of enumerated and reserved powers. The Supreme Court's resolution of the clash, in a 7–2 opinion with no written dissents, was to declare that not only did the treaty power prevail over conflicting state police powers, it could be employed to validate congressional legislation that would otherwise be unconstitutional as trespassing on state reserved power prerogatives.

Contemporary readers, after unraveling Holmes's opinion in *Missouri v. Holland,* could have come to two quite different conclusions. One was that Sutherland's extraconstitutional theory of foreign relations powers was correct. The acts of treaty-making and ratification by the national government demonstrated that there were certain subjects that were so important to the existence of "every civilized government,"[99] and so inherently international in their nature, that they constituted acts of the United States in its sovereign capacity and were thus subject to no constitutional limitations. The other was that the treaty-making power, despite prevailing over competing state police powers in *Missouri v. Holland,* remained subject to constitutional limitations and, by implication, that the foreign relations powers of the federal government would continue to be exercised in an enumerated and reserved power framework.

Missouri v. Holland was a challenge by the state of Missouri to congressional legislation implementing a 1916 treaty between the United States and Great Britain (representing Canada), which established protection for migratory birds.[100] Efforts to protect birds had surfaced in Congress as early as 1904, when proposed federal legislation was introduced to that effect. A federal statute eventually did pass both houses of Congress in 1913 and was signed by President Taft.[101]

In the course of debates in Congress over federal protective legislation for migratory birds, both supporters and opponents suggested that the constitutional status of any such legislation was highly questionable.[102] Their concerns rested on several doctrinal propositions taken to be established at the time. First, a line of Supreme Court cases had treated birds (included in the legal category of *ferae naturae*) as property under the control of the states in their capacity as trustees for their citizens.[103] Second, the Commerce Clause had not been read in a sufficiently sweeping fashion to permit birds flying across state lines to be treated as articles in interstate commerce, especially since there was very little evidence that birds were actually transported across state lines, as distinguished from flying across them on their own volition. Nor did the fact that birds were sometimes killed in a state and subsequently sold outside it, and that state laws regulated the conditions under which birds were killed and sold, mean that birds under early twentieth-century Commerce Clause doctrine were objects of interstate commerce.[104] Finally, an argument that federal power to regulate birds for the benefit of all American citizens followed from the inability of individual states to adequately protect birds foundered on the enumerated powers assumption.

As early as January 1913, Senator Elihu Root of New York, in the course of debates over federal migratory bird legislation, had suggested that negotiation of a treaty for the protection of such birds might give "the Government of the United States . . . constitutional authority to deal with this subject."[105] By July of that year a resolution recommending such a treaty passed the Senate,[106] and in 1916 the treaty itself was negotiated and ratified.

As the treaty was being ratified and enabling legislation was being passed in the years between 1916 and 1918, challenges to the 1913 federal migratory bird legislation had been working their way up to the Supreme Court. After the ratification of the migratory bird treaty the Department of Agriculture, which had been reluctant to enforce the 1913 legislation for fear of a successful court challenge, began enforcing regulations passed in light of the treaty more vigorously.[107] Among the prosecutions for violation of those regulations were indictments against two citizens of Missouri. These prompted the state of Missouri to bring a bill in equity against Ray P. Holland, the federal game warden who had enforced the regulations, to prevent further enforcement of the 1918 enabling legislation. The indicted persons demurred to their indictments, and the United States government moved to dismiss Missouri's bill. The trial judge overruled the demurrers and dismissed the bill on the grounds that the 1918 legislation was constitutional, stating at the same time that it would have been unconstitutional if not made pursuant to a treaty.[108] Missouri appealed to the Supreme Court.

There was more to *Missouri v. Holland* than the question of whether the treaty power trumped conflicting reserved state police powers in a Constitution whose framework was taken to be governed by the enumerated powers assumption. There was the additional question of whether migratory birds were a proper subject for a treaty at all. Since that question was not obviously answered in the affirmative—the disposition of game having been traditionally regarded as a local rather than an international matter—*Missouri v. Holland* required attention to the origins of subject matter limitations on the treaty power. Did those limitations originate in the Constitution's text, read as being governed by the enumerated/reserved allocation of powers in the American system of government? Or did they originate somewhere else, perhaps in a tacit understanding of the limited range of "inherent" powers derived from national sovereignty?

Early in Holmes's opinion he wrote a lengthy paragraph that contained some remarkable general comments about the nature and sources of the treaty power. Although he intended the comments to be taken sequentially, as part of an integrated argument, they deserve separate treatment, especially since some of his sequential connections seem embryonic at best. The first comment stated:

> Acts of Congress are the supreme law of the land only when made in pursuance of the Constitution, while treaties are declared to be so when made under the authority of the United States. It is open to question whether the authority of the United States means more than the formal acts prescribed to make the convention. We do not mean to imply that there are no qualifications to the treaty-making power; but they must be ascertained in a different way. It is obvious that there may be matters of the sharpest exigency for the national well being that an act of Congress could not deal with but that a treaty followed by such an act could . . .[109]

Up to this point in the opinion, Holmes, despite his statement that the "qualifications to the treaty-making power" must be ascertained in a "different way," had not identified any limitations on the treaty power that rested on the enumerated/reserved powers framework. If anything, the passage suggested that the "different way" in which he was approaching limitations on the treaty power was to bypass the enumerated powers framework altogether. Nor did his next set of comments introduce any limitations. He wrote:

> We are not yet discussing the particular case before us but are only considering the validity of the test proposed. With regard to that we may add that when we are dealing with words that also are a constituent act, like the Constitution of the United States, we must realize that they have called into life a being the development of which could not have been foreseen completely by the most gifted of its begetters. It was enough for them to realize or to hope that they had created an organism; it has taken a century and has cost their successors much sweat and blood to prove that they created a nation. The case before us must be considered in the light of our whole experience and not merely in that of what was said a hundred years ago.[110]

Despite the breadth of this passage, it was designed to relate only to "the validity of the test proposed," a test designed to formulate the scope and limits of the treaty-making power. Holmes had, at the place in the opinion where he wrote the passage, only identified one feature of that test unambiguously: a treaty needed to govern "matters requiring national action" to pass constitutional muster.[111] Thus, the context of the passage suggests that, notwithstanding its rhetorical flourishes, it can be reduced to an argument that even though the framers might not have explicitly said that the protection of migratory birds was a matter requiring national action, the "whole experience" of the United States since the founding of the Constitution, including "much sweat and blood" to prove that the United States was now "a nation" rather than merely "an organism," demonstrated a national interest in the protection of migratory birds.

That argument, however, seemed directed more toward confirming the breadth of the treaty power than to ascertaining any limitations on it, since that power could now be taken to extend to subjects that those who drafted the Treaty Clause did not contemplate as being matters of national concern.[112] So by this point in his opinion Holmes, although intimating that he would be ascertaining "qualifications to the treaty-making power," had not identified any significant qualifications, and had hinted that the treaty-making power might rest on some inherent sovereign powers and might not be subject to constitutional limitations at all.

Holmes then mentioned some constitutional limitations: "The treaty in question does not contravene any prohibitory words to be found in the Constitution. The only question is whether it is forbidden by some invisible radiation from the general terms of the Tenth Amendment. We must consider what this country has become in deciding what that Amendment has reserved."[113] These limitations would not have been particularly comforting to those who believed that the combination of treaty and statute challenged in *Missouri v. Holland* amounted to an amendment of the Constitution through the treaty process. Direct prohibitions on the conduct of the federal government are few and far between in the constitutional text, and only some of them appear to involve matters likely to be the subject of treaties. In addition, Holmes had defined the Tenth Amendment as restraining federal power only through "some invisible radiation." He had reversed the general presumption of the enumerated/reserved powers framework, that power was retained in the states or the people unless it had been specifically conferred on the national government. His presumption was that the exercise of federal powers consistent with nationhood could extend rather deeply into the residuum of state powers.

Thus, Holmes's application of his test for determining the limitations on the treaty-making power amounted to assertions that "a national interest of very nearly the first magnitude" in the protection of migratory birds existed, and that this interest could be "protected only by national action in concert with that of another power." In the context of *Missouri v. Holland,* this amounted to saying that when the national government wanted to achieve some goal and believed that the states would resist it, it could induce a foreign power to agree to a joint articulation of that goal in a treaty to surmount the difficulty. Since nothing about the protection of migratory birds suggested that it was an essentially national or international undertaking, Holmes's "matters requiring national action" requirement for the constitutional validity of treaties did not suggest any subject matter limits to the treaty-making power. Moreover, his analysis of the reserved power limitations on the treaty-making power—the "invisible radiations" that now flowed from a Tenth Amendment interpreted against a backdrop of increasing national power—did not suggest any federalism limitations.

Finally, along the way Holmes had raised, and not discounted, two other theories on which the treaty-making power might be sustained: the absence of an explicit reference to constitutional limits on that power in the Supremacy Clause and the presence of something like an "inherent" federal police power, which "must belong to and somewhere reside in every civilized government." If those two theories were embraced along with Holmes's other arguments in *Missouri v. Holland,* the scope of the treaty-making power seemed virtually unlimited, especially given its very extensive subject matter range. The essential ambiguity of *Missouri v. Holland* was that Holmes had acted as if he were conducting his inquiry into the limitations on the treaty-making power within the orthodox enumerated/reserved powers framework, but his opinion suggested that the treaty-making power might not be affected by that framework at all.

In light of the sweeping implications of Holmes's opinion in *Missouri v. Holland,* the reaction of contemporary commentators to the decision was surprisingly mild. Prior to the decision Charles Butler,[114] Westel Willoughby,[115] Edward Corwin,[116] and of course Sutherland[117] had endorsed the proposition that the treaty power prevailed over conflicting reserved powers in the states, and after *Missouri v. Holland* was announced two law review articles[118] and four student notes[119] either openly supported it or found its conclusions unexceptionable. One article[120] and two student notes[121] were highly critical, raising arguments similar to those made by Henry St. George Tucker in his 1915 treatise on the treaty power, where Tucker had concluded that "if the treaty power were permitted to take the police powers of the states *ad libitum,* they would be unlimited in number, for the treaty power may embrace any and all subjects."[122]

The reaction to *Missouri v. Holland,* embodied in Quincy Wright's blunt conclusion that "[t]he 'reserved powers' of the states . . . do not limit the treaty-making power,"[123] requires some explanation, given the implications of a broad reading of Holmes's opinion. Had the reserved power consciousness that dominated the orthodox constitutional jurisprudence of foreign relations suddenly evaporated after World War I? Why didn't *Missouri v. Holland* precipitate more dissents or engender a larger degree of commentator protest?

Two explanations seem possible. The first is that the ambiguities in Holmes's opinion resulted in few contemporary readers taking it as an unqualifiedly broad statement of the scope and subject matter coverage of the treaty power, as Holmes may have meant it to be. The opinion could have been understood within the conventional enumerated powers/reserved powers framework and, as such, as simply reasserting the unexceptionable proposition that the treaty power could extend to subjects in which the national government had a serious interest. Holmes's hints that the language of the Supremacy Clause might have obviated any limitations on the treaty power, or that an "inherent" power in the federal government to exercise "sovereign" powers existed, might not have been taken seriously, since there was little historical support for the former and a 1907 decision of the Court, admittedly in a domestic context, had decisively repudiated the latter.[124] It seemed hard to imagine migratory bird legislation serving as the opening wedge of an attack designed to install a federal Leviathan.

So the decision might have been read in a minimalist fashion, despite Holmes's sweeping language. It seems more plausible, however, that the decision was read not so much as minimalist but as confined by the constitutional "understandings" to which Wright alluded. In this reading *Missouri v. Holland* could have been taken at two levels. It was a decision sustaining the constitutionality of federal migratory bird legislation enacted pursuant to a treaty. It was also an endorsement of the proposition that the treaty power, and possibly other federal foreign affairs powers, inevitably prevailed over reserved state powers. The first level was unexceptionable; the second level was potentially revolutionary. The second level, however, was qualified by constitutional understandings.

A sense of that qualification can be gleaned from remarks Wright made just after discussing *Missouri v. Holland* in his 1922 treatise.[125] "[A]ny respect that is shown by the treaty-making power to 'reserved powers' of the states," he announced,

> is merely by virtue of an understanding of the Constitution. In fact such respect has often been shown and it was thus to safeguard the interests of the states that the Senate was made such an important element in treaty-making. This function the Senate has recognized, and . . . has frequently exercised a veto upon treaties thought to violate states' rights . . . The practice of the Senate, the opinions of statesmen and dicta of the courts indicate that, except for the most cogent reasons, the treaty power ought to exercise its powers in such a way as not to interfere with the control by the states of their own land, natural resources, and public services and not to interfere unnecessarily with the enforcement by the state of its own policy with reference to the protection of public safety, health, morals and economic welfare.[126]

In Wright's view constitutional understandings suggested that the revolutionary potential of a broad reading of *Missouri v. Holland* was not likely to be realized. The question of the scope of foreign affairs powers, both with respect to separation of powers concerns and with respect to federalism concerns, were at bottom questions of politics, not questions of constitutional doctrine. One-third of the members of the Senate stood as representatives of the reserved powers of the states or as representatives of the autonomy of Congress or the Senate itself. Exercises in foreign policymaking could not fail to take into account the concerns of those representatives of the federal legislature and of the states, so long as their presence continued to be necessary to give constitutional legitimacy to the acts of the policymakers. The practices, the opinions, and the powers of senators were part of the set of understandings that placed parameters on constitutional foreign relations jurisprudence. According to this view, *Missouri v. Holland* was just a case about migratory birds, not a case revolutionizing the relationship between the federal government and the states in the conduct of foreign affairs.

There was, however, an unstated premise in Wright's conclusion that *Missouri v. Holland* needed to be read in light of constitutional understandings. The premise was one deeply ingrained in the orthodox regime: most foreign policymaking activities would continue to involve the Senate because they would continue to take the form of treaties. With that premise in place Wright could treat as unexceptionable potentially revolutionary formulations of constitutional doctrine, since they would be tempered with constitutional politics. This seemed appropriate to a commentator writing in the 1920s because the landscape of constitutional foreign policymaking appeared to combine increased international activity on the part of the executive branch with the continued presence of the Senate as guardian of internal domestic interests.

The idea that questions of constitutional foreign relations jurisprudence ultimately reduced themselves to the politics of constitutional understandings, however, proved capable of spawning a logic that pointed in quite a different direction. By the time of Wright's treatise there was an increasing sphere of American foreign policymaking that did not include treaties and thus did not include the Senate. If one of the implications of *Missouri v. Holland* was that the entire regime of foreign policymaking, not simply the treaty power, had been entrusted to the federal government and forbidden to the states, it might be that the absence of significant constitutional limitations on the treaty-making power also pertained to other federal foreign relations powers. If that were the case, it was hard to summon up any constitutional understandings restricting the exercise of those powers. Perhaps there was no such locus, and thus there were no restraints on the powers of the national government. Perhaps Sutherland's theory that federal foreign affairs powers were extraconstitutional provided a more accurate description of the terrain.

This logic, which had already surfaced in the early twentieth-century discussions of the relationship between treaties and executive agreements, was to take on new urgency in the 1920s. That decade was marked by the continuation of two trends that opponents of American entanglements in world affairs had hoped might be reversed by the end of World War I and the refusal of the United States to join the League of Nations. First, American businesses continued to increase their participation in international markets, and United States foreign policymakers remained concerned with furthering and maintaining international political stability in the rest of the world.[127] Second, aggressive foreign states in Europe and Asia continued to make encroachments on their neighbors, reviving an atmosphere of international tension that was heightened for Americans by the fact that many of the aggressive states had adopted totalitarian forms of government.

Those trends suggested that the foreign policy ventures of the United States were likely to increase and to be delicate and potentially dangerous as the twentieth century progressed. By the early 1930s, in fact, foreign policy initiatives had become one of the chief preoccupations of the national executive branch. With those initiatives the stress lines in the orthodox regime of constitutional foreign relations jurisprudence were accentuated. In an atmosphere where the political maps of Europe, Asia, and even Latin America seemed capable of changing rapidly, the swift, flexible, unencumbered conduct of foreign policy by the executive branch seemed a natural response.

It appeared by the 1920s that the constitutional jurisprudence of foreign relations was no longer a reflection of the essentialist conceptions of constitutional powers and limitations that had governed nineteenth-century foreign and domestic cases. It appeared, rather, to be a unique blend of pervasive federal power and constitutional "understandings" that qualified that power. Constitutional understandings could change. In the face of an altered international context and altered confidence about the national executive's capacity to respond to international conflict, they did change, providing a jurisprudential space for Sutherland's extraconstitutional theory of national foreign relations power to take hold and for the principle of executive discretion in foreign affairs policymaking to become entrenched. The result was the transformation of twentieth-century constitutional foreign relations jurisprudence.

3

The Triumph of Executive Discretion in Foreign Relations

In the sixteen years between *Missouri v. Holland* and the next significant constitutional foreign relations decision by the United States Supreme Court, *United States v. Curtiss-Wright Export Co.*, the efforts of American foreign policymakers to secure and to preserve a stable international climate for the expanding global business ventures of American citizens ran up against another set of expansionist global forces. Totalitarian states had emerged in the wake of economic and political dislocations in Europe and Asia in the years after World War I. The first such state to surface was the Soviet regime in Russia, which had cemented its authority by the year *Missouri v. Holland* was decided. By the early 1930s additional totalitarian regimes, comparable to the Soviets in their authoritarian, antidemocratic systems of government, were in place in Italy, Germany, and Japan. All of these regimes featured massive state involvement with the economy, aggrandizement of the state's military forces, aggressive nationalistic and expansionist rhetoric, and hierarchical, state-controlled politics. Their structure enabled them to subsume the international political and economic ventures of their citizens in the foreign policy goals of their leaders.

The emergence of totalitarian states posed a variety of difficulties for Americans who sought to engage in international business transactions in the 1920s and thirties and for United States policymakers dedicated to the maintenance of a favorable climate for such transactions. Of those difficulties, two were to have particularly significant ramifications for the early twentieth-century constitutional jurisprudence of foreign relations. One involved the Soviet Union's determined effort, as part of its centralized control of the Russian economy, to nationalize the property holdings of corporations and individuals located within Russia, including those holdings in which American citizens had a stake. The other involved the efforts of American armaments manufacturers to profit from the increased trade in weapons that accompanied the expansion of the military forces of totalitarian regimes. By

1937 both of these side effects of the growth of global totalitarianism in the 1920s and 1930s had produced cases that gave the Supreme Court of the United States opportunities to dramatically increase the substance, and the scope, of the transformation of constitutional foreign relations jurisprudence.

The accession of the Soviets to power in Russia was officially treated by the United States government as an event that had not happened. From 1920 to 1933 the United States declined to recognize the Soviet Union, with a policy statement issued by Secretary of State Bainbridge Colby in 1920 forming the basis of nonrecognition. Colby had emphasized that the Soviets were not a popularly elected government; that they had violated "every principle of honor and good faith, and every usage and convention underlying the whole structure of international law" in seizing power; and that they were identical to the Third International of the Communist Party, which believed in world revolution and subversive propaganda.[1]

Although it was obvious that the Soviets remained in political control of the territory formerly known as Imperial Russia during the years following Colby's pronouncement, at the time of the presidential election of 1932 the policy of nonrecognition remained in place, and the traditional bases of that policy remained essentially unchanged. After coming to power the Soviet government regularly declared its commitment to world revolution, repudiated debts incurred by the former Russian government to the United States, and issued nationalization decrees that confiscated the Russian property of American citizens. These actions served to reinforce Colby's proposition that nonrecognition of Soviet Russia was a matter of principle. By the early 1930s, however, the question of affording official recognition to the Soviets was subjected to reexamination,[2] and in 1933 official recognition came in the form of an exchange of diplomatic letters between President Franklin Roosevelt and Commissar for Foreign Affairs Maxim Litvinov.[3]

Between 1920 and the Second World War, the official attitude of the United States toward the Soviet Union had a significant impact on the constitutional jurisprudence of foreign relations. The initial policy of nonrecognition precipitated a series of lawsuits that prompted a reconsideration of the principles and understandings of the orthodox constitutional regime. In those suits, which were primarily concerned with the domestic distribution of assets claimed by Russian citizens, Russian or American banks, or American citizens holding property in Russia, orthodox separation of powers and federalism paradigms were placed under pressure. Then, after 1933, the Litvinov Agreement created additional constitutional dimensions for those lawsuits.

In the period between the Bolshevik Revolution and the Litvinov Agreement, New York City was the center of international economic transactions involving the Soviet Union and American citizens, American citizens and Russian banks, and Russian citizens and American banks. A number of legal disputes involving assets affected by the Soviet government's treatment of Russian corporations and property in Russia found their way to the New York Court of Appeals during that period.[4] Sometimes the cases involved claims by or against Russian corporations that had been dissolved by decrees of the Soviets but continued to do business in New York;[5] sometimes they involved claims to ownership of property in Russia that had been seized by the Soviets and sold to American companies.[6]

In those cases the Court of Appeals frequently noted the dissonance between the State Department's official position that the Soviet government did not exist and that government's political control of the territory formerly known as Imperial Russia. This dissonance, the Court of Appeals noted, made a juristic characterization of the Soviet government difficult: in one case it asked whether the Soviets were "a de facto" government or "a band of robbers."[7]

In each of its Russian recognition decisions the Court of Appeals emphasized the need for courts to defer to the discretionary powers of the federal executive in foreign affairs. But although lip service was paid to that posture, the actual stance of the Court of Appeals can more accurately be described as consistent with independent determinations by state courts on the legal consequences of nonrecognition of the Soviet government. A fair reading of the New York recognition cases between the early 1920s and 1933 would treat them as compatible with a constitutional foreign relations jurisprudence in which judges continued to exercise independent review of legal questions raised by foreign policy decisions of the executive, and in which federalism constraints on such decisions were taken seriously, at least at the level of constitutional understandings.

In one case Judge Irving Lehman, for a majority of the court, noted that although the Soviet government was notoriously in existence, that nation had not been recognized by the United States. The absence of official recognition, Lehman felt, meant that American courts need not "ascribe to [Soviet] decrees all the effect which inheres in the laws or orders of a sovereign," and that the State Department, whatever its policies toward the Soviets, "cannot determine how far the private rights and obligations of individuals are affected by a body not sovereign, or with which our government will have no dealings." A question of the effect of Soviet nationalization decrees on the disposition of Russian assets in New York, Lehman declared, "does not concern our foreign relations. It is not a political question, but a judicial question. The courts in considering that question assume as a premise that until recognition these acts [of the Soviets] are not in full sense law."[8]

Lehman's statement assumed that until the United States government had recognized the Soviets, New York courts were entirely free to decide for themselves how the "private rights and obligations" of citizens affected by dealings with the Soviet government would be disposed of within New York state. Such questions were not questions "of foreign relations" nor "political" questions. They were domestic common law questions, to be decided on the basis of New York law and policy. Although particular New York common law decisions involving American or foreign citizens affected by the acts of the Soviet government might be consistent with the State Department's refusal to afford de jure status to that government, they need not be. New York law and policy governed those decisions, not the foreign relations of the federal government.

This posture was consistent with the orthodox, limited view of international political questions in early twentieth-century foreign relations jurisprudence. State courts had a fair amount of latitude to decide private rights and obligations that had become contested because of acts by foreign governments. Although a state court might give legal weight to a decree of an unrecognized government in political control of territory, the fact that the United States had not recognized that government did not provide a reason for the Supreme Court of the United States to review the state court's decision on the ground that it might run counter to the foreign policy of the national government. Such a decision did not affect foreign relations at all.

The decisions of New York courts in Russian recognition cases were noted by commentators in the 1920s and early thirties, who, on the whole, concluded that the officially unrecognized status of the Soviet regime was not a fruitful starting point for assessments of the rights and responsibilities of Russian nationals, Russian citizens, and the Russian government in American state courts.[9] More than one commentator argued that there was no compelling reason why the State Department's fiction that the "Russian government" continued to be composed of refugee representatives of the Czarist or Provisional regimes should be indulged in by courts that were aware of the actual state of affairs in Russia. At the same time, more than one commentator suggested that the nationalization decrees of the Soviet regime need not bind American courts if public policy considerations dictated otherwise.[10] In sum, most commentators endorsed the proposition that state courts could reserve judgment about the weight given to acts of unrecognized foreign governments.

In a 1933 monograph, *Judicial Aspects of Foreign Relations,* Louis Jaffe, eventually to become a distinguished member of the Harvard law faculty, noted a potential consequence of treating the federal government as the exclusive architect of foreign policymaking. By a certain logic, Jaffe suggested, all the legal questions raised in domestic cases in which foreign governments or citizens were parties could be seen as "international political questions." According to this logic "[t]he power to make treaties, to declare war, and to receive ambassadors is expressly vested in the 'political organs' of the Government, and so it is said that any disputed questions logically related to or presupposed in the exercise of these powers are 'political' and that by the same token they are withdrawn from the courts, whose constitutionally granted functions are a-political, i.e. judicial."[11] But in a survey of potential "international political questions" cases that had focused on the New York Russian recognition decisions, Jaffe had discovered that "[m]any matters relating to foreign affairs which under this logic would be 'political' are, in fact, handled by the courts. Courts determine whether a claim of sovereign immunity is properly asserted; they interpret treaties . . . They may do these things in the absence of relevant executive action; they may do it in the face of executive action already taken."[12]

Jaffe found that the Court of Appeals could have concluded (and occasionally did) that it had no jurisdiction over cases interpreting acts of the Soviets, or over cases in which the Soviet government was a plaintiff or defendant, because the Soviet government had not been recognized. Such a position would have been consistent with executive policy and with the logic of the political questions doctrine. But on the whole the Court of Appeals heard, and decided, such cases. Not only that, it reserved the option to acknowledge the existence of the Soviet regime, despite the State Department's refusal officially to do so, and to treat the acts of that regime as binding, or not binding, based on their effects on state public policy.

In his analysis of the New York Russian recognition cases Jaffe devoted no attention at all to their federalism dimensions. He assumed that the fact that the national government had declined to recognize the Soviets had no definitive federalism consequences. State Department policy toward the Soviets did not prevent New York courts from making their own determinations of the rights and responsibilities of those affected by Soviet decrees nor did it create any "federal questions" in the cases for potential Supreme Court review. This conception of state common law decisions in cases where foreign nationals or governments were parties was consistent with the orthodox federalism paradigm. Jaffe was so convinced that state court dispositions of claims involving actions of the Soviets did not raise federal questions that his study did not even have an index entry for "federalism" issues.

Thus, as late as 1933 the numerous Russian recognition cases decided in the New York courts were still being conceptualized as domestic common law cases in which judges could treat the attitude of the United States government toward the Soviet Union as having no legal effect. But once the United States officially recognized the Soviets, that recognition significantly influenced the state of constitutional foreign relations jurisprudence. The widespread consequences of that recognition, as they materialized in Supreme Court decisions over the next several years, were a result not only of the fact of recognition but of the form it took.

In a November 16, 1933 exchange of letters between President Roosevelt and Soviet Commissar of Foreign Affairs Maxim Litvinov, the United States agreed to grant the Soviets diplomatic recognition in exchange for a partial settlement of the Russian government's outstanding debts to the United States. The Soviets also agreed to forgo claims they had made for damage done by United States troops who had been dispatched to Russia in 1918 to aid the counterrevolutionary "White Armies" in their efforts to displace the Bolsheviks.

The process that concluded in the Litvinov Agreement began on October 10, 1933, when President Roosevelt wrote a letter to Soviet President Mikhail Kalinin suggesting that "frank friendly conversations" be held between himself and representatives of the Soviet government, with a view toward resolving differences between the two powers.[13] A week later Kalinin replied, accepting the proposal to discuss matters of mutual interest and stating that "the abnormal situation [of no diplomatic relations] . . . has an unfavorable effect not only on the interests of the two states concerned, but upon the general international situation."[14] Litvinov was designated the official representative of the Soviets for a series of conferences in Washington in November, and on November 16 he and Roosevelt released the texts of letters they had exchanged.

The most important provision of the Litvinov Agreement for constitutional foreign relations jurisprudence was a letter from Litvinov to Roosevelt in which the Soviets released and assigned to the United States government all amounts that previous court decisions had concluded were owed by American nationals to the Russian government.[15] This meant that the Soviets pledged not to enforce any claims or settlements Russian governments held against Americans. Since an officially recognized Soviet government succeeded to the previous claims of any Russian regime, this was a potentially significant concession,[16] as was the Soviets' agreement not to press any claims against the United States for damage from American troops supporting the White Armies. Those claims did not approach the amount of the unpaid debts owed the United States for loans in connection with World War I (which were not covered by the Litvinov Agreement), but they nonetheless might have been considerable.

The Litvinov Agreement was a protocol, not requiring Senate ratification. Given the general goodwill of the Roosevelt administration in its first term and the continued presence of opposition to recognition of the Soviets in

Congress, the protocol form was not surprising. But the form of the Litvinov Agreement, and the potential effect of its assignment provisions on the disposition of Russian assets in American courts, opened up some significant questions for the constitutional regime of foreign relations jurisprudence. The Litvinov Agreement clearly amounted to a policy statement of the United States government on the status of certain claims to assets in Russia derived from Soviet nationalization and confiscation decrees. But that statement of policy had not been made in a treaty nor in a process involving significant congressional oversight. Moreover, American state courts, as the New York recognition cases suggested, had not previously regarded cases involving the distribution of assets derived from property holdings in Russia as "foreign relations" cases.

Thus, the passage of the Litvinov Agreement raised three potentially momentous questions. One was whether an executive agreement with little congressional oversight occupied the same constitutional status as a treaty. A second was whether, if the Litvinov Agreement did occupy that status, it had the same potential as the treaty in *Missouri v. Holland* to displace state law if its assignment provisions conflicted with any state policies as to the disposition of Russian assets. A final question involved the continued validity of the New York Court of Appeals' long-standing assumption that state cases raising domestic common law issues, in which international subjects happened to be parties, were not by virtue of that fact transformed into "foreign relations" cases, in which courts needed to defer to the foreign affairs policies of the United States government.

The first question tested the continued relevance of the orthodox separation of powers paradigm of foreign relations jurisprudence; the second tested the continued relevance of the orthodox federalism paradigm. The last question asked judges to consider whether the foreign relations policies of the federal government, whether embodied in the form of treaties or in executive agreements, could displace state law in state common law disputes. If all those questions were to be answered in favor of plenary federal power, two results would ensue: a major change in the constitutional jurisprudence of foreign relations and the emergence of a federal common law of foreign relations cases, derived primarily from national executive policies.

Those questions surfaced in a series of cases, stretching from 1936 to 1945, in which the Supreme Court revisited the starting assumptions of the orthodox regime. The collective product of those cases and related commentary was a transformation of American constitutional foreign relations jurisprudence to a form largely resembling its current state. In that transformation a reconstituted principle of federal executive discretion in foreign relations was established, with discretion functioning as a surrogate for judicial deference to the policies of the national executive.

The first question raised by the Litvinov Agreement was resolved in a case related to the impact of international totalitarian states on American foreign relations in the 1920s and 1930s. Totalitarian regimes were predicated on a massive military apparatus. That apparatus provided jobs, helped cement the authority of a regime's leaders, reinforced the concept of hierarchical discipline, and was consistent with an aggressive, expansionist foreign policy. The growth of military forces in totalitarian states also expanded the markets for arms sales, and American entrepreneurs responded to those markets. By the early 1930s a number of American firms were engaged in international armaments ventures.

At the same time as the international appeal of totalitarian regimes widened, certain nations in Latin America gave evidence of adopting totalitarian-style governments, with Argentina the largest nation to do so. This trend, coupled with the outbreak of border wars among neighboring Latin American nations, gave rise to concern, in Congress and elsewhere, that unstable political conditions in Latin America could pose a potential threat to the security of the United States. An ominous example was the Chaco War between Paraguay and Bolivia, which had begun in 1932 and had featured atrocities on both sides.

In May 1934 President Roosevelt introduced, and Congress approved, a joint resolution giving the president the power to suspend American arms sales to the Paraguayan and Bolivian governments.[17] The joint resolution[18] authorized the president to proclaim an embargo on the shipment of arms from American manufacturers to either Paraguay or Bolivia if he found that such a prohibition might "contribute to the establishment of peace between those countries." It provided that violators of the embargo could be subject to fines and imprisonment.[19]

In January 1936 four corporate officers of the Curtiss-Wright Export Corporation, along with the corporation itself and two affiliated companies, were indicted for conspiring to sell aircraft machine guns to Bolivia in violation of the 1934 joint resolution and accompanying proclamation. Among the grounds on which the defendants contested the indictment was an argument that the joint resolution, which had allowed the president to issue the embargo and its associated criminal penalties simply on a finding that American arms sales to Bolivia or Paraguay would jeopardize the establishment of peace between those countries, amounted to an unconstitutional delegation of legislative power to the executive branch.[20] The case was tried in federal court for the southern district of New York, where the defendants' demurrer to the indictments was sustained on the unconstitutional delegation ground.[21] Under the Criminal Appeals Act of 1907, the United States could appeal directly from a federal district court to the Supreme Court when a decision sustaining a demurrer to an indictment was based on the invalidity of the criminal statute upon which the indictment had been founded.[22] Thus, the *Curtiss-Wright* case was heard by the Supreme Court in November 1936 and handed down in December of that year. By a seven-to-one count, with Sutherland writing the majority opinion, McReynolds dissenting without opinion, and Stone not participating, the Court reversed.

Two sets of developments that had taken place between the 1933 Litvinov Agreement and the 1936 indictment of the corporations and their officers in *Curtiss-Wright* furnished the context for Sutherland's opinion. The first involved a series of foreign policy measures initiated by the executive without the consent of the Senate but with the apparent blessing of Congress.[23] These included multilateral executive agreements on currency[24] and commodities[25] and a 1934 Reciprocal Trade Agreements Act.[26] The currency and commodities agreements, responses to depressed economic conditions, did not generate much controversy. The 1934 tariff legislation, however, treated presidential action on tariffs as binding without congressional oversight for three years and did not require the president to submit any trade agreements to the Senate. As such it went further in the direction of executive autonomy than any previous reciprocal trade agreement and was challenged on constitutional grounds.[27] Opponents of the Act argued that it violated the delegation principle and unduly departed from the treaty model of foreign affairs policymaking.[28] Supporters of the Act simply voted its passage without confronting those arguments.[29]

The second set of developments involved the Supreme Court's response to delegation of legislative powers arguments in domestic cases between 1934 and late 1936. In three challenges to early New Deal regulatory legislation, significant majorities of the Court struck down the statutes, twice on unconstitutional delegation grounds.[30] Sutherland voted with the majority each time and wrote the Court's opinion in the last of the cases, *Carter v. Carter Coal Co.* Although Sutherland's central argument for invalidating the legislation in *Carter Coal* was premised on reserved powers limitations on the Commerce Clause, he had inserted a suggestive sentence that had implications for the delegation issue.[31] The cases, taken together, demonstrated that in the domestic arena a solid majority of the Court had signaled that it was not only committed to significant federalism limitations on the regulatory powers of the national government; it was also committed to significant separation of powers limitations embodied in the nondelegation doctrine.[32] In the popular parlance, it was seen as an anti–New Deal Court.

In the sentence in *Carter Coal,* a challenge to a 1935 congressional statute seeking to set minimum prices and to establish collective bargaining in the coal industry, Sutherland, after maintaining that the legislation could not be justified on Commerce Clause grounds, considered the possibility that the importance of coal to the national economy and the existence of a severe economic crisis might justify some "inherent" federal regulatory powers akin to state police powers. His response was that the federal government possessed "no *inherent* power in respect of the internal affairs of the states."[33] He then went on to say, "The question in respect of the inherent power of that government as to the external affairs of the nation and in the field of international law is a wholly different matter which it is not necessary now to consider."[34] *Carter Coal* had been argued in March 1936 and handed down on May 18 of that year; six months later Sutherland would revive that sentence.

A number of elements were coalescing in the time interval between *Carter Coal* and *Curtiss-Wright* to make the latter case a potentially momentous one. The nondelegation doctrine, apparently dormant for much of the early twentieth century, had been revived as a potential major constitutional barrier to New Deal legislation. At the same time the international situation appeared increasingly foreboding, as Nazi Germany and Fascist Italy continued to build up their military forces and began efforts to expand their territory. The obvious contempt the Soviets had shown for previous treaty obligations of the Russian government suggested that totalitarian states might have a different attitude toward binding international obligations than that embodied in such 1920s documents as the Kellogg-Briand Pact. Finally, the experiments of the first Roosevelt administration with expanded government, even though their constitutionality remained an open question, had apparently received popular endorsement in Roosevelt's landslide victory in the 1936 presidential election. Thus, one possible effect of a delegation challenge to a New Deal-inspired extension of presidential prerogatives in the foreign affairs area might be to precipitate a clash between the constitutional jurisprudence of the domestic and foreign affairs realms.

As it turned out, no such clash occurred. In *Curtiss-Wright* Sutherland produced an opinion upholding the 1934 joint resolution and proclamation that precipitated only an inarticulate dissent from McReynolds.[35] The strong support for Sutherland's opinion, given its breathtakingly broad scope and dubious use of authorities, is one of the most interesting features of the

Curtiss-Wright decision. We shall return to that feature subsequently; at this point the structure of Sutherland's argument, including his use of the *Carter Coal* sentence, deserves attention.

Given the rapidly changing scope of international politics in the 1930s, the resolution and proclamation being challenged in *Curtiss-Wright* did not appear to be foreign policy initiatives of great moment. The Chaco War between Bolivia and Paraguay, which in 1934 had looked like a volatile bloodbath near American borders, had fizzled out by 1936, and the proclamation Roosevelt had issued in May 1934 had been withdrawn in November 1935.[36] But in terms of its constitutional ramifications, the legislative-executive understanding challenged in *Curtiss-Wright* appeared to depart significantly from the orthodox means by which foreign relations powers were exercised. The resolution authorized the president to make his own judgment about the connection between prohibiting American arms sales to Paraguay and Bolivia and the reestablishment of peace between those countries. Having made that judgment, and without any consultation of Congress, he could issue a proclamation embargoing arms sales at any time and withdraw that proclamation if and when he saw fit. He could also make exceptions to the implementation of the resolution, or set limits to its terms, without any congressional oversight.

The only standard against which the president's discretion was to be evaluated was a requirement that he find the requisite connection between an embargo of arms sales and continued peace between Paraguay and Bolivia. That finding seemed to be the equivalent of the president's opinion. The ordinary characteristics of a legitimate delegation, as implicitly defined by the Court in its 1935 decisions striking down New Deal statutes as unconstitutional delegations of congressional power, seemed to be lacking in *Curtiss-Wright*.[37] Congress had not instructed the president to find any detailed facts necessary to the triggering of legislative policies nor had the legislative policies themselves been spelled out. Instead, the president had, in effect, been given the discretion to indict American arms manufacturers whenever he thought their sales jeopardized peace between two Latin American nations.

Sutherland opened the central portions of his opinion in *Curtiss-Wright* with a sentence that provided an echo of his sentence in *Carter Coal:* "Whether, if the Joint Resolution had related solely to internal affairs it would be open to the challenge that it constituted an unlawful delegation of legislative power to the Executive, we find it unnecessary to determine."[38] This comment prepared readers of Sutherland's opinion for the distinction between the internal and external powers of the national government on which it would be centrally grounded. The orthodox constitutional jurisprudence was not controlling in *Curtiss-Wright* for a simple reason: the foreign affairs powers of the national government were conceptually distinct from its domestic powers. In the foreign affairs realm most broad delegations of power to the national executive branch, or broad encroachments by that branch into the residuum of reserved state powers, were constitutionally unproblematic. This was because most exercises in foreign relations policy-making by the national government rested not only on constitutional enumerations but on inherent powers of sovereignty that were not subject to constitutional restraints at all. The distinction between internal and external affairs, and the existence of inherent national powers in the latter realm, were vital, clarifying jurisprudential concepts.

From these opening sentences the remainder of Sutherland's opinion flowed as if it had been written before. And of course much of it had, for much of it rehearsed his previous arguments on behalf of an inherent, extra-constitutional set of national powers in the foreign affairs realm. Sutherland repeated his 1910 distinction between internal and external powers.[39] He summoned up the same sources he had employed in 1910 and 1919 in support of the propositions that "the powers of external sovereignty" were never held by the states, had always existed in the federal government, and were extraconstitutional in origin, the equivalent of "inherent" powers possessed by all international sovereigns.[40] To say, as one commentator did ten years after *Curtiss-Wright*, that Sutherland was "in the happy position of being able to give [his] writings and speeches the status of the law"[41] was not an overstatement.

The logic of Sutherland's stark separation of external from internal powers, and his grounding of the former powers on the extraconstitutional basis of international sovereignty, suggested that he might not regard the nondelegation doctrine, whose origins lay in a constitutionally enumerated separation of powers among the branches of American government, as even germane to the foreign affairs realm. But he nonetheless devoted some attention in *Curtiss-Wright* to buttressing the legitimacy of what he called "the very delicate, plenary and exclusive power of the President as the sole organ of the federal government in the field of international relations."[42]

Sutherland's arguments for the proposition that the executive was the primary repository of foreign relations power were extremely attenuated. The arguments were of three sorts: arguments from extraconstitutional principles, arguments based on practical considerations of international policymaking, and arguments based on what he called the "unbroken legislative practice" of deferring to executive discretion in foreign affairs. The fact that the latter two sets of arguments were noticeably devoid of any constitutional buttressing highlighted their dependence on the first set of arguments.

Sutherland noted that the president alone negotiated treaties with foreign governments, and that neither the Senate nor Congress could involve itself in the negotiation process.[43] He asserted that "embarrassment—perhaps serious embarrassment" might occur if the president were not given "a degree of discretion and statutory restriction" in delicate international transactions.[44] He claimed that the president had a better opportunity than Congress to "know . . . the conditions which prevail in foreign countries" because "he has his confidential sources of information" and "his agents in the form of diplomatic, consular and other officials."[45] He suggested that secrecy was often the essence of international relations, so that to involve members of the legislative branch in the processes of diplomacy might be "productive of harmful results."[46] All of these considerations revealed "the unwisdom of requiring Congress in this field of governmental power to lay down narrowly definite standards by which the President is to be governed."[47]

Having made these claims about the nature of foreign affairs policymaking, Sutherland suggested that they amounted to "principles" justifying broad delegations of legislative power to the executive in the foreign affairs realm. He then proceeded to sketch the "overwhelming support" for such legislation in a legislative practice "which has prevailed almost from the inception of the national government to the present day."[48] "Practically every volume of the United States Statutes," Sutherland maintained, "contains one or more acts or joint resolutions of Congress authorizing action by the President in respect of subjects affecting foreign relations, which either leave the exercise of the power to his unrestricted judgment, or provide a standard far more general than that which has always been considered requisite with regard to domestic affairs."[49]

The problem with this array of examples of legislative practice was that, as Chief Justice Charles Evans Hughes had pointed out in *Panama Refining v. Ryan*, one of the 1935 domestic delegation cases, the examples did not support a conclusion that Congress believed it had an unqualified power of delegation in the realm of foreign affairs. The examples amounted to a series of instances in which Congress had taken a collective position on an international matter and had simply delegated power to the executive to implement its wishes. The practice was only evidence, Hughes concluded, that the president had regularly been asked to execute congressional policies.

Nonetheless, Sutherland concluded that "a legislative practice such as we have here . . . goes a long way in the direction of proving the presence of unassailable ground for the constitutionality of the practice, to be found in the origin and history of the power involved, or in its nature, or in both combined."[50] The convoluted language of that sentence suggested the shaky constitutional basis of his conclusion. The practical reasons he had given for executive discretion in foreign affairs had no constitutional basis; the legislative acts he cited did not provide support for the kind of broad delegation given to the president in the 1934 joint resolution; and his "proof" of the "unassailable ground for the constitutionality of the practice" rested, ultimately, on the "origin," "history," and "nature" of the federal foreign relations power.

If that power was "inherent" in a sovereign nation, and the federal government the sole representative of that sovereignty, then there was no gainsaying that the federal foreign affairs power was plenary, if not necessarily executive-centered. But the "inherent" foreign relations power of the federal government was extraconstitutional. And Sutherland had previously stated in *Curtiss-Wright* that executive power in the field of foreign relations, "like every other governmental power," needed to be "exercised in subordination to the applicable provisions of the Constitution."[51] So the nature of the foreign relations power did not itself provide a justification for executive discretion unless that statement were to be disregarded. As for the "origin" and "history" of the federal foreign relations power, more than one student of the historical evidence has concluded that Sutherland's theory of the extraconstitutional origins of that power was "shockingly inaccurate."[52]

The fundamental difficulty with Sutherland's theory of the nature and origins of the foreign relations powers of the federal government was that it ignored the distinction on which Quincy Wright had built his entire 1922 treatise: the sovereignty of the United States as a nation in the international community is not the equivalent of the sovereignty of the federal government under the United States Constitution. The American government has a status as an international entity, and certain "powers" follow from that status. But those powers do not give the federal branches of that government corresponding powers to exercise plenary control over the states or over American citizens without constitutional limitations. If they did, the foreign affairs provisions of the Constitution would necessarily have been worded differently. One could imagine some master provision along this line: "The power to conduct all aspects of foreign affairs shall be exclusively invested in the President, anything to the contrary in this Constitution notwithstanding." But no such provision exists or ever has existed.

Sutherland had promulgated in *Curtiss-Wright* the "radically more liberal" interpretation of federal foreign affairs powers that he had called for in his Columbia lectures. This enabled him not only to resolve the delegation issue in that case but to give a very broad hint as to *Curtiss-Wright*'s implications for future cases in which federalism as well as separation of powers issues might be implicated. If the president's foreign affairs powers primarily rested on an extraconstitutional basis, a whole series of potential executive decisions on foreign policy did not require a senatorial check, did not raise significant delegation issues, and were not subject to reserved powers scrutiny. Indeed, the logic of Sutherland's analysis in *Curtiss-Wright* produced a stunning anomaly. His opinion left treaties *more* vulnerable to constitutional attack than other foreign policy measures initiated by the executive, since however broadly the *Curtiss-Wright* opinion was read, it had not abolished the Treaty Clause.

Given the sweepingly revisionist character of Sutherland's *Curtiss-Wright* opinion, it might have been expected to engender some polemical commentary. This did not, on the whole, take place, at least not in the short run. Several law journals commented on the decision shortly after it was handed down and, taken together, the commentators recognized most of its larger implications.[53] Although the tendency of the commentators was to focus on the delegation issue,[54] they noted Sutherland's separation of the "internal" and "external" realms of constitutional analysis,[55] his grounding of federal foreign affairs powers on an extraconstitutional basis,[56] and his emphasis on the particular expertise of the executive branch in foreign relations, where decisions often required secrecy and dispatch.[57] In addition, they raised the possibility that the Court might be treating the entire subject of embargoes as "political in nature and beyond judicial consideration."[58] One comment concluded that "[o]n the face of it the case is a long step toward executive autonomy in the field of foreign relations."[59] But no commentator seemed particularly disturbed by any of these features of *Curtiss-Wright*.

The most extended immediate reaction to *Curtiss-Wright*, in fact, applauded its promise as a charter of executive autonomy. In a 1937 essay in the *American Journal of International Law,* James Garner of the University of Illinois, a member of the journal's board of editors, defended a proposal to give the president discretionary authority to impose embargoes on American exports if he concluded that the embargoes might help keep the United States out of war.[60] Garner's essay can be seen as an effort to recast *Curtiss-Wright* as a decision that unambiguously established the principle of executive discretion in constitutional foreign affairs jurisprudence. It amounted to a paraphrase of Sutherland's arguments in *Curtiss-Wright* and his Columbia lectures, including references to the same historical sources Sutherland had invoked.[61] Garner's conclusion was particularly telling:

> It is clear from this summary that the discretionary power which the President has, either as civil executive or commander-in-chief of the armed forces, is [already vast] . . . If this augmentation of his power in the domain of international relations will make him a potential dictator, . . . consistency would seem to require that he should be deprived of the far greater and potentially more dangerous powers which he already possesses . . . It would seem that, if there is a discernible tendency, it is the

direction of increasing rather than diminishing the President's power in the domain of international relations. The Supreme Court in its opinion in the recent Chaco arms embargo case pointed out that if embarrassment—perhaps serious embarrassment—is to be avoided in the conduct of the foreign affairs of the country, it is necessary to accord to the President a degree of discretion and freedom which would not be admissible in the conduct of domestic affairs.[62]

A scholar sympathetic to the New Deal had lionized Justice Sutherland.[63]

Sutherland's opinion in *Curtiss-Wright* had suggested, although it had stopped short of holding, that executive agreements and treaties had an identical constitutional status. That suggestion, given *Missouri v. Holland,* had federalism as well as separation of powers implications and seemed to have the potential for investing the Litvinov Agreement with enhanced constitutional significance. Indeed, only five months after *Curtiss-Wright* had been handed down, a case involving the effect of the Litvinov Agreement on the disposition of Russian assets in New York found its way to the Supreme Court. The case was *United States v. Belmont,*[64] in which Sutherland continued his reframing of orthodoxy. When Sutherland's opinion for the Court was issued, an international executive agreement, neither ratified by the Senate nor made pursuant to a congressional directive, had trumped the Constitution's Just Compensation Clause. Moreover, the existence of any state public policy with respect to the claims of debtors holding property within that state had been found to be irrelevant once the property had been affected by an international agreement. One commentator noted that "[t]he curious result of the Belmont opinion [was] that . . . Soviet confiscatory decrees [were] given an extraterritorial effect in the United States—although not in any other country."[65]

These consequences of the *Belmont* decision were a product of Sutherland's apparent determination to deconstitutionalize foreign affairs jurisprudence. *Belmont* was in some respects a good case in which to pursue that strategy. The Petrograd Metal Works, a Russian corporation, had deposited some money with the New York banking house August Belmont & Co. prior to the outbreak of the 1918 revolution. The assets of the Petrograd Metal Works, however, had been appropriated by the Soviet government in one of its 1918 nationalization decrees, which extended to property of pre-Soviet corporations, wherever situated.

As a result of the Litvinov Agreement, the United States was assigned all amounts due to the Soviet government from American nationals between 1918 and 1933, including the Petrograd Metal Works' deposit account with Belmont & Co. When the United States made a demand on Belmont's executors for the assets in that account, the executors refused. The government then brought suit in federal district court, and the executors made a motion to dismiss its claim on the ground that it had no cause of action. The motion to dismiss was based on the fact that the account was located in the state of New York; that it was thus not property within Soviet territory and hence not properly subject to any nationalization decree; that the public policy of New York was not to give effect to extraterritorial claims on property owned by American citizens within its jurisdiction; and that to enforce the Soviet nationalization decree would be to take property without just compensation. The district judge granted the motion to dismiss, and the United States Court of Appeals for the Second Circuit affirmed that judgment.[66]

Sutherland began his majority opinion, for five other justices,[67] with a remarkable sentence:

> We do not pause to inquire whether in fact there was any policy of the State of New York to be infringed, since we are of opinion that no state policy can prevail against the international compact here involved.

The Litvinov Agreement had not been ratified by the Senate; it had simply been an exchange of diplomatic correspondence. The Constitution did not prevent the states from entering into international compacts themselves, and orthodox reserved powers jurisprudence, in the domestic realm, treated the states as having very strong interests in making rules for the disposition of property located within their borders, especially property held by American citizens. Sutherland concluded that these considerations were simply irrelevant to the *Belmont* case.

His arguments supporting that conclusion made use of disparate doctrinal elements but ended up having an unexpressed common theme. He invoked the "act of state" doctrine, first articulated by the Supreme Court in an 1897 case,[68] for the proposition that the courts of one country could not sit in judgment on the governmental acts of another. But the Soviet Union's seizure of the assets of the Petrograd Metal Works had been the act of an unrecognized government, only made legitimate by the fiction, once de jure recognition of the Soviet regime came with the Litvinov Agreement, that all the previous acts of a newly recognized regime were valid. In the leading case Sutherland cited as authority for the act of state doctrine, the 1918 decision in *Oetjen v. Central Leather Co.*, the property involved had been located in the foreign country. In *Belmont*, Sutherland was extending the *Oetjen* doctrine to property within New York state, even though the New York courts had been sitting in judgment of Soviet nationalization decrees since the early 1920s and declining to extend them to property within that state.

Thus far Sutherland had contented himself with establishing that the "act of state" doctrine might apply to a decree of a then unrecognized, but subsequently recognized, foreign government even if it pertained to property within the boundaries of the United States. Now he moved to expand the breadth of his opinion, sketching out its implications for both the separation of powers and the federalism dimensions of traditional constitutional foreign affairs jurisprudence. The separation of powers issue in *Belmont* was whether an executive agreement that had not been ratified by the Senate had the status of a "treaty" for constitutional purposes; the federalism issue was whether the agreement could prevail over competing state policies or laws. Sutherland's discussion intertwined the issues.

He began by repeating his conceptual division between the domestic ("internal") and foreign relations ("external") realms. "Governmental power over internal affairs is distributed between the national government and the states," he maintained, but "[g]overnmental power over external affairs is not distributed, but is vested exclusively in the national government."[69] He then noted the category of "international compact[s]" that were not treaties, such as protocols, modi vivendi, "and agreements like that now under consideration." Such agreements, he maintained, had the same constitutional status as treaties: they were supreme over state laws.[70] "[W]hile this rule in respect of treaties is established by the express language of cl. 2, Art. VI of the Constitution," Sutherland claimed, "complete power over international affairs is in the national government and is not and cannot be subject to any curtailment or interference on the part of the several states. Compare *United States v. Curtiss-Wright Export Corp.* . . . In respect of all international negotiations and compacts, and in respect of our foreign relations generally, state lines disappear."[71]

Sutherland's attention had hitherto seemed to be primarily directed toward separation of powers issues. But now he read *Curtiss-Wright* (on its face a separation of powers case) for the proposition that in the foreign relations realm national power was not just plenary but very possibly exclusive. Not only in "international negotiations and compacts" but in "our foreign relations generally," state lines disappeared. Sutherland particularized: "And when judicial authority is invoked in aid of such consummation, state constitutions, state laws, and state policies are irrelevant to the inquiry and decision. It is inconceivable that any of them can be interposed as an obstacle to the effective operation of a federal constitutional power. Cf. *Missouri v. Holland*."[72]

The states, by Sutherland's account, had ceased to become actors in the realm of constitutional foreign affairs jurisprudence. But his citations of *Curtiss-Wright* and *Missouri v. Holland* together in his *Belmont* opinion added up to more than simply the obliteration of reserved powers restraints on the conduct of foreign policy. They amounted to virtual carte blanche for the executive to establish plenary control of foreign relations on its own accord. In *Missouri v. Holland* a treaty had been necessary to cure the constitutional deficiency of federal migratory bird legislation. After *Belmont* it appeared that an executive agreement alone could trump competing reserved powers. The power Sutherland found established in the executive to supplant state laws through an international compact had been labeled a "federal constitutional power." And yet the power itself was ultimately grounded on Sutherland's "inherent," extraconstitutional conception of federal foreign affairs powers.

There was one more possible difficulty in *Belmont*, the Takings Clause argument. Sutherland fudged that difficulty. "[T]he answer" to the argument that in the Litvinov Agreement the United States had taken private assets without just compensation, Sutherland announced, was "that our Constitution, laws and policies have no extraterritorial operation, unless in respect of our own citizens." "What another country has done in the way of taking over property of its nationals, and especially of its corporations," he went on, "is not a matter for judicial consideration here."[73] He claimed that the executors in *Belmont* were merely custodians of the money and that only the rights of the Petrograd Metal Works were affected.[74] That claim finessed the question of what would be done with the assets, which now presumptively passed to the United States government. Edwin Borchard of Yale Law School, reacting to the *Belmont* decision shortly after it was handed down, found this one of its most troubling aspects. "The net result, if the United States title is deemed to prevail over the private title," Borchard wrote, "is that the United States engages with Soviet Russia to seize the proceeds of a Soviet confiscation of money in New York and hand them over to American corporations and citizens who have been despoiled in like manner in Russia. A profound principle is thus impaired, not for the benefit of the United States, but presumably of private investors who in the long run have nothing to gain from a confiscatory policy."[75]

Belmont showed the first stirrings of concern among Sutherland's fellow justices for the breadth of his revisionist effort. Stone wrote a separate concurrence, joined by Brandeis and Cardozo, in which he disassociated himself from Sutherland's use of the act of state doctrine and from his implication that a contrary state policy would invariably be overridden by an international executive agreement. Stone read the act of state doctrine as only meaning that when an American citizen's property located in a foreign government was confiscated by that government, American courts would honor the action. Where an extraterritorial transfer of property located within an American state was concerned, Stone suggested, that state might "refuse to give effect to [the] transfer . . . if the transfer is in conflict with its public policy." It could also "disregard the transfer where the subject of it is a chose in action due from a debtor within the state to a foreign creditor, especially where, as in the present case, the debtor's only obligation is to pay within the state, on demand." In particular, Stone felt, there was no reason for the majority opinion in *Belmont* to have concluded that "in respect of all international negotiations and compacts . . . the State of New York does not exist."[76]

It seems worthwhile, at this point, to step aside momentarily from the narrative of transformation to explore the relationship of the *Curtiss-Wright* and *Belmont* decisions to the conventional account of early twentieth-century constitutional history, which, as noted, has been centered on domestic developments. The *Curtiss-Wright* opinion, handed down on December 21, 1936, and the *Belmont* opinion, handed down on May 3, 1937, represent, according to the conventional historiographical view of constitutional developments in that year, snapshots out of place in the album. By the latter months of the 1935 Term, so runs the conventional account,[77] the "Three Musketeers," Brandeis, Cardozo, and Stone, had become a solid bloc in opposition to the "Four Horsemen," Butler, McReynolds, Sutherland, and Van Devanter, who were resolutely opposing any attempted extension of the regulatory powers of the federal government. Two months before *Belmont* had come the apparent capitulation of the Court to the momentum of regulatory legislation with *West Coast Hotel v. Parrish*,[78] in which Hughes and Roberts joined the Three Musketeers. Three weeks before *Belmont,* the case of *National Labor Relations Board v. Jones & Laughlin Steel Corp.* [79] was handed down, with the same lineup sustaining the National Labor Relations Act.

Before this "constitutional revolution" had even been launched, but after the divisions between the Horsemen and Musketeers were in place, had come *Curtiss-Wright,* in which Brandeis and Cardozo joined Sutherland's majority opinion and McReynolds dissented from it. Then in the midst of the constitutional revolution came *Belmont,* in which the Three Musketeers declared themselves far less inclined than Sutherland, the other Horsemen, and Hughes and Roberts to extend the plenary regulatory powers of the federal government at the expense of the states. Whereas Sutherland and other justices conventionally thought of as opponents of the New Deal were perfectly comfortable with the use of an executive international agreement to confiscate private property situated in a state, without any concern for potentially competing state interests, Stone and the other conventionally described supporters of increased federal regulation expressed some misgivings about that prospect.

The insertion of *Curtiss-Wright* and *Belmont* within the more familiar late

1930s cases emphasized by the conventional account is intended to fore-shadow some broader conclusions about the transformation of the constitutional regime of foreign relations in the early twentieth century. Those conclusions will subsequently be sketched in more detail. It is enough at this point to recognize that conventional political labels applied to justices in the domestic arena do not work well in the realm of foreign affairs, at least for the period under consideration in this book. One reason the conventional domestic labels do not capture judicial perspectives in the foreign relations realm is that many of Sutherland's contemporaries, whatever their views on domestic issues, seem to have shared his intuitive belief that the foreign relations sphere was "different" from the domestic sphere, jurisprudentially, politically, and perhaps constitutionally.

It remains to probe that belief in more detail after the narrative of transformation is concluded. But it is worth mentioning at this stage that if one discards the stereotypical labels of the conventional account, but at the same time continues to emphasize the chronological as well as the doctrinal dimensions of the Court's early twentieth-century constitutional foreign relations cases, it becomes clear that the same majority of justices that actively resisted the extension of national powers in the domestic arena in the late 1930s had already committed themselves to a much more potentially broad extension of national powers in the arena of foreign affairs.

One might be tempted to see this judicial tolerance for extended national powers in foreign relations as a precipitating cause of the eventual tolerance for extended national powers in the domestic arena exhibited by a majority of the Court by the early 1940s. Some of the constitutional arguments invoked as barriers to the extension of national domestic power, such as the nondelegation doctrine and respect for the residuum of reserved state powers, were first swept away in the very foreign relations cases we have been considering; all of these, if one includes *Missouri v. Holland,* predated, sometimes by a significant amount of time, the great bulk of the domestic cases highlighted in the conventional account of the constitutional revolution. But we have already seen that if *Curtiss-Wright* and *Belmont* were dress rehearsals for a domestic revolution, they were initiated by a judge who had no sympathy for that revolution, retained an orthodox, category-driven conception of constitutional jurisprudence, and had repeatedly declared, since 1910, that the constitutional realm of "internal" powers was utterly different from its "external" powers counterpart. In sum, the standard labels of the conventional account obfuscate rather than facilitate our understanding of the narrative of transformation being set forth.

In seeking to assess the relationship of constitutional foreign relations cases to the dramatic changes in other areas of constitutional jurisprudence that took place in the late 1930s and 1940s, we need to look beyond historio-graphic labels to the attitudes of contemporaries at the time. Here it becomes apparent that some commentators on *Belmont* sensed the breadth of Suther-land's revisionist perspective and recognized its subversive implications for the orthodox regime, but others felt that the revised meaning of executive discretion in foreign affairs policymaking was appropriate for a world marked by increasingly treacherous international relations.

In addition to that of Edwin Borchard, three critiques of the majority opin-ion in *Belmont* appeared in 1937. Philip Jessup, writing in the *American Journal of International Law,* agreed with Borchard that Sutherland's treat-ment of some central issues had been both sweeping and cursory. Jessup pointed out that since the Soviet confiscation decree had not yet been exe-cuted against any account in New York, it was possible that New York "may well decline on the basis of its own public policy to assist the foreign sover-eign in reducing to possession a *res* over which it has no physical control." For Sutherland to treat New York's interests as entirely irrelevant seemed troublesome.[80]

Jessup also noted the majority's equation of the constitutional status of executive agreements and treaties, and the fact that the opinion "barely skirt[ed] the fringe of the interesting question whether the United States through the treaty-making power may take private property without com-pensation notwithstanding the provisions of the Bill of Rights." In short, Jessup found that on "the highly complicated legal situations which have arisen out of the Soviet nationalization decrees and subsequent recognition of the Soviet Government," Sutherland's *Belmont* opinion "[led] off in an unsatisfactory direction"[81] by assuming that exercises of foreign affairs pow-ers by the national government reduced other constitutional concerns to a minimum.

A student note in the *Yale Law Journal* expressed similar reservations about Sutherland's blithe equation of executive agreements and treaties for constitutional purposes, and about his conclusion that confiscatory legisla-tion outside the United States could affect property within it because any state policy to the contrary would simply be ignored. "If the agreement had been a treaty, made with the advice and consent of the Senate," the note sug-gested, "there is little doubt but that it could override state law or state policy, for a treaty is 'the supreme law of the land.'" But "the status of an ex-ecutive agreement made without congressional authorization or senatorial ratification" was "not so certain." Nonetheless, "by implication" *Belmont* had "confirm[ed] the executive's power to make [such agreements] and at the same time [held] that they are to have the same force as treaties in their supremacy over state law or policy." The note was noncommittal about the efficacy of those dimensions of the *Belmont* case but clearly recognized them as departures from the traditional separation of powers and federalism baselines of constitutional foreign affairs jurisprudence.[82]

Stefan Riesenfeld, writing in the *California Law Review*, was able to weave the various skeins of Sutherland's *Belmont* opinion into a single thread. Riesenfeld understood that *Belmont* was a departure from both of the paradigms of the orthodox regime. It was "the first case in which the Supreme Court has dealt with an [executive] agreement reached without authorization by Congress,"[83] but Sutherland had not treated that fact as having any effect on the Litvinov Agreement's constitutional status. It was also the first case to treat an unauthorized executive agreement as taking on the powers of a treaty to displace countervailing state powers.[84] As such, Riesenfeld understood *Belmont* to be a charter for executive discretion in twentieth-century constitutional foreign affairs jurisprudence. As he put it:

> It is certainly a liberal construction of the constitutional powers to hold that the President, without even congressional authorization, merely on the strength of his position as chief executive vested with the conduct of foreign relations, may override state law and public policy. Without doubt the majority opinion in the *Belmont* case represents one of the most extreme extensions which could be accorded to the power of the President in the field of international relations.[85]

Despite the uneasiness of such commentators about the implications of *Curtiss-Wright* and *Belmont*, the idea of discretionary executive power in the realm of foreign affairs increasingly appeared to be one whose time had come as the world moved closer to a second global conflict.

In a July 1941 article in the *California Law Review*, Harry Willmer Jones took stock of the roles of the president and Congress in foreign relations. The occasion for his survey was the "Lend-Lease" Act of March of that year, in which Congress authorized the president to enter into financial transactions with foreign governments when he "deem[ed] it in the interest of national defence." Jones described the Act as "confer[ring] upon the President a measure of discretionary authority unequalled in the history of the United States." He suggested that "if the same test of constitutionality were applied as in the case of statutes imposing domestic regulation, a strong argument could be made that the broad grant of power contained in the lend-lease statute vests the President with just the sort of a 'roving commission' struck down in the [case of *Schechter Poultry Corp. v. United States*]."[86]

Jones, however, identified himself as a supporter of the lend-lease statute. He proceeded to summarize the case for executive discretion in the realm of foreign affairs as it then existed. Drawing on work by Corwin and Sutherland, including *Curtiss-Wright*,[87] Jones noted the increased participation of the executive branch in foreign affairs policymaking, often without the approval or even consultation of the Senate, and the innate advantages of flexibility, circumspection, and administrative efficiency that were associated with executive decisionmaking in foreign affairs.[88] He concluded: "Crisis conditions call for resolute and consistent leadership, and initiative in the foreign policy field must come from the executive department . . . This is not, unfortunately, a parliamentary age, and the great impersonal pressures of the dynamic world situation may preclude executive consultation with the Congress prior to the taking of particular emergency measures."[89]

Sutherland's opinions in *Curtiss-Wright* and *Belmont* had been written in the context of increased international tension, extending to the Soviet Union and to Latin American nations; Jones's article was written with World War II breaking out all around him and Pearl Harbor only eight months away.[90] When *Curtiss-Wright* and *Belmont* had been handed down, Roosevelt was late in his first or early in his second terms, with his legislative agenda still largely unrealized. By the time Jones wrote, Roosevelt had been elected to an unprecedented third term, in part because of the deteriorating international situation and the unanticipated positive economic effects of defense-related industrial activity on the United States economy. The idea of a powerful executive, exerting leadership on a variety of fronts, seemed more natural in a world where totalitarian states were both common and threatening. Sutherland and others had already identified the realm of foreign relations as particularly well suited to executive leadership.

Thus, by the time the Supreme Court decided *United States v. Pink*,[91] which had been argued eight days after Pearl Harbor, the reconstituted principle of executive discretion in the realm of constitutional foreign affairs jurisprudence had already become a mainstream proposition. Nevertheless, Justice Douglas's opinion, for an attenuated Court,[92] further extended the scope of the transformation of such jurisprudence.

The process by which *Pink* reached the Supreme Court was an unusual one. *Belmont,* despite Sutherland's broad language, had not expressly reached the question of whether New York public policy about the distribution of Russian assets within the state conflicted with any distribution contemplated by the Litvinov Agreement.[93] That question was raised in a subsequent New York case, *Moscow Fire Insurance Co. v. Bank of New York & Trust Co.*,[94] in which the New York Court of Appeals concluded that the Litvinov Agreement had expressed no intent to contravene any state laws or policies on the distribution of extraterritorial assets of Russian insurance companies.[95]

Moscow Fire found its way to the Supreme Court in 1939[96] and was a potentially momentous case, raising not only the issue left open in *Belmont* but the issue of whether federal courts, sitting in cases with internationalist dimensions, were bound to follow the common law of the states in which they sat.[97] *Moscow Fire* produced no definitive resolution of those issues, however, because the eight sitting justices were evenly divided, affirming the Court of Appeals' judgment.[98] With that disposition, the question whether an international executive agreement purporting to affect assets within the United States could be enforced in the face of a conflicting state policy about the distribution of those assets remained open. A new majority of the Supreme Court signaled that it was eager to decide that issue, and the *Pink* case quickly gave it an opportunity.

In 1925 the New York superintendent of insurance, Louis Pink, had taken possession of the assets of the First Russian Insurance Company, established in New York since 1907, when the company ceased to do business in the state. Following standard New York asset distribution procedure, Pink paid off the claims of all domestic creditors of the company and retained about a million dollars. Various foreign creditors filed claims, and in 1931 the New York Court of Appeals directed that those claims be paid and that any surplus be given to a quorum of the board of directors of the company.[99]

By the date of the Litvinov Agreement most of the million dollars remained with Pink. The United States claimed an immediate right to the assets as the successor to the Soviet government, which had confiscated the company's assets in one of its nationalization decrees. The United States brought an action in federal district court to recover the assets in November 1934 and, after that action was eventually dismissed on technical grounds by the Supreme Court,[100] sued in a New York trial court, naming Pink and the foreign creditors of the First Russian Insurance Company who had presented claims in the earlier New York liquidation proceeding. An answer to the United States' bill of complaint was filed in March 1938, and in April 1939 the New York Court of Appeals decided *Moscow Fire.*

Then an extraordinary series of developments occurred.[101] Pink moved for an order to dismiss the complaint on the ground that the United States' complaint in *Moscow Fire* was identical to that against him. The United States responded that a petition for certiorari in the *Moscow Fire* case was about to be filed. A New York trial court granted Pink's motion and dismissed the complaint in June 1939. In September of that year the *Moscow Fire* petition for certiorari was filed; in October it was granted; and on February 12, 1940, the New York Court of Appeals' decision was upheld as a result of the Court's equal division. This prompted the Appellate Division of the Supreme Court of New York, and subsequently the New York Court of Appeals, to affirm the dismissal of the United States' complaint. In a per curiam opinion accompanying the dismissal, the Court of Appeals stated that its *Moscow Fire* decision "left open no question which has been argued" in *United States v. Pink*.

Nonetheless, the United States filed another petition for certiorari, and in May 1941 the Supreme Court granted it. It heard argument in the *Pink* case on December 15, 1941, and handed down an opinion in the case about six weeks later. The Court's decision to hear the *Pink* case, in the face of the New York courts' determination to treat *Moscow Fire* and *Pink* as raising identical issues, was a clear signal that the justices were interested in attempting to reach a more definitive resolution of the issues originally raised in *Moscow Fire*.

That signal was made even clearer by Douglas's opinion in *Pink*, which proceeded as if all of the implications of the Litvinov Agreement for constitutional foreign relations jurisprudence should be fleshed out. The opinion consisted of a series of efforts to invest each of Sutherland's earlier intimations about the breadth of federal foreign affairs powers with the status of definitive principles of constitutional law. It also consisted of a remarkable interpretation of the scope of the Litvinov Agreement. In that exchange of diplomatic correspondence, Douglas concluded, the Soviet government and the United States had agreed that the Soviets' confiscatory decrees extended to property of Russian corporations located in the United States, and that the United States government, in being assigned Soviet assets, would become part of the confiscatory process.

The first set of assertions was striking because Douglas gave no evidence for his reading of *Belmont* other than citations to that decision. The second set of assertions—couched as an interpretation—was, arguably, even more striking because there was no evidence, other than a self-serving declaration after the fact by the Soviet government,[102] that the Soviets' nationalization decrees were intended to apply to Russian property located in other countries. Moreover, there was overwhelming evidence that international law, American common law, and the United States Constitution supported the principle that American courts would not enforce the confiscatory decrees of another nation where those decrees affected property within the borders of the United States.[103]

Douglas began his *Pink* opinion by stating that "[w]ith one qualification . . . the Belmont case is determinative of the present controversy." He then went on to find that "[t]he Belmont case forecloses any relief to the Russian corporation." He quoted Sutherland to the effect that "our Constitution, laws, and policies have no extraterritorial operation, unless in respect to our own citizens . . . What another country has done in the way of taking over property of its nationals, and especially of its corporations, is not a matter for judicial consideration here." This statement alone did not take Douglas very far because New York had clearly already taken the interests of foreign creditors of the First Russian Insurance Corporation into account, having ordered distribution of some of its funds to them. Douglas conceded this, and referred to the Fifth Amendment's protection being applied to aliens.[104] But he then sought to reassure his audience as to what exactly was going on in *Pink*.

"The contest here," Douglas pointed out, "is between the United States and creditors of the Russian corporation who, we assume, are not citizens of this country and whose claims did not arise out of transactions with the New York branch. The United States is seeking to protect not only claims which it holds but also claims of its nationals."[105] One was supposed to understand, as a result of those remarks, that if the United States government was given title to the disputed assets in *Pink*, the losers would be Russian nationals identified with the First Russian Insurance Company and other foreign creditors of the corporation. The winners, in contrast, would be American citizens.[106] Not only would their government have possession of about a million dollars, but American nationals who had their property in Russia confiscated by the nationalization decrees might benefit from the United States collecting some money once allegedly claimed by the Soviets. It did not matter, apparently, that the State Department had stopped well short of guaranteeing that any assets it collected pursuant to the Litvinov Agreement would be used to help compensate American citizens with unsatisfied claims against the Soviets.[107] The point was that American citizens would win and Russian nationals would lose.

Douglas had one more issue to dispose of in *Pink*, the Fifth Amendment's requirement that property could not be taken for public use without just compensation.[108] It seemed that by taking an assignment from the Soviet Union of assets of Russian nationals located in New York, the United States was literally violating that Amendment. Douglas disposed of the argument with a two-pronged response. First, he declared that the Litvinov Agreement embodied a federal policy of "securing for [the United States] and our nationals priority against . . . creditors who are nationals of foreign countries and whose claims [arise] abroad." There was "no Constitutional reason," Douglas asserted, "why this Government need act as the collection agent for nationals of other countries when it takes steps to protect itself or its own nationals . . . it matters not that the procedure adopted by the Federal Government is globular and involves a regrouping of assets."[109] Thus, there was a federal policy that clashed with the New York policy of marshaling and paying the claims of foreign creditors to property within its borders.

Second, Douglas pointed out that if the United States had signed a treaty with Russia that gave American claims priority to those of foreign nationals, "there would have been no doubt as to its validity." The "same result obtain[ed]" with an executive agreement, even one that Congress had not authorized. Here both *Curtiss-Wright* and *Belmont* were cited for the propositions that "the President . . . is the 'sole organ of the federal government in the field of international relations'" and that "international compacts and agreements such as the Litvinov Assignment have a similar [constitutional] dignity to treaties."[110] To cap off his argument, Douglas resorted to a sweeping statement of federal executive discretion in foreign affairs that Sutherland, who was still alive when the *Pink* opinion was handed down, must have found heartening:

> We repeat that there are limitations on the sovereignty of the States. No State can rewrite our foreign policy to conform to its own domestic policies. Power over external affairs is not shared by the States; it is vested in the national government exclusively . . . And the policies of the States become wholly irrelevant to judicial inquiry, when the United States, acting within its constitutional sphere, seeks enforcement of its foreign policy in the courts. For such reasons, Mr. Justice Sutherland stated in [*Belmont*], "In respect of all international negotiations and compacts, and in respect of our foreign relations generally, state lines disappear. As to such purposes the state of New York does not exist."[111]

Separation of powers and federalism limitations on the conduct of foreign relations by the federal executive had virtually disappeared. The transformation of orthodox constitutional foreign affairs jurisprudence was nearly complete.

Reaction to *Pink* was swift, extensive, and mainly unenthusiastic. Stone dissented, arguing that if a federal policy was to displace the policies of New York with respect to the distribution of assets within that state, it needed to have been clearly expressed in the Litvinov Agreement. He further asserted that "the pronouncements in the Belmont case, on which the Court relies, . . . are without the support of reason or accepted principles of law."[112] His position would resonate with several commentators, but it is worth noting that the effect of *all* of the opinions in *Pink* was to affirm the principle of federal executive discretion in foreign affairs. Stone had declared that "[i]t is not for this Court to adopt policy, the making of which has been by the Constitution committed to other branches of government." Although the immediate point of this comment was to suggest that Douglas had inappropriately read the Litvinov Agreement as entirely displacing New York state policy, as a general proposition it outlined an even more deferential role for the Court in undertaking constitutional review of foreign policy decisions by the executive.

Of the numerous reactions of contemporary commentators to *Pink*,[113] that of Edwin Borchard was the most critical and arguably the most searching. Borchard, a frequent contributor to the *American Journal of International Law* since the early 1920s, had observed with increasing incredulity the displacement of the traditional assumptions of the constitutional jurisprudence of foreign relations with revisionist ones. His comment, "Extraterritorial Confiscations," in the April 1942 issue of the *American Journal of International Law,* consisted of a series of increasingly astringent characterizations of the *Pink* majority's approach, adding up to the conclusion that "the court has upset and parted with international law, as heretofore understood, gravely impaired or weakened the protection to private property afforded by the Fifth Amendment, . . . endowed a mere executive agreement by exchange of notes with the constitutional force of a formal treaty, misconstrued the agreement, and . . . confused that foreign policy of the United States in whose alleged support this revolutionary decision was thought necessary."[114]

Perhaps the worst feature of the *Pink* decision, Borchard felt, was that very few people in a position to influence the constitutional regime of foreign relations jurisprudence seemed to be upset with the fact that revisionism had become orthodoxy. Two years after his critique of *Pink*, Borchard noted "considerable propaganda . . . emanating from Washington and elsewhere designed to prove that the treaty-making power . . . is too cumbersome, slow, and 'undemocratic,' . . . and that by a 'usage' which supposedly has imperceptibly developed it is now possible and preferable to substitute for the Constitutional treaty the executive agreement, without Congressional approval if possible." This "effort to bring about a change in the Constitution, either with or without formal amendment," Borchard claimed, "has . . . supposed moral support from the Supreme Court."[115]

The dominance of the principle of national executive discretion in foreign affairs had come incrementally. The *Chinese Exclusion Cases* and the *Insular Cases* had produced doctrines that had transformative potential as departures from the enumerated powers framework, but they were decisions made squarely within the boundaries of the orthodox regime. *Missouri v. Holland*, despite the breadth of Holmes's language, was a logical extension of the treaty-making power and had been anticipated by commentators at the opening of the twentieth century. Sutherland's extraconstitutional theory of foreign relations powers had been derived within the orthodox, category-driven structure of foreign and domestic constitutional powers. It was not until the broad suggestions about executive discretion made by Sutherland in *Curtiss-Wright* were taken up, and their federalism as well as their separation of powers ramifications revealed in *Belmont* and *Pink,* that the momentum of the transformation process began to take on a life of its own.[116]

In the conventional account the New Deal has been prominently identified as the formative event in reshaping twentieth-century constitutional jurisprudence. None of the stereotyped characteristics associated with the New Deal and its relationship to the "constitutional revolution" of the late 1930s, however, helps make sense of the transformation in foreign affairs jurisprudence, and the timing of that transformation is very awkward for any hypothesis emphasizing the New Deal as a formative episode.

Some elements in the transformative jurisprudential mix had surfaced as early as the first decade of the twentieth century. The potential interchangeability of treaties and executive agreements, and Sutherland's effort to posit a rigid separation of "external" and "internal" governmental powers, had been articulated in commentary before World War I. The possible displacement of reserved state powers by federal legislation enacted pursuant to the treaty power had been anticipated in commentary before *Missouri v. Holland* and had been constitutionally legitimated by the Supreme Court nine years before the stock market crashed. The established separation of powers and federalism paradigms of the orthodox regime of constitutional foreign relations jurisprudence were under severe pressure by the early 1920s. One of the stereotyped judicial opponents of the New Deal had gone on record as championing a "radically more liberal" judicial construction of the foreign relations powers of the national government by 1919.

When one shifts to the heart of the New Deal period, things do not get any more promising for an explanation that would associate changes in the constitutional jurisprudence of foreign relations with the political and economic realignments conventionally identified with the New Deal. The attitude toward the constitutionality of delegations from Congress to the executive exhibited by the Court in *Curtiss-Wright* and *Belmont* cannot be reconciled with its attitude toward domestic delegations in the same time frame. *Curtiss-Wright, Belmont,* and *Pink* were each recognized as major departures from traditional constitutional foreign relations principles, and were justified by appeals to the imperatives of world war and a deteriorating international situation. Not a single contemporary commentator, remarking on the changed jurisprudential climate in the foreign affairs realm, associated it with developments in domestic economics or politics. If anything, the commentary was striking for its internalization of Sutherland's conviction that the realms of domestic and foreign affairs policy were constitutionally separate.

So the early twentieth-century transformation of constitutional foreign affairs jurisprudence cannot easily be engrafted onto the explanatory map supplied by the conventional account of constitutional change in that time period. That transformation has been ignored, a myth of continuity in foreign relations jurisprudence has been created, and the dominant paradigms of the orthodox regime, still extant in the 1930s, have largely been lost from view.

The disappearance of this transformation has not simply been a function of its awkward historiographical fit with the conventional account's emphasis on the New Deal as the primary force driving constitutional change. It has also been lost because one of the starting premises driving the revision of orthodox constitutional foreign relations jurisprudence—that a rapidly changing international order underscored the consummate importance of human flexibility and discretion in the delicate and dangerous realm of international relations—has been widened to include not merely foreign relations policymaking but any form of legal decisionmaking in the modern world of American constitutional government.

Under this widened version of the premise, judicial interpretations of the enumerated or reserved powers of the Constitution, whether in the foreign affairs or domestic realms, are taken to be a species of policy exercises in which human officials attempt to adapt the American governmental apparatus to changing conditions. The fact that judges, between the 1920s and the close of the Second World War, allowed Congress and the executive to circumvent reserved power limitations through treaties, and permitted the executive to bypass congressional or senatorial oversight by negotiating international executive agreements, is perceived as no more remarkable than judges allowing state legislatures to impose wage and hours restrictions on private contracts or allowing Congress to regulate the home consumption of food under the Commerce Clause. A central conviction that principles of constitutional law cannot be fruitfully separated from the policies of governmental officials has served to make the transformed state of constitutional foreign relations jurisprudence appear as if it has always been the norm.

But that central conviction and the assumptions flowing from it were not present in the orthodox regime of constitutional foreign relations law. That regime's very identity was related to its essentialist conceptions of law, constitutional law, and constitutional powers, which fostered a limited view of judicial creativity. Those conceptions were not confined to the realm of domestic legal issues: orthodox late nineteenth- and early twentieth-century constitutional jurisprudence did not assume any meaningful separation between the foreign and domestic constitutional realms. When early twentieth-century state judges assumed that they did not have to defer to State Department policies in applying state common law principles governing the distribution of assets within a state, they did not make that assumption because they held a strong belief in their capacity as creative lawmakers. On the contrary, they made it because they believed that clear, preordained spheres of federal executive and state judicial power had been established by the Constitution.

One can best understand Sutherland's determined efforts to separate the external from the internal affairs of the national government, and to identify the sources of federal foreign relations powers as extraconstitutional, by realizing that those efforts took shape within the assumptions of orthodox early twentieth-century constitutional jurisprudence. Sutherland's efforts were necessary because he continued to hold to an essentialist view of constitutional powers, while at the same time grasping the increasingly expansive and foreboding character of the emerging twentieth-century international order. Once he came to believe that the complex and dangerous world of twentieth-century international relations required flexible, unencumbered decision-making by foreign relations specialists, he felt it was necessary to view the foreign policy decisions of officials of the national government as primarily grounded on the inherent sovereign powers of a nation to defend itself from foreign threats. He thus set out to show that foreign relations was a unique arena to which the constitutional strictures governing domestic issues did not apply. Had those strictures applied, the federal executive would have been prevented from bypassing the concerns of Congress or from blithely overriding the judgments of state legislatures and state courts.

We will see that the sensibility exhibited by Sutherland in his efforts to reshape early twentieth-century constitutional foreign relations jurisprudence was exhibited by many of his legal and judicial contemporaries in several other areas of constitutional law. They were attempting to make sense of some dramatic and frightening features of modernity from a perspective that included a set of orthodox, essentialist conceptions about constitutional law and judging. As they strove to understand the constitutional implications of the conditions of twentieth-century life they were experiencing, they began their inquiries with those conceptions intact, and the constitutional issues that they regarded as particularly contested were issues that placed pressure on those conceptions. As subsequent generations have abandoned the conceptions, their sense of the awkward and painful accommodation of constitutional orthodoxy to modernity has been lost, and with it an accurate sense of the frame of reference from which Sutherland and his contemporaries approached early twentieth-century constitutional issues. Recovering the early twentieth-century transformation of the constitutional jurisprudence of foreign relations thus amounts to more than recreating a lost episode in American constitutional history. It also begins the process of exploring the striking perceptual differences between those who participated in that history and their twentieth-century successors who have narrated it.

4

The Emergence of Agency Government and the Creation of Administrative Law

One of the major themes of the conventional account of early twentieth-century constitutional history has been the growth of administrative agencies as important units of government in modern America. The emergence of agencies, particularly those affiliated with the federal government, has been portrayed as symbolizing the widespread acceptance of new theories of governance, theories that stressed the pervasiveness and importance of the state as a regulatory and bureaucratic presence and as a force for expertise. The growth of agencies has also been identified with the emergence of a field of law, administrative law, whose special focus has been on the relationship between agencies as governing units and courts that review agency decisions on constitutional grounds. Both the growth of agencies and the emergence of administrative law have a defining moment in this history, the passage of the Administrative Procedure Act in 1946, in which Congress allegedly signaled the entrenchment of the agency form of government by establishing a system of uniform, fair, and efficient procedures for federal agencies.

The common account of agency growth has tracked the stages of the broader conventional history of early twentieth-century constitutional jurisprudence. Like that history, the account has original, mainstream, and reconstructed versions, representing stages in which successive narrators approached the emergence of agencies from different perspectives but perpetuated its central themes. The first-stage narrators saw themselves as partisan advocates of a largely new governmental form, and as such attempted to suppress the constitutional novelty of agencies while advancing extraconstitutional justifications for their presence.[1] The mainstream narrators treated administrative agencies as permanent features of American government and equated administrative law with a particularistic conception of that field, centering on the scope of judicial review of agency decisionmaking under the Administrative Procedure Act.[2]

Reconstructed narratives of the role of administrative agencies in twentieth-century constitutional history have been less concerned with defending the agency form of government or with debating whether judicial review of agency decisions has been, or should be, broad or narrow.[3] They have been interested in examining the growth of agencies as a cultural phenomenon. Recent studies have emphasized the initially contested status of agencies in late nineteenth- and early twentieth-century America, the arguments employed to justify their existence as governmental units, and their close connection to an agenda of governance that placed faith in the capacity of expanded governmental institutions, staffed by experts, to manage the emerging social and economic problems of modern life. An inference of some of these studies is that this faith in the promise of agencies as symbols of expanded government has not been kept, so that the original vision of an expansive modern American regulatory state has not fully materialized.[4] This work on administrative agencies can be called reconstructionist in that it seeks to revive some important cultural reasons why modern America needed—and by implication still needs—the agency form of government.

All of the versions of the common account of agency growth present a narrative in which agencies have emerged as legitimate governing institutions despite initially being regarded as constitutional misfits. The cumulative effect of this narrative is to produce a story in which the growth of agency government in America is a function of the superiority of agencies over other prospective managerial units of government in modern America, especially the courts. The establishment of agencies as permanent features of the American governmental landscape is identified with the extraconstitutional reasons why agencies were acknowledged to be superior instruments in the modern state: their expertise, their flexibility, their ability to take a proactive rather than a merely reactive stance toward emerging social problems. The narrative, in its successive versions, tends to juxtapose constitutional objections to agencies against these extraconstitutional arguments on their behalf. In that juxtaposition the constitutional objections reveal themselves to be rigid and outmoded, and they are gradually overcome or modified out of existence.

The growth of agency government thus becomes a story of the absorption into the American system of constitutional governance of an institution that once had no constitutional legitimacy. And since the large-scale emergence of federal administrative agencies took place in the early 1930s, and the constitutional legitimation of agency government is associated with the passage of the Administrative Procedure Act in 1946, the story is another example of the formative role of New Deal experiments with expanded government in the creation of a "constitutional revolution."

My narrative of the constitutional legitimation of administrative agencies, and of the consequent establishment of the field of administrative law, attempts to complicate that story. As in the case of early twentieth-century foreign relations jurisprudence, I have sought to present a more accurate picture of the universe of early twentieth-century constitutional jurisprudence in which debates about the agency form of government took place. I have attempted to recover the intellectual underpinnings of a jurisprudential orthodoxy that regarded agencies as alien units of government and to describe the orthodox constitutional objections to the agency form, as well as the arguments employed by proponents of agency government in seeking to deflect those objections. Although the conventional account of agency growth has paid considerable attention to the last set of arguments, it has tended to ignore the arguments associated with orthodoxy. By unearthing those arguments, I hope to show that the eventual legitimation of the agency form and the resultant creation of administrative law were as much a product of the continued vitality of orthodox objections to agencies as they were of the resonance of arguments on their behalf.

Early twentieth-century objections to the agency form of government were derivative of the orthodox framework of late nineteenth-century constitutional jurisprudence. That framework, as we have seen, featured essentialist conceptions of enumerated and reserved governmental powers, an interpretive map of the Constitution featuring spheres and boundaries of power, and guardian judicial review, which assumed that judges would monitor those boundaries to preserve the integrity of the system. This judicial monitoring ("pricking out the boundary") extended to two distinguishable sets of cases. We have encountered one set, conventionally called federalism cases, in the last two chapters: those cases involved the allocation of power between the states and the federal government and, on occasion, between both of those entities and the people. Our concern here is with the other set of cases, conventionally called separation of powers cases. Here the guardian function of the judiciary was also to preserve spheres and prick out boundaries, but the spheres and boundaries were those established by the Constitution's enumeration of powers for the designated branches of the federal government.

In separation of powers cases the focus of judicial review was on purported invasions by one national branch into the sphere of authority of another rather than on purportedly unwarranted extensions of national power into the sovereign realms of the states or the people. The general justification for judicial monitoring in separation of powers cases, however, was the same as that in federalism cases, that is, to prevent the evils of tyranny and arbitrariness associated with unconstrained invasions of individual liberty by government. In separation of powers cases those evils came from too ambitious an exercise of the powers of one branch of the national government.

In orthodox late nineteenth- and early twentieth-century constitutional jurisprudence judicial monitoring invariably began with the relevant essentialist categories of the constitutional text. In separation of powers cases, this meant that judges would be expected to refer to the enumerated powers of the national branches of government, whose scope they assumed to have been intelligibly set forth, and whose nature to have been implicitly defined, in the Constitution. The idea of enumerated national powers, combined with the idea of separating power among distinct governmental branches and the maxim that all governmental power had been parceled out among the respective sovereign entities identified in the Constitution, yielded some governing separation of powers principles. The powers given to the respective branches of the national government were not to be intermingled, and they were complete powers, not to be delegated. The purpose of the arrangement was to forestall the concentration of power in a single unit of government.

The governing principles of orthodox separation of powers jurisprudence were understood to have immediate application to federal administrative agencies. One principle suggested that an organ of the federal government could not simultaneously exercise "legislative" and "judicial," or "legislative" and "executive," or "executive" and "judicial" functions. We have seen how new forms of foreign policymaking in the early twentieth century posed difficulties for this principle. A similar strain on the presumption that enumerated federal powers could not be combined in a single unit of government was created by the emergence of federal agencies, whose opponents sometimes described them as simultaneously performing executive, legislative, and judicial functions.

The second principle had already been embodied in a late nineteenth-century constitutional doctrine designed to facilitate judicial monitoring. Characterized in late nineteenth-century commentary as "[o]ne of the settled maxims of constitutional law," it prevented the legislative branch of government from delegating its lawmaking powers to another enumerated branch or to some other governmental unit, unless that unit was clearly an agent of the legislature.[5] The "nondelegation doctrine"[6] primarily came into play in constitutional challenges to programs where Congress entered into a relationship with a newly created unit of government but failed to establish sufficiently clear standards by which the unit was to govern. In the foreign relations area, we have seen, delegations from Congress to the president to make changes in tariff rates or to prohibit the exporting of armaments had been attacked on constitutional grounds. The first effort by Congress to delegate power to a domestic federal administrative agency, the Interstate Commerce Commission, which it created in 1887, precipitated similar attacks. Critics of the ICC charged that it combined legislative, adjudicative, and enforcement powers in a single unit of government, and several commentators suggested that it could only operate as a moral force.[7]

Nonetheless, by the early twentieth century, the Interstate Commerce Commission had become an established unit of government, sanctioned by the Supreme Court of the United States. In 1921, on the death of Chief Justice Edward White, his successor, William Howard Taft, described White's contributions to the "new field of administrative law," singling out cases reviewing actions of the ICC. Taft said that

> [t]he Interstate Commerce Commission was authorized to exercise powers the conferring of which by Congress would have been, perhaps, thought in the earlier years of the Republic to violate the rule that no legislative power can be delegated. But the inevitable progress in exigencies of government and the utter inability of Congress to give the time and attention indispensable to the exercise of these powers in detail forced the modification of the rule. Similar necessity caused Congress to create other bodies with analogous relations to the existing legislative, executive, and judicial machinery of the Federal Government, and these in due course came under the examination of this court. Here was a new field of administrative law which needed a knowledge of government and an experienced understanding of our institutions safely to define and declare.[8]

That paragraph contained the orthodox constitutional objections to the agency form and the elements of two extraconstitutional arguments on behalf of agencies. It also confirmed that the Supreme Court intended to play a role in the creation of administrative law. A detailed reading of the paragraph will serve to illustrate.

Taft began by asserting that Congress's authorization of the Interstate Commerce Commission to exercise certain powers would have, "in the earlier years of the Republic," been conventionally thought of as "violat[ing] the rule that no legislative power can be delegated." In that sentence he sought to emphasize the unorthodox constitutional status of federal regulatory commissions. Among the constitutional objections to the ICC that surfaced at the time of its creation were that in determining the reasonableness of rates, and sometimes establishing alternative rates,[9] it was exercising "legislative" powers, and that the "just and reasonable" standard Congress entrusted to it as a basis for rate regulation was too broad to constitute an appropriate delegation of those powers.[10]

But, Taft noted, the "inevitable progress in exigencies of government" and the "utter inability of Congress" to exercise detailed legislative oversight of the railroad industry "forced the modification" of the nondelegation doctrine when the ICC was created. In that sentence he had identified two of the three principal arguments in an extraconstitutional critique of traditional governmental institutions that begun to surface in the last three decades of the nineteenth century.

"[T]he inevitable progress in exigencies of government" was a way of representing the perception that the American economy and American society generally were increasingly "complex" mechanisms, making the tasks of industrial management or social governance more exacting and demanding. In the hearings and debates related to the passage of the Interstate Commerce Act of 1887, speakers had referred to the "complexity" of the railroad industry and, consequently, of governmental solutions to its problems.[11] The term "complexity," in such arguments, was used in a double sense. It not only signified a recognition of the tendency of mature industrialism to contribute to rapid changes in the scope and functions of business enterprises; it also signified a perception that the process of governing such enterprises was no longer a "simple" exercise. The increasing "complexity" of American life undercut the universality of externally grounded theories of law or the economy, and revealed the increased importance of human discretion in governing industrial enterprise.

Another phrase employed by Taft in the same sentence introduced a second element in the critique of traditional American governmental institutions. The attribution of "complexity" to the railroad industry and its governance meant that hands-on attention to the details of the industry's organization, structure, and practices was necessary to master its complex nature. Congress, given its preoccupation with elections, political parties, and patronage, was not well equipped to devote that attention; more specialized governmental units were required. Taft noted that Congress had responded to this state of affairs by "crea[ting] . . . bodies with analogous relations to the existing legislative . . . machinery of the Federal Government."

The passage from Taft's remarks on White did not invoke the third, and arguably most central, argument in the extraconstitutional critique of traditional governmental institutions that surfaced in the late nineteenth and early twentieth centuries. That argument can also be seen in the hearings and debates on the Interstate Commerce Act of 1887. It was premised on the assumption that the "complex" problems of railroad regulation "would be much better handled by a body of experts."[12] The concept of expertise would function as the centerpiece in a critique in which the perceptions of social and economic complexity, and of the inadequacy of traditional governmental institutions as overseers of a modern industrial order, were fused to demonstrate the comparative advantage of agencies as units of governance.

Expertise came to signify a combination of specialized knowledge, training in the professional techniques for acquiring that knowledge, and a stance of objectivity and detachment toward the subjects of learned inquiry. The last dimension of expertise had originated in the idea that "scientific" methods of acquiring and classifying knowledge required a dispassionate stance on the part of the scientist so that techniques of observation, deduction, and generalization were not tainted by dogma or human bias.[13] Expertise, with those associations, was to become the central rationale for administrative agencies as twentieth-century units of government.

Finally, Taft's 1921 comments on administrative law signaled that the new administrative bodies created by Congress to assist it in the process of governing an increasingly complex modern society had come "under the examination of this court." The comments, along with his conclusion that administrative law presupposed "a knowledge of government and an experienced understanding of our institutions," indicated that judicial review of the actions of administrative agencies could be anticipated as an ongoing feature of the new field. When these comments were coupled with Taft's earlier recognition of the problematic status of federal agencies as constitutionally legitimate units of government, his paragraph could be said to contain nearly all the jurisprudential elements whose mix was to give administrative law its distinctive identity.

Taft's remarks had been made against a backdrop of several decades, stretching from the creation of the ICC in 1887 to the 1920s, in which extraconstitutional justifications for federal administrative agencies had been advanced in response to arguments opposing them on constitutional grounds. By the 1920s additional federal agencies had been created, and the Supreme Court had exhibited a slight tendency to relax its constitutional scrutiny of agency decisions.[14] But constitutional discussions about agencies continued to be framed by orthodox jurisprudential assumptions.

The debates in Congress over the Hepburn Act of 1906, which sought to broaden the rate-making powers of the ICC,[15] provide an illustration of the early twentieth-century constitutional discourse in which discussions of government by federal agencies were set. The Hepburn Act proposed that the ICC be empowered to establish future standards of "reasonable" railroad rates on a particular line. Its rate-setting orders were to go into effect immediately rather than requiring court enforcement. They could be challenged in court, but the burden was on railroads to establish their invalidity. The proposed standard under which the ICC was to set rates was whether they were "just, reasonable, and fairly remunerative." No provision explicitly defined the scope of judicial review of ICC decisions, and it was not clear whether, or to what extent, courts could issue injunctions preventing immediate implementation of challenged ICC rates.

All of those features of the Hepburn Act stimulated constitutional objections.[16] The first set of those objections stressed the merger of governmental functions in the ICC. Its power to set rates prospectively was taken to be "legislative," and the fact that its rate orders were treated as presumptively valid in courts suggested that it was exercising "judicial" functions as well. In a series of hearings and debates over the Hepburn Act, stretching from 1902 to 1906, opponents and supporters of the legislation commented on its apparent merger of constitutionally separated powers in one governmental institution. Even one of the ICC commissioners, Charles Prouty, felt that "the executive, the administrative and the judicial functions . . . ought [not] to [be] combine[d] in the same body." [17]

Prouty's remarks demonstrated that supporters as well as opponents of the Hepburn Act recognized that merging governmental powers in the ICC was constitutionally dubious. One supporter, Congressman F. C. Stevens, expressed concern that "quasi-judicial and quasi-legislative powers are conferred upon an executive tribunal." He proposed establishing separate "executive" and "legislative" tribunals to deal with railroad regulation, as well as establishing "full judicial power" in courts.[18] Another, Congressman William Sulzer, wanted to establish the adjudicatory and executive powers of the ICC in other institutions. He described the ICC's power to establish rates, subject to judicial review, as "an administrative function," which "should be the sole and only power under the constitutional limitations of our Government conferred" on it.[19]

In addition to the constitutional objections to the ICC that were based on its merging of separate powers, there were objections based on its being delegated rate-making power–traditionally a "legislative" power—without any precise enforcement standards. Congressman S. W. McCall stated that "the hitherto accepted notions of the function of legislation will have to be radically revised" if "the making of railroad rates is a legislative function which can be delegated by calling it administrative."[20] And Senator Joseph Foraker made explicit what, in his view, the ICC's extended rate-making powers would mean: "All that Congress can do, if it has power to make rates at all, is to fix just and reasonable rates. If we confer that power on the Commission, we have divested ourselves of every particle of the rate-making power we have and given it all to the Commission. And yet Senators tell me there is no delegation by this provision of legislative power."[21]

Eventually the debate over the Hepburn Act moved from the merger of functions and delegation issues to center on the scope of judicial review of the ICC's rate-making orders. Senator Foraker argued that the Hepburn Act, in not explicitly providing for judicial review of ICC determinations that rates were "just," "reasonable," or "fairly remunerative," had ignored due process requirements.[22] Senator J. W. Bailey objected on constitutional grounds to the presumptive validity of ICC rates, claiming that Congress, in creating that presumption, was attempting to strip the courts of their power to issue injunctions against unconstitutional deprivations of property.[23] After a lengthy debate over an amendment that would have explicitly limited judicial review to situations where rates were arguably confiscatory, the Senate reached a compromise in which the term "fairly remunerative" was dropped as a guideline for ICC rate-setting, and judicial review of the ICC's decisions by federal district courts was explicitly provided for, but its scope not defined.

The Hepburn Act debate was to foreshadow the treatment of federal agencies for the next two decades. As legislation proposing the creation of the Federal Trade Commission and the Federal Power Commission was introduced, precisely the same sets of extraconstitutional arguments on behalf of those agencies—the growing "complexity" of American industrial life, the inadequacy of Congress or the courts as hands-on overseers of the technical problems of specific industries, the consequent need for experts as regulators—were made,[24] and precisely the same sorts of constitutional objections, centering on excessive delegations and inappropriate combinations of powers, were advanced.[25] And in each case the eventual creation of a new agency was accompanied by a procedure for judicial review of its decisions that afforded the agencies substantive discretion but allowed due process challenges to its decisionmaking procedures.[26]

The extraconstitutional arguments on behalf of agencies, and the constitutional arguments in opposition to them, had also become part of the mainstream discourse of the legal profession by the time Taft made his 1921 comments. Three comments on administrative agencies made by prominent lawyers can serve as illustrations. In his presidential address before the American Bar Association in 1916, Elihu Root noted that "as any community passes from simple to complex conditions, the only way in which government can deal with the increased burdens thrown upon it is by the delegation of power to be exercised in detail by subordinate agents." He felt that "such agencies furnish protection to rights and obstacles to wrong doing which under our new social and industrial conditions cannot practically be accomplished by the old and simple procedure of legislatures and courts." At the same time he insisted that "[i]f we are to continue a government of limited powers these agencies of regulation must themselves be regulated."[27]

That same year Charles Evans Hughes, then practicing law in New York City, referred to "the intricate situations created by expanding enterprise" and to the "deepening conviction of the impotency of Legislatures with respect to the most important departments of law-making." The "complex situations" of modern life required "expert investigations": the "ideal which has presented itself in justification of these new agencies" was that of "special knowledge, flexibility, [and] disinterestedness." Nonetheless, Hughes noted, the creation of agencies clashed with "[t]he doctrine that the Legislature cannot delegate its power," which had the potential to "make needed adaptation of legislation impossible."[28]

A year later George Sutherland, having been defeated for the Senate in the 1916 election, addressed the American Bar Association on the same subject. His emphasis was more on the potential "danger[s] to the citizen" associated with the growth of agencies. He also recited the standard extraconstitutional arguments for agency government. A "tremendous increase in the extent and complexity of our social, economic, and political activities," he noted, had made "additions to the extent of governmental operations inevitable and necessary." The increased complexity of American life had made "it more difficult for the legislative authority to deal directly and completely with many matters which come within its powers," resulting in the formation of "bureaus and commissions . . . of a highly specialized character." Sutherland worried about "the commingling of [governmental] powers" that he saw embodied in "the multiplication of bureaus and commissions," and about the potential "failure . . . of the legislative authority to lay down explicitly . . . the primary standard which fixes the limits [of their] power."[29]

Thus, by the time of Taft's remarks in 1921 agencies appeared to have become an established unit of American government despite continuing to be seen as constitutional misfits. As the emergence of agency government began to be recognized, academics turned their attention to a prospective development Root had identified in 1916, "the creation of a body of administrative law." The "system of administrative law," Root had noted, "is still in its infancy, crude and imperfect." What was to be the focus of administrative law, and what would be the governing principles systematizing that field and giving it a scholarly and professional identity? Legal scholars, some of whom had first shown an interest in those questions in the late nineteenth century, turned to them in earnest in the 1920s.

The earliest legal scholarship directed toward administrative agencies had focused on the substantive decisions made by agency officials in their respective areas of governance and on the particular deliberative processes of individual agencies. Late nineteenth- and early twentieth-century works by Frank

Goodnow, Bruce Wyman, and Ernst Freund[30] had anticipated that the tasks of administrative law scholars would resemble those of the existing cottage industry of legal academics who analyzed the common law decisions and the procedures of courts. The growth of federal agencies in the years after World War I was expected to present potential administrative law scholars with ample materials for those tasks.

The model of administrative law as a subject concerned with the internal deliberations and substantive decisions of agencies was not, however, the model that was to emerge in American academic life during the 1920s and 1930s. Instead, the subject of "administrative law," as understood by most legal scholars, came to be distinguished from the subject of "administration," which largely passed out of the consciousness of legal academics. The model of administrative law that was eventually established was centered on a recurrent debate between the extraconstitutional arguments that had helped legitimate agencies and reframed versions of the original constitutional objections to them. The crux of that debate was the scope of judicial review of administrative action on constitutional grounds. Its central arguments surveyed the comparative merits and demerits of agency expertise, and the comparative costs and benefits of judicial guardianship of orthodox separation of powers principles.

This model for administrative law had been anticipated by a line of scholarship produced by Roscoe Pound between 1905 and the early 1920s, years in which he taught at the University of Nebraska, Northwestern, the University of Chicago, and Harvard Law Schools, becoming dean of Harvard in 1916. In several articles Pound rehearsed the standard extraconstitutional arguments on behalf of agencies and at the same time recognized their novel constitutional status and their potential threat to liberties. He concluded that the superior capacity of agencies to solve "complex" problems in governance justified them despite their capacity to produce "lawless" decisions.[31] Pound's central concern in this line of scholarship was the accommodation of the agency form of government to the governing principles of orthodox separation of powers jurisprudence.

Felix Frankfurter was to echo this concern in a 1927 essay intended as an introduction to a new series of monographs entitled Harvard Studies on Administrative Law. His essay, published in the *University of Pennsylvania Law Review*,[32] described the "administrative law" as dealing with "the field of legal control exercised by law-administering agencies other than courts, and the field of control exercised by courts over such agencies."[33]

Because of "the danger of arbitrary conduct in the administration application of legal standards," Frankfurter concluded, "our administrative law is inextricably bound up with constitutional law." He associated constitutional

"safeguards" with "flexible, appropriate, and economical [agency] procedure," and identified judicial review of administrative discretion as the principal mechanism for safeguarding constitutional liberties.[34] He also felt, however, that to understand "the problems subsumed by 'judicial review'" of
agency decisions, one needed to be familiar with "the nature of the subject
matter under review as well as . . . the agency which is reviewed." Hence
he called for "a physiological study of administrative law in action," which
would focus on "the processes, the practices, the determining factors of administrative decisions . . . now left obscure by the printed pages of courts'
opinions."[35] The Harvard series on administrative law, he implied, would include both legal analyses of judicial decisions reviewing the scope of agency
discretion and "intensive scientific studies" of administrative decisions themselves.

But when John Dickinson's *Administrative Justice and the Supremacy of
Law,* supervised by Frankfurter, appeared shortly after Frankfurter's essay,[36]
its central focus was on "the boundary between the province of administrative adjudication and the courts," not on the actual decisions made by administrative agencies. Dickinson's monograph was an exploration of "the difficult points in the law of judicial review" of administrative action,[37] and its
normative thrust was to maintain aggressive judicial oversight of the constitutional dimensions of agency decisionmaking. Although Dickinson departed
from orthodox separation of powers jurisprudence by conceding the multiple
functions of agencies and justifying them on expertise grounds, he anticipated that not all agency decisions could be grounded on the discretionary
authority that followed from expertise, and in those instances searching judicial review was appropriate.

After surveying the areas in which, by the 1920s, agency governance had
been established,[38] Dickinson concluded that "if law [was] to be developed in
a field given over to regulation by administrative bodies," that process could
not primarily "be carried on by the administrative bodies themselves." The
"limited and specialized nature of [the] work" of agencies tended to make
them "unfit . . . for the task of developing general rules of law." The "narrow
angle" from which "an expert body of specialists" viewed the problems that
regularly came before it, and the fact that those problems were often "purely
technical," meant that such findings needed to be "touched off into greater
generality by a tribunal which has under its jurisdiction the whole field of legal relations."[39] In other words, judicial review of agency decisions should remain a vital feature of administrative law.

As Dickinson's work appeared, Frankfurter was approaching the trade-off
between expertise and the rule of law from another angle. He was engaged,
throughout the 1920s and early 1930s, in a campaign to reframe separation

of powers objections to the agency form. In a 1924 article in the *Harvard Law Review*, written with James Landis,[40] Frankfurter had attacked essentialist readings of the enumerated federal powers. He asserted that the "practical demands of government preclude[d] . . . [a] doctrinaire application" of the separation of powers principle, which needed to be applied with "latitude" in "a work-a-day world." "The accommodations among the three branches of government," he felt, were "not automatic." To "speak of *lines* of demarcation is to use an inapt figure."[41]

This reframing of essentialist separation of powers jurisprudence was crucial, Frankfurter believed, to the development of administrative law. But his conclusion that the field's identity was dependent on the modification of essentialist constitutional orthodoxies presupposed that its central issues would remain issues in constitutional jurisprudence. This presupposition was still in place in 1932, when Frankfurter, in connection with J. Forrester Davison,[42] published the first edition of a casebook on administrative law. The preface to the first edition declared that "the inevitable response of government to the needs of modern society" had resulted in "powers [being] lodged in a vast congeries of agencies." The growth of agency government had created "a process, still largely unconscious and unscientific, of adjusting the play of these powers to the traditional system of Anglo-American law and courts." The "concern of Administrative Law" was with the "systematic exploration of these problems."[43]

For Frankfurter this "systematic exploration" of the problems of the field of administrative law meant attention to constitutional issues, notably separation of powers objections to agency decisionmaking. Over half of the first edition of his casebook was devoted to cases and other materials on separation of powers issues; the remainder of the book covered specific areas of administrative regulation that had been reviewed by the courts. The casebook continued Frankfurter's effort to reframe orthodox separation of powers jurisprudence: its sections on judicial review of administrative action featured cases that had been used, in Frankfurter and Landis's 1924 article, to illustrate instances in which courts had adopted antiessentialist interpretations of separation of powers doctrines or had engaged in notoriously essentialist readings.[44]

The appearance of Frankfurter and Davison's casebook prompted a 1933 symposium on administrative law in the *Iowa Law Review*, which revealed that the identity of the field and its relationship to constitutional law were still deeply contested issues among academic specialists. The symposium, the first devoted to administrative law in an American law journal, had been generated by Paul L. Sayre, a former student of both Frankfurter and Ernst Freund. Frankfurter wrote a general introduction to the symposium,[45] which featured three reviews of the first edition of the Frankfurter and Davison casebook[46] and a review of Freund's 1932 treatise, *Legislative Regulation*.[47]

The symposium had two common themes. One was the tacit or explicit recognition by all the participants that agency government had become an established alternative to traditional American governmental forms, but that discretionary decisionmaking by agency officials required constitutional checks. Edwin Borchard crystallized that theme, noting that two significant characteristics of administrative government in America were "its extraordinary growth and the concomitant necessity of the individual for protection against it." Borchard felt that the growth of agencies had "placed a severe strain on . . . the traditional views concerning the separation of powers."[48]

The appropriateness of Frankfurter's constitutionally based conception of administrative law was the second common theme of the Iowa symposium. That conception was juxtaposed against another definition of the field, one primarily identified in the symposium with the work of Ernst Freund. Freund had died just before the symposium appeared in print, and several contributors contrasted his model of administrative law with that of Frankfurter and his disciples.

Freund's scholarship had emphasized the process of administrative rule-making, the technical requirements of agency practice, and the administrative remedies afforded by agencies to persons affected by their decisions. It was a study of the details of "administration," administrative law being grounded in those details. In contrast, as one reviewer noted, Frankfurter's casebook was "not a casebook on administrative law" but "a . . . collection of cases on the separation and delegation of powers, and judicial review of administrative action." A "book on a highly specialized branch of constitutional law" and a "course on administrative law," that reviewer concluded, "were two different things."[49]

The appearance of Frankfurter and Davison's casebook was a signal that by the early 1930s American administrative law, as a nascent field for practitioners and a developing subject for academics, was undergoing a kind of identity crisis. The extraconstitutional critique of traditional American governing institutions had resulted in the appearance of new units of government, generically referred to as administrative agencies. Despite the constitutionally awkward status of agencies, they had begun to build a collective body of decisions, procedures, and practices. Their decisions had, from the outset of their existence, been reviewed by courts.

Administrative law was surely more than the set of decisions by which courts had determined the constitutional legitimacy of agencies. But those decisions had been a regular feature of the growth of administrative government in America, regular enough to fill the pages of Frankfurter and

Davison's casebook. Moreover, those decisions were of the sort with which American lawyers and legal academics were familiar: the decisions of trial and of appellate courts, addressing questions of constitutional law and judicial procedure. In contrast, the nonconstitutional "administrative law" of agencies was a mass of technical rules and proceedings, not all of them easily accessible to the average lawyer and some not even regularly published. The threat to "administrative law" posed by Frankfurter and Davison's casebook was a real one. The appearance of that casebook signified how much the identity of administrative law had been created out of constitutional objections to the agency form.

As Frankfurter and Davison were preparing the second edition of their casebook, an unexpected development had given even greater momentum to the conception of administrative law as a specialized branch of constitutional law. For a two-year period beginning in 1935, traditional separation of powers theory revived itself on the Supreme Court, as efforts by Congress to create additional federal agencies were struck down on delegation grounds.

The development had been unexpected because, on the whole, the Supreme Court had been relatively receptive to federal agencies in the years between the Hepburn Act and the early 1930s. After Congress strengthened the ICC's powers in 1906, the Court assumed a largely deferential posture in reviewing that agency's administrative discretion, one that a commentator in 1924 described as "a statesmanlike comprehension of the purpose and function of administrative enforcement, and of the importance of expert decision upon questions of great economic importance."[50] The Federal Trade Commission got off to a rockier start,[51] but a few years after its creation that same commentator thought that the Court was inclined to exhibit a similar deference toward its decisions.[52]

In addition, the Court, in the first two decades of the twentieth century, promulgated some specialized administrative law doctrines that had the effect of limiting review, such as the "negative order doctrine," which insulated from review refusals of an agency to grant relief on the hearing of a complaint;[53] limitations on the standing of potential claimants before agencies;[54] and the distinction between agency rulemaking and adjudication, which limited judicial review only to the latter type of decision.[55] By 1931 a study of the Interstate Commerce Commission concluded that between 1906 and that year "the scope of judicial interference" with that agency had "progressively narrowed."[56]

One of the first examples of experimental legislation proposed by the Roosevelt administration, after having been swept into office in the 1932 election, was the National Industrial Recovery Act. The theory of the NIRA, whose drafters were influenced by the federal government's experience in controlling industrial production in World War I, was that excessive, cut-throat competition was a major source of the depressed economy of the early 1930s. The NIRA created "codes" establishing cooperative prices for certain American industries. The codes were drafted by the industries themselves, in connection with a federal agency, the National Recovery Administration.[57]

One of the industries singled out in the NIRA was the petroleum industry, which had grown significantly in certain states in the 1920s with the discovery of oil and natural gas wells. Section 9(c) of the NIRA, designed to prevent petroleum producers in oil-rich states from exceeding state production quotas and funneling their excess capacity into interstate commerce, authorized the president to "prohibit the transportation in interstate or foreign commerce of petroleum . . . produced or withdrawn from storage in excess of the amount permitted to be produced or withdrawn from storage by any state law or valid regulation."[58]

Roosevelt then issued four executive orders in July and August 1933 regulating the production and shipping of petroleum. By October 1933, as officials of the Petroleum Administrative Board had begun to enforce the regulations, two small producers, one of them the Panama Refining Company, filed suit in federal court in the eastern district of Texas challenging the constitutionality of the NIRA's petroleum codes and its delegation of power to the president to regulate production in the petroleum industry.

As that challenge, *Panama Refining Co. v. Ryan*,[59] began to work its way up through the court system, three arguments on behalf of the constitutionality of the NIRA surfaced in government circles. Two of those arguments were grounded on the federal government's power to regulate interstate commerce; the third argument was responsive to a potential challenge on delegation grounds. The last argument invoked a line of Supreme Court cases, extending back to the nineteenth century, in which federal legislation had been upheld against delegation challenges. Government lawyers believed that those cases stood for the proposition that whenever Congress articulated some "policy" and specified its implementation by a governmental agency, the delegation was constitutionally valid.[60]

But when the Court's opinion in *Panama Refining* came down in January 1935, it was apparent that a sizable majority of the Court (only Justice Benjamin Cardozo dissented) was prepared to resurrect the nondelegation doctrine, and in so doing to remind those engaged with the field of administrative law that the ubiquity of agencies did not mean that their constitutional legitimacy was inevitably assured.

Chief Justice Hughes's opinion, for the Court, found Section 9(c) of the NIRA, taken together with the declaration of congressional policy in Section 1, an unconstitutionally broad delegation of Congress's power to the president. He characterized Section 9(c) as "giv[ing] to the President an unlimited authority to determine the policy and to lay down the prohibition, or not to lay it down, as he sees fit."[61] He also found that Section 1 could not be regarded as saving the statute by reciting a policy that could be invoked as a ground for limiting the president's authority. It was "simply an introduction to the Act."[62]

Hughes conceded that

legislation must often be adapted to complex conditions involving a host of details with which the national legislature cannot deal directly. The Constitution has never been regarded as denying to the Congress the necessary resources of flexibility and practicality, which will enable it to perform its function of laying down policies and establishing standards, while leaving to selected instrumentalities the making of subordinate rules within prescribed limits and the determination of facts to which the policy as declared by the legislature is to apply.[63]

Here were two of the extraconstitutional arguments for agency government—flexibility and hands-on expertise. But they could not transgress "the limitations of the authority to delegate, if our constitutional system is to be maintained." According to Hughes, none of the Court's previous pro-delegation opinions had ignored those limitations. They had maintained the distinction, obliterated by Section 9(c) of the NIRA, between Congress's delegating power "to make the law, which necessarily involves a discretion as to what it shall be," and Congress's "conferring authority or discretion as to its execution."[64]

Panama Refining suggested that orthodox separation of powers strictures, embodied in the nondelegation doctrine, had survived almost fifty years of efforts to modify their impact. There was, however, a passage toward the end of the opinion that hinted that the simple attachment of a few procedural safeguards to congressional delegations might assuage the Court's constitutional concerns. Hughes wrote, "If the citizen is to be punished for the crime of violating a legislative order of an executive officer, or of a board or commission, due process of law requires that it shall appear that the order is within the authority of the officer, board or commission, and if that authority depends on determinations of fact, those determinations must be shown."[65]

Some enthusiasts for administrative regulation, after the issuance of *Panama Refining*, equated this definition of "due process of law" with minimal procedural requirements. They took "due process" concerns to be satisfied if

Congress declared its policies and supplied standards to implement them. Acting on that assumption, New Deal supporters designed a new statutory framework for retaining the identical structure for regulating the petroleum industry that had been challenged in *Panama Refining*.[66] But before any such statute could be enacted, the Court declared the entire NIRA invalid in *Schechter Poultry Corp. v. United States*,[67] which was heard and decided in May 1935, only four months after *Panama Refining* had been handed down. The heart of the *Schechter* decision was the Court's conclusion that the "codes of fair competition" established for industries by the NIRA were unconstitutional delegations because they provided no clear enforcement standards.[68]

Hughes, this time for a unanimous Court, with Cardozo writing separately, once again emphasized that "the wide range of administrative authority which has been developed . . . cannot be allowed to obscure the limitations of the authority to delegate, if our constitutional system is to be maintained."[69] Hughes found that Section 3 of the NIRA, which provided for the creation of "codes of fair competition" to be proposed by representatives of an industry and, once approved by the president, enforced by administrative officials, did not even approach the threshold of constitutional adequacy.

First, he maintained, the term "fair competition" was not given a sufficiently precise legal definition. It was simply a device by which those who had drafted a code, or possibly the president himself, justified "provisions for the government of the trade or industry" as being "wise and beneficent."[70] The term "fair competition" meant, in effect, whatever a group of industry representatives and the president said it meant.[71]

In addition, the nature of the delegation in the NIRA was unprecedented. The drafters of the code provisions were not members of the government at all: the codes were to consist of "rules of competition deemed fair for each industry by representative members of that industry." Such a delegation of legislative power was "unknown to our law and . . . utterly inconsistent with the constitutional prerogatives and duties of Congress."[72]

Hughes thus struck down Section 3 of the NIRA, and with it the entire implementing machinery ostensibly created to further the general policies Congress had declared in Section 1. And if there was any doubt that the limits of a permissive Court stance toward congressional delegations had been reached with the *Panama Refining-Schechter* sequence, it disappeared with Cardozo's concurrence in *Schechter*. Cardozo found the combination in Section 3 of a standardless definition of "fair competition," together with delegation of code promulgation to private groups, an example of "delegation run riot."

The Court continued its revival of delegation objections to agency government in *Carter v. Carter Coal Co.*,[73] which was argued in March 1936 and decided in May of that year. In his opinion for the Court in *Carter Coal*, which invalidated the Bituminous Coal Conservation Act of 1935, Sutherland intimated that any congressional delegation of power to private groups was unconstitutional. A labor relations section of the Act had delegated the power to fix maximum hours and minimum wages in the bituminous coal industry to two-thirds of the coal producers and a majority of the miners in specified coal districts. Mine owners who did not accept the wage or hour agreements made by those groups were subjected to a 15 percent excise tax on their coal, and the United States government was prohibited from buying coal from them.

Sutherland described the "power conferred upon the majority" by the labor relations section as "the power to regulate the affairs of an unwilling minority." He characterized it as "legislative delegation in its most obnoxious form; for it is not even delegation to an official or an official body, presumptively disinterested, but to private persons whose interests may be and often are adverse to the interests of others in the same business. . . A statute which attempts to confer such power undertakes an intolerable and unconstitutional interference with personal liberty and private property."

Thus, at the conclusion of the 1935 Term it appeared that a decisive majority of the Court was presumptively disinclined to sustain federal legislation delegating lawmaking power to private groups, would insist that Congress prescribe relatively specific standards for agency decisionmaking, and in many contexts would require the president to make specific findings of fact, related to congressional policies, before making further delegations of his powers. The *Panama Refining, Schechter,* and *Carter Coal* decisions obviously required courses in administrative law to give serious attention to constitutional limitations on the agency form.

The decisions also prompted those concerned with the drafting of congressional legislation to reexamine the character and composition of federal agencies that had survived Court scrutiny. The prominent examples were all independent regulatory agencies: the ICC, the Federal Trade Commission, the Federal Power Commission, and the Federal Communications Commission. Each of those agencies had certain common characteristics. They had been given a statutory standard for regulation (sometimes a quite broad one, such as the FCC's "public interest, convenience, and necessity"), which had been tied to a constitutionally enumerated federal power (typically the commerce power). Their regulatory process was administered by a board or commission of independently appointed officials, none of whom were representatives of the industry being regulated. Although their administrative structure assumed some discretion in agency officials to find facts and issue rules, agency decisions were ultimately subject to judicial review, sometimes of a searching nature. None of the agencies had been successfully challenged on delegation grounds.

It was therefore no surprise that the next regulatory statute passed by Congress in the wake of the *Panama Refining* and *Schechter* decisions created a National Labor Relations Board, self-consciously modeled on the Federal Trade Commission,[74] which had an independent staff and exercised discretion in fact-finding and rulemaking but was subject to having its decisions and its procedures reviewed in court. The NLRB was created in 1935, and after *Carter Coal* was decided its asserted power to regulate local labor disputes because of their connection to interstate commerce was expected to be challenged.[75] But when that challenge came in a series of 1937 cases, commerce power issues occupied the Court's opinions; delegation issues were not given any attention.[76] So long as agencies followed the form of the NLRB and its extant predecessors, constitutional objections to them seemed to have shifted away from separation of powers concerns.

To academic observers who were sympathetic to New Deal experiments with expanded agency government, the above sequence of Court decisions made it clear that the judiciary was reasserting its "own capacity to review governmental action in accordance with the doctrines of constitutional law," particularly "the principles and theories of the separation of powers" and "those principles which restrict the right to delegate any of the traditional functions of [the three branches of government] to administrative agencies."[77] Devotees of the agency unit of government thought that unless courts exercised "judicial self-limitation,"[78] the result of the Court's revival of the constitutional limitations on agency decisionmaking would be "to render Congress and the President impotent to deal with the conditions designed to be regulated."[79]

Instead of reading the *Panama Refining/Schechter/Carter Coal* sequence of decisions as unmistakable evidence that administrative law would develop against the backdrop of principles and doctrines identified with orthodox constitutional jurisprudence, some commentators, who were sympathetic to the growth of agencies, treated the decisions as confirming the constitutional legitimacy of the agency form and providing blueprints for the creation of new agencies. Reuben Oppenheimer, after surveying *Panama Refining, Schechter, Carter Coal,* and four additional administrative law cases decided by the Court in 1935 and 1936, agreed with other commentators about the significant constitutional dimensions of administrative law and also about the intrusive quality of the Court's reviewing stance. But the major implication Oppenheimer took from the Court's activity was that "the quasi-judicial or quasi-legislative administrative tribunal has been recognized and approved as a permanent instrument of government."[80]

The Court's striking down of Section 9(c) of the NIRA on delegation grounds in *Panama Refining*, Oppenheimer argued, was caused by "the fact that the statute of itself provided no administrative machinery."[81] The *Schechter* decision's "outstanding feature" was "the emphasis which the Court place[d] upon the development of administrative machinery through the sorts of tribunals which it has in the past held valid."[82] The "chief importance of the *Carter* case" was the "undisputed finding of the three [dissenting] Justices that Congress can make provisions for a code of industry when proper standards and administrative machinery are provided."[83]

The most influential of the group of commentators who read the Court's 1935 and 1936 delegation decisions optimistically for agency government was James Landis, who had evolved from being a Frankfurter protégé to chairman of the Securities and Exchange Commission and, by 1937, dean of Harvard Law School, replacing Roscoe Pound. Landis's 1938 book, *The Administrative Process*, is best known as an aggressive defense of agencies and agency discretion, accompanied by a prediction that agencies would become the prime symbols of an expanded governmental regulatory presence in modern industrial America.[84] Landis's work, however, had another, arguably more significant, dimension. It was the first major example of the conventional twentieth-century account of agency growth in America, the first to see the emergence of agencies as part of a history that made their appearance inevitable despite constitutional objections to them.

Landis's strategy in *The Administrative Process* unfolded in three steps. He first sought to identify the emergence of agencies as part of a historical process in which American policymakers responded to the presence of modernity by expanding the role of government as a regulatory force. This invested agency growth with an historical inevitability and shifted discussions of the legal dimensions of agency decisionmaking from a context in which agency government was treated as dubious to one in which it was treated as natural and necessary.[85]

Having established agencies as historically inevitable institutions, Landis next reviewed the standard constitutional objections to them, which he found to be grounded on models of government that were unrealistic in a modern industrial society. Traditional separation of powers jurisprudence, he concluded, was based on the limited conceptions of government associated with a far less industrialized and less democratic social order than that which early twentieth-century Americans were experiencing. Since the very purpose of expanded government in America was to respond effectively to the new conditions and problems of modern life, the institutions of that government should assume a shape that best enabled them to facilitate that response. Essentialist constitutional conceptions of the branches of government needed to yield, in this context, to pragmatic ones.

Further, Landis stressed the comparative advantages of agency government over traditional institutions in dealing with the social issues generated by an industrial democracy. He identified the comparative advantages of agencies as governmental institutions with expertise.[86] Like previous supporters of the agency form, he emphasized the scientific training of agency officials, their specialized grounding in the areas of industrial enterprise they were expected to regulate, their nonpartisan status, and their independence from the conventional political process, features that made them "experts."[87] But the final step of his argument for agency government sought to employ the concept of expertise in a novel fashion.

Agency expertise, Landis suggested, provided a check on the potential for tyrannical or arbitrary exercise of power that opponents of the agency form had associated with the combination of traditionally separate governmental functions in one institution. Since experts derived their status from their mastery of specialized knowledge and scientific techniques of inquiry, they could be expected to take on the values of the early twentieth-century scientific community, in which careful empirical observation, the unbiased evaluation of data, and an attitude of objectivity toward one's investigations defined the role of an expert scientist. Agency expertise, in Landis's hands, had evolved from being an extralegal argument for administrative discretion to being the equivalent of a legal check on that discretion.[88]

When Landis's paean to the administrative process had concluded, some constitutional checks on agency discretion remained in place. In *The Administrative Process* Landis quoted with approval a 1936 definition by Justice Brandeis of the checks on administrative decisionmaking necessary to maintain the principle of "[t]he supremacy of law." Brandeis had required an "opportunity to have some court decide whether an erroneous rule of law [had been] applied" by an agency or "whether the proceeding in which the facts were adjudicated was conducted regularly."[89] Landis called this definition "modern," and noted that it had been "made in protest" against an insistence by a majority of the Supreme Court that findings of fact made by an administrative agency could be independently determined by a reviewing court.[90] But the definition nonetheless anticipated that reviewing courts retained power to scrutinize the decisions of agencies on what amounted to due process grounds. Even Landis, with his great faith in the connections between specialization, expertise, and impartial decisionmaking, implicitly acknowledged that even expert administrators were capable of arbitrariness and tyranny, and their "erroneous" or "irregular" decisions could be reversed.[91]

Thus, one can observe, in the midst of Landis's aggressive defense of the exercise of administrative discretion on an unprecedentedly broad scale, a kernel of the constitutional checks on that discretion that had been derived from a jurisprudential orthodoxy in which agencies were seen as alien forms of government. And as Landis's muted concession that even government experts were capable of procedural or substantive abuses became stated more loudly and categorically in the late 1930s, the theme of constitutional restraints on agency decisionmaking was once again sounded, assuring that as administrative law entered the decade of the 1940s it would still be significantly concerned with the constitutional implications of agency decisions.

As early as 1933 efforts to curb administrative discretion had begun to surface.[92] That year Senator Mills Logan of Kentucky introduced a bill providing for an administrative court that would hear appeals from decisions of all the federal agencies. The ostensible purpose of the bill was to create a more formal record of the deliberations of agencies, which at that time did not publish most of their decisions. Congress took no action on the bill.[93]

The same year also witnessed the first appearance of the American Bar Association's Special Committee on Administrative Law, which was subsequently to emerge as a consistent opponent of agency discretion. The Committee began issuing annual reports, which emphasized constitutional objections to the agency form of government,[94] from 1933 through the Second World War. The objections centered on the merger of traditionally separated governmental functions in agencies and on the absence of judicial review of many agency decisions.[95]

In 1937 the context of antiagency sentiment changed. That year the Court sustained the constitutionality of two statutes creating federal agencies, suggesting that its earlier invalidations of comparable legislation might have been centered on loose statutory language rather than on fundamental separation of powers principles.[96] Those decisions signaled that federal agencies might well become common units of government. But at the same time the Roosevelt administration exhibited some political vulnerability in Congress for the first time since it came into office, having failed to enact legislation providing for a governmental reorganization in which several independent agencies would be swept under executive control. Finally, the combination of an economic recession and the growth of totalitarian governments in Europe revived political opposition to the New Deal and gave more credence to arguments identifying the expansion of the federal government with autocratic tendencies in those regimes.[97]

The last two developments enabled those who were politically or jurisprudentially unsympathetic to agency government to pose a reframed challenge to Landis's ideal of an expanded administrative state. The challenge had two related dimensions, one rhetorical and the other legislative. The ABA Committee was involved with both dimensions of the challenge. Its members advanced characterizations of agency government that fused older constitutional objections with contemporary concerns about totalitarianism. At the same time they drafted legislation to modify the structure of decisonmaking by federal agencies.

The vision of those challenging agency government was captured in a passage from the 1938 report of the ABA's Special Committee on Administrative Law, drafted by Roscoe Pound, who had been recruited to chair the Committee that year. Pound, after alluding to the constitutionally mandated separation of powers and strong judicial checks on the activities of other governmental branches, which served to identify the American system of government, then declared that

> [t]he antithesis is the proposition recently maintained by the jurists of Soviet Russia that in the socialist state there is no law but only one rule of law, that there are no laws—only administrative ordinances and orders. The ideal of administrative absolutism is a highly centralized administration set up under complete control of the executive for the time being, relieved of judicial review and making its own rules. This sort of regime is urged today by those who deny that there is such a thing as law (in the sense in which lawyers understand the term) and maintain that this lawyer's illusion will disappear in the society of the future.[98]

Some of this rhetoric was to find its way into the 1939 session of Congress, as the ABA Committee and its allies introduced a bill designed to impose significant constraints on federal agencies. The legislation, known as the Walter-Logan Act, was virtually identical to a bill drafted by the ABA Committee in 1937.[99] It sought to reduce agency discretion through the promulgation of a uniform code of procedure for all agencies, which would include more formalized agency internal processes, a separation of some agency functions, and expanded judicial review.

The appearance of the Walter-Logan Act signified a new stage in the long-standing debate between those who viewed federal administrative agencies as constitutionally alien units of government and those who saw them as symbols of the increased need for expert management of social problems in a modern industrial democracy. The framers of the Walter-Logan Act took for granted that federal agencies had acquired some constitutional legitimacy. At the same time, however, they rejected Landis's argument that the expertise of administrators itself furnished the basis of their accountability. In rejecting that argument, they insisted that the experience, specialized knowledge, and scientific techniques of administrators were not sufficient grounds to insulate agency decisions from scrutiny. The sponsors of the Walter-Logan Act sought to telescope essentialist objections to the agency form into procedural checks on agency discretion, and to insist that the existence of such checks, rather than expertise alone, were necessary to make agency government constitutionally legitimate.

The Walter-Logan Act nearly became law. It was initially passed by the House of Representatives in April 1940 and by the Senate in November of that year. Roosevelt vetoed the bill on December 2, 1940, and on December 18 the House voted 153–127 to override the veto, falling 34 votes short on the necessary two-thirds majority. The change in congressional sentiment toward agencies reflected in the appearance of the Walter-Logan Act meant that the momentum of expanding, discretionary agency government, which Landis had heralded in *The Administrative Process,* had slowed. At the same time the central focus of debates about agency government had shifted from the constitutionally alien status of agencies to their "absolutist" tendencies. This meant that administrative law would continue to have a recurrent constitutional component, but that component would primarily manifest itself in debates about the scope of procedural checks on agency discretion.

Before the Walter-Logan Act reached Congress, the Roosevelt administration had created the Attorney General's Committee on Administrative Procedure as a response to the growing attacks on government by federal agencies. The ostensible purpose of the Committee was to conduct a study of federal agencies and propose its own version of congressional legislation; its actual purpose was to head off the ABA Committee's assault. The membership of the Committee included a solid majority of New Deal supporters, and its research director, Walter Gellhorn of Columbia Law School, was a strong advocate of agency government and an outspoken critic of attempts to replace agencies with courts.[100] But despite the Committee's mandate, one of its recommendations evolved into the Administrative Procedure Act of 1946, which conclusively defined the field of administrative law as centering on the scope of procedural checks on agency discretion, notably the scope of judicial review of administrative action on constitutional grounds. With the passage of the Administrative Procedure Act a residuum of the original constitutional objections to agency government became entrenched in the practice of twentieth-century federal agencies and the jurisprudence of administrative law.

In late January 1941, a month after the Walter-Logan Act had failed to be revived in the House, the Attorney General's Committee submitted its report,[101] which contained two draft bills designed to establish uniform procedural guidelines for all federal agencies. The first bill, which was endorsed by a majority of the Committee's members, did little to alter the state of federal administrative procedure that had existed at the time the Walter-Logan Act was first introduced. It did not provide for any additional judicial review of agency decisions nor did it impose any additional procedural requirements on agencies.[102]

The other bill presented in the Committee's report, the so-called "minority" bill, resembled the Walter-Logan bill in its efforts to impose formal controls on agency decisionmaking. It required notice and comment procedures for all rulemaking by agencies.[103] It also required that all agency rules and regulations be published in the Federal Register.[104] Its standard of judicial review, which required courts to uphold agency decisions only if they were found to be based on "substantial evidence . . . upon the whole record," and permitted courts to reverse decisions they found "arbitrary and capricious,"[105] was clearly more intrusive than that anticipated by the majority bill, which had taken no position on the standard by which courts should evaluate agency decisions.

The minority bill's approach would eventually prevail in the Administrative Procedure Act of 1946, typically seen as the modern charter of agency government in America. The path from the appearance of the Committee report in 1941 to the passage of the Administrative Procedure Act was a lengthy one. First, a chorus of praise greeted the issuance of the Committee report in academic journals, and even the *Journal of the American Bar Association* gave the report a qualified endorsement.[106] This kept alive the possibility that Congress would address the procedural dimensions of agency decisionmaking in some comprehensive fashion, and gave the ABA Special Committee the option of backing a fairly comprehensive set of restrictions on agency discretion that was identified with the Roosevelt administration rather than the ABA itself. Eventually the ABA's membership voted to endorse the minority bill in the Committee report, reasoning that a more restrictive bill would have virtually no chance of being endorsed by Congress in the face of opposition by the Roosevelt administration.[107]

In 1944 a bill drafted by the ABA Committee, closely resembling the minority bill in the Attorney General's Committee report, was introduced into the Senate and the House.[108] The bill established a uniform procedural code for all federal agencies. In endorsing the 1944 bill the ABA Committee stated that "it define[d] the minima of administrative procedural requirements" and provided for judicial review of a scope as "broad as can now be required," given that it would require cooperation from the Roosevelt administration for passage.[109]

Over the next two years the 1944 bill became the standard text from which negotiations occurred between the ABA, representatives of the agencies, and the Roosevelt and Truman administrations. Modifications of the 1944 bill took place, most in the direction of relaxing some of the requirements imposed on informal agency rulemaking proceedings and slightly relaxing the bill's proposed standard of judicial review, which now advised courts to defer to agencies whose decisions were based on "substantial evidence on the whole record."[110]

Finally, in 1946, the bill, now known as the Administrative Procedure Act, passed both houses of Congress unanimously and was signed into law by President Truman on June 11. The unanimity of Congress concealed the fact that those who had originally favored a significant judicialization of the administrative process, as well as those who were determined to preserve agency discretion, remained unsure about whether the standard of judicial review imposed by the Act was a tightening of, or simply a continuation of, existing practices. As a consequence all sides sought to build after-the-fact "legislative histories" into the Act, and then to interpret those histories to their advantage.[111] Members of the Truman administration suggested that the APA merely "declare[d] the existing law concerning the scope of judicial review,"[112] but Senator Pat McCarran, the chairman of the Senate Judiciary Committee and a critic of agencies, wrote in the *American Bar Association Journal* that "it would be hard . . . for anyone to argue that [the APA] Act did anything other than cut down the 'cult of discretion' so far as federal law is concerned."[113]

Although McCarran was perhaps banking on stricter judicial scrutiny of agency decisionmaking than the APA's standard required, his comment was nonetheless a fairly accurate description of the thrust of the Administrative Procedure Act. Although the APA was not the equivalent of the Walter-Logan bill, it established three levels of checks on agency discretion that had not been uniformly established before its passage. First, agencies had to publish their decisions. Second, their officials could no longer combine prosecutorial and adjudicatory functions in their job descriptions. Third, at every stage in an agency's deliberations it either had to offer affected parties an opportunity to comment on prospective decisions or an opportunity to have those decisions reviewed in a court of law. Those procedural safeguards that the Administrative Procedure Act imposed on agencies can be seen as the remnants of orthodox constitutional objections to agency government, reframed and built into the administrative process to constrain the discretion of expert administrators.

The creation of modern administrative law in America was thus not simply the product of the inexorable triumph of extraconstitutional arguments that demonstrated the superiority of agency government. It was the product of a complicated interplay between those arguments and the essentialist premises of traditional constitutional jurisprudence. Yet the interplay has largely disappeared from conventional accounts of the growth of agency government in the twentieth century. It remains to explain the sources of this lost history.

We have seen that the original versions of the common account of agency growth surfaced at the very moment when some decisions of the Supreme Court, some members of Congress, and the ABA's Special Committee were signaling that the growth of agency discretion raised troublesome constitutional issues. This was not fortuitous. Landis's creation of a historical pedigree for agencies in *The Administrative Process* dovetailed neatly with the more detailed history of the commission form of government presented in Robert Cushman's *The Independent Regulatory Commissions* (1941). Landis's assertion of the comparative superiority of agencies over courts as social managers was echoed by Robert Jackson in *The Struggle for Judicial Supremacy* (also 1941). All of those works invoked the standard extraconstitutional arguments for agency government; all emphasized the role of agencies as an embodiment of the philosophy of expanded governmental involvement in the social problems of a modern industrial democracy; all implied that in light of those arguments, and of the triumph of that philosophy, the challenges to the agency form that had surfaced in the late 1930s were outmoded and misguided.

The above accounts were in place when, in the wake of the Administrative Procedure Act's passage in 1946, participants in the debates over agency discretion that had taken place in the late 1930s and 1940s began to fashion their versions of the APA's legislative history. As we have seen, several "histories" of the APA's formation were advanced, and one of the sources on which those histories could draw was a monograph by Walter Gellhorn, the research director of the Attorney General's Committee on Administrative Procedure, which had appeared in 1941. In that monograph, *Federal Administrative Proceedings*, Gellhorn offered a framework in which the APA could be seen as the culmination of the growth of agency government in America.

Gellhorn declared that at the time of the appearance of *Federal Administrative Proceedings* "administrative law [had] entered into its third great phase," in which "concern is addressed chiefly not to constitutional divisions of power, not to appropriate boundaries of judicial review, but to the procedure of administration itself."[114] He argued that "bad administrative decisions" should be alleviated not by judicial review but by internal procedures "which give assurance that matters will receive full and fair administrative consideration."[115] The decision by the Attorney General's Committee to study and report on the internal procedures of several agencies, he felt, should be taken as a signal that any lingering constitutional objections to the agency form could be alleviated simply by improving those procedures.

If one adopted Gellhorn's division of early twentieth-century administrative law into phases in which constitutional issues progressively receded in significance, eventually becoming subsumed in streamlined agency procedures, the Administrative Procedure Act could be characterized as simply a codification of procedures and standards of review that already existed. This characterization, which complemented the Justice Department's 1947 conclusion that the APA merely declared existing rules of administrative law and procedure, was precisely the characterization that mainstream versions of the conventional account of agency growth were subsequently to adopt. Mainstream narrators also adopted Landis's and Jackson's pejorative characterizations of those who advanced constitutional objections to agencies.

One example can be found in a 1978 article by Paul Verkeuil, who acknowledged the help of Walter Gellhorn in its preparation.[116] Verkeuil's account of the developments between 1938 and 1946 began by characterizing the ABA's successive efforts to curb agency discretion as hysterical denunciations of "administrative absolutism" rather than efforts to "creat[e] working principles of administrative procedure."[117] He saw the proposals as "a reversion to the earlier view of the substantive and procedural tyrannies of administrative law" and oriented toward an "apotheosis of the judiciary."[118] The "forces in favor of the [Walter-Logan] bill were undoubtedly led by those who were substantively opposed to . . . the New Deal programs." They "must have believed that if they could reassert the procedural analogue to nineteenth-century liberalism . . . they might succeed in frustrating the substantive solutions proposed by the welfare programs of twentieth-century liberalism."[119]

But the ABA's opposition to agencies, Verkeuil claimed, had been predicated on "a mistake." The "New Deal period was [not] characterized by administrative arbitrariness." It was a time of "procedural innovation." The period of the 1930s introduced "the concept of the administrator as an agent for the public," working "to ensure that the . . . goals [of affirmative governmental policy] were fulfilled." This "innovative thinking about administrative procedure . . . would ultimately lead to the emergence of an independent procedural model for administrative law."[120]

When the Attorney General's Committee report appeared, Verkeuil suggested, it was quickly understood to be "a vindication of New Deal procedural solutions," as well as "the best study of federal administrative procedure ever prepared." It had been undertaken by staff who "approached the administrative process without preconceptions and studied it empirically." This focus moved "administrative law into its third and mature phase," in which "[a]utomatic and unexamined reliance upon the judicial model would never again satisfactorily resolve debate."[121]

Verkeuil then used these characterizations as the basis of an explanation of the significance of the Administrative Procedure Act. Although "[o]n the face of it" the APA "looked like a victory for the old Walter-Logan forces who had earlier sought unsuccessfully to judicialize administrative procedure," it was not. The APA "was passed in a period of reconciliation and relative agreement about its goals and techniques." It "amounted to something of a catharsis for long contending forces." And it reflected "much of the progressive thinking about administrative law that emerged from the 1940s."[122] In short, the passage of the APA demonstrated the coming of age of the administrative agency as a unit of government, and the substitution of procedural checks on agencies for substantive judicial review of agency decisions on constitutional grounds.

Another example of the mainstream account can be seen in the emergence, in the years after the APA's passage, of the Department of Justice's 1947 *Manual on the Administrative Procedure Act*,[123] which was prepared by staff members of the solicitor general's office during the Truman administration,[124] as the authoritative exegesis on the relationship of the APA to preexisting administrative law. Although the *Manual* was simply one of the numerous "legislative histories" of the APA created after its passage, it came to be treated as the definitive account, and other efforts were ignored. The *Manual* asserted that "the main origins of the present [APA]" could be "found in [the Attorney General's Committee's Final] Report,"[125] declining to point out that the APA most resembled the framework endorsed by a minority of the Attorney General's Committee. The *Manual* then engaged in a series of interpretive glosses on sections of the APA that concluded that the legislation merely codified the existing state of administrative law prior to its passage.[126] This confirmed Gellhorn's view of the evolution of administrative law. Agencies were already established as constitutionally legitimate institutions by the 1930s, the *Manual*'s glosses suggested, and had begun to build procedural checks into their deliberative processes. All the APA did was to make those checks somewhat more regular and uniform. Subsequent courts and commentators, including the Supreme Court,[127] have taken this suggestion at face value and treated the *Manual*'s interpretations of the APA as definitive.

A third set of examples of the mainstream account comes from participant histories of the formation of the APA by Walter Gellhorn and Kenneth Culp Davis, who served with Gellhorn on the Attorney General's Committee. Gellhorn's and Davis's histories were prompted by the fortieth anniversary of the APA's passage in 1986.

In Gellhorn's history the Administrative Procedure Act was "approved . . . with no indication of dissent, . . . in an atmosphere of happy accord."[128] The Act "had been begun in an exercise of the imagination," which he identified with the Attorney General's Committee. The path from that Committee's report to the passage of the APA demonstrated that "[i]nvective had given way to investigation."[129] Gellhorn ridiculed the ABA Special Committee. "Their level of penetration into the mysteries of administrative processes was . . . barely . . . below the surface."[130] The concept of "administrative absolutism" amounted to "contemplat[ing] their respective navels and . . . com[ing] up with some proposition of a philosophical character or grab[bing] some idea from the heavens." Their reform proposals simply sought to "transfer everything from administrative agencies to an administrative court."[131]

Davis's account was similar to Gellhorn's. He characterized the Attorney General's Committee on Administrative Procedure as a group of "distinguished practitioners, judges, and professors" who "set about its tasks in scholarly fashion." In contrast to the ABA Special Committee, it "went after the facts." It produced "[a] detailed monograph" on each agency. It issued an "elaborate report" that, as late as 1958, was "still a primary source of information about the federal administrative process."[132] In contrast, the ABA, which in Davis's view was from 1933 to 1941 "a pernicious organization," simply took an "extreme political attitude." The ABA "of the thirties," Davis felt, "was not merely conservative, but extreme conservatives were dominant."[133] Despite the ABA's fulminations against agencies, the Administrative Procedure Act embodied very few of the ABA's reformist goals.[134]

From the late 1930s through the 1980s, then, a particularistic reading of the sequence of events that began with Taft's 1921 description of the "new field" of administrative law, and culminated in 1946 with the passage of the Administrative Procedure Act, has been entrenched. Originally perpetuated by persons who took the inevitability of expanded government in modern, "complex" societies as a given, identified administrative agencies as especially promising forms of active government, and in some instances were directly involved with the Roosevelt's administration's response to challenges to the agency form, the reading has amounted to a self-fulfilling prophesy.

This chapter has set forth an alternative interpretation of the emergence of agency government and the creation of administrative law, emphasizing that orthodox constitutional objections to the agency form played a far more prominent role in the gestation processes than the conventional account has suggested. I have drawn on three sets of evidence in fashioning that alternative interpretation. One set has consisted of academic commentary in the first three decades of the twentieth century. Taken collectively, that commentary reveals the alien constitutional status of agencies and, accordingly, the prominent attention given to the constitutional dimensions of administrative law by commentators. By the early 1930s, an earlier conception of administrative law as the detailed study of the internal rules and deliberations of agencies was on its way to being supplanted by a conception that centered the field's core issues around a tension between the growth of administrative discretion grounded on expertise and the need to maintain judicially imposed constitutional safeguards on agency decisionmaking. Modern American administrative law has thus always had an important constitutional dimension, despite efforts on the part of advocates of agency discretion to minimize that dimension.

A second set of sources buttressing my interpretation has consisted of debates in Congress, stretching from 1906 through the 1940s, in which orthodox constitutional objections to the agency form were articulated and reframed. Some of the orthodox objections found their way into Supreme Court decisions invalidating New Deal agencies on constitutional grounds, and even after the Court seemed prepared to accept certain forms of agency government, the objections, now centering on the apparently limitless scope of agency discretion, resurfaced. Instead of Congress and the courts accepting agencies, in the wake of the New Deal, as natural, uncontroversial, modern substitutes for traditional American institutions of government, one sees, as late the 1940s, the continuation of a rhetorical dialogue between extraconstitutional arguments for agencies, especially ones grounded on the concept of expert administrative discretion, and arguments derived from orthodox assumptions about the constitutionally alien character of governmental institutions whose decisions were effectively insulated from scrutiny by other branches.

The third set of evidence has been employed to historicize the contributions of those who originated and perpetuated the conventional account. Its sources provide reasons why such narrators might have been inclined to stress the cogency or historical resonance of extraconstitutional arguments on behalf of agencies and to ignore or caricature constitutional objections to them. In some instances contributors to the conventional account were themselves participants in debates about the constitutional legitimacy of agencies during the New Deal years. Landis, Cushman, Jackson, Gellhorn, and Davis can each be placed in that category. As partisans this group of contributors consistently had to confront, and attempt to deflect or reframe, traditional constitutional objections to agencies. When some of them later came to sketch histories of the debates in which they had participated, they tended to reinforce their perceptions of the triumph of agency government by treating those objections as not deserving much weight, and consequently not worthy of much attention in accounts of the growth of administrative law.

By identifying orthodox constitutional objections to agencies with stereotyped images of the courts, personified by the "nine old men" on the Supreme Court who struck down New Deal agencies in the *Panama Refining/ Schechter/Carter Coal* sequence, the conventional account has successfully associated those objections with an ascribed resistance of the Supreme Court to all early twentieth-century efforts to expand the reach of government. The growth of federal agencies thus becomes linked to other efforts to respond to the problems of modernity through an expanded governmental presence, and the Court's resistance to that growth is thought of as of a piece with its general disinclination to adapt twentieth-century constitutional jurisprudence to the needs of a modern society.

With this stereotype of judicial resistance to progressive government-sponsored regulation in the New Deal period in place, the sequence of events leading to the passage of the Administrative Procedure Act can be presented as a struggle between progressive supporters of agencies and reactionary devotees of the courts. Instead of the Walter-Logan Act being portrayed as a source of ideas later embodied in the APA, the Act is caricatured as an effort to transfer all the decisionmaking powers of agencies to the judiciary. Hence the voicing of concerns about the scope of administrative discretion in Congress in the 1940s appears the equivalent of the Supreme Court's unsuccessful threats to destroy the New Deal in the 1930s.

Given this portrayal of events, the APA *had* to have been simply a codification of the existing informal procedures of agencies rather than the imposition of significant procedural checks on agency discretion, because otherwise the reactionary forces who sought to use courts to prevent the growth of affirmative government would have accomplished in administrative law what they had failed to accomplish in other areas of constitutional jurisprudence.

The last step in the common account's history of administrative law, then, was to define the passage of the APA as the moment when the central issues of administrative law became ones of minimalist constitutional procedure rather than essentialist, orthodox, constitutional law. As such the creation of modern administrative law symbolized the apparently permanent establishment of an expanded apparatus of modern American government. The extra-constitutional arguments on behalf of the agency form had finally prevailed.

Administrative law, in its modern form, has been taken to signify the presence and constitutional legitimacy of expansive agency government in America. With that premise in place, it seems unnecessary to recall previous constitutional objections to the agency form or to emphasize their importance in shaping administrative law itself. It is far easier to fashion a historical account in which the creation of administrative law is associated with the inevitable emergence of agencies in a complex modern world, one whose problems require the affirmative interventions of governmental experts. But the fashioning of that history leaves out at least half of the story.

5

The Emergence of Free Speech

Previous chapters have sought to complicate the causal relationship between the New Deal and changes in the early twentieth-century constitutional jurisprudence of foreign relations and administrative law. This chapter considers the relationship between the New Deal and the emergence, over the course of the twentieth century, of expanded constitutional protection for free speech, especially in the context of what could be called diminished constitutional protection for rights and liberties associated with economic activity.

We have seen that in the areas of foreign relations and administrative law, intuitive associations have been made between the appearance of a jurisprudential tendency to remove constitutional limits from the exercise of national regulatory powers and the emergence of an expanded conception of the role of government in modern society, personified by a variety of New Deal initiatives. Although such associations have served to overrate the causal significance of the New Deal and to create oversimplified characterizations of the constitutional changes that were taking place, one can readily see how the associations might seem plausible. If one notices that persons making public policy in the early twentieth century have come to believe that efforts to respond to the problems of modernity require a more expansive governmental apparatus or greater discretion for federal officials than orthodox constitutional doctrines would permit, one might expect—especially if one thinks of judicial decisions as exercises in public policy—the doctrines to be modified. In fact, such an expectation has been at the core of the conventional account of early twentieth-century constitutional change and has served to elevate the importance of the New Deal as a transformative force.

The emergence of heightened constitutional protection for free speech in the twentieth century, however, would not appear to represent a jurisprudential transformation that paralleled, and was reinforced by, the surfacing of a philosophy of expanded government. Unlike the transformations in foreign

128

affairs and administrative law, that in free speech jurisprudence had the effect of curtailing the regulatory power of the federal government or the states through heightened constitutional constraints. At the close of World War I, Congress, despite the First Amendment, was regarded as having quite substantial powers to regulate speech perceived as threatening national interests, and the states were regarded as having comparable latitude under their police powers. By the close of the Second World War the First Amendment's categorical statement that Congress "shall make no law . . . abridging the freedom of speech" had been held to apply to the states as well, and a number of governmental efforts to regulate speech had been struck down by the Supreme Court.

Despite the difficulties in connecting increased judicial protection for free speech with the constitutional legitimation of expanded government, historians of twentieth-century constitutional law have seen the growth of expanded judicial protection for free speech as another by-product of the "constitutional revolution" of the late 1930s. They have reached this conclusion though a series of interconnected, anachronistic readings of the Court's early twentieth-century constitutional decisions.

The first step in those readings has been for commentators to note that since the Second World War the prevailing stance of constitutional review adopted by the Supreme Court has been one of bifurcated review rather than guardian review. That posture, we have seen, results in judicial deference toward most forms of legislation regulating economic activity and heightened judicial scrutiny of legislation restricting certain civil rights and liberties, prominent among those the right of free speech.[1]

The next step in the process has been to use bifurcated review as a basis for classifying most of the Court's significant constitutional decisions since the Second World War. The classification scheme has been designed to replicate the Court's method of scrutinizing legislation challenged on constitutional grounds. That method posits a "presumption of constitutionality" for all such legislation, which results in challenged laws being upheld if the Court can derive a "rational basis" for them. It also identifies certain kinds of challenges in which the presumption of constitutionality is departed from, resulting in heightened scrutiny of the legislation being reviewed. In the period between the early 1940s and the present, the most enduring example of constitutional challenges triggering heightened scrutiny has been challenges based on constitutional provisions protecting freedom of expression. By tracing examples of this method of constitutional review at work, commentators have suggested that the crucial step in any case in which the Court reviews legislation on constitutional grounds is the choice to follow or depart from the presumption of constitutionality.[2]

Having employed deferential or heightened constitutional review as a basis for classifying the Court's mid and late twentieth-century constitutional decisions, commentators have then sought to identify the origins of bifurcated review and to connect its emergence to the "constitutional revolution" of the New Deal period. They have identified a case decided by the Court in 1938, *United States v. Carolene Products,*[3] as the origin of the Court's adoption of a bifurcated review posture. In *Carolene Products* Justice Harlan Fiske Stone, after stating that "regulatory legislation affecting ordinary commercial transactions is not to be pronounced unconstitutional" if resting on a rational basis, inserted a footnote in which he identified three instances in which "[t]here may be narrower scope for operation of the presumption of constitutionality." The first of which occurred "when legislation appears on its face to be within a specific prohibition of the Constitution," and the remaining two when it "restricts those political processes which can ordinarily be expected to bring about repeal of undesirable legislation" or when it rested on "prejudices against discrete and insular minorities."[4]

The *Carolene Products* footnote, handed down at the outset of the "constitutional revolution," has provided a link between the emergence of bifurcated review and the New Deal. It has enabled one commentator, emphasizing Stone's presumption of constitutionality for legislation "affecting ordinary commercial transactions," to claim that "the timing of the footnote is important" because "the Great Depression . . . and the Court's war against Roosevelt's New Deal had left laissez-faire—and the nation—in shambles," and "[b]y 1938, the Court had retreated, saying it would presume economic regulation to be constitutional."[5] It has also enabled another commentator, emphasizing Stone's footnote listing examples of when the presumption of constitutionality might be departed from, to suggest that "[t]he Constitutional Revolution of 1937 altered fundamentally the character of the Court's business . . . After 1937 the most significant matters on the docket were civil liberties and other personal rights."[6]

Such readings, which are common to most late twentieth-century constitutional commentary, have resulted in all of the Court's early twentieth-century constitutional decisions being seen in the context of the eventual triumph of bifurcated review, with *Carolene Products* serving as the symbol of that emergence and the New Deal and the "constitutional revolution" serving as precipitating causes. This foreshadowing has had a particular effect on the way in which the Court's early twentieth-century free speech decisions have been characterized. Since free speech cases were prominently cited in the *Carolene Products* footnote as examples of cases triggering heightened scrutiny, commentators have seen judges who advocated expanded protection for free speech in early twentieth-century cases as implicitly forsaking guardian for bifurcated review. In addition, commentators have needed to provide explanations for why heightened judicial scrutiny in free speech cases would have surfaced in an atmosphere in which a chastened Court was purportedly deferring to legislative judgments about the efficacy of expanded government. Their explanations have drawn upon the rationales for heightened scrutiny mentioned in the *Carolene Products* footnote, which emphasize the occasional tendency of majoritarian governmental policies to curtail individual rights or to discriminate against minorities.[7] Those explanations have then been applied to libertarian free speech decisions before *Carolene Products* and the "constitutional revolution."

The result has been a loss of two of the defining features of early twentieth-century free speech jurisprudence. One feature was that early twentieth-century free speech cases, whether they produced opinions restricting or expanding protection for speech rights, were not conceived of as cases requiring judicial treatment different from any other constitutional cases. They were approached from a posture of guardian review, not bifurcated review, and speech rights were not treated as a special class of rights requiring heightened judicial solicitude.

The other obscured feature of early twentieth-century free speech jurisprudence relates to the relationship of protection of free speech to majoritarian democracy. The standard *Carolene Products* arguments for heightened scrutiny emphasize the failures and imperfections in a majoritarian legislative process, producing tyrannies of the majority that inappropriately restrict civil rights or liberties and require judicial correction. But the principal rationale for enhanced protection for free speech, from the 1920s through the 1940s, was that expanded protection for free speech reinforced the ideal of majoritarian democracy. Heightened judicial scrutiny in speech cases was triggered, according to that rationale, because of the special nature of the right of speech itself. That rationale—summed up in the claim that speech rights occupied a "preferred position" in American constitutional jurisprudence—was resisted by some judges, such as Justice Frankfurter, who were strong supporters of the New Deal and advocates of judicial deference.

In sum, to understand the emergence of expanded judicial protection for free speech in the early twentieth century it is necessary to abandon the conventional view that the Court, in the wake of the New Deal's constitutional revolution, suddenly abandoned guardian review for bifurcated review. It is necessary to separate the justifications for scrutinizing legislation restricting speech claims severely from the justifications for relaxing scrutiny of legislation regulating economic activity, rather than seeing them as, as anachronistic readings of Stone's *Carolene Products* opinion might suggest, two integrated parts of the same jurisprudential development. This alternative way of looking at the emergence of heightened protection for free speech produces a fresh understanding of the original meaning of the *Carolene Products* case.[8]

As late as 1915 the Supreme Court of the United States continued to treat free speech cases as ordinary police power cases. Two venerable doctrinal formulations continued to control free speech jurisprudence. One was the position, represented in the 1897 case of *Robertson v. Baldwin*,[9] that the First Amendment did not institute "any novel principles of government" but simply codified "certain guaranties and immunities which we had inherited from our English ancestors, and which from time immemorial had been subject to certain well-recognized exceptions." This meant that speech that was regarded as libelous, blasphemous, obscene, indecent, or "injurious to public morals or private reputation" could be suppressed.

The other formulation confined constitutional protection for free speech to freedom from governmentally imposed "prior restraints," such as the censorship of publications before they were issued. This position dated back at least to William Blackstone's *Commentaries,* where Blackstone had defined "the liberty of the press" as protection only from "laying no *previous* restraints upon publications," as distinguished from "freedom from censure for criminal manner when published."[10] In a 1907 case, *Patterson v. Colorado,* in which a newspaper editor had been convicted of contempt of court for publishing articles and a cartoon impugning the motives of justices of the Colorado Supreme Court, the Court, in an opinion by Justice Holmes, upheld the conviction, holding that even factually accurate ("true") criticism of judicial officials that tended to interfere with the administration of justice could be criminally punished.[11]

The approach taken by the Supreme Court in *Patterson,* and in additional cases up to World War I,[12] was embodied in the so-called "bad tendency" test, in which a court asked if the expression in question had a tendency to injure public morals or private reputation or to lead to other socially injurious acts. This test was not conceptually different from other standard judicial inquiries in police power cases: states were assumed to have power to regulate expressions that offended against public morality, just as they regulated activities that had that effect.

The First Amendment did not play a significant role in free speech cases prior to World War I. The absence of federal legislation restricting speech (other than the ancient Alien and Sedition Acts, which had never been enforced) meant that there was virtually no category of cases in which the language of the First Amendment, which applied to Congress, was directly relevant. Moreover, the First Amendment had not been "incorporated" in the Fourteenth Amendment's Due Process Clause: that would not occur until 1925.[13] Orthodox free speech jurisprudence was inconsistent with the incorporation of First Amendment rights against the states because it treated speech liberties as having existed, as part of English common law, prior to the Amendment's passage. The content of "liberty" in the Fourteenth Amendment's Due Process Clause was thus unaffected by the existence of the First Amendment: "liberty of speech" meant the ancient rights of expression enjoyed by English subjects, no more and no less.

Recent scholarship, however, has unearthed, alongside the relatively speech-restrictive tendency of orthodox early twentieth-century free speech jurisprudence, a tradition of libertarian commentary on issues implicating freedom of expression that can be traced back to the years before the Civil War. In particular, scholars have shown that libertarian theories of individual thought and expression had been articulated in late nineteenth- and early twentieth-century commentary; that groups such as the Free Speech League and the International Workers of the World had initiated, by the early years of the twentieth century, the practice of scrutinizing and challenging restrictions on speech in the press and in public debate; and that by the early twentieth century libertarian theories of free speech had begun to appear in mainstream academic writing.[14]

Late nineteenth-century and early twentieth-century libertarian free speech theory can nonetheless be seen as consistent with the framework of orthodox constitutional jurisprudence. Freedom of speech was seen in that commentary as a "liberty" similar to other potential due process liberties in police power cases. It was a private right that in some contexts had important public ramifications because it involved the dissemination of information or opinions on public issues. The public weal, as interpreted by the legislature through its police powers, might be advantaged or disadvantaged by certain forms of speech, just as it might be advantaged or disadvantaged by certain forms of economic activity. Police power analysis could prick out the boundaries in liberty of speech cases as well as in other due process cases. Libertarian commentary on free speech was consistent with greater protection for expressive activity, but it did not suggest that speech liberties were intrinsically different from other sorts of liberties nor that the existence of the First Amendment had any effect on the police power analysis required in speech cases.

Nonetheless, late nineteenth-century libertarian interpretations of free speech came to take on enhanced significance around World War I. In 1917 and 1918 Congress passed two statutes, affected by the wartime atmosphere, that criminalized speech tending to encourage resistance to the war effort or to undermine respect for the government and its operations.[15] Indictments under those statutes raised the question, dormant for so many years, of what the First Amendment's imprecation that "Congress shall make no law . . . abridging speech" meant. Challenges to the statutes expanded the potential scope of free speech jurisprudence by including, in an arsenal of arguments on behalf of freedom of expression, the fact that speech had been singled out for protection against the government in a provision of the constitutional text.

In *Schenck v. United States* [16] and *Abrams v. United States,*[17] prosecutions under the Espionage and Sedition Acts, Holmes announced a test for at least some free speech cases that, at least in its *Abrams* version, was more protective of freedom of expression than the "bad tendency" test. In *Schenck,* for a unanimous Court, he said that "the question in every [subversive advocacy] case is whether the words are used in such circumstances and are of such a nature as to create a clear and present danger that they will bring about the substantive evils that Congress has a right to prevent."[18] In *Abrams,* in dissent, he restated the "clear and present danger" test as "the United States may constitutionally punish speech that produces or is intended to produce a clear and imminent danger that it will bring about forthwith certain substantive evils that the United States constitutionally may seek to prevent."[19]

A majority of the Court continued to employ the "bad tendency" test in speech cases for nearly twenty years after Holmes's *Abrams* dissent. Nonetheless, Holmes's opinions in *Schenck* and *Abrams* revealed that the Espionage Act and Sedition Act cases of the years following World War I had served as a fulcrum for a reconsideration of nineteenth-century free speech jurisprudential orthodoxy. That reconsideration, energized by Harvard law professor Zechariah Chafee's commentary on Holmes's opinions, served to integrate and to give new meaning to the diverse strands of free speech commentary that were in existence by World War I. It also served to supply free speech jurisprudence with its first modern set of theoretical apologetics, which associated protection for speech with a "search for truth" in a democratic society. Nonetheless, Chafee's reconsideration of free speech theory continued to assume that free speech cases were a species of police power cases.[20]

The Espionage Act decisions of 1919 were handed down in an important transition period in the history of twentieth-century American jurisprudence. As the approach of World War I dawned, some commentators who thought of themselves as "progressives" became increasingly concerned with the implications of dissident speech for political and cultural solidarity.[21] Dissident speech, in their view, became linked to anticapitalist economic ideologies and to criticism of the war effort. They also expressed skepticism about the ability of modern nation-states to function efficiently and to achieve "progressive" goals without a degree of homogenous, expert-based policymaking. These beliefs were consistent with a restrictive approach toward speech, personified by the "bad tendency" test, which many progressives endorsed.[22]

At the same time other progressive theorists had begun to invest the concept of free speech with enhanced seriousness and to advocate more speech-protective theoretical formulations. One of the political goals of the Progressive movement in national politics was to broaden the base of popular involvement in government and to encourage larger numbers of citizens to participate in public discourse, even though many who supported Progressive candidates held a selective view of who those citizens should be.[23] The enhanced significance of the idea of "freedom" was a thread linking many policies endorsed by Progressives, ranging from increased bargaining power for workers in the industrial marketplace to opposition to machine politics to enthusiasm for new scientific techniques that would relieve the drudgery of workplace and household routines.[24] Freedom of speech from this perspective signified freedom of political participation and freedom of inquiry.

In this context Zechariah Chafee, who thought of himself as a "progressive," began a reformulation of free speech jurisprudence. Critical to Chafee's reformulation, which appeared in his 1920 treatise, *Freedom of Speech,* was the disengagement of free speech "liberties" from the tradition of protection for constitutional liberties associated with economic activity in police power cases. Free speech liberties, Chafee suggested, should receive enhanced constitutional protection not because they were individual, prepolitical rights along the lines of "liberty of contract," but because they were associated with a "social interest" in enhanced public participation and informed public debate in a democracy. By conceptualizing protection for free speech as a "social interest," Chafee sought to complicate the analysis of what "police power" in speech cases meant. If the social interests in protecting safety or public morality by suppressing expressions that had "bad tendencies" were offset by other social interests in achieving the accurate and informed discussion of public issues through a broad circulation of viewpoints, the strength of police power arguments for restricting speech was diminished.

The normative end of Chafee's proposed reformulation of free speech jurisprudence, which he derived from an analysis of *Schenck* and *Abrams,* was that "the great interest in free speech should be sacrificed only when the interest in public safety is really imperiled, and not, as most men believe, when it is barely conceivable that it may be slightly affected." Chafee suggested that even in wartime speech should be protected "unless it is clearly liable to cause direct and dangerous interference with the conduct of the war."[25] This formulation asserted a "great" social interest in free speech, a comparable social interest in public safety, and then looked to empirical analysis on which to ground a rational process of offsetting those interests. Alongside that formulation the "bad tendency" test ("when it is barely conceivable that [public safety] may be slightly affected") appeared unduly vague and subjective as well as irrationally underprotective of speech in wartime.

In the short run, Chafee's reformulation had far greater impact on the level of theory than of doctrine. His proposed test for determining whether speech should be protected, which was influenced by Learned Hand's holding in *Masses Publishing Co. v. Patten,*[26] was not adopted by the Supreme Court in the Espionage Act cases. Chafee had roundly criticized the "bad tendency" test in free speech cases,[27] but even Holmes had employed it for the Court in all the Espionage Act cases except *Abrams,* where the majority employed it. At least until *Abrams,* Holmes did not appear to treat his celebrated "clear and present danger" dictum in *Schenck* as incompatible with the "bad tendency" test.[28]

Chafee, however, intimated that the Court had adopted his reformulation as early as the Espionage Act cases. He repeated in *Freedom of Speech* a conclusion he had earlier advanced in a 1919 article entitled "Freedom of Speech in War Time" in the *Harvard Law Review.*[29] There Chafee had written that in *Schenck* and the companion Espionage Act cases, in order to give force to the First Amendment, Holmes had drawn "the boundary line very close to the test of incitement at common law and clearly ma[de] the punishment of words for their remote bad tendency impossible."[30] This was what Chafee took Holmes to mean by "clear and present danger."

Holmes had written, in his *Abrams* dissent, that

> when men have realized that time has upset many fighting faiths, they may come to believe even more than they believe the very foundations of their own conduct that the ultimate good desired is better reached by free trade in ideas—that the best test of truth is the power of the thought to get itself accepted in the competition of the market, and that truth is the only ground upon which their wishes safely can be carried out. That at any rate is the theory of our Constitution.[31]

Chafee was enthusiastic about this passage because Holmes had elevated the "social interest" in the search for truth as a foundation for civic policymaking over any "individual interest" in expression. The "ultimate good," Holmes suggested, was "free trade in ideas" rather than the "foundations" of individual conduct. Individual "faiths" were ephemeral, but the search for truth in the marketplace of ideas was permanent, since truth was "the only ground" upon which policy could "safely" be made.

Holmes's articulation in *Abrams* of the "search for truth" rationale for protection of speech has regularly been celebrated as a defining moment in the modern history of the First Amendment. But there has been little discussion of the role played by the search for truth rationale in a jurisprudential universe in which free speech cases continued to be designated as a species of police power cases.

It is possible to read Holmes's *Abrams* dissent as a forthright expression of majoritarian fatalism—true ideas are simply those a majority adopts—a reading some of his own comments tend to support.[32] But this would suggest that Holmes should tolerate legislative efforts to *repress* speech, when his reformulated version of free speech theory pointed in exactly the opposite direction. A more satisfactory conclusion is that Holmes, along with Chafee, sought to distinguish the social interest in the spread of truth from the social interest in implementing the views of majorities. Part of Holmes's rationale for allowing expressions such as those suppressed in *Abrams* into the marketplace was based on an assumption that patently foolish expressions—the "silly leaflet[s]" and "poor and puny anonymities" that Holmes chose to protect in *Abrams*[33]—would by their very foolishness reveal their "falsity" and permit more sensible alternatives to emerge. At least at this stage in his free speech jurisprudence,[34] Holmes seems to have been including, within his "search for truth" metaphor, both a commitment to the free exchange of ideas and information in a democracy and an elitist reading of that exchange process, in which the surfacing of "truth" would be accompanied by a discarding of foolish ideas for rational ones.

This paradoxical conception of freedom of speech—allowing many expressions to enter the marketplace of ideas so that their abject foolishness could be discerned, thereby deterring the future articulation of such expressions—demonstrates the importance of speech being labeled a social rather than an individual interest. "Free speech" meant the opportunity for all citizens, in a democratic society, to express their views. But the primary purpose of an unfettered exchange of views was not to encourage diversity of individual expression; it was to filter out "true" from "false" beliefs and policies so that America could be governed more effectively. Holmes and Chafee buttressed their claim that free speech served important social interests by a supposition that, ultimately, rational elites controlled the marketplace of ideas. Some ideas would be deemed superior to other ideas because they expressed an accurate and rational understanding of the defining social and economic "facts" of a civilization at a point in its history. As such they would be recognized by elites as having the character of "truth" and would form the basis of social policies.

Despite Chafee's and Holmes's efforts, the marketplace theory of free speech and the clear and present danger formula for speech cases were not accepted as orthodoxy during the remainder of Holmes's tenure on the Supreme Court. A majority of the Court continued to equate "clear and present danger" with the established "bad tendency" test,[35] so that by the time of Holmes's retirement from the Court in 1932 only Justice Louis Brandeis had joined him in repudiating the "bad tendency" formula.[36]

One difficulty with the "clear and present danger" test, as a more speech-protective alternative to the "bad tendency" test, was that it did not necessarily enable judges to draw clear boundary lines between protected and unprotected speech claims, as Chafee had claimed that it would. Cases such as *Gitlow v. New York,* which reviewed a New York statute providing criminal penalties for those who advocated "that organized government should be overthrown by force, or violence or any unlawful means,"[37] appeared to pose particular problems for boundary pricking in police power speech cases. In such cases legislative majorities had made the "social interest" assessment in advance, deeming the espousal of a particular ideological position "subversive" to democratic institutions and thus not a contribution to the search for truth in a democracy.

Thus, Holmes's and Chafee's approach to speech claims in police power cases appeared in need of a reformulation to retain its speech-protective character. Two possible reformulations suggested themselves. One was to reframe the central rationale for protecting speech to make it clear that the marketplace of ideas was not the equivalent of collective majoritarian prejudices but rather the distilled wisdom of rational elites. This reformulation had the practical disadvantage, for those who found orthodox free speech jurisprudence insufficiently speech-protective, of opening the door for traditionally limited judicial definitions of speech rights to be perpetuated.

An alternative was to reframe the rationale for protecting speech so as to link speech more closely to the idea of democratic government itself, especially the feature of democratic government that emphasized broad participation in public affairs by an informed citizenry. In this formulation the primary importance of protecting free speech rights in a democracy was, rather than a search for collective truth, the creation of expanded opportunities for citizens to participate in the democratic process. This reformulation was to receive a considerable boost from doctrinal developments in twentieth-century free speech jurisprudence that took place after *Gitlow.*

In 1927 Brandeis, in his concurring opinion in the case of *Whitney v. California,* wrote a passage on free speech that has come to rival that from Holmes's dissent in *Abrams* in its canonical status. The *Whitney* case raised the constitutionality of Anita Whitney's conviction, under a California criminal syndicalist statute, for attending a convention held in Oakland to create a California chapter of the Communist Labor Party.[38] In upholding Whitney's conviction, the Court majority adopted conventional police power analysis, concluding that the state of California had a strong interest in suppressing the advocacy of doctrines designed to foment revolution; that the Communist Labor Party platform had that tendency; and that Whitney had associated herself with the party. Although concurring in the result, Brandeis and Holmes declared that Whitney had a constitutional right to associate with a political party that was advocating "the desirability of a proletarian revolution by mass action at some date necessarily far in the future."[39]

In his concurrence Brandeis, after suggesting that the clear and present danger test rather than the bad tendency test should control the Court's evaluation of speech claims, wrote the following:

> Those who won our independence believed that the final end of the state was to make men free to develop their faculties; and that in its government the deliberative forces should prevail over the arbitrary. They valued liberty both as an end and a means . . . They believed that freedom to think as you will and to speak as you think are means indispensable to the discovery and spread of political truth; . . . that the greatest menace to freedom is an inert people; that public discussion is a political duty; and that this should be a fundamental principle of the American government . . . Believing in the power of reason as applied through public discussion, they eschewed silence coerced by law—the argument of force in its worst form. Recognizing the occasional tyrannies of governing majorities, they amended the Constitution so that free speech and assembly should be guaranteed.[40]

Brandeis's paragraph achieved a fusion of two sets of arguments justifying protection for free speech. One set rehearsed the now familiar search for truth position. The other identified freedom as both "an end" and "a means," and associated "freedom to think as you will and to speak as you think" with "public discussion." Notable in the passage were arguments on behalf of speech as part of the process by which American citizens learned how to govern themselves.

Brandeis's intuitions about First Amendment jurisprudence provide an embryonic response to the principal problems encountered by Chafee's and Holmes's search for truth rationale as a basis for enhanced protection for speech. His response, when coupled with doctrinal changes in free speech jurisprudence, eventually achieved the separation of free speech cases from other "liberty" cases in police power jurisprudence and pointed the way toward the accommodation of robust free speech theory to deferential constitutional review.

Brandeis made three assertions about the value of speech in America in *Whitney:* that it signified a commitment to a broader ideal of human "freedom" itself; that it furthered the discovery and spread of truth; and that it fostered public discussion. But the assertions were not treated as separable. Freedom "to think as you will and to speak as you think" was linked to *political* truth, and political truth, as well as the "duty" of citizens to participate in government, was linked to *public* discussion. Thus, the *Whitney* concurrence can be read as subsuming the search for truth rationale in a rationale that identified the principal function of speech as promoting self-governance in a democratic society. In addition, the *Whitney* concurrence can be read as offering the principle of public discussion as a basis for channeling and limiting freedom of expression as well as a basis for furthering it.

In one stroke Brandeis was attempting to supply a rationale for the protection of speech that cleansed it of any lingering overtones of the doctrine of "liberty of contract." The rationale for protecting speech was its extraordinary value in promoting free and rational public discussion; speech as an embodiment of other liberties was implicitly less central. The normative goal of protection for speech need not enlist any arguments identified with other individual liberties in orthodox police powers jurisprudence.

Brandeis was also attempting to modify Chafee's analytical methodology in free speech cases. Although he retained clear and present danger as an evaluative standard for speech claims, his *Whitney* concurrence did not refer to any process of offsetting competing social interests. Brandeis spoke of courts "fix[ing] the standard by which to determine when a danger shall be deemed clear; how remote the danger may be and yet be deemed present; and what degree of evil shall be deemed sufficiently substantial to resort to abridgment of free speech and assembly."[41] He announced that "[o]nly an emergency can justify repression" of speech, and that "[s]uch must be the rule if authority is to be reconciled with freedom."[42]

Brandeis's methodology retained the categorical inquiries judges made in police power cases, using the concept of public discussion as his touchstone for classification. He anticipated two sorts of categorical inquiries in free speech cases. At the level of doctrinal application, judges, employing the clear and present danger formula, were to categorize cases as involving or not involving "emergencies." At the level of normative theory, judges were to categorize speech claims as related or unrelated to public discussion. To make the implications of the latter inquiry clear, Brandeis said in *Whitney* that "[t]he power of the courts to strike down an offending law" was "no less" in cases implicating "the fundamental personal rights of free speech and assembly" than in cases "where the denial of liberty was that of engaging in a particular business."[43] By "no less" he meant "possibly greater."

Although Brandeis's methodology employed the techniques of orthodox police power analysis, its speech-protective thrust was to receive considerable reinforcement from an apparently uncontroversial development in free speech jurisprudence that had taken place two years before *Whitney*. This was the almost casual agreement on the part of the Court's majority in the *Gitlow* case that the First Amendment's imprecation that Congress should make no law abridging the freedom of speech also applied to the states. The First Amendment's freedom of speech clause, the Court declared in *Gitlow*, was one of those provisions of the Bill of Rights that had been "incorporated" in the Due Process Clause of the Fourteenth Amendment, and thus amounted to a constitutional restriction on state legislatures comparable to that which restricted Congress.

The offhand fashion in which the justices who decided *Gitlow* endorsed the incorporation of the First Amendment's freedom of speech clause in the Fourteenth Amendment's Due Process Clause[44] requires some explanation, given the state of orthodox constitutional jurisprudence at the time. We have noted that judicial glossing of the term "liberty" in the Fourteenth Amendment had become an established practice under guardian review. Free speech arguments had been employed against state statutes directed at subversive advocacy, and in the analysis of such cases judges had, prior to *Gitlow*, indicated that speech claims might be treated as "liberties" within the meaning of the Due Process Clause.[45] No Supreme Court decisions prior to *Gitlow*, however, had invalidated state statutes restricting speech, and one 1922 decision had categorically stated that "neither the Fourteenth Amendment nor any other provision of the Constitution of the United States imposes on the states any restrictions about 'freedom of speech.'"[46]

It was nonetheless clear by the time of the *Gitlow* decision that the content of "liberty" in the Fourteenth Amendment's Due Process Clause was to be determined by judges in the context of individual cases. Since "liberty" in that clause had already been taken to include a "fundamental" right to enter into employment relations on the terms one chose, it seemed uncontroversial to interpret "liberty" to include other "fundamental rights." In fact, the Court had, two years prior to *Gitlow*, stated that "liberty" denoted not only freedom to contract but freedom to acquire useful knowledge or to worship God according to the dictates of one's conscience[47] and, in a case decided just before *Gitlow*, had extended "liberty" to include a right in parents to direct the education of their children.[48]

Both the majority's bad tendency test in subversive advocacy cases and Holmes's and Brandeis's clear and present danger test assumed that First

Amendment speech rights imposed some substantive limitations on congressional efforts to regulate expression. If the First Amendment no longer meant simply freedom from prior government censorship but freedom from subsequent punishment for the expression of controversial viewpoints—as Holmes, for a unanimous Court, had declared in *Schenck*—speech had become a "fundamental" liberty, includable within the Fourteenth Amendment's Due Process Clause.

Moreover, the judicial incorporation of First Amendment free speech rights within the Fourteenth Amendment's Due Process Clause was uncontroversial because nothing initially followed from it. In *Gitlow* and *Whitney* the allegedly subversive speech being suppressed was treated, alternatively, as a police power liberty of the sort identified by the Court in pre-*Gitlow* decisions or as an "incorporated" liberty, but the majority's police power analysis sustained the state statute criminalizing controversial speech. Thus, so long as guardian review remained the Court's posture, and any expression having a subversive tendency could be suppressed by states in the exercise of their police powers, incorporation of the free speech provisions of the First Amendment into the Fourteenth Amendment's Due Process Clause only had the effect of making federal and state speech cases analytically of a piece.

But the casual incorporation of First Amendment rights into the Fourteenth Amendment was subsequently to have great significance. As, after *Gitlow,* Holmes and Brandeis continued to advance speech-protective rationales in free speech cases, and at the same time to identify themselves as critics of the "liberty of contract" gloss,[49] incorporation provided an alternative basis for protecting free speech rights: they were singled out for protection by the text of the Constitution. When Brandeis spoke in his *Whitney* concurrence of the "fundamental personal rights of free speech and assembly," the label "fundamental" drew upon the exalted status in American jurisprudence of enumerated guaranties in the Constitution's text.[50] When guardian review itself came to be criticized as arrogating too much discretionary interpretive power to unelected judges, the Court could point to the text of the Constitution as having already singled out specific rights for protection.

The methodology recommended for speech cases by Brandeis in *Whitney* was thus an effort to modify the substantive orientation of judicial glossing of "liberties" in police power due process cases. Instead of treating free speech as an incidental example of due process liberties, whose more prominent examples came from the realm of economic relationships, Brandeis suggested that speech, being a textually protected right that was incorporated against the states as well as against the federal government, was a particularly "fundamental" constitutional liberty. He underscored the special constitutional status of speech by associating it with a foundational value of American democracy, self-governance through the participation of citizens in public affairs. By connecting the liberty of speech with effective self-governance in a democratic society, Brandeis could imply that speech rights might possibly be given *greater* protection against legislative infringement than rights associated with economic activity.

Although Brandeis intended the association of free speech with political self-governance to enhance the scope of protection for speech rights, it could also be taken as a basis for distinguishing between speech claims that embodied the core of the constitutional meaning of freedom of speech and claims of a more peripheral character. Holmes's and Chafee's marketplace of ideas rationale had not, at least on its face, contained a comparable limiting principle. Brandeis had articulated a potentially narrower category of protected speech that closely connected to self-governance or the political process. His rationale was eventually to facilitate the separation of liberty of speech cases from cases involving other police power liberties and the eventual detachment of free speech cases from police power jurisprudence.

By the 1930s the Court's free speech jurisprudence had taken on a more speech-protective character. For the first time in the twentieth century, free speech claims were made the basis for striking down police powers legislation. A Minnesota law authorizing injunctions against newspapers previously found to have made defamatory statements against public officials was invalidated as a prior restraint; an advertising tax imposed on Louisiana newspapers above a certain circulation was likewise invalidated; and a majority of the Court, in a January 1937 decision, adopted "clear and present danger" as the governing test for subversive advocacy cases.[51]

This group of speech-protective decisions by the Court presents difficulties for any hypothesis linking expanded constitutional protection for speech rights with the New Deal or the Court-packing crisis. Two were handed down in 1931, before the New Deal was launched; the other two were decided in 1936 and January 1937, before the Court-packing plan was announced. The cases were consistent, however, with the growing jurisprudential momentum for speech rights that incorporation of First Amendment provisions had produced: they all involved the invalidation of state statutes whose constitutionality was attacked on the ground that they offended incorporated Fourteenth Amendment "liberties."

Meanwhile, the Court, in the years after *Gitlow*, had continued to incorporate additional First Amendment provisions into the Fourteenth Amendment's Due Process Clause, such as those protecting freedom of the press,[52] the free exercise of religion,[53] and the freedom to assemble peaceably,[54] and showed signs that it might be inclined to incorporate some other Bill of Rights provisions as well.[55] In a 1937 case, *Palko v. Connecticut*,[56] the Court attempted to articulate its criteria for discerning which provisions of the original Bill of Rights qualified for incorporation. The criteria it settled on in *Palko* were not particularly helpful as guidelines—provisions eligible for incorporation were those that could be associated with "fundamental principles of liberty and justice" and were "of the very essence of a scheme of ordered liberty."[57] The effect of *Palko*, however, was to shift the focus, in police power due process cases, from a general inquiry into the meaning of "liberty" in the Fourteenth Amendment's Due Process Clause to an assessment of the constitutional weight of the specific liberty that was the basis of a due process claim. This appeared to require a more precise judicial characterization of particular liberties as "fundamental," or less than fundamental, to "the scheme of ordered liberty" envisaged by the Constitution.

The end product of the above two developments was an interlude in the twentieth-century history of free speech jurisprudence in which shifting majorities of the Court entertained the possibility that First Amendment rights, in their dual capacity as textual provisions of the Bill of Rights and incorporated due process rights, might occupy a "preferred position" in the American constitutional order, and thus require heightened judicial protection. Although the idea that First Amendment rights were "preferred" to other rights never became an established feature of twentieth-century constitutional jurisprudence, the playing out of the "preferred position" rubric in cases between 1937 and the early 1950s had the effect of permanently disengaging free speech cases from police power jurisprudence.

The "preferred position" cases have conventionally been seen as evidence of the Court's sudden adoption of a stance of bifurcated review after 1937, and the decisions themselves have been taken as the culmination of tendencies on the Court, going back as far as Holmes's Espionage Act opinions and illustrated in *Carolene Products*, to regard speech rights as far more deserving of judicial solicitude than economic rights.[58] But the preferred position cases can be better described as an initial experiment in developing the stance that eventually became bifurcated review. They were decided in a jurisprudential environment in which the Court was wrestling with two discrete but related issues. One issue had been spawned by *Gitlow*: which provisions of the Bill of Rights should the Court incorporate against the states as due process "liberties"? The other was related to the emergence of deferential review in cases where legislation affecting ordinary economic transactions was being challenged. If a principal justification for relaxing judicial scrutiny of such legislation was that in a democratic society the economic theories of legislators should be given more weight than the economic glosses of constitutional provisions by unelected judges, what justified selective judicial incorporation of Bill of Rights provisions in the first place? Why was the process that produced the *Palko* criteria for incorporating Bill of Rights provisions any more constitutionally defensible than the process that had resulted in the Court's glossing "liberty" in the Due Process Clauses as "liberty of contract"?

In wrestling with these two issues shifting Court majorities advanced two rationales for continuing a heightened scrutiny of challenges to legislation restricting freedom of expression. The first rationale was not stressed in preferred position cases because it was taken for granted: challenges to legislation restricting free speech, free press, and freedom of religion "liberties" were severely scrutinized because those liberties were textually protected, whereas economic liberties were not. The second rationale received more overt emphasis, although it often consisted of a single rhetorical assertion. Freedom of expression bore an "indispensable connection" to democracy in America. As such, judicial decisions that upheld free speech challenges to majoritarian legislation reinforced democratic theory rather than being inconsistent with it.

As a doctrinal development, the preferred position episode was cryptic and abortive. Between 1937 and the early 1950s various justices on the Court declared openly, or implied, that free speech occupied a preferred position in the pantheon of constitutional rights. Their scattered remarks, although invoked by majority opinions in subsequent cases, neither clarified the precise doctrinal meaning of "preferred position" nor provided any extended justification for why freedom of speech or related freedoms of religion and assembly should be given preferred status. Eventually the Court implicitly abandoned the term "preferred position" altogether and explored other interpretive techniques for retaining a high level of scrutiny for speech-based challenges to legislation.

The theme of free speech as a foundational liberty had been sounded in the *Palko* case itself. Justice Cardozo, for the Court, noted that "liberty" in the Fourteenth Amendment had "been enlarged . . . to include liberty of the mind as well as liberty of action," and defined free speech as "the matrix, the indispensable condition, of nearly every other form of freedom."[59] He stopped short of suggesting that free speech rights, by being a "matrix" of other rights, were to be preferred over all other constitutional guaranties, but in a case in which the Court was seeking to identify Bill of Rights freedoms that were "of the very essence of a scheme of ordered liberty,"[60] freedom "of thought and speech" was first on the list.

Between *Palko* and the close of the Second World War the Court came to consider a number of free speech challenges to state and municipal regulations brought by members of the Jehovah's Witnesses sect. Many Witness sects believed that the Old Testament's First Commandment, forbidding the worship of any graven image, prevented them from participating in flag-salute ceremonies. Jehovah's Witnesses were the petitioners in one of the Court's most controversial set of decisions in the 1940s, *Minersville School District v. Gobitis*[61] and *West Virginia State Board of Education v. Barnette*,[62] in which the justices reversed themselves on the constitutionality of compulsory flag-salute laws and overruled an opinion that had been rendered only three years previously and had engendered only one dissent. The flag-salute cases also provided the basis for an eventual critique of the preferred position rationale by Justice Felix Frankfurter, who initially had associated himself with that rationale.

As early as 1939 Jehovah's Witnesses cases began to test the effect that incorporation and *Palko*'s effort to identify "fundamental" constitutional provisions would have on orthodox police power analysis in speech cases. In *Schneider v. Irvington*[63] the constitutionality of an antilittering ordinance directed against the distribution of Witness literature was tested. Justice Owen Roberts, for the Court majority, defined the *Schneider* case as pitting the "duty" of municipalities "to keep their streets open and available for movement of people and property" against "the guarantee of freedom of speech or of the press." The Court's role in such cases, Roberts said, was "to weigh the circumstances and appraise the substantiality of the reasons advanced in support of the regulation of the free enjoyment of the rights."[64] He made it clear that the identity of the particular constitutional liberty being infringed would weigh heavily in that analysis:

> This court has characterized the freedom of speech and freedom of press as fundamental personal rights and liberties . . . Legislative preferences or beliefs respecting matters of public convenience may well support regulation directed at other personal activities, but may be insufficient to justify such as diminishes the existence of rights so vital to the maintenance of democratic institutions.[65]

Not only were First Amendment freedoms indispensable and fundamental, they had been explicitly linked to the ideal of democracy.

A year after *Schneider* the first of the flag-salute cases was handed down. Both Frankfurter's majority opinion, sustaining the constitutionality of a mandatory public school ceremony paying homage to the American flag, and Stone's dissent, finding the practice a violation of the religious freedom of objecting Jehovah's Witness families, attempted to justify their positions by connecting constitutionally protected freedom of expression to democracy. Frankfurter asserted that "personal freedom is best maintained—so long as the remedial channels of the democratic process remain open and unobstructed—when it is . . . not enforced against popular policy by the coercion of adjudicated law."[66] Stone countered that "[t]he Constitution expressed more than the conviction of the people that democratic processes must be preserved at all costs. It is also an expression of faith and a command that freedom of mind and spirit must be preserved, which government must obey, if it is to adhere to that justice and moderation without which no free government can exist."[67]

The Frankfurter-Stone exchange suggested that the ideal of democracy could be translated into support for majoritarian policies restricting speech as well as support for an individual's speech rights as the embodiment of freedom. As the Court developed those alternative conceptions of speech and democracy, it continued to review Jehovah's Witnesses cases, many involving municipal regulations on the distribution of leaflets.[68] In those cases certain justices began to reflect on the relationship of a posture of heightened scrutiny for speech cases to their general stance of constitutional review.

In the 1942 case of *Jones v. Opelika*,[69] a 5–4 majority of the Court upheld municipal license fees directed against Witness pamphlets by characterizing the distributions as commercial transactions, and thus not implicating speech rights, and the fees as reasonable restraints on economic activity. In his dissent Stone was not content simply to challenge the majority's characterizations of the municipal regulations. He announced:

The First Amendment is not confined to safeguarding freedom of speech and freedom of religion against discriminatory attempts to wipe them out. On the contrary, the Constitution, by virtue of the First and the Fourteenth Amendments, has put those freedoms in a preferred position. Their commands are not restricted to cases where the protected privilege is sought out for attack. They extend . . . to every form of taxation which, because it is a condition of the exercise of the privilege, is capable of being used to control or suppress it.[70]

Stone's dissent in *Jones v. Opelika* made it clear that the "speech dimensions" of the leaflets conveyed special protection to those who distributed them. By "preferred position" he meant that "every form of taxation" and other economic regulation that could be seen as infringing free speech rights would receive heightened judicial scrutiny. When one relates this categorization of preferred position rights to the two principal rationales for giving those rights special attention—their textually protected status and their indispensable connection to the maintenance of democratic principles—it becomes clear that Stone was suggesting that speech rights reinforced democracy in a way that economic rights did not. Thus, for Stone, the Court's analysis in due process cases where the challenged "liberties" were incorporated speech rights need not be the same as its analysis in economic due process cases.

This reading of Stone's dissent in *Opelika* is supported by an unusual memorandum issued in the case by Justices Murphy, Black, and Douglas, all of whom had joined Stone's dissent. In that memorandum the three justices stated that "the opinion of the Court sanctions a device which in our opinion suppresses or tends to suppress the free exercise of religion practiced by a minority group."[71] They then announced that they had changed their mind about the Court's decision in *Gobitis,* the first flag-salute case, which they had each joined. Although *Opelika* had nothing to do with compulsory flag salutes, the three justices saw the two cases as raising the same issue, whether a legislative majority could restrict the religious views of minorities. As they put it, "our democratic form of government, functioning under the historic Bill of Rights, has a high responsibility to accommodate itself to the religious views of minorities, however unpopular and unorthodox those views be."[72] In that sentence the textually protected status and the democratic status of speech rights were once again intertwined.

A personnel change on the Court in 1942 provided additional support for the theory that speech rights should occupy a "preferred position" in a modern democratic society. *Murdock v. Pennsylvania,*[73] another Jehovah's Witnesses license case handed down a little over a year later, vacated *Opelika* and invalidated all municipally imposed "flat taxes" on the distribution of religious literature. The majority in *Murdock* consisted of the four dissenters in *Opelika* plus newly appointed Justice Wiley Rutledge, who had replaced James Byrnes in the 1942 Term. The remaining members of the majority in *Opelika* (Frankfurter, Roberts, Reed, and Jackson), three of whom had joined the majority opinion in *Gobitis,* dissented.

Justice Douglas, for the majority in *Murdock,* declared that "[f]reedom of press, freedom of speech, [and] freedom of religion are in a preferred position." The context of his statement made it clear that he meant "preferred" to refer to a distinction between speech and commercial activity. "A license tax," he argued, "certainly does not acquire constitutional validity because it classifies the privileges protected by the First Amendment along with the wares and merchandise of hucksters and peddlers and treats them all alike."[74]

The Court now returned in *Barnette* to the issue of compulsory flag salutes, as the national counsel for the Witnesses challenged a policy imposed by the West Virginia Board of Education on all state public schools.[75] Frankfurter's position, which had once commanded the votes of eight justices, now, three years later, commanded the votes of only three. As the opinions in the second flag-salute case unfolded, it was apparent that two themes were on the justices' minds: the "indispensable" connection between free speech and democratic theory and the implications of conferring a "preferred" position on speech rights for their constitutional review jurisprudence.

Justice Robert Jackson's opinion for the Court, after noting that "[t]hose who begin coercive elimination of dissent soon find themselves exterminating dissenters," announced that "the First Amendment . . . was designed to avoid these ends by avoiding these beginnings . . . We set up government by consent of the governed, and the Bill of Rights denies those in power to coerce that consent."[76] Having identified the First Amendment's democratic philosophy as in opposition to that of the totalitarian states with whom the United States was at war, he then turned to the implications of treating the Constitution as withdrawing "certain subjects," such as "free speech [and] freedom of worship," from "the vicissitudes of political controversy."[77] Why should those "liberties" be shielded from regulation by majorities, when other liberties need not be?

The justification for heightened scrutiny for speech rights, Jackson concluded, was that they were incorporated due process rights, based on specific provisions of the Constitution's text, whereas most other due process "liberties" were simply products of judicial glossing in police power cases. As he put it,

> it is important to distinguish between the due process clause of the Fourteenth Amendment as an instrument for transmitting the principles of the First Amendment and those cases in which it is applied for its own sake . . . Much of the vagueness of the due process clause disappears when the specific prohibitions of the First become its standard. The right of a State to regulate, for example, a public utility may well include, so far as the due process test is concerned, power to impose all the restrictions which a legislature may have a "rational basis" for adopting. But freedoms of speech and of press, of assembly, and of worship may not be infringed on such slender grounds. They are susceptible of restriction only to prevent grave and immediate danger to interests which the state may lawfully prevent.[78]

Jackson's doctrinal conclusion was unmistakable: where free speech rights were involved, the presumption of constitutionality Stone had referred to in *Carolene Products* would be departed from, and the legislation under review would have to pass a version of Holmes's and Brandeis's clear and present danger test.

Frankfurter, dissenting in *Barnette*, immediately took up the question of whether a preferred position for speech rights was necessary once one concluded that free speech bore an "indispensable" connection to democratic theory. His answer was that placing speech rights in a preferred position was not only unnecessary but dangerous:

> The Constitution does not give us greater veto power when dealing with one phase of "liberty" than another . . . Judicial self-restraint is equally necessary whenever an exercise of political or legislative power is challenged . . . Our power does not vary according to the particular provision of the Bill of Rights which is invoked. The right not to have property taken without just compensation has, so far as the scope of judicial power is concerned, the same constitutional dignity as . . . freedom of the press or freedom of speech or religious freedom.[79]

Frankfurter's dissent in *Barnette* was not simply an emotional reaction to seeing one of his opinions overruled three years after it had been issued. It was also part of a flirtation he had undertaken in the 1930s and 1940s with the preferred position rubric as an experiment in bifurcated review. In 1938, before being appointed to the Court, Frankfurter wrote Stone that he had just finished a series of lectures on Holmes "in which I've tried to reconcile his latitudinarian attitude toward constitutionality in cases other than civil liberties . . . with his attitude in civil liberties cases," and that "I was extremely excited by your note 4 [in *Carolene Products*]," which "is extremely suggestive and opens up new territory."[80] In his lectures on Holmes Frankfurter had concluded that "the liberty of man to search for truth was of a different order than some economic dogma," and "therefore Mr. Justice Holmes attributed very different legal significance to those liberties of the individual which history has attested as the indispensable conditions of a free society from that which he attached to liberties which derived merely from shifting economic arrangements."[81]

Two years later Frankfurter found himself writing the majority opinion in *Gobitis*. He wrote Stone, after the latter had circulated a draft dissent, that "I am aware of the important distinction which you so skillfully adumbrated in your footnote 4 . . . in the *Carolene Products Co.* case. I agree with that distinction; I regard it as basic."[82] And as late as 1941 he was prepared to declare, for the Court, that judges should approach efforts to restrict freedom of discussion in labor disputes "with a jealous eye," and to cite footnote 4 in *Carolene Products* for that proposition.[83]

But Frankfurter had also told Stone, in his *Gobitis* letter, about his "anxiety that, while we lean in the direction of the libertarian aspect, we do not exercise our judicial power unduly . . . In other words, I want to avoid the mistake comparable to those whom we criticized when dealing with the control of property."[84] And after being humiliated in the flag-salute sequence,[85] he signaled that any inclination he once had to endorse the preferred position experiment had been withdrawn. Eventually, after Stone died in 1946, he decided to mount an open attack on the preferred position experiment itself.

The case was *Kovacs v. Cooper,* [86] a 1949 decision in which a plurality of the Court sustained a Trenton, New Jersey ordinance prohibiting the use of sound trucks that issued "loud and raucous noises." In *Kovacs* Justice Stanley Reed, for a plurality that included Justices Fred Vinson and Harold Burton, endorsed what he called "[t]he preferred position of freedom of speech in a society that cherishes liberty for all,"[87] but found that the state interest in protecting the privacy and tranquility of its citizens overrode the free speech claim. Frankfurter and Jackson concurred in the result in *Kovacs,* with Black, Douglas, Rutledge, and Murphy dissenting.

In his concurring opinion Frankfurter launched an attack on the preferred position rubric. He called "preferred position" a "mischievous phrase" that had "uncritically crept into some recent opinions of this Court."[88] He then set forth a history of the preferred position experiment, including not only cases where the characterization was explicitly used but cases in which he concluded that the Court was adhering to a bifurcated standard of review. The result of this historical exegesis, for Frankfurter, was that "the claim that any legislation is presumptively unconstitutional which touches the field of the First Amendment . . . has never commended itself to a majority of this Court."[89] He then concluded with the following sentence: "In considering what interests are so fundamental as to be enshrined in the Due Process Clause, those liberties of the individual which history has attested as the indispensable conditions of an open as against a closed society come to this Court with a momentum for respect lacking when appeal is made to liberties which derive merely from shifting economic arrangements."[90] This was, of course, an almost verbatim rendering of the characterization of Holmes's jurisprudence that he had made in 1938, in the course of an argument that "the liberty of man to search for truth was of a different order than some economic dogma defined as a sacred right."[91]

Frankfurter's reaction to the preferred position experiment reveals that he had internalized both of the central rationales for heightened protection for speech rights. They were "fundamental" rights in two respects: textually protected and indispensably connected to democratic theory. But at the same time Frankfurter had recognized that the open judicial declaration that some due process "liberties" were to be constitutionally preferred over other liberties was reminiscent of the judicial glossing that had produced "liberty of contract." He was not confident that the Court could openly adopt a double standard of scrutiny for constitutional claims, which he took the "preferred position" rubric to be implementing. Consequently, he called for the abandonment of the rubric.

After *Kovacs* the phrase "preferred position" virtually disappeared from the Court's free speech cases, showing up only once more in a throwaway line by Douglas in a 1953 case.[92] The short life of the preferred position experiment, however, concealed its significance for the early twentieth-century history of free speech jurisprudence and for the transition from guardian to bifurcated review.

Both Chafee and Brandeis had hinted, but not explicitly suggested, that the search for truth and self-governance rationales for the protection of speech were connected to educating American citizens to make informed and intelligent decisions about questions of public concern. Although their formulations sought to channel the freedom to learn about and to discuss issues along the paths of civic awareness and citizen participation, they had not explicitly suggested that the central justification for protecting speech was its reinforcement of democratic theory and a democratic model of political governance.

By openly identifying the basis of special constitutional protection for speech as the indispensable connection between free expression and democratic theory, and at the same time distinguishing between speech and liberties deriving from "shifting economic arrangements," the preferred position cases had sought to link free speech with the idea of America as a democratic society and to disengage protection for economic liberties from that idea. "Preferred position" meant a preference for a freedom that had a particularly close association with the model of democratic politics that had surfaced in modern American society. It also meant, implicitly, that the freedoms associated with an economic model of unregulated capitalism were less democratic and hence less preferred.

There were, as the flag-salute cases suggested, some difficulties with grounding a preferred position for speech rights in the expanded meaning of America as a democratic society. These lay in the tension between democratic theory as bolstering freedom of expression and democratic theory as embodied in majoritarian policymaking. If a justification for legislative regulation of economic activity was that legislatures, as representative of the majority of citizens, were appropriate institutions to make policies affecting the distribution of benefits in the economic marketplace, why were they not equally appropriate institutions to determine the forms of expression that a majority wanted to restrict as well as protect? Yet the very cases announcing that free speech rights should be placed in a preferred position because of the close connection between free speech and the ideal of democracy were cases in which legislatures, on behalf of their majoritarian constituency, had restricted speech.

Thus, it appeared that a further particularization of which types of speech were indispensable to a democratic society, and which were not, might be required. Since a democratic model of politics presupposed that policymaking should be majoritarian, that model, on its face, gave no guidelines for determining the sorts of expressions that were presumptively immune from legislation to which majorities had subscribed. How, then, did one identify those sorts of expressions? An answer emerged from the rhetorical thrust of the preferred position cases: speech that itself could be said to be indispensable to the functioning of a democratic polity should be protected.

In a search for indispensable democratic speech neither the search for truth formulation nor its accompanying metaphor of a constantly expanding marketplace of ideas seemed to provide much guidance. Letting more speech into the market did not clarify which expressions a majority could, and could not, suppress consistent with the ideal of democracy. It was not particularly surprising, then, that, after the preferred position episode, the next development in twentieth-century free speech jurisprudence abandoned the "marketplace of ideas" rationale and accentuated the self-governance rationale as a basis for refining the meaning of "democratic" protected speech.

In 1948 Alexander Meiklejohn, then the president of Amherst College, published a book, *Free Speech and Its Relation to Self-Government*.[93] The "most general thesis" of *Free Speech*, Meiklejohn announced in his first chapter, "is . . . that our civil liberties, in general, are not all of one kind. They are of two kinds which, though radically different in constitutional status, are easily confused . . . One of these is open to restriction by the government. The other is not open to such restriction."[94] As examples Meiklejohn offered the liberty "of religious or irreligious belief," which "the government is unqualifiedly forbidden to restrict," and "the liberty of an individual to own, and use the income from, his labor or his property," which was "a limited one."[95]

Meiklejohn located the constitutional source of these two types of "liberties" in the juxtaposition of the First and Fifth Amendments. The First flatly prohibited the abridgment of freedom of speech. The Fifth prohibited the deprivation of liberty without due process of law. Liberty in the Fifth Amendment had been construed by the Court to include speech, but it could still be limited so long as due process was accorded. There were thus two classes of liberties in the Constitution, nonabridgable and abridgable liberties, and speech could be included in both. It was crucial to determine what sorts of speech belonged in each class.[96]

Meiklejohn was not a lawyer, and commentators with legal training have attacked his effort to distinguish unabridgable First Amendment speech rights from abridgable Fifth Amendment speech rights as confused and even incoherent.[97] He may have confused the Fifth and Fourteenth Amendments, and have been thinking of a distinction between unincorporated and incorporated Fourteenth Amendment rights of expression, since some early twentieth-century cases, such as *Meyer v. Nebraska,* had spoken, prior to *Gitlow,* of a Fourteenth Amendment "liberty" to teach or to be taught. If so, he had intuitively grasped how the Court's process of incorporating provisions of the First Amendment in the Fourteenth Amendment's Due Process Clause had strengthened the constitutional weight of speech rights.

Undeterred by the dubious constitutional basis of his distinction between First Amendment speech rights and other speech rights, Meiklejohn proceeded to make a further characterization based on that distinction. He asserted that speech as a Fifth Amendment "liberty," because of the language of that provision, was to be correlated to rights such as life and property, private rights also mentioned in the Fifth Amendment. By contrast speech in the First Amendment referred to public speech, the freedom of public discussion. Thus, "[t]he constitutional status of a merchant advertising his wares, of a paid lobbyist fighting for the advantage of his client, is utterly different from that of a citizen who is planning for the general welfare."[98] The question in every case was whether the speech was public or private, unabridgable or abridgable.

It is readily apparent that Meiklejohn's distinction between public and private speech was designed to provide textual support for a bifurcated standard of constitutional review that would give greater protection to noneconomic than to economic liberties. For all its analytic deficiencies, Meiklejohn's interpretation represented an ingenious effort to accommodate heightened scrutiny of legislation restricting free speech with a deferential approach to most other legislation. By replacing judicial formulas such as "clear and present danger," which smacked of guardian review in police power cases, with a judicial obligation to protect all "public" speech, the approach ostensibly limited the opportunities for the selective application of speech rights. At the same time the approach, by emphasizing that "private" speech was to receive no judicial protection, suggested that those whose economic activities had been given an undue freedom from legislative regulation by an older line of police power due process cases would not be able to resurface as free speech claimants.

This second feature of Meiklejohn's approach also appeared to preserve much of the doctrinal framework of free speech jurisprudence, including the more libertarian subversive advocacy cases and the preferred position cases. It was well settled, at the time of the appearance of *Free Speech,* that the protections of the First Amendment did not apply to a variety of expressions, including commercial speech,[99] libel and slander,[100] obscenity,[101] and unauthorized disclosure of "private" information.[102] By describing each of these expressions as private speech, Meiklejohn avoided the intrusion of the First Amendment into a number of established common law doctrines.

Finally, Meiklejohn's approach also promised to clarify the meaning of the democratic speech singled out for protection in the preferred position cases. He explicitly associated public speech with the processes of education and responsible citizenship in a democracy. The metaphoric construct that he employed to introduce his theory of free speech was not the marketplace of ideas but the New England town meeting: a public forum in which all citizens participated and spoke freely about civic affairs.[103] In his portrait of the town meeting no private or commercial issues corrupted the discussion; only public matters such as roads, schools, poorhouses, and public health were on the agenda. The speech that he was seeking to protect was that associated with the quintessentially public and democratic act of voting on noncommercial community issues.

Meiklejohn's interpretation offered a way out of the apparent dilemma between protection for speech rights and a commitment to the principle of majority rule in a democracy. If the central purpose of speech was to foster individual citizen participation in a democracy, an equation of majoritarian policies with the collective will of the democratic citizenry was dependent on that participation not being restricted. Otherwise a majority was not truly representative and its decisions not truly democratic. Majoritarian decisions restricting speech rights were thus open to the charge that they were seeking to block the very channels of citizen participation that justified majority rule. At this point Meiklejohn's interpretation associated itself with another of the *Carolene Products* criteria for departing from the presumption that most challenged legislation was constitutional. Statutes that restricted "public" speech not only were in facial conflict with provisions of the Constitution, they obstructed remedial opportunities that might be opened up by the process of democratic exchange.

But for all the apparent ingenuity of Meiklejohn's approach, it contained a significant internal tension. If protection for free speech was so indispensable an element of American democracy, it would appear that freedom of expression itself was to be cherished, regardless of its content. Since the principle of majority rule was dependent on full participation by all citizens in the "town meeting," some of whom eventually composed a majority, majoritarian efforts to restrict any form of speech would appear to threaten the integrity of the process of self-government. Why, then, had Meiklejohn offered so limited a definition of protected speech? He insisted that democratic theory only required a wide latitude for individuals to speak on *public* subjects, and that speech on other subjects could be restricted at will.

In making a powerful argument that individual public speech in a democratic society trumped majoritarian efforts to restrict it, Meiklejohn had raised the possibility that the self-education of individual citizens could not easily be confined to his limited definition of public expression. Speech connected to the desire of individual citizens to learn more about themselves and the world around them might have value in a democracy whether or not it appeared to be directed toward public issues. The capacity of humans to effectively govern themselves might be a product of qualities, such as self-fulfillment, that were not easily labeled "public" or "private." The "self" component of Meiklejohn's self-governance rationale for protecting speech bore an uneasy relationship to his insistence on limiting that protection to "public" expressions. The issues that Meiklejohn's theory of free speech had difficulty solving were to become the central issues of free speech jurisprudence for the remainder of the twentieth century.[104]

At the beginning of that century free speech jurisprudence was firmly grounded in doctrinal orthodoxies whose cumulative effect was to limit the scope of constitutional protection for expression. Doctrinal exegesis of First Amendment cases read the amendment as merely codifying existing common law liberties and as affording protection only against prior governmental censorship of speech. To the extent that liberty in the Fourteenth Amendment's Due Process Clause was taken to include freedom of thought and expression, that liberty was squarely placed within the framework of police power analysis, a framework in which legislative restrictions on speech to protect the safety or morals of the citizenry were taken as commonplace. In short, within the orthodox regime of early twentieth-century constitutional jurisprudence there was nothing special about free speech.

There was still nothing constitutionally special about free speech in the years immediately following World War I. In fact as late as the mid-1920s, notwithstanding Chafee's treatise and Holmes's *Abrams* dissent, the Supreme Court was continuing to treat First Amendment speech cases as governed by the bad tendency test, which gave considerable weight to the federal government's interest in restricting subversive speech, and to treat Fourteenth Amendment speech claims as indistinguishable from other police power liberty claims. Judicial incorporation of First Amendment rights had not yet occurred.

By the appearance of *Free Speech* in 1948 Meiklejohn was able to treat both the clear and present danger test and heightened scrutiny of claims based on First Amendment provisions as established features of free speech jurisprudence. In fact, he was prepared to suggest that the first feature was insufficiently attentive to the Constitution's unqualified protection for public speech, so that heightened scrutiny, in at least one class of free speech cases, should invariably lead to the judicial validation of speech claims.

Meiklejohn's effort to group speech cases into instances of "public" or "private" expression was eerily reminiscent of the categorical groupings made by earlier twentieth-century judges undertaking guardian review in police power cases. But his approach extracted one entire category of cases—those raising "public speech" claims—from the domain of police power analysis altogether, thus allowing the remaining speech cases to be governed by whatever form of deferential review the Court chose to adopt. The Court's preferred position cases had intuitively sought a similar extraction of speech cases from orthodox police power analysis, but had difficulty in distinguishing speech claims from other claims based on textually based rights, and democratic speech from other forms of speech. Meiklejohn did not believe that such distinctions were difficult. "Public" speech, as he formulated it, was speech related to the discussion of public issues in a democracy and, being a "fundamental," textually based liberty, could not be abridged. All other forms of speech would be as regulable as economic activity.

At this point we are in a position to grasp how the evolution of twentieth-century free speech jurisprudence served to undermine the integrity of guardian review and make bifurcated review constitutionally credible. As speech became transformed from a relatively weak police power liberty to an increasingly robust textually protected liberty, and the practice of judicial incorporation of Bill of Rights liberties highlighted its special constitutional status, justices on the Court began to consider whether speech rights occupied a preferred constitutional position. That development, which involved a comparison among the putative strength of specific constitutional provisions that had been designated as candidates for incorporation, changed the focus of due process cases from generalized judicial glosses on "liberty" to inquiries about the relative "fundamentality" of particular provisions. As the fundamental status of speech rights was reinforced by their association with democratic theory and practice, the judicial analysis of speech claims was progressively detached from police power analysis. By the appearance of Meiklejohn's *Free Speech* a category of speech claims—where "public" speech was at issue—had been identified as having nothing to do with police power jurisprudence.

Meanwhile, in the same time period, the Court had been progressively urged to adopt a more deferential posture toward legislative restrictions on economic activity, and by the early 1940s was beginning to exhibit that posture, stressing the presumption of constitutionality and requiring only that such restrictions be reasonable exercises of state or federal regulatory powers.[105] This development, taken together with the transformation of free speech jurisprudence, meant that the Court's core function in police power cases, pricking out the appropriate constitutional boundary between the "public" and "private" spheres of activity, had virtually disappeared. Due process cases were either incorporated rights cases, requiring a high level of judicial scrutiny, or ordinary police power cases, requiring only deferential review. The new boundary lines in constitutional analysis were being drawn by the constitutional text, the incorporation doctrine, and the special cultural status afforded speech rights in a democracy.

It remains to underscore why, in this narrative of the emergence of free speech and of the replacement of guardian constitutional review with bifurcated review, the New Deal and the Court-packing crisis have played minor roles, and the role of the *Carolene Products* decision has been recast. Those conclusions can be accentuated by a brief recapitulation of the narrative's central themes.

The early twentieth-century attribution of special cultural and constitutional significance to speech rights was the end product of three interrelated factors. One was the recognition by some courts and commentators, shortly after World War I, that protection for freedom of speech had beneficial social effects in a democratic society whose citizens were encouraged to inform themselves about public issues and to participate in the discussion of those issues. This rationale for protecting speech, which was articulated at a time when free speech claims were still regarded as the equivalent of police power liberties, became more prominent when federal and state statutes sought to suppress subversive speech in the aftermath of the war. Some Supreme Court justices and commentators, notably Holmes, Brandeis, and Chafee, began to use subversive speech cases as a basis for articulating the "social interests" in furthering the "search for truth" or in encouraging civic participation.

This development had the effect of enhancing the constitutional significance of speech rights, which in orthodox late nineteenth- and early twentieth-century police powers jurisprudence had been treated as eminently regulable "liberties," not gaining any constitutional weight from the existence of the First Amendment. Although free speech cases continued to be treated as police power cases, the Court's recognition that the First Amendment afforded more protection to speech rights than merely freedom from prior restraint, when coupled with the articulation of a "social interest" in protecting free speech in a democracy, increased the stature of "liberties of speech." The result, eventually, was that the Court concluded that the same substantive limitations First Amendment provisions placed on the federal government ought to be imposed on states by the Due Process Clause of the Fourteenth Amendment. Speech became an "incorporated" liberty.

This second factor in the early twentieth-century emergence of speech rights to a position of constitutional and cultural prominence at first appeared to have no effect on the analysis of free speech claims. But because the continuing judicial incorporation of additional Bill of Rights protections into the Fourteenth Amendment required the Court to focus on specific textual provisions, and was selective, it required justices, in their analysis of "liberty" claims in police power due process cases, to attach some comparative weight to the Bill of Rights provisions on which particular claims were based. Eventually, the Court confirmed, in *Palko v. Connecticut,* that this shift from generalized judicial glossing to specific investigations of the comparative stature of textually based rights was now its approach in police power cases. In that same case it concluded that the textually based rights most "indispensable" to the American constitutional system of "ordered liberty," and therefore the most obvious candidates for incorporation, were those protecting freedom of thought and speech.

At the same time Justice Cardozo's opinion for the Court in *Palko* explicitly linked the "fundamental" status of liberties related to thought and speech to the identity of America as a democratic society. Both the "preferred position" cases that followed *Palko* and Meiklejohn's conclusion that public democratic speech, as he defined it, enjoyed absolute constitutional protection were logical extensions of the recognition that textually based, incorporated, democratic liberties were not subject to the ordinary framework of police power analysis. Legislation restricting those liberties was not only in facial conflict with constitutional provisions; it was obstructing the process by which democratic majorities were assembled.

The emergence of this third factor in the Court's decisions meant that many speech-based challenges to legislation were extracted from guardian review-style police power analysis. Simultaneously the Court was urged to take a more relaxed approach toward legislation affecting ordinary commercial transactions. Thus the conception of a Court adopting a consistent posture of guardian review toward all forms of challenged legislation no longer seemed to capture what the justices were doing. What they were doing was groping toward a posture of bifurcated review.

In this narrative the New Deal, the Court-packing crisis, and the 1938

Carolene Products decision have received very little attention. But if one focuses on the most significant consequence of the transformation of early twentieth-century free speech jurisprudence, the substitution of bifurcated review for guardian review as the Court's orthodox stance in constitutional law cases, one can see how both the New Deal, and especially the *Carolene Products* decision, might be invested with causal significance.

The establishment of bifurcated review as the Court's operative stance in constitutional cases raises a central question. In light of the mounting critique of the Court's early twentieth-century "liberty of contract" decisions, the opposition to the Court's invalidation of early New Deal legislation, and the apparent pressure placed on the Court by the introduction of the Court-packing plan, why was guardian review not abandoned for deferential review in all cases testing the constitutionality of legislative regulations? Footnote 4 in *Carolene Products* had offered a series of justifications for bifurcated review, and the *Carolene Products* case was handed down a year after the Court-packing crisis. Even a narrative that associates enhanced judicial protection for free speech with developments that largely took place before the New Deal came into existence needs to consider the possibility that it was those justifications, advanced in the shadow of the New Deal, that really launched bifurcated review as a successor to the now discredited stance of guardian review.

There is even a stock explanation, as we have seen, for the emergence of a double standard of constitutional review around the time of the *Carolene Products* decision. The explanation suggests that the increased presence of government as a force regulating economic activity, symbolized by the New Deal, led to a heightened concern about the potential of government to restrict noneconomic rights and liberties. But that answer presupposes that the period in which bifurcated review was first seriously entertained as an alternative to guardian review—the years in which the preferred position rubric was formulated on the Court—was one in which a heightened general concern for the civil rights and liberties of minorities existed in America. There is little evidence of that general concern.[106] But even if it existed, this chapter has shown that heightened review in constitutional cases, from the late 1930s through the 1940s, was almost exclusively confined to *incorporated First Amendment* rights. The development of heightened judicial scrutiny of other types of legislation, such as that discriminating against minorities on racial, ethnic, or gender grounds, has been a later twentieth-century development.

If one keeps in mind that the only area in which the Court had retained heightened review, after it began to adopt a deferential posture toward the constitutionality of legislative regulations, was in cases where the challenges were based on incorporated provisions of the First Amendment, the justifications for heightened review advanced in *Carolene Products* can be seen in a different light. *Carolene Products,* we have noted, was a deferential review case, in which Stone, for himself and three of the Court's nine justices,[107] stated that regulatory legislation affecting ordinary commercial transactions would be presumed to be constitutional if it rested "upon some rational basis within the knowledge and experience of the legislators." His celebrated accompanying footnote to that statement ran as follows:

> There may be narrower scope for operation of the presumption of constitutionality when legislation appears on its face to be within a specific prohibition of the Constitution, such as those of the first ten amendments, which are deemed equally specific when held to be embraced within the Fourteenth. See Stromberg v. California; Lovell v. Griffin.
>
> It is unnecessary to consider now whether legislation which restricts those political processes which can ordinarily be expected to bring about repeal of undesirable legislation, is to be subjected to more exacting judicial scrutiny under the general prohibitions of the Fourteenth Amendment than are most other types of legislation. On restrictions upon the right to vote, see Nixon v. Herndon; Nixon v. Condon; on restraints upon the dissemination of information, see Near v. Minnesota; Grossjean v. American Press Co; Lovell v. Griffin; on interference with political organizations, see Stromberg v. California; Fiske v. Kansas; Whitney v. California; Herndon v. Lowry; and see Holmes, J. in Gitlow v. New York; as to peaceable assembly, see De Jonge v. Oregon.
>
> Nor need we inquire whether similar considerations enter into the review of statutes directed at particular religious, Pierce v. Society of Sisters, or national, Meyer v. Nebraska; Bartels v. Iowa; Farrington v. Tokushige, or racial minorities, Nixon v. Herndon; Nixon v. Condon; whether prejudices against discrete and insular minorities may be a special condition, which tends seriously to curtail the operation of those political processes ordinarily thought to be relied upon to protect those minorities, and which may call for a correspondingly more searching judicial inquiry . . .[108]

We have seen that Stone advanced three different sorts of justifications for heightened judicial review of legislation in the above paragraphs. His first justification, in the first paragraph, emphasized the particular constitutional basis under which legislation was challenged. When legislation appeared on its face to violate a prohibition specifically identified in the Bill of Rights, which, Stone felt, was "equally specific when held to be embraced within the Fourteenth," there "may be narrower scope for . . . the presumption" that it was constitutional. Both of his examples, *Stromberg v. California*[109] and *Lovell v. Griffin,*[110] involved police power legislation in which the challenges were based on incorporated First Amendment provisions. Thus, his first justification can be seen as reducing itself to the proposition that free speech challenges to legislation should trigger higher scrutiny because free speech rights were textually based, incorporated rights.

In contrast, the justifications offered for heightened review in the second and third paragraphs of the footnote emphasized imperfections in the legislative process that prevented the full participation of affected persons or imperfections that could be associated with animus toward minorities. In such instances, Stone implied, heightened review might be in order because the legislature, by restricting the involvement of certain groups or stigmatizing them, had departed from democratic ideals. These justifications were to become influential in the Court's equal protection decisions in the 1950s and sixties. But in 1938 Stone had almost no case support for them. Nearly all the cases that he mentioned in connection with those justifications, in fact, were free speech cases supporting his first justification.

Other than two cases, *Nixon v. Herndon* and *Nixon v. Condon,* in which Texas explicitly attempted to bar black voters from eligibility in primary elections, the cases Stone listed in connection with the final two paragraphs of his footnote were of two classes. One class consisted of three pre-*Gitlow* police power cases, *Pierce, Meyer,* and *Bartels v. Iowa,* and a Fifth Amendment due process case, *Farrington v. Tokushige,* in which the Court had read "liberty" to include freedom of speech or thought as evidenced in the decisions of parents about their children's education. The other class, which made up all of the remaining cases cited by Stone in his footnote, consisted of cases in which various provisions of the First Amendment had been deemed to have been incorporated against the states for the purpose of police power analysis.[111] Despite the fact that Stone associated these two classes of cases with his comments about imperfections in the legislative process, they were all pre- or post-*Gitlow* examples of free speech cases.

Thus, the *Carolene Products* opinion, including its footnote, can be seen as communicating the following messages at the time it was handed down. It announced, for less than a majority of the Court, that the standard of review in cases testing the constitutionality of legislation "affecting ordinary commercial transactions" would be deferential. As we will subsequently see, this statement remained a controversial one in 1938, but it would eventually become unquestioned orthodoxy. It also suggested that a deferential standard of review would very likely not be followed in all constitutional cases, but departures from the presumption of constitutionality required some justification. At that point it summoned up a number of post-*Gitlow* incorporated

First Amendment cases and a handful of other heightened scrutiny cases, all but two of which implicated freedom of thought or speech, and scattered them around as support for a series of tentative justifications for enhanced review. All of those justifications have resonated with later twentieth-century courts and commentators. But only one—that heightened judicial scrutiny made sense where legislation specifically affected a textually grounded, incorporated provision of the Constitution—was a common part of the discourse of constitutional jurisprudence in 1938. And that justification was grounded on incorporated First Amendment cases, whose incorporation had been launched before deferential review had become an established judicial posture.

Thus, it was crucial to the development of bifurcated constitutional review in twentieth-century constitutional jurisprudence that free speech rights had come to be treated as "liberties" with significant constitutional and cultural weight *before* deferential review was seriously entertained as an alternative to guardian review of regulatory legislation. And, as this chapter has shown, free speech rights had come to occupy that position prior to the 1930s, and Court majorities had shown evidence of developing a speech-protective jurisprudence between 1931 and early 1937.

So if we look at the early twentieth-century history of free speech jurisprudence with an eye toward identifying the central factors that fostered the emergence of free speech to a position of constitutional and cultural prominence, and consider the first stirrings of bifurcated review in the 1930s with that history in mind, we are able to come to two perhaps unexpected conclusions. The New Deal and the Court-packing crisis had very little causal connection to the emergence of free speech. But the emergence of free speech bore a significant connection to the famous footnote in *Carolene Products* and, more fundamentally, to the substitution of bifurcated review for guardian review as the approved stance for judges in twentieth-century constitutional cases.

II

The Constitutional Revolution as Jurisprudential Crisis

At this point some stocktaking seems in order. Previous chapters have identi-fied a conventional narrative of early twentieth-century constitutional history and have suggested that it inadequately describes major transformations in constitutional law that took place in the first four decades of the century. The narrative's undue emphasis on short-run political events associated with the emergence of the New Deal, and on changes in constitutional law as judicial responses to those events, has produced some causal difficulties and some mischaracterizations of doctrinal changes.

But although the precise nature of early twentieth-century changes in con-stitutional law has been imperfectly understood and the conventional expla-nation for those changes appears inadequate, the fact remains that every ma-jor doctrinal area of American constitutional law was significantly altered in the first four decades of the century. Moreover, although doctrinal change over time was a common feature of American constitutional jurisprudence, contemporaries in the 1940s remarked on the unusual magnitude of changes that were taking place and the Court's relaxation of its scrutiny of regulatory and redistributive legislation. It seemed to those observers that these devel-opments were truly "revolutionary": not only was the Court reversing many of its previous decisions in Commerce Clause cases, due process cases, and Contracts Clause cases, but it was adopting a radically different conception of its obligations to act as a constitutional check on other branches of govern-ment.

Thus, the question that remains, after one has concluded that the "constitu-tional revolution" of the early twentieth century cannot be satisfactorily ex-plained as a short-term judicial response to external political pressures gener-ated by the New Deal, is how one can account for it. Chapters 6 and 7 explore an alternative way of thinking about the constitutional revolution.

165

6

The Restatement Project and the Crisis of Early Twentieth-Century Jurisprudence

Thus far the term "jurisprudence" has been employed to characterize the collective doctrinal and theoretical developments that took place in particular areas of early twentieth-century constitutional law. That usage is atypical. Most commentators, when referring to early twentieth-century American jurisprudence, have used the term in a broader sense and have not focused on constitutional law. For them the study of "jurisprudence" in that time period emphasizes particular perspectives held by judges and legal scholars on the nature of law, or judging, or the relationship of law to its social context, as illustrated in analyses of common law cases.[1]

In particular, scholars writing about early twentieth-century American jurisprudence have emphasized the presence of two such perspectives that competed with one another in the first four decades of the century. The perspectives have been labeled "Formalism" and "Realism," with the history of early twentieth-century American jurisprudence presented as a narrative in which Formalism overshadowed, contested with, and was eventually displaced by Realism as the dominant jurisprudential perspective.

Formalism has been characterized as a perspective that sees legal principles as essentialist, foundational entities, embodied in cases, and that takes new cases to be exercises in the "formal" (noncreative and nondiscretionary) judicial application of existing principles. In most instances such application was routine: a new case would simply be seen as an illustration of an existing principle. But in some instances, either because of the perceived novelty of the issues raised in a case or because the case seemed capable of being decided by either of two competing principles, application required the governing boundaries of a particular principle to be expanded or contracted or, on rare occasions, required the formulation of an exception to the principle. Such instances demonstrated the capacity of the common law to respond to changing circumstances that produced novel legal issues, without altering the essentialist content of its governing principles or the formal process by which those principles were articulated by judges in cases.

Realism, by contrast, has been characterized as a perspective that treats preexisting legal principles as abstract "concepts" having no essential meaning independent of the context of cases in which they are applied. For Realists it was meaningless to conceive of judicial decisionmaking as a formal exercise in the application of existing principles to new cases: all common law "principles" were utterly dependent on the facts and consequences of the cases in which they had been formulated. Instead of characterizing the "common law" of particular fields as a collection of principles, successively embodied in cases, judges and commentators should regard it as an aggregate of cases with their distinctive settings and policy implications.

With the above characterizations of Formalism and Realism in place, scholars have produced a series of studies, many of them illuminating, about the relationship of Formalism and Realism to one another and to the changing doctrinal patterns of private law subjects in the early twentieth century.[2] Their elucidation of the contrasting perspectives of Formalism, Realism, and of the relationship of those movements to one another has assumed that the impact of the movements was primarily on common law fields.[3] In particular, those describing the contrasting perspectives of Formalism and Realism have identified the central contested issue in early twentieth-century American jurisprudence to be whether judges could appropriately claim that the legal principles they articulated in the process of deciding common law cases were preexisting, essentialist sources of authority, even though they represented extractions from previous judicial decisions.

Thus, the so-called "Formalist/Realist debate," taken as the defining feature of early twentieth-century American jurisprudence, has been portrayed as a debate grounded in common law subjects, and a debate whose ultimate concern was the nature and legitimacy of *judicial* authority. This portrayal has seemed intuitively plausible because contemporary participants in the debate regularly illustrated their positions with references to judicial opinions in common law cases, and because common law fields are distinguished by the absence of any governing legal authority other than the preexisting decisions of judges.

But we have seen in preceding chapters that the methodology of judicial decisionmaking in constitutional cases in the early twentieth century was not fully consistent with an assumption that judges were simply reciting and following the imperatives of the Constitution's text. The stance of guardian review in constitutional cases was seemingly designed to give judges a fair amount of latitude to extract meaning from broad and indeterminate constitutional provisions through glosses that yielded the equivalent of legal principles (such as "liberty of contract"). Moreover, the prevailing conception of the Constitution's text as allocating spheres of power to the federal government and to the states, and as reserving a sphere to the people that was "private" and not appropriate for governmental regulation, required continual judicial monitoring of the boundaries between those spheres. Boundary pricking involved judicial reconsideration, in the context of new cases, of allocations of power that were preexisting and essentialist, and assumed that in drawing new boundary lines judges would invoke principles that could fairly be extracted from particular textual provisions. This process closely resembled the judicial extraction of principles from previous judicial decisions in common law cases.

In addition, criticism of certain controversial early twentieth-century constitutional decisions sounded themes that scholars have associated with a Realist jurisprudential perspective. Attacks on the Court's line of liberty of contract decisions, for example, emphasized the unsatisfactorily abstract nature of the concept of "liberty of contract" and its dissonance with the "facts" of modern American industrial life, implying that judicial applications of the liberty of contract principle represented an otherworldly version of "formal" decisionmaking.[4] In response, defenders of the liberty of contract decisions characterized them as appropriate applications of the essentialist constitutional principle, embodied in the term "liberty" in the Due Process Clause, that decisions about the terms of private employment should be made by individuals rather than by the government.

It would appear, then, that to treat the central issues of early twentieth-century American jurisprudence as principally associated with common law cases, or as principally involving debates about the nature of judicial authority, is to advance too narrow a definition of those issues and debates. Suppose one were to broaden the boundaries of early twentieth-century American jurisprudence to include constitutional law as well as common law fields and to pose the central contested issue differently. Suppose one were to assume that the central contested jurisprudential issue of the first four decades of the twentieth century was the nature and legitimacy of *legal* authority. Suppose one were to assume that the fundamental question being debated was whether any purportedly authoritative legal source—any "principle" extracted by a court from a previous judicial decision, a statute, or the Constitution—could be said to derive its authority from sources independent of the persons who formulated it and independent of the context in which it was articulated.

If jurisprudential debates in the first four decades of the century are seen as centering on the nature and legitimacy of legal authority, the fact that the clash between those holding Formalist and Realist perspectives was largely focused on the relationship between principles and cases in private law subjects does not mean that the Formalist/Realist debate was not part of the universe of early twentieth-century constitutional jurisprudence. This chapter suggests that, on the contrary, the controversy conventionally rendered as a struggle between Formalist and Realist approaches to common law subjects had important implications for early twentieth-century constitutional law.

The chapter examines an episode that brought the Formalist/Realist debate sharply into focus and that can be seen as illustrative of a crisis in early twentieth-century American jurisprudence. The episode began with the formation of the American Law Institute in 1923 and the ALI's commissioning of textual "Restatements" of the common law principles of particular private law subjects. It culminated with the appearance of the first group of those Restatements in the 1930s and the critical reaction their appearance engendered. That criticism initially revealed itself in skepticism about the usefulness of the Restatement project's effort, then broadened and deepened to reveal profound divisions among early twentieth-century legal scholars about the intelligibility of legal principles as essentialist, universal sources of authority. The broader dimensions of the crisis radiated into constitutional law, where an analogous debate, centering on the implications of "adapting" the Constitution to changing external conditions, was simultaneously taking place. This chapter traces the crisis as it evolved in a common law setting; the next chapter considers its relationship to debates about the meaning of constitutional change.

The formation of the American Law Institute and the launching of the Restatement project have received a fair amount of scholarly attention, but there has been sharp disagreement on the Restatement project's role in the history of early twentieth-century American jurisprudence. One line of scholarship has pictured the project as a conservative, rearguard action, seeking to reassert the primacy of orthodox nineteenth-century conceptions of law and legal subjects in the face of early twentieth-century pressure for change.[5] Another line has emphasized the reformist orientation of the American Law Institute, associating its formation with a "progressive-pragmatist" tradition of protest against jurisprudential orthodoxy that is taken to be a defining element of twentieth-century American jurisprudence.[6] From the perspective of this chapter, this lack of consensus on the jurisprudential orientation of the Restatement project is not surprising because the formation of the Institute itself and the commissioning of the project were symbols of the fundamentally contested state of jurisprudential ideas in the 1920s.

In the course of analyzing the Restatement project as the common law setting in which a crisis in early twentieth-century American jurisprudence emerged, I have examined the starting assumptions that precipitated the Restatement project, the jurisprudential conceptions animating the first set of Restatements, and the scholarly reaction to those Restatements. Before plunging into details, it seems useful to supply an overview of my central findings.

The starting point of the Restatement project was its founders' assumption that the American legal system was suffering from difficulties related to its increased "uncertainty" and "complexity." That diagnosis unwittingly brought to light the simultaneous existence of a number of trends within the legal profession that had come to the surface just after World War I. One trend was the declining usefulness of techniques associated with a pristine late nineteenth-century version of "law as a science" as devices for analyzing and synthesizing common law subjects. A second was the explosion of common law jurisdictions, a process spawned by population growth, the entrance of new states into the Union, and the persistence of a pre–*Erie v. Tompkins* jurisprudence, in which federal and state courts often promulgated different common law rules for the same subjects. Both trends were related to each other, and to a third: the increased prominence, in law as well as a number of other early twentieth-century academic disciplines, of an epistemological attitude that rejected "simple," externally based theories of causal explanation in the universe, treating the meaning of experience as more human-centered and more "complex."

The formation of the American Law Institute, whose principal purpose was identified by its founders as producing "restatements" of the law of common law subjects, was a response to those trends. The ALI's Restatement project sought to deal with the epistemological problems of uncertainty and complexity though authoritative compilations of the rules and doctrines governing common law fields. In addition, the distinctive methodology employed in the production of Restatements, which consisted of the appointment of visible scholars as Reporters for designated common law subjects, their authoring of volumes in which the "black letter"[7] principles governing legal issues in each of those subjects were set forth, and the oversight of those volumes by "Advisors," other persons regarded as learned in the subjects, was an effort to ensure that the inevitable doctrinal changes taking place in the common law could be fitted into comprehensive syntheses produced by experts.

So described, the formation of the American Law Institute and the launching of the Restatement project can be thought of as efforts to resist as well as to embrace perceived changes in early twentieth-century American law and the legal profession. But the launching of the Restatement project was also the catalyst for strident criticism of the jurisprudential assumptions on which the project was founded. The conception of law as a body of core fundamental principles that animated the first Restatements of common law subjects was attacked as incoherent and unsound. The methodological approach of the Restatements was likewise dismissed as outmoded and "unscientific."

In the course of this criticism of the Restatement project an alternative conception of law was articulated. That conception stressed the impermanent and contextual quality of legal rules and principles. It rejected nineteenth-century conceptions of law as a "science" that was logically self-contained and self-referential, such as geometry, or taxonomic, such as the natural sciences. It asserted that to the extent law was a science, it resembled the social sciences, its organizing generalizations resting on evolving empirical data. Eventually, as this conception of legal science as akin to other early twentieth-century social sciences displaced older conceptions, it served to undermine essentialist definitions of the nature of legal authority. Instead of authoritative legal sources being treated as the equivalent of inexorable external forces in the universe or fundamental scientific principles, they came to be treated as provisional efforts on the part of human "social engineers" to make sense of and to govern their current environment.

A close analysis of the epistemological and juristic dimensions of the Restatement project and critical reaction to it reveals that, over the course of the first two decades of the twentieth century, a well-established nineteenth-century jurisprudential distinction between the authoritative sources of law and the authoritative interpreters of law had broken down. That distinction was the product of attitudes that emphasized the causal primacy of inviolable external forces and entities in the universe. Law was one such entity. The inviolability of law and its role as an external causal agent were related to its established presence in every society that had renounced tyranny as a principle of social organization. Because law was the principal mechanism for resolving human conflict, it was treated as an authoritative source of wisdom. And because law was an antidote to tyranny, its authority was external to human will, independent of the authority of those who laid down the legal rules that governed disputes.

This set of attitudes toward law acknowledged that the rules and principles that were applied as sources of authority in the resolution of disputes were often mysterious and unintelligible to the average citizen. Certain persons, most conspicuously judges, would, by virtue of their training and their professional roles, be given special authority to discern, interpret, and apply legal principles. But the authority of that class of persons came from their status as savants and from the obligations of impartiality and disinterestedness that accompanied their professional role. Their authority to declare which principles of law governed a given dispute, and to apply those principles to the resolution of that dispute, was of a different order than the authority of the principles themselves. That authority was imminent in law itself; it was external to human will. The sources of law were distinct from the interpretations of those sources by judges in cases.

Those involved in the Restatement project were motivated by a sense of the uneasiness of the distinction between the authority of legal sources and the authority of legal interpreters. They sought to shore up that distinction in the Restatements by treating the compiled "black letter" law as essentialist principles rather than collections of decisions rendered by judges. But the necessarily abstracted form in which black letter summaries were rendered, and the decision on the part of the founders of the Restatement project to eliminate commentary on those summaries from the Restatement volumes, had the effect of convincing critics that the black letter summaries were not essentialist principles: they were overly generalized and attenuated renderings of the tendencies of judicial decisions in particular lines of cases. Eventually those critics concluded that the abstracted form of the Restatement volumes demonstrated that legal principles, treated as independent of the cases in which they were applied, were unintelligible. There was thus no meaningful distinction between the sources of law and its interpreters: the common law was what the judges said it was. Any "scientific" approach to legal subjects needed to be predicated on observations of what was "really" being decided in cases, not on some taxonomic arrangement of allegedly preexisting principles.

The collapse of the distinction between the authority of legal sources and the authority of those who interpreted the sources had obvious and significant consequences for the jurisprudence of constitutional law. It suggested that the glossing of constitutional provisions frequently engaged in by judges exercising guardian review was not simply the application of preexisting principles embodied in those provisions. It was a series of creative interpretations of constitutional language, whose "meaning" could not easily be divorced from the circumstances in which a particular provision was being interpreted and applied. Instead of being relatively passive figures who applied the core principles of the Constitution to new situations as they arose, judges engaged in constitutional interpretation were active figures who were asked to determine the changed meaning of principles such as "due process of law," "equal protection of the laws," and protection for "free speech" in light of contemporary conditions. In interpreting constitutional provisions judges were "adapting" the Constitution to the demands of current American society, and in the process of judicial adaptation the meaning of the Constitution changed.

Those conclusions about constitutional interpretation and constitutional adaptivity had significant implications for the legitimacy of constitutional decisionmaking by judges in a democratic society. If judges were constrained by the external, timeless nature of legal principles themselves, the fact that they were not accountable officials in the conventional political sense did not pose any difficulty. Their authority to declare the meaning of constitutional principles and to apply them to cases came from their status and expertise: they were a species of savants in the legal profession. If, however, the distinction between authoritative sources of law and authoritative interpreters of law was illusory, so that law, constitutional or otherwise, was the equivalent of the decisions of humans holding lawmaking power, it was difficult to find a justification for allowing lawmaking to be conducted by unelected, unaccountable judges, particularly when the lawmaking took the form of judicial invalidation of legislation on constitutional grounds. Thus, as we have seen, arguments for judicial deference to legislation subjected to constitutional challenges began to surface in early twentieth-century constitutional commentary.

The specific implications for early twentieth-century constitutional jurisprudence of the emergence of alternative conceptions of the sources of law, the meaning of legal interpretation, and the authority of legal interpreters will be spelled out in a subsequent chapter. At this point I turn to a detailed treatment of how those conceptions surfaced in connection with the American Law Institute's Restatement project.

Christopher Columbus Langdell's 1887 declaration that "law is a science, and . . . all the available materials of that science are contained in printed books,"[8] was not a novel statement in the sense that it has commonly been taken to be. The novelty lay in his claim that "printed books"—by that phrase Langdell principally meant the reported decisions of appellate courts—contained all the relevant data of the field of law. His characterization of law as a science had been made at least since the middle of the eighteenth century in America, and earlier than that in Europe.[9] The ideal of the science of law had been a recurrent concept for Langdell's American predecessors, including Joseph Story, David Hoffman, and Daniel Mayes.[10] Langdell's innovation was to exclude relentlessly anything except reported judicial decisions as sources of "scientific" legal principles. Earlier jurists had included the laws of nature, history, religion, and "first principles" of government as relevant sources for the legal scientist to draw upon.[11]

Langdell's conception of science modified the "geometric analogy" that had dominated mid-nineteenth-century definitions of "scientific" methodology in law. In that analogy legal "first principles" were taken to be the equivalent of geometric axioms, and legal reasoning was treated as deductive. In Langdell's modification, influenced by methodological developments in the natural sciences, legal principles were rearranged taxonomically in a logical hierarchy oriented toward producing a self-contained system of classification for legal subjects. Evidence (cases) was then fitted into that system. When Langdell said that "the number of legal doctrines is much less than commonly supposed,"[12] he meant to locate doctrines within a taxonomic hierarchy. His goal was to "select, classify, and arrange all the cases" according to the degree to which they "had contributed . . . to the growth, development or establishment of . . . essential doctrines."[13] The critical step in his system was his taxonomic labeling of certain doctrines (embodied in cases) as "essential."

The methodology of Langdell's system was consistent with his epistemological perspective. He wished to tighten the database of his system to make it more "scientific," focusing on cases and ruling out other potential sources of doctrinal principles. That innovation sharply delineated the field of legal expertise, transforming law into a self-contained professional enterprise with its secularized, "scientific" data, vocabulary, and reasoning patterns. It demonstrated, as Langdell put it, that law as a science was more than a "species of handicraft."[14]

For Langdell, essentialist status for a legal principle was not a function of its regular appearance in cases, as his system assumed that certain doctrinal formulations would be discarded as "wrong." The essentialist status of principles was connected to an intuitive hierarchical ordering of sources of legal authority, based on the collective political and philosophical assumptions of Langdell and his fellow legal scientists. This ordering resulted in certain legal doctrines—those taken to embody very significant cultural values, such as individual autonomy or the sanctity of property—being designated as "fundamental" and judicial decisions invoking them being designated as "correct."[15]

Eventually the step in Langdell's version of legal science wherein some legal principles were implicitly designated as "fundamental" was exposed, scrutinized, and labeled incoherent, causing the collapse of his methodology as a jurisprudential orthodoxy. But that critique was not related to the epistemological turbulence that accompanied the commissioning of the Restatements. A less cosmic element in Langdell's conception of legal science was directly tied to the founding of the Restatement project. Langdell had assumed that "all the cases" in an area of common law could be rearranged in a hierarchical classification system that would reveal that the number of essential legal prin-

ciples was far fewer than commonly supposed. As judicial decisions proliferated in twentieth-century America, and the increased reporting of those decisions vastly increased the database of legal commentators, it became apparent
that many aspiring legal scientists were having difficulty fitting new cases
neatly into hierarchical, taxonomic classification systems.

When the American Law Institute came into being, its founders addressed
the problem of "uncertainty" in the law and sought to particularize its
causes. In a 1923 policy statement they identified "the most important"
cause of uncertainty as a "lack of general agreement on [the] fundamental
principles" of the common law.[16] But they felt that this lack of consensus on
fundamental principles was endemic to a system in which "[i]t is not the duty
of . . . courts to set forth the principles of the common law in an orderly manner," even though those principles were "developed by the slow process of
judicial decision."[17] Even though this endemic uncertainty might have suggested that "fundamental" legal principles had a limited intelligibility outside
of the concrete contexts in which they were invoked, the founders did not
pursue that suggestion.

Instead, the founders of the ALI identified a series of factors at the opera-
tional end, as distinguished from the conceptual end, of the common law system that were fostering "uncertainty." These factors included "the great volume of recorded decisions,"[18] "ignorance of judges and lawyers,"[19] "the
number and nature of novel legal questions,"[20] and "attempts to distinguish
between two cases where the facts present no distinction in the legal principles available."[21] They argued that if these factors could be addressed, uncertainty could be reduced.

These factors, according to those who urged the creation of Restatements
of common law subjects, were a symptom of early twentieth-century American life. The founders of the ALI saw the "complexity" of contemporary
American society, itself one of the causes of "defects" in the law,[22] as related
to the growth and diversification of the American economy, a development
that had produced "novel legal questions" and had increased the "volume of
recorded decisions." The increased number of cases, and of "novel" issues in
those cases, the founders felt, had interacted unfortunately with the "ignorance of judges and lawyers." While that "ignorance" was partially inevitable,
given the increased volume and complexity of issues before the courts, it was
also a product of a lack of understanding of the nature of legal principles. The
founders noted that in cases in which the application of an established principle to a "novel" set of facts was perceived as "produc[ing] injustice," courts
attempted to distinguish the cases "on account of some immaterial difference
in their respective facts." The result was "that we have no clear statement of
any legal principle, the law on the subject being left confused and uncertain."[23]

The proposed Restatements of common law subjects were designed to respond to these deficiencies in the operation of the system. If the principles of the common law were carefully and authoritatively formulated, the task of the courts in applying principles to cases would be greatly simplified. "Ignorance" would be thereby reduced, and the problem of immaterial distinctions solved. Moreover, the proliferation of litigated and reported cases, even cases presenting "novel" issues, need not result in "uncertainty" about the law, since properly formulated principles would cover such cases, unless they were wholly novel, in which instances new principles covering them would come into being.

Of two alternative responses to the problem of uncertainty in the law, the founders of the Institute had opted for a response that was consistent with the epistemological assumptions of orthodox late nineteenth-century jurisprudence. They had identified two quite different causes of uncertainty: endemic epistemological uncertainty and contextual, applicational uncertainty. Having mentioned the former, they identified it as inevitable in any system in which legal principles were declared in individual cases, and directed their attention to the latter. But in attempting to alleviate applicational uncertainty they reaffirmed one of the governing assumptions of Langdell and his contemporaries, that the number of fundamental legal principles was smaller than commonly supposed, and therefore most cases could be seen as exercises in the application of already existing principles. The choice of the Restatement format as a response to uncertainty was consistent with that assumption. Restatements would be more precise, more hierarchically ordered, and therefore more authoritative statements of "fundamental" common law principles, making the application of those principles in individual cases a less uncertain task.

The founders of the ALI made a similar response to the problem of "complexity." Their 1923 statement maintained that "complexity" in the law "may denote one of two things."[24] It might signify that "a number of rules of law apply to a given situation," or that "in order to ascertain the law applicable thereto many elements of fact have to be considered."[25] As an example, they offered the duty of a railway company to take care of its passengers. If that duty was described as "reasonable care under the circumstances," the application of that duty to a given case might require a "complex" analysis of the steps the railroad and its officials had taken to safeguard passengers, together with the situations in which particular passengers had been exposed to various risks. In the example the "rule of law" was not complex, but the facts to which it applied might be. If, however, the duty of a railway varied with the kind of conduct it engaged in, or the kind of passenger injured, or the conduct of that passenger, the rules of law governing the liability of railroads for accidents to their passengers could be said to be "complex" because, as the founders put it, "the rules of law affecting the carriage of passengers are more numerous."[26]

As in the case of uncertainty, complexity in the law was treated by the ALI's founders as partially inevitable. Complexity in the law, they asserted, was to an important extent a product of "the complexity of the conditions of life"[27] in twentieth-century America. Such conditions "must either increase the number of the rules of law . . . or the number of factors which must be taken into consideration to determine . . . legal responsibility."[28]

Here again, however, the founders believed that a careful articulation and ordering of legal rules would result in the governing principles of an area seeming less "complex" than might first appear. Just as "ignorant" judges and lawyers had contributed to uncertainty by attempting to make meaningless distinctions between cases in order to avoid the possible injustice of following an established principle in a "novel" situation, they had precipitated "illogical distinctions" in order to respond to complexity, articulating rules that "violated general principles established in other cases." This had precipitated a "lack of systematic development in the law."[29] The Restatements of common law subjects would address this problem by reformulating principles so that they had sufficient breadth and generality to cover a variety of situations. Emphasis would then shift to a careful analysis of the facts of "novel" cases, which would reveal that many such cases were really not novel after all, being analogous to situations governed by an established common law principle.

A defining feature of the Restatement response to uncertainty and complexity, then, was the founders' avoidance of alternative readings of those conditions that would have undermined the orthodox late nineteenth-century conception of legal science. The alternative reading of uncertainty suggested that legal principles were multivalent entities, containing mutually contradictory applications, one of which was suppressed in the articulation. Uncertainty was inherent in a system that applied such principles to cases. The alternative reading of complexity suggested that legal principles were inherently dependent on the facts to which they were applied, so that simplicity was not gained by statements of principles in the abstract.[30]

Both readings threatened the epistemological integrity of the Langdellian meaning of the concept of legal science, which rested on the distinction between the essentialist authority of sources of law and the expertise-based authority of interpreters of law. The alternative reading of uncertainty radically changed the meaning of a legal "principle," suggesting that it was not a certain, predictable, finite entity but rather a cluster of opposing and contradictory values, pointing in different directions depending on the context of their application. The alternative reading of complexity even more radically stripped "principles" of any determinate content, since their meanings not only varied with the context in which they were applied but were the creations of that context. With principles denuded of their essentialist and universalist qualities, the derivation of common law rules shifted quite sharply to the actions of judges in particular cases. A good deal of the energy of Langdellian science had been directed toward the formulation of a few discernible and finite principles capable of very wide application. The alternative readings of uncertainty and complexity in modern American law intimated that such energy had been significantly misplaced, and to chart the "common law" of various private law subjects one needed to look at the very cases whose proliferation had furnished an impetus for the Restatement project.

The ALI founders' choice to treat uncertainty and complexity as defects at the epistemological periphery, rather than at the core, of orthodox nineteenth-century jurisprudence helps clarify the form the "crisis" of early twentieth-century jurisprudence took for them. In their view the crisis did not stem from inherent difficulties in discerning the meaning of essentialist legal principles or from applying principles to cases without changing their meaning. It simply stemmed from the increased volume of cases and clumsy techniques in the process of discerning and applying principles. The Restatement project was directed toward improving those techniques. It was directed at the expertise-based authority of legal interpreters, not the essentialist authority of legal sources.

The choice of the Restatement format as the solution to uncertainty and complexity provides an additional illustration of the ALI founders' governing jurisprudential assumptions. There were three other responsive projects the founders could have adopted without radically departing from American jurisprudential traditions. One would have continued the early nineteenth-century tradition of disseminating law primarily through the production of academic treatises on common law subjects, such as William Blackstone's *Commentaries* or the works of James Kent, Joseph Story, and a host of other contemporaries and successors.[31] A second project would have drafted a uniform national code of legal subjects, thereby borrowing from the civil law tradition and reviving numerous proposals for codification that had appeared in the nineteenth century. A third project would have encouraged codification of common law principles through the passage of statutes at the state level, with such statutes being designed to integrate and to clarify the common law of particular jurisdictions.

The founders of the ALI were aware of each of these alternatives. This conclusion can be drawn not only from the early discussions of the ALI's membership but from the fact that the ALI, in the course of its subsequent history, was eventually to produce versions of each of the alternatives. The founders of the ALI initially anticipated that the Reporters they commissioned to produce Restatements of various common law fields would also produce accompanying treatises that would serve as authoritative support for and commentary on the black letter principles formulated in their Restatement volumes.[32] After launching the Restatement project, the ALI expanded its operations to commission the creation of uniform laws on certain subjects, such as the Uniform Commercial Code, which amounted to minicodes for the nation. And although the ALI's founders made clear in their early deliberations that they had no intention of delegating the reformulation of common law subjects to state legislators,[33] they assumed that the ultimate proof of the authoritativeness of the Restatements (and, subsequently, of the uniform laws) would come from their acceptance in state courts and state legislatures.

Nonetheless, the founders did not anticipate that treatises, codes, and state statutes would displace the Restatements as primary authoritative sources of common law principles. In making that choice they revealed that their assumptions about the nature of legal authority remained the assumptions that lay behind Langdell's conception of law as a science.

We have noted that the jurisprudential system bequeathed by Langdell and his contemporaries to the founders of the ALI anticipated that judges and others who participated in the development of law—Langdell referred to the latter as jurisconsults—would maintain the integrity of legal principles by learned applications and scientific classifications of rules and doctrines. Although principles might be refined and purified in their application or scientific elucidation, so that their intelligibility or comprehensiveness might be increased in the process, their essentialist, fundamental nature remained unchanged. The fact that the meaning of sources of legal authority could be better understood after judges had invoked those sources in deciding cases, or commentators had arranged them in a logical order, did not make them any less finite.

Langdell's model of legal science continued to be an analog to the models employed in geometry or taxonomy, featuring the application of fundamental axioms or the defining characteristics of species. The early twentieth-century physical and social sciences, however, had come to think of scientists not simply as observers and recorders of data but also as promulgators of scientific generalizations based on that data, which had some predictive value. They were learned authorities who were attempting to make sense of the scientific fields they studied. If the role of legal scientists was assumed to be comparable to that of other twentieth-century scientists, the Restatements of common law subjects were expected to result in the principles of those subjects being set forth in a more comprehensive, less complex, and less uncertain form. They were expected to be sources of legal authority.

Critics of the Restatement project would eventually treat its version of legal science as failing to recognize that "restating" common law principles necessarily altered the content of those principles, blurring the distinction between the sources of law and those who claimed authority as interpreters of those sources. But the founders of the ALI did not think of their version of legal science as having this effect. Instead, they proceeded along two lines that were consistent with the established jurisprudential separation of the authority of legal sources from that of legal interpreters. First, they sought to respond to "uncertainty" and "complexity" through a modified version of Langdell's techniques, the restatement of governing principles in common law subjects. Such principles were apparently independent of the context of the cases in which they were applied and the judges who applied them. They were detached from human agency, even though they had been compiled by human commentators.

At the same time the founders of the ALI entrusted the "restating" of common law subjects to handpicked elite members of the legal profession. This decision was at the very heart of the Restatement project. The founders assumed that uncertainty and complexity in the law had a far better chance of being reduced if the reformulation of governing legal principles was undertaken by the best minds in the legal profession. They continued to separate the essentialist authority of the black letter principles being compiled by authors of Restatement volumes from the expertise-based authority of the compilers.

We have previously seen that a belief in expertise was a defining component of other early twentieth-century efforts to respond to modernity by designing legal institutions, such as administrative agencies, whose effectiveness was identified with the specialized knowledge and mastery of the techniques of empirical observation and analysis of the humans who staffed them. But, in contrast, those who launched the Restatement project did not associate expertise with a grounding in the methods of modern social science. The attention of the Reporters and Advisors who produced Restatements of common law subjects was directed toward careful linguistic formulations of authoritative legal principles, with the hope that improved statements of black letter rules would provide an antidote to complexity and uncertainty. This methodological choice of the Restatement project's founders takes us closer to the center of the developing crisis in early twentieth-century American jurisprudence.

The Institute founders' emphasis on relieving doctrinal uncertainty, and their apparent commitment to Langdell's version of law as a science, tended to minimize the fact that their methodological approach to the relationship between principles and cases in common law subjects was quite different from that of Langdell. Langdell, as we have seen, had responded to what the ALI founders termed "uncertainty" through radical simplification, a process by which certain principles would be elevated as "fundamental," cases embodying those principles noted, and cases illustrating contradictory principles discarded as "wrong." The ALI founders' analysis of the "defects" of early twentieth-century American law suggested that they held a different view of the relationship of principles to cases. Their designation of the growing number of "novel legal questions" as one of the causes of uncertainty in the law indicated that they conceived the common law system as one constantly adopting itself to change, as distinguished from one working itself pure by refining its core principles. Their designation of legal questions as "novel" suggested that on some occasions they perceived the existing doctrinal structure of common law subjects as not providing easy guidance to the resolution of disputes.

This methodological orientation was shared by many of the early twentieth-century legal scholars who had continued Langdell's enterprise of mapping out the relationship between common law principles and cases. Rather than engaging in radical simplification of their subjects, scholars such as Samuel Williston, Arthur Corbin, and John Wigmore had begun to devote regular attention to new and "novel" cases in common law fields. Williston and Wigmore did not abandon a conception of law as a body of principles that could be scientifically arranged, but they came, in varying degrees, to see common law doctrines as relatively fluid and responsive to changing social conditions. Corbin especially proposed that the heart of legal analysis lay in the testing and modification of existing principles in "novel" fact situations. Under such analysis the jurist's task was a delicate accommodation of principles to new cases.[34]

Although this group of early twentieth-century legal scholars assumed that the content of legal doctrine was constantly changing, they did not conclude that common law principles were therefore meaningless apart from the contexts of cases. On the contrary, they believed that by carefully adapting the terminology employed in the articulation and classification of principles to take account of new fact situations and novel issues, the jurisprudential integrity of the system could be preserved. As Jeremiah Smith of Harvard put it in a 1912 essay on causation in the law of torts:

> [O]ur present purpose is . . . to bring out the most important elementary principles underlying . . . decisions. The decisions contain the rough material from which the leading principles are to be evolved; but a detailed statement of each separate decision is not equivalent to a state-

ment of the leading principles . . . [I]t is not desirable to attempt to add subsidiary rules sufficiently numerous and sufficiently minute to point out unerringly the exact decision in every conceivable specific case.[35]

Smith's methodology retained Langdell's conception of law as a collection of "important elementary principles underlying decisions" but at the same time defined cases as "the rough material from which the leading principles are to be evolved." The clear implication of Smith's approach was that cases were the source of principles rather than vice versa, and yet Smith declined to equate "a statement of each separate decision" with "a statement of the leading principles." This might require "numerous" and "minute" "subsidiary rules," which Smith found "not desirable" to formulate.

With Smith's comment in mind, it is possible to see how the proliferation of cases in the early twentieth century had created "uncertainty" for those aspiring to be legal scientists in the Langdellian tradition. An expert understanding of developments in common law subjects increasingly required a recognition of the proliferation of cases and how these new cases, themselves mirroring the increased "complexity" of modern American life, raised new issues. Consequently, judicial decisions in those cases were not always easily incorporated into an established body of legal principles or discarded as "wrong." Judicial decisions nonetheless continued to be thought of merely as illustrations of underlying principles. How did a system that subordinated cases to essentialist principles, but was confronted with an increasing number of new cases and issues, avoid the formation of a multiplicity of rules and doctrines that undermined its integrity and coherence?

Of a number of possible alternative responses to this "uncertainty," ranging from the elaborate codification of "numerous and minute subsidiary rules" to Langdell's radical simplification of governing principles, the founders of the Restatement project concluded that uncertainty and complexity could be best addressed by the formulation of a more precise and uniform legal terminology. The Restatements were to clarify the meaning and shore up the stature of common law principles by stating them as precisely and categorically as possible. Reporters were to survey common law fields, extract principles from cases, refine them by defining legal terms with great clarity, and state "the law as it is." They were to avoid textual commentary, case citation, and ambiguity: those matters were for accompanying treatises. Their black letter formulations were designed to be sufficiently general, but at the same time precise enough, to encompass cases as they evolved. No case was so novel that it could not be incorporated in the analytical and linguistic terminology of the Restatements.

It might appear from the above comments that the Restatement project's approach was intended to be a reincarnation of Langdell's methodology. One could hardly state principles as integral generalizations unless one read inconsistent cases out of the system, treating them as "wrong." But the founders of the Institute did not anticipate that the Reporters would be engaging in Langdellian radical simplification. Instead, they expected the Reporters to employ a methodology that would permit the ingenious application of properly formulated black letter principles to new cases as they appeared over time.

Several of the founders of the ALI were inspired by Wesley Hohfeld's description of "fundamental legal conceptions in judicial reasoning" in two articles in the *Yale Law Journal* between 1913 and 1917.[36] Hohfeld's concern in those essays was to rephrase some recurrent terms in the corpus of established common law rules to make them more precise and more certain, and thus more of a practical guide to deciding cases.

Hohfeld recast terms that consistently appeared in common law doctrines, such as "right," "duty," "privilege," or "immunity," as "fundamental legal conceptions" that transcended the doctrinal contexts in which they had appeared. In Hohfeld's usage the terms served as universal descriptions of the legal expectations or obligations of parties in disputes. Each time one of the terms was employed to describe the legal status of a party, it implicitly defined the correlative status of the other party. The attribution of a legal "right" to one party, for example, meant that the other party had a correlative legal "duty"; the attribution of a "privilege" created a correlative "no-right"; the attribution of an "immunity" created a correlative "disability." Hohfeld believed that if the terminology of legal doctrines emphasized these "fundamental legal conceptions" and their "jural correlatives," the practical significance of common law decisions and their predictive value would be increased.[37]

One can see how Hohfeld's approach would have excited those launching the Restatement project. Hohfeld was suggesting that if one used terms such as right, duty, privilege, or immunity in the statement of black letter common law rules, the use of that language would serve as a guide to the legal position of all actors in cases where the rules were applied to legal disputes. This would have the effect of endowing compilations of black letter principles with the kind of intelligibility and capacity for generalized application that the founders of the ALI sought to achieve in Restatement volumes.

By 1933 tentative drafts of several Restatement volumes had appeared and were being circulated among Advisors and the general membership of the American Law Institute. That year George R. Farnum, a member of the ALI, published an article in the *Boston University Law Review* entitled "Terminology and the American Law Institute." The purpose of Farnum's article was to associate the methodology employed in the Restatement project with that outlined by Hohfeld. Farnum asserted that "the categorical imperative of a useful process of administering justice" was the derivation of "a scientific terminology" for the statement of legal rules, identified Hohfeld's "comprehensive reexamination and restatement of certain fundamental legal conceptions implicated in judicial reasoning" as a model of such terminology, and characterized "[t]he work of the American Law Institute" in producing Restatements of common law subjects as creating an "arena in which the decisive battle over the practical value of Hohfeldian terminology seems to be in progress."[38]

Farnum was committed both to the central importance of precise legal terminology and to the promise and practical value of the Hohfeldian classification system. But his article, which surveyed the reception of Hohfeld's system among the Reporters working on Restatements, demonstrated the inability of those engaged in the Restatement project to come to agreement on any uniform system of terminology or classification for legal subjects.

Farnum began by noting that the ALI's first director, William Draper Lewis, had signaled that he found Hohfeld's terminological approach promising. When the first Tentative Draft of the Law of Property was submitted to the members of the ALI in a May 1929 meeting, Farnum reported that Lewis, in response to a question Farnum had put to him, stressed "the great importance of having a word, especially those which relate to fundamental legal conceptions, always used in the same sense throughout the entire Restatement."[39] Farnum added that the Reporter of the Restatement of Property, Professor Harry Bigelow, had stated at the same meeting that "we very definitely took Mr. Hohfeld's ideas as the basis upon which we framed . . . definitions."[40]

But this enthusiasm for Hohfeldian terminology, Farnum found, had not played itself out in the actual definitions of legal rules and principles in drafts of Restatements. Bigelow himself had conceded that the Hohfeldian terms sounded "more or less strangely" when used in statements of black letter rules, and Lewis, the Reporter for the Restatement of Business Associations, appeared in his draft to have confused the term "right" with another of Hohfeld's "fundamental legal conceptions," the term "power."[41] Those lapses were mild, however, compared to the terminology employed in other Restatements.

For example, Farnum reported that in the Restatement of Contracts, for which Samuel Williston had been the Reporter and Hohfeld's colleague Arthur Corbin had been Special Advisor, "Right and duty are constantly and consistently employed as correlatives throughout. Power and privilege are frequently used and invariably in the sense designed by Hohfeld. [But] [t]he concepts implied in immunity and disability are accurately expressed though seldom, if ever, labelled by these terms . . . [R]esort to the term . . . liability . . . has been avoided."[42]

Other Restatements were even less faithful to Hohfeld's terminology. Austin Scott, the Reporter for the Restatement of Trusts, was, according to Farnum, "reputed to hold Hohfeld's work in considerable esteem and to regard his terminology as excellently adapted to clear analytical thinking over legal distinctions." But when tentative drafts of the Restatement of Trusts appeared, Farnum noted that it was "difficult to detect any pronounced trace of Hohfeld's influence." The Hohfeldian terms "immunity and disability are not in evidence," Farnum reported, and "liability is used in a sense quite other than that accorded it by Hohfeldian prescription."[43]

Farnum felt that "the subject of Agency was one in which the Hohfeldian terminology could be utilized to particular advantage." But in reviewing several tentative drafts of the Restatement of the Law of Agency, written by two Reporters, Floyd Mechem and Warren Seavey, Farnum found in Seavey's drafts only "some approximation to Hohfeldian predilections," and in Mechem's drafts that "the influence of Hohfeld cannot be traced with any satisfactory certainty at all."[44]

As for the remaining Restatements that had been commissioned, the situation for Hohfeldian enthusiasts was even worse. Francis Bohlen, the Reporter for Torts, had "condemned and rejected . . . the terminological part of [Hohfeld's] technique."[45] Joseph Beale's Restatement of Conflict of Laws featured "crisp diction and succinct enunciation of the rules in the black letter sections," but "[t]he influence of Hohfeld is nowhere apparent."[46] And when Arthur Corbin, an enthusiastic supporter of Hohfeld's work,[47] ventured a tentative encapsulation of the Restatement project as the first Restatement volumes neared publication, he concluded that

> each jurist and scholar, however eminent, and however accustomed to the writing of law books, is continually surprised and frequently chagrined to find that his most cherished and careful generalizations, his dearest formulas, and the legal verbiage to which he has been most religiously wedded convey no clear and definite idea to the benighted minds of the judges, lawyers, and scholars who constitute the other members of the various committees and the Council of the Institute.[48]

The ALI's experiment with Hohfeldian terminology brought to the surface two defining characteristics of the Restatement project as the first volumes of Restatements of common law subjects began to appear in print in the early 1930s. First, the quixotic belief among the founders of the Restatement project that Hohfeld's highly schematic system of "fundamental legal conceptions" and their "jural correlatives" could be made the basis for synthesizing common law doctrines revealed how desperately they hoped to find a methodological approach that would invest those doctrines, restated as black letter principles, with the regularity and predictability that could redress "uncertainty" and surmount "complexity." Second, as Farnum's report had unwittingly demonstrated, neither the Hohfeldian system nor any other ubiquitous terminological classification could achieve that goal. Precise, uniform statements of comprehensive black letter principles not only threatened to become rapidly obsolete as cases with novel legal issues proliferated, but they seemed difficult to achieve in the first place, given the variety and ambiguity of language.

As the Restatement volumes appeared, the inability of authors to arrive at any uniform terminology to describe the general principles of common law subjects had the effect of undermining the essentialist nature of those principles. The black letter summaries offered in Restatements seemed to be, at bottom, compilations of common law decisions, gathered by a handful of experts and reflecting the shared terminology and collective prose of those experts. The erudition displayed in Restatement volumes may have served to strengthen the expertise-based authority of their authors. But the Restatement format did not serve to strengthen the essentialist authority of legal principles. Instead, it served to undermine the separation between the authoritative status of law and the authoritative status of legal savants as interpreters of law, on which orthodox early twentieth-century American jurisprudence had insisted. The stage was thus set for a line of critical commentary of Restatement volumes that denied the intelligibility of any effort to separate "law" from its authoritative human interpreters.

When the first published Restatement, that of Contracts, appeared in 1932, it became apparent that the Institute had made a decision to limit the substance of the Restatements to black letter paragraphs, omitting any commentary. This decision was the result of an ongoing debate within the ALI about the purpose and function of the Restatements and their relation to other legal authorities.

The founders of the Restatement project had originally anticipated that the Restatement volumes on common law subjects would likely be accompanied by treatises on those subjects, with the treatises providing discussions of contested points, citations of authorities, and justifications for the substantive positions endorsed in black letter paragraphs. As the Restatements evolved, this goal was abandoned. Some Reporters, such as Beale on Conflict of Laws,

Williston on Contracts, and Bohlen on Torts, had already written treatises on their subjects and felt that further production of treatise volumes would be superfluous. They did produce running commentaries, and for most of the gestation period of the first Restatements it was anticipated that those commentaries, which would include interventions by Advisors and other interested persons and would be accompanied by citations to cases, would be published along with the black letter summaries. But the leadership of the Institute eventually decided not to publish commentaries along with the Restatements, citing the expense and the lack of interest by a majority of the ALI's members.[49] When the final drafts of Restatements appeared in published form, they contained no citations; black letter paragraphs were accompanied primarily by illustrations of a particular legal rule.

The choice of a black-letter-only form for the Restatements had a particularly unfortunate interaction with developments in the legal academy taking place at the same time. Between 1923 and 1930 jurisprudential undercurrents surfaced at elite law schools that were eventually to result in the self-conscious promulgation, by Karl Llewellyn and Jerome Frank, of a school of "Realistic" jurisprudence and the identification of certain scholars as "Realists."[50] As the Realist movement gained momentum in the early 1930s, its participants defined one of their common starting jurisprudential premises as skepticism about the intelligibility of what Llewellyn called "traditional prescriptive rules."[51] A belief that "the announced rules are the paramount thing in the law," Frank asserted in his influential 1930 book, *Law and the Modern Mind,* only fostered "the phantasy of a perfect, consistent, legal uniformity."[52]

When academics who had embraced Realism were confronted with the ALI's Restatements, most concluded that in attempting to reframe the common law to keep pace with modern life, the Institute had only demonstrated the futility of centering that effort on black letter rules. This conclusion encouraged Realist scholars to use the appearance of the Restatements to attack the purportedly universalistic nature of legal rules as entities having some essential meaning independent of the contexts in which they appeared.

In 1937, in a review of the Restatement of Property in the *Illinois Law Review,* Myers McDougal of Yale Law School surveyed a number of earlier critical reviews of Restatement volumes and found some common features. McDougal's summary provides a demonstration of how far some legal theorists in the 1930s had moved from Hohfeld's belief that "fundamental legal conceptions" recurrently occurred in common law cases. McDougal found certain "commonplace criticisms" of the Restatements:

Some reviewers have pointed to naivete in fundamental assumptions—assumptions that certainty is obtainable and obtainable by high abstractions, that certainty is more important than flexibility, that "substantive law" is all-comprehensive, . . . that the defects of "the law" can be cured by restating it as it is . . . [O]thers have deplored the omission of historical, economic, and sociological backgrounds . . . a failure to study the social consequences of institutions and doctrines, the omission of supporting authorities, reasoned discussion, and contrast of conflicting opinion, the use of "doctrinal" rather then "factual" classifications.[53]

McDougal added that the Restatement of Property's assumption "that the judicial handling of property problems in contemporary America can be made more predictable by an authoritative canonization and rationalization of ancient feudal-conditioned concepts and doctrines" was "little short of fantastic."[54]

McDougal's summary of the criticism leveled at early Restatement volumes[55] revealed three common critical themes. One was "naivete in fundamental assumptions" about the nature of law, particularly the assumption that legal doctrines were abstractions, as distinguished from being inextricably related to the facts of discrete cases. A second was the failure of the Restatements to place legal doctrines in any kind of social context, whether "historical, economic, [or] sociological." A third was the decision of the drafters of the Restatement simply to state the black letter law without "supporting authorities, reasoned discussion, [or] contrast of conflicting opinion."

These deficiencies of the Restatements led their Realist critics to conclude that the entire project was a demonstration of the futility of forestalling uncertainty through a uniform terminology dedicated to the authoritative promulgation of universal legal principles. In drawing this conclusion they were not simply suggesting that the methodological apparatus of the Restatement project was flawed. They were also suggesting that the starting jurisprudential assumptions of those engaged in the Restatement project were wrongheaded. A search for essentialist common law principles, no matter how expertly conducted, would be fruitless because "law" was nothing but the aggregate of legal decisions made by human officials in a changing social context.

In review after review of the early Restatements critics demonstrated their disaffinity with the jurisprudential assumptions guiding the ALI's project. In one of the earliest reviews, Charles Clark, in the course of his assessment of the Restatement of Contracts, called the Institute's "general purpose of clarification and simplification" of common law subjects "certainly fallacious." "Our civilization," Clark claimed, "is complex and our law, if it is to keep abreast of business and social life, cannot be simple." Moreover, the black letter form of the Restatements was equally fallacious, "an unreality."

"[W]ithout interpretation, or background against which meaning can be discovered," Clark suggested, "the black letter statements are not understandable."[56]

Leon Green, in his review of the Restatement of Torts, juxtaposed the Institute's black letter approach against what he found to be a far more accurate description of torts cases, a "process" in which the procedural posture of a case, its factual elements, its social context, the inclinations of the judge who decided it, and the doctrinal options available to advocates and to the court combined to produce decisions. If classification was to take place in the law of torts, Green believed, it should be along "functional" lines, reflecting the various interests and entities involved in a line of cases rather than being based on the kind of "overelaborated [doctrinal] generalizations" that characterized the Torts Restatement.[57]

Green's "functional" approach had explicitly incorporated some of the methodology of early twentieth-century empirical social science. Ernest Lorenzen took a similar approach in his 1935 review of the Restatement of Conflicts. Lorenzen began by attacking "the old rationalistic absolutist conception of law" on which Joseph Beale's Conflicts Restatement was premised. Beale had described the common law as "a philosophical system, a body of scientific principle which has been adopted in each of the common law jurisdictions." In making decisions, Beale asserted, common law courts were "attempting to apply this general body of principles" in their respective jurisdictions. Sometimes they "misconceived it and misstated it," which resulted in "errors," producing "local peculiarit[ies]." Nonetheless, "the general scientific law remains unchanged in spite of these errors."[58]

Lorenzen characterized Beale's conception of law as a science as "now generally discredited." He quoted with approval an earlier attack on Beale's "scientific" approach to conflicts by Walter Wheeler Cook. Cook had described "such writers" of the Bealian persuasion as beginning their approach by "establishing to their own satisfaction the general or essential nature of law and legal rights." This led them "to certain general or fundamental principles, supposed to flow from the nature of law or legal rights as thus established." The fundamental principles produced ancillary rules, which enabled jurists to reach the conclusion that "for every situation dealt with in the conflict of laws there is always some one and only one 'law' which has 'jurisdiction.'"[59]

In Lorenzen's view this approach reversed the logical order in which legal issues ought to be examined. He preferred to look at the context of a particular issue, weigh the competing interests at stake, and give the judge discretion to make a decision that seemed to further the administration of justice. In his view the subject of conflict of laws should be properly seen not as a collection of rigid rules or all-encompassing principles but as a collection of particular decisions in which the choice of applying the laws of one state or another was fairly weighed by human actors. His image of "science" in conflicts law was contextual rather than conceptualistic, behavioral rather than taxonomic.

In the same year that Lorenzen's review appeared, Edward Robinson, a psychologist who had recently joined the Yale law faculty, argued that the entire Restatement project was based on an erroneous notion of what "law" was. Robinson dismissed the Restatements' "general philosophy" as "founded upon the belief that too much truth about the law is disastrously confusing." The Restatement volumes, Robinson claimed, amounted to "an authoritative suppression of the facts rather than . . . better education of the public and the bar as to the actual psychological and sociological nature of the law."[60] The "abstract propositions" announced in the Restatement volumes, Robinson felt, made the task of learning law "hideously difficult." He concluded that "it would be easier and more satisfactory to learn law by random sampling of the cases with all their contradictions and complexities" than by reading the black letter paragraphs in the Restatements.[61]

Robinson's last conclusion was particularly provocative to those who had invested in the Restatement project, given their association of the carefully wrought black letter prose of Restatement paragraphs with the promotion of a scientific approach to common law subjects. "The notion that one can learn law better by random examination of the cases than by reading the propositions in the Restatement," Dean Herbert Goodrich of the University of Pennsylvania Law School, a member of the ALI Council, said of Robinson's suggestion, "will seem fantastic to lawyers."[62]

After observing the exchange between Robinson and Goodrich, Yale law professor Thurman Arnold concluded that the gap between Realists and those who had invested in the Restatement project was a product of their differing conceptions of law as a science. Arnold asserted that the most exciting prospects for future research about law and legal institutions lay in a "science about law," as distinguished from a "science of law."[63] By a "science about law" Arnold meant scholarship exhibiting an "objective or naturalistic" perspective on the legal profession. This included "observations on the psychology of [legal] institutions," evaluated "from the standards of diagnosis of a complicated mental case."[64]

Arnold was seeking to distinguish the version of science that he felt had been codified in the Restatement project from a science that would locate legal institutions in their external culture, draw upon the techniques of the behavioral sciences, and employ the perspective of the dispassionate "observer," the "naturalist." One can get a sense of Arnold's distinction between a "science of law" and a "science about law" by looking at two analogies he employed in elaborating it.

In the first analogy Arnold likened the activities of those who prepared the Restatements to priests interpreting the scriptures. "The idea behind religious dialectic," he said, "was to dig truths out of the Bible by the light of pure reason, and it was sustained by the faith that the more truths that were dug out, classified and stored away, the less doubt there would be in the world, and the clearer religion would become."[65] In the analogy persons who had made an investment in an intellectual system (the Bible as a fountain of reason and truth) were confronted with the problem of complexity in the application of the system. They responded not by challenging the premises of the system but by "restating" them, believing that in the process they were achieving clarity and simplicity. But religious dogma, far from being made clearer by the process, was undermined as a source of authority.

What was required, Arnold felt, was a reorientation of first premises, which he felt could be produced by a science about law. Here Arnold propounded his second analogy. Replacing a science of law with a science about law was like "[t]he so-called Copernican revolution," which "had a significance in human culture far beyond the specific astronomical discovery. For the first time, in ceasing to think of the earth as the center of the universe, men began to look at it from the outside. Amazing advances in man's control over his physical environment followed that change of attitude. Discoveries were made which would have been impossible for men bound by fetters of earlier preconceptions."[66] Arnold then made the parallel to early twentieth-century developments in jurisprudence explicit:

> Today there is beginning to dawn a similar change in attitude towards creeds, faiths, philosophies and law. Looked at from within, law is the center of an independent universe with economics the center of a coordinate universe. Looked at from outside, we can see what makes the wheels go round and catch a vision of how we can exercise control not only of the physical environment but of the mental and spiritual environment. When men begin to examine philosophies and principles as they examine atoms and electrons, the road to discovery of the means of social control is open.[67]

At a surface level, Arnold's analogies were intended to suggest that a "science of law" simply refined and restated a set of unexamined, insular, professional premises, whereas a "science about law" looked at that set of premises "from [the] outside," with a view to seeing how orthodox jurisprudence was rooted in its contemporary environment. At a deeper level, Arnold's analogies revealed a consciousness that the demands of modernity required, and were producing, human efforts to control the course of changing external events and to shape the future through a purposive use of law. As part of this process, modernity had redirected the focus of law as a science, resulting in the collapse of Langdellian radical simplification, or the restatement of essentialist common law principles by experts, as useful scientific methodologies for lawyers, legal scholars, or judges. Further, modernity, with its emphasis on purposive legal decisionmaking by human officials in changing social contexts, had made the traditional separation of the authority of legal sources from the authority of their interpreters an unintelligible starting point for legal science.

In the minds of their Realist critics, the founders of the Institute had shown a dim awareness of the truth of the modern legal universe. They had sought to combat uncertainty and complexity, but the forces of modernity had created a cultural landscape that was inherently complex and uncertain. In such a landscape legal decisions were bound to be inconsistent and even random; legal doctrines were fated to be constantly under stress. The proper response was to see such a landscape as it "was," and ask how legal institutions should respond to it. That question was a pragmatic, instrumentalist, contingent one. But if based on a properly acquired understanding of "reality," it could result in rational answers.

For Realists the ALI in its Restatement project had intuited the right observations about the American legal system in the early twentieth century: the system was getting more complex and more uncertain. But those engaged with the Restatement project had made a hopelessly wrongheaded response. Instead of embracing the truths of complexity and uncertainty, they had ended up attempting to suppress them in a perfected version of Langdellian legal science. The result was a series of massive Restatements containing collections of outdated, hopelessly abstract dogma.

The launching of the American Law Institute's Restatement project was a pivotal episode in the history of early twentieth-century American jurisprudence. It marked the decisive abandonment of the distinction between sources of law and authoritative interpreters of law, with a reframing of the definition of law as science serving as the vehicle for that change. The reception of the Restatements by academic critics in the 1930s demonstrated that, even in modified form, the conception of law as a science established by Langdell and his contemporaries could no longer furnish an adequate description of the contemporary American legal universe.

In the critical responses to the first generation of Restatements of common law subjects the factors of uncertainty and complexity in law were transformed from "defects," as they had been identified by the founders of the Restatement project, to, if not "virtues," at least "realities." In that transformation law ceased to be thought of as an entity that existed apart from its immediate social context to one that necessarily reflected that context, and was thus constantly changing. The science of law was also transformed, from an exercise in organizing and clarifying preexisting principles to an exercise in observing and making sense of the behavior of humans who made legal decisions in an uncertain and complex modern world.

Treating the Restatement project within the parameters of a conventional narrative of the triumph of Realism over Formalism is likely to produce a distorted sense of the project's historical significance. The Restatement project was not "formalist" in the orthodox, Langdellian sense; it was an effort to reframe Langdellian legal science, the radical simplification of governing principles, in an improved version of legal terminology and analysis that would take into account the constantly changing variety and novelty of common law cases in modern America. Those who launched the project assumed that if a crisis in early twentieth-century jurisprudence existed, it had been precipitated by a proliferation of cases and an attendant difficulty in discerning and applying preexisting principles. They did not assume that the crisis stemmed from the unintelligibility of legal principles as essentialist entities that were independent of the context of their application.

The Realists, in contrast, made that assumption. Their version of legal science abandoned taxonomy and terminological refinements because they believed that the legal concepts that the Restatement project sought to reframe and to clarify were meaningless abstractions when divorced from the actual judicial decisions in which they were invoked. This meant that for Realists the authority of legal principles could not be separated from the authority of those who had the power to apply them. It did not mean, however, that law could not be studied scientifically. The techniques of the twentieth-century social sciences, especially psychology, sociology, and economics, could be expected to yield a better understanding of the context of judicial decisions, and possibly a new set of governing principles of legal decisionmaking, principles based on scientific generalizations about human behavior and the tendencies of institutions wielding power in a modern society.

The Realists' legal science was every bit as driven by their conceptions of scientific truth as the legal science of Langdell or the Restatement founders. But conventional narratives of the "Formalist/Realist debate" in early twentieth-century jurisprudence have privileged the Realists' behavioralist theories of law and judging. Thus, the Realists' descriptions of themselves as scientific observers of law as an exercise in policymaking in discrete contexts by officials holding positions of legal authority have been taken to be the natural responses of persons who had come to understand what law "really" is. Privileging the Realists' conceptions of scientific truth makes the "triumph" of Realism over Formalism inevitable. In a legal universe in which law is taken to be synonymous with the decisions of human officials exercising power, a Formalist-inspired distinction between the sources and the authoritative interpreters of law seems otherworldly, whereas the Realist equation of "law" with human power-wielding seems the equivalent of truth. The taxonomic science of Formalists becomes dogma; the behavioralist science of the Realists becomes a guide to legal decisionmaking.

This chapter has suggested that by describing early twentieth-century American jurisprudence as a struggle between adherents of Formalism and Realism, conventional narratives have misunderstood the relationship of the ALI's Restatement project to that "debate," and consequently misunderstood the jurisprudential crisis to which the Restatement project was a response. The crisis was precipitated by the awkward interaction of a long-established jurisprudential distinction between the sources of legal authority and the authority of legal interpreters with pressures on the American legal system generated by the advent of modernity. Both the founders of the ALI and the Realists recognized those pressures, symbolized by a proliferation of legal decisions, the apparent surfacing of numerous cases raising "new" and "novel" issues, and the "uncertainty" and "complexity" these developments produced for a system whose principal decisionmaking mechanism consisted of judicial applications of common law rules to cases.

Those who invested in the Restatement project were not simply aware that the "uncertainty" and "complexity" of judicial decisionmaking in modern America might produce the application of diverse and contradictory rules to cases. They were also aware that the proliferation of such rules might undermine the belief that authoritative legal principles were essentialist entities whose authority any properly learned judge was bound to recognize. A meaningful separation of the essentialist authority of legal principles from the expert-based authority of their official interpreters could only be maintained if judges knew the precise meaning of the principles they applied in their decisions. Thus, the ALI devoted its efforts to terminological restatements of common law principles in order to increase the potential breadth of their applicability. The more judges understood the essential and fundamental nature of such principles, the founders of the ALI assumed, the more likely they were to apply them widely. This would not only help solve the problem of proliferating contradictory rules, it would buttress the separation between the authority of principles and the authority of interpreters because the expansion of courts, cases, and judicial decisions produced by modernity would not result in an expansion of authoritative principles.

The taxonomic and terminological refinements of the Restatements were thus efforts to make Langdell's radical simplification of essentialist legal principles more scientific. The Realists started from the same set of observations about the impact of modernity on the American legal system, and from the same perceptions of increased jurisprudential "uncertainty" and "complexity." But the model of legal science that framed their observations of the proliferation of cases, decisions, and judicially imposed rules was radically different from that of the ALI founders. It was a model that centered on the human, institutional, and social contexts of judicial decisions rather than on essentialist legal principles. The behavioralist emphasis of the model rejected any meaningful separation between the rules applied to cases and the process by which judges applied those rules. In the Realists' model of legal science the context of legal rules—the discrete facts of a case, its social implications, the temperament and ideology of the judge who decided it, the institutional patterns of the jurisdiction in which it was decided—were so determinative of their content that it was meaningless to speak of rules or principles as essentialist abstractions.

Although the Realist critics of the Restatements were convinced of the futility of shoring up essentialist legal principles through taxonomic and terminological refinements, they were relatively vague about their own projects in a "science about law," contenting themselves with proposals for "observations on the psychology of legal institutions." But the principal impact of their critique of the Restatements was not to launch a series of behavioralist-inspired studies of law. It was to highlight the very crisis in the nature of legal authority to which the Restatement project had sought to respond, and to suggest that a behavioralist theory of legal decisionmaking revealed the true reason that crisis had surfaced. The crisis had surfaced because legal decisionmaking had never consisted of the disinterested application of essentialist legal principles, by judges who grasped the fundamental nature of those principles, to cases necessarily governed by them. It had always consisted of discretionary choices by judges to apply one existing rule or another or to fashion a new rule, choices driven by the contexts, broadly defined, of cases. A behavioralist model of judging, properly understood, obliterated the distinction between the authority of legal sources and the authority of their interpreters. "Law" as a collection of essentialist principles was illusory; law as a collection of context-driven decisions by persons holding official authority was "real."

If we posit the surfacing of a crisis in American jurisprudence in the period between the World Wars and center it on the intelligibility of an established distinction between the sources of law and its authoritative interpreters, we will be in a better position to understand the nature of the "constitutional revolution" that has been described as taking place in the same time period.

For it will become apparent that the crisis that was brought to the surface in common law jurisprudence by the launching of the Restatement project also surfaced in a debate about constitutional interpretation, centering on the nature and legitimacy of judicially created changes in the "meaning" of the Constitution, and on the Constitution's capacity to "adapt" to changing social conditions. That debate was to have a significant impact on the constitutional decisions that have been prominently featured in the conventional account's Court-packing tale.

7

The Constitutional Revolution as a Crisis in Adaptivity

In the conventional account of early twentieth-century constitutional history the center of the "constitutional revolution" of the New Deal period lies in doctrinal changes in the constitutional jurisprudence of political economy cases. The most celebrated of those changes occurred in two police power due process cases, *Morehead v. New York ex rel. Tipaldo* and *West Coast Hotel v. Parrish,* in which Court majorities, in decisions sandwiched around the introduction of the Court-packing plan in February 1937, struck down[1] and then sustained[2] state statutes imposing minimum wage levels: the switch in time that saved nine. But a number of other political economy cases have been singled out in the "constitutional revolution" narrative. Some of those cases have been decision sequences that preceded and followed the introduction of the plan, such as the contrastingly narrow and broad interpretations of the federal government's power to impose collective bargaining on industries engaged in interstate commerce advanced in *Carter v. Carter Coal* (1936)[3] and *National Labor Relations Board v. Jones & Laughlin Steel Corp.* (April 1937),[4] or the similarly contrasting interpretations of the federal commerce and general welfare powers advanced in *Railroad Retirement Board v. Alton Railway Co.* (1935)[5] or *United States v. Butler* (1936)[6] and the paired decisions, *Stewart Machine Co. v. Davis*[7] and *Helvering v. Davis* (May 1937)[8].

Other sequences of political economy cases, stretching over a longer time frame, have been cited as evidence of a transformation in the Court's attitude toward governmental regulation of economic affairs during the period of the New Deal. Examples have been drawn from decisions in Commerce Clause cases, such as the sequence extending from *Schechter Poultry Corp. v. United States* (1935)[9] and *Carter Coal* to *United States v. Darby* (1941)[10] and *Wickard v. Filburn* (1942),[11] in which the Court virtually abandoned the idea of federalism limitations on congressional legislation based on the commerce power. They have also been drawn from contrasting decisions in due process

198

cases, such as *Adkins v. Children's Hospital* (1923)[12] and *West Coast Hotel v. Parrish* (1937), where a majority of the Court replaced its aggressive scrutiny of federal or state minimum wage legislation with a deferential posture. Finally, the Court's 1934 Contracts Clause decision, *Home Building & Loan Association v. Blaisdell,*[13] has been singled out because that decision, permitting a state to relax obligations imposed by preexisting home mortgages in the face of a stipulated economic "emergency," ran squarely counter to previous interpretations of the Contracts Clause as an absolute bar to legislation that attempted to modify previous contractual obligations. The above decisions have been offered as evidence that the three orthodox constitutional barriers to federal or state economic regulation—the Commerce, Due Process, and Contracts Clauses—had been dismantled by the Court between the early 1930s and the early 1940s. As one version of the conventional account puts it, those decisions signaled "a revolution in jurisprudence that ended, apparently forever, the reign of laissez-faire and the arrival of the Leviathan State."[14]

Of all the changes in constitutional jurisprudence that occurred in the early twentieth century, those affecting doctrines in Contracts, Due Process, and Commerce Clause cases have been the ones most easily associated with the hypothesis that the New Deal was a political force that the Supreme Court needed to reckon with. The changes in the Court's posture toward political economy cases between the mid-1930s and the mid-1940s, when viewed in the context of a plan to pack the Court by an administration with a broad popular mandate, have helped enhance the appeal of the Court-packing thesis.

Moreover, only an eccentric student of Contract, Commerce, and Due Process Clause decisions between 1933 and 1943 would deny that the Court significantly altered its doctrinal posture in those areas. And because the alteration of the Court's posture ushered in a far more extensive role for the federal and state governments as regulators of economic activity or redistributors of economic benefits, the period, when contrasted with the time spans between 1923 and 1933 or 1943 and 1953, can be seen as a "revolutionary" interval, at least in the twentieth-century constitutional jurisprudence of political economy cases. In attempting to explain why the years between 1933 and 1943 produced revolutionary doctrinal changes, historians have looked for suggestive features in the external context of the Court's decisions, and there, between 1933 and 1937, lie the advent of the New Deal, the Court's invalidation of some early New Deal legislation, Roosevelt's electoral mandate in 1936, and the introduction of the Court-packing plan.

The durability of the conventional claim that the Court-packing crisis precipitated a constitutional revolution thus rests in part on its ability to provide an externally based explanation for sudden jurisprudential change in a particular time interval. But the conventional explanation's success has also been dependent on the naturalness and uncontroversiality of its starting assumptions about politics, judging, and constitutional interpretation.

The conventional explanation has been predicated on a particular view of the role of judges as constitutional interpreters. That view characterizes judges, in interpreting the Constitution, as acting in a fashion similar to political actors making decisions about questions of public policy. Like those actors, judges have ideological agendas and are mindful of their constituents, and, like those actors, their ideological inclinations and their awareness of constituent pressures affect their decisionmaking. The view also assumes that the political inclinations and goals of judges have a decisive effect on constitutional law because it rejects, as antiquated or misguided, any conception of judges as constitutional interpreters and that treats the authority of the Constitution's text as separate from the authority of those given the power to interpret it. Since the meaning of the Constitution is synonymous with the current interpretations of its provisions by judges, and those interpretations are affected by political events and political pressures, the hypothesis that the Supreme Court changed its constitutional political economy jurisprudence in response to pressure placed on it by the Roosevelt administration, in the form of the Court-packing plan, appears eminently plausible.

If one assumes that most mid and late twentieth-century constitutional scholars have subscribed to a behavioralist view of judges as constitutional interpreters, one can see how the conventional explanation of the constitutional revolution has been so durable a feature of early twentieth-century constitutional history. With 1937, the fulcrum of constitutional change, established as a jurisprudential watershed, early twentieth-century constitutional history can be arranged into segments featuring an "older," eventually discarded, line of cases and their "new," "revolutionary" successors. The history can even be seen as a morality play, in which the revolution stimulated by the Court-packing crisis becomes the basis of a more enlightened judicial approach to legislation increasing the role of government as a regulator of economic affairs or a redistributor of economic benefits.

To be sure, those adhering to a behavioralist explanation of judicially induced changes in constitutional law have had to confront a number of statements made by early twentieth-century justices in which they described their function in constitutional interpretation as discerning existing constitutional principles and applying them to new cases. Several such statements, as well as comments in which early twentieth-century judges declared that their role as interpretive guardians of constitutional principles was utterly inconsistent with "lawmaking" in the legislative sense, have been quoted in earlier chapters.

But a behavioralist theory of judging does not need to take such statements very seriously. The behavioral sciences have provided explanations for posited tendencies on the part of humans to engage in disingenuous, obfuscatory, or self-deluding justifications for their actions. With those explanations in place, one can characterize judges as having strong incentives to disclaim any ideological component in their interpretations. Sharp distinctions between judicial interpretations of the Constitution and ordinary forms of policymaking by other public officials serve to forestall inquiries into the limited political accountability of unelected judges with life tenure. They also serve to reinforce those elements of judicial authority that are associated with the impartiality and disinterestedness of the office of judge. Thus, judges might well avoid equating their role as constitutional interpreters with the policymaking roles of other public officials even if they believed that in interpreting the Constitution they were performing as a species of political actors.

The behavioralist grounding of the Court-packing thesis has helped its proponents dismiss a large sample of contemporary evidence contradicting its conclusions as the self-serving, defensive, or misguided statements of judges who could not be expected to confess the true reasons for their participation in a constitutional revolution. This particular weapon of those invested in the Court-packing tale has enabled them to treat their largely undocumented conjectures about judicial motivation as having even greater weight, as explanations for constitutional change, than the contrary testimony of judges themselves. Behavioralist conceptions of judging lend credibility to the conjectures, and at the same time undermine the credibility of the judicial statements. Small wonder why, in a late twentieth-century climate in which behavioralist theories of judging have been widely held, the Court-packing thesis has remained resonant.

But in the midst of all this success a few problems have recently surfaced for the Court-packing thesis in its area of greatest intuitive applicability, political economy cases. First, the explanation's attempt to posit a causal link between the Court-packing crisis and specific "revolutionary" decisions has encountered some severe difficulties. One of the decisions most commonly identified as exhibiting a major change in the analysis of police power/due process cases, *West Coast Hotel v. Parrish,* was decided before the Court-packing plan was introduced, even though it was handed down after the plan's announcement. Two others mentioned as signals of an altered judicial attitude toward orthodox constitutional barriers to legislation regulating economic affairs, *Home Building & Loan Association v. Blaisdell* and the 1934 decision in *Nebbia v. New York,*[15] came down three years before the plan, and two years before another event featured prominently in the conventional explanation, Roosevelt's landslide victory in the 1936 presidential election, which allegedly encouraged him to attack the Court.[16] The most "revolutionary" of the Court's new line of political economy cases, the decisions in which the Court effectively abandoned any constitutional scrutiny of congressional regulation of the economy under the commerce power, did not surface until four years after the Court-packing episode.[17] When those decisions were handed down, the composition of the Court bore almost no resemblance to its composition in the 1936 Term.[18]

In addition to these burdens, the conventional explanation has been shown to rest on an exceptionally thin, and possibly misleading, doctrinal base of Supreme Court decisions. Since timing is so important to the conventional explanation, it has been helpful for its proponents to identify a "switch" in the Court's constitutional jurisprudence that can be placed in the crucial time interval between February 1937, when the plan was announced, and June 1937, when the Court's 1936 Term ended.[19] Particularly helpful to the conventional explanation has been the fact that the Court's personnel remained constant during the sequences of pre- and post-Court-packing decisions—*Tipaldo/Parrish, Carter Coal/Jones & Laughlin, Alton* and *Butler/* Social Security cases—so that the only significant external developments affecting the Court between those pairs of decisions were the 1936 presidential election and the subsequent introduction of the Court-packing plan. The change in the outcome in the *Tipaldo/Parrish* sequence has been described as particularly suggestive, since it was produced by Justice Roberts' having voted with the majority in both cases.[20]

Unfortunately, the case law support for the "switch in time that saved nine" consists only of the above paired cases. This raises difficulties because the constitutional revolution associated with the New Deal and the Court-packing crisis has been taken to be an exceptional occurrence in American constitutional history, qualitatively different from the general tendency of the Supreme Court's constitutional jurisprudence to change with time. If the time frame is broadened, adherents of the Court-packing thesis are able to contrast a fairly large sample of pre-1937 decisions with several post-1937 decisions, illustrating changes in constitutional law doctrines. But that sort of exercise can be undertaken, if a sufficient time interval is employed, for any period in the Court's history.

The relative lack of decisional support for the proposition that the Court suddenly and dramatically altered its constitutional jurisprudence in the wake of the Court-packing crisis, coupled with the general tendency of the Court's constitutional law decisions to change with time, brings us back to the question of why contemporaries in the late 1930s and early 1940s thought that they were witnessing a constitutional revolution at all. If it is unlikely that the changes in the Court's constitutional political economy jurisprudence were short-term accommodations to external political pressures, and if changes in constitutional law doctrines have been habitual in the history of the Court, why did observers attach special significance to changes in the late 1930s and early 1940s? And was their perception that the changes were truly revolutionary accurate?

A recent work by Barry Cushman concludes that a constitutional revolution in the Court's political economy cases did take place in the time interval between 1933 and 1943, but argues that the revolution had little to do with the Court-packing crisis. After Cushman's critique, the Court-packing thesis appears discredited, and the intellectual groundings for revolutionary changes in the Court's political economy jurisprudence can be better appreciated. But the timing of the revolution remains to be fully explained.

Cushman argues that the constitutional revolution in political economy cases that took place between 1933 and 1943 was the culmination of a gradual disintegration, in place since the 1920s, of the integrity of the orthodox judicial doctrines and formulas governing those cases. Pivotal for Cushman's account is the collapse of the established distinction between "private" and "public" spheres of economic activity in police power cases. The unraveling of that distinction in the 1934 case of *Nebbia v. New York,* Cushman suggests, reconfigured orthodox police power analysis and had important secondary effects on the doctrinal formulas employed in minimum wage cases, cases involving the organization of labor, and Commerce Clause cases. When a new set of justices, having less of an investment in the orthodox early twentieth-century constitutional jurisprudence of political economy cases, came on the Court in the late 1930s and early 1940s, they were relatively free to fashion a new set of doctrinal approaches.[21]

Along the way Cushman rejects external explanations for alterations in the Court's doctrinal changes, including the linchpin of the Court-packing thesis, Justice Owen Roberts's "switch" in the *Tipaldo/Parrish* sequence. After examining internal Court correspondence and the briefs and arguments in *Tipaldo* and *Parrish,* Cushman concludes that Roberts voted with the majority in *Tipaldo* only out of deference to the weight of *Adkins* as an established precedent, and would have been prepared to vote the other way had the Court been asked to flatly overrule *Adkins.*[22] Although Cushman relies on some documents written after the fact, and concedes that his reconstruction of Roberts's motivation is conjectural, his alternative reading of the *Tipaldo/Parrish* sequence has the effect of undermining the conventional explanation's strongest causal claim.[23]

Cushman's alternative explanation for the constitutional revolution in political economy cases threatens the very center of the conventional account of early twentieth-century constitutional history. If one assumes that constitutional change in the years between 1933 and 1943 was the result of doctrinal disintegration and reformulation, that change could have taken place regardless of whether the Court was paying attention to external political developments or not. In Cushman's account the causal significance of the Court-packing plan virtually disappears, and the causal significance of the New Deal begins to recede. But the "constitutional revolution," with its particular time interval, remains. Cushman is more concerned with demonstrating its doctrinal origins than with explaining why it occurred when it did.

For example, Cushman suggests that the appointment to the Court between 1930 and 1932 of three new justices, noticeably younger than the men they replaced, may have hastened the collapse of the orthodox constitutional jurisprudence of political economy.[24] But he does not speculate as to why this particular group of justices should have been implicitly confident of their ability to implement qualitatively significant doctrinal change. Nor does he explore why some holdover justices on the Court in the 1930s and early 1940s, who resisted changes in the constitutional jurisprudence of political economy cases, described those changes as not only doctrinally unsound but as amounting to radical assaults on their understanding of how the Constitution should be interpreted.

My concern in this chapter is with those last two sets of questions. I am interested in the constitutional revolution of the 1930s and 1940s as an interpretive revolution, one centering on what I am calling a crisis in the meaning of constitutional adaptivity. As in preceding chapters, the time frame of my explorations will extend both backward and forward from the 1930s. As in Chapter 6, I will be investigating changes in the perceived meaning of authoritative sources of law, in this instance the Constitution itself. My focus again will be on academic commentary, the rhetoric of judicial opinions, and their interrelationship. My ultimate goal is to explain why the Court's approach to constitutional political economy cases could have fairly been described by contemporaries in the early 1940s as revolutionary.

❧

Reconstruction of the interpretive universe in which early twentieth-century constitutional political economy cases were considered requires attention to a lost attitude toward constitutional interpretation itself. That attitude toward interpretation, and the methodologies accompanying it, had been almost entirely abandoned by the Supreme Court by the early 1940s. This very abandonment has made the attitude and methodologies more difficult to reconstruct. As a result mid and late twentieth-century commentators have paid relatively scant attention to the rhetorical arguments in political economy cases identified with the constitutional revolution, especially the rhetoric of justices opposing doctrinal change. If one returns to that rhetoric, however, one finds the lost attitude intact.

The attitude can be captured in a jurisprudential proposition animating much of the resistance to New Deal legislative experimentation: the Constitution was not designed to change with time. Its principles were universal, and thus its "meaning" at a generalized level was fixed. Its structure and language were not altered by events but accommodated events. Events were seen as precipitating restatements of fundamental constitutional principles.

The constitutional revolution that took place between the late 1920s and the mid-1940s was not only a doctrinal revolution but an interpretive revolution. As an interpretive revolution it altered the jurisprudential framework in which constitutional decisions by Supreme Court justices took place. It also altered the professional function of the judge in constitutional interpretation. Finally, it altered the manner in which authoritative legal sources in American jurisprudence, of which the text of the Constitution was the archetypal example, were treated by the judges who applied those sources to legal disputes. The end result of this interpretive revolution was a new orthodox conception of constitutional adaptivity.

The constitutional revolution, as an interpretive revolution, also had significant practical ramifications. Prior to the late 1930s Supreme Court justices, in their role as interpreters of the Constitution, were seen as guardians of fundamental constitutional principles, some of which were taken to erect barriers against legislative excesses; since then justices and legislatures have been seen as partners ensuring that the Constitution be responsive to changing economic and social conditions. An important function of judges in constitutional cases affecting government and the economy has been to implement a conception of the Constitution as an adaptive document, one whose "meaning" could change to reflect the context and mores of its times. This conception of the Constitution, and of the theory of constitutional interpretation accompanying it, was embodied in the phrase "the living Constitution," which began to appear in constitutional discourse just prior to the New Deal period.[25]

By the 1920s commentators were advancing a theory of the Constitution as a "living" document, one whose meaning was capable of changing with time. The construct of a "living Constitution" had implications for two distinct features of constitutional interpretation. One, the feature emphasized by most commentators, was the capacity of the Constitution to respond to changed conditions: its adaptivity. American jurists had long emphasized the Constitution's adaptivity, a prominent example being Chief Justice John Marshall's characterization of the Constitution, in *McCulloch v. Maryland*, as capable of being "adapted to the various crises of human affairs."[26]

In the 1920s Marshall's characterization was used by some commentators to support arguments that the fundamental principles of the Constitution *did not* change with time: constitutional adaptivity involved the restatement of universal first principles in new contexts. This was faithful to Marshall's usage.[27] Other commentators, however, were beginning to treat constitutional adaptivity as signifying something quite different: that constitutional principles themselves could be modified in response to the demands of modern American life. The latter conception of adaptivity illustrated a radically different set of assumptions about the nature of constitutional interpretation.

The other feature of constitutional interpretation emphasized by the appearance of "living Constitution" commentary was the human character of the Constitution's judicial interpreters. This was the less overtly stressed, but for our purposes more significant, feature. We have seen that the orthodox guardian role for judges in constitutional interpretation rested on a strong distinction between what Marshall once called the "will of the law and the will of the judge,"[28] which was often articulated in republican constitutional theory as the distinction between a government of laws and a government of men. American constitutional republicanism, embodied in an enduring written Constitution, was taken as a quintessential example of a government of laws, personified by an enduring written Constitution. A central reason why orthodox constitutional jurisprudence conceived of constitutional principles as essentialist, fundamental, and unchanging—even when those principles were declared by judges—was because otherwise America would cease to be a government of laws.

Despite repeated judicial pronouncements that judges "make no laws, . . . establish no policy, [and] . . . never enter into the domain of public action" because "[t]heir functions . . . are limited to seeing that popular action does not trespass upon right and justice as it exists in written constitutions and natural law,"[29] an increasing number of early twentieth-century commentators asserted that laws were, at bottom, the policy judgments of humans holding power, and thus the distinction between a government of laws and a government of men was potentially meaningless.[30] But those assertions, especially when applied to constitutional interpretation by judges, were sharply contested in the early twentieth century.

As the Supreme Court began to confront New Deal legislation in the 1930s, some opponents of that legislation suggested that its constitutional unsoundness was related to its violation of fundamental social and economic principles that the Constitution embodied and that humans were powerless to alter. The lawyer and former presidential candidate John W. Davis, in a 1934 attack on New Deal efforts at economic regulation, asked, "Who can doubt that there are natural laws in the social and economic as well as the physical worlds, and that these cannot be overridden without courting disaster?"[31] That same year Justice Sutherland gave a speech before the New York State Bar Association expressing similar sentiments. Sutherland said that

[t]here is nothing more unfortunate in governmental administration than a policy of playing fast and loose with great economic and political principles which have withstood the strain of changing circumstance and the stress of time and have become part of our fundamental wisdom . . . Conditions which such a principle governs may change—indeed, in this forward moving world of ours, they must change—but the principle itself is immutable . . . There are certain fundamental social and economic laws which are beyond the power, and certain underlying governmental principles, which are beyond the right of official control, and any attempt to interfere with their operation inevitably ends in confusion, if not disaster.[32]

The views expressed by Davis and Sutherland represented one of two sharply divergent perspectives during the 1920s and 1930s on the integrity of universal, externally based governing principles and their embodiment in the Constitution. Several years before Davis's and Sutherland's comments, the closely timed appearance of two influential books on the Constitution had demonstrated that the jurisprudence of constitutional interpretation was in considerable ferment, and that the fissures between opposing camps ran very deep.

The first of the books was *The Constitution of the United States* by James M. Beck, solicitor general of the United States.[33] Beck's treatment of the Constitution, which he described as a document embodying "a great spirit" of "conservative self-restraint,"[34] struck a deep nerve among some of his contemporaries. President Calvin Coolidge wrote an introduction to a condensed edition designed for schools and libraries, stressing that reverence for the Constitution was the equivalent to support for "a government of law,"[35] and Senator William E. Borah, in a 1924 letter, said that he wished Beck's book "could be in the hands of every young person in the United States," since "God knows how dearly we need a constitutional revival."[36]

In contrast, critics of *The Constitution of the United States* described it as reflecting an indiscriminately pious devotion to universalist constitutional principles that deterred enlightened thinking about constitutional interpretation. In two reviews of successive editions of the book, Thomas Reed Powell, known for his penetrating critiques of the reasoning of Court opinions,[37] turned his powers of ridicule on Beck. In the first of the reviews he likened Beck's work to a "prayer book," designed to elicit a "mystical adulation of the Constitution in the pious faith that it contains in itself the saving grace that will shield the interests of the worshipers from the ambitions of those whose interests are adverse." Noting that Beck had likened the Constitution to a floating dock, remaining secure in its moorings while adjusting to the tides, Powell said that Beck's "idea seems to be that while [the Constitution] does not move forward or backward, it jiggles up and down."[38] His second review opened, "Here is a new kind of book about the Constitution. You can read it without thinking."[39]

Powell's was not the only public criticism that appeared. The *Nation,* the *New York Times,* the *New York Tribune,* the *New York Evening Post,* and the *New York Call* also voiced dissatisfaction with what they took to be Beck's indiscriminate worship of universal constitutional principles, the *Times* calling him one of the "high priests" of constitutional fetishism.[40] One commentator suggested that although Beck claimed that the principles of the Constitution were timeless, they bore a remarkable resemblance to "what conservative lawyers conceived [the Constitution] to be about 1901."[41]

Some of the reaction to Beck, who was closely identified with the center of the Republican Party in the 1920s, was simple partisanship. But another theme of Beck's critics was that his claim that constitutional principles existed independent of the views of those who interpreted the Constitution amounted to jurisprudential naivete. By caricaturing the argument that America was a government of laws rather than men, Beck, his critics believed, had demonstrated its essential emptiness. Law was itself the creation of humans, reflecting the changing context and the changing theories of governance that accompanied that context.

Beck's theory of constitutional interpretation, his critics maintained, had confused permanence with fundamentality. They conceded that the Constitution was a fundamental document, the ultimate source of legal authority in the American system of government. But judges as constitutional interpreters, they asserted, were not simply mouthpieces for preexisting legal principles. This was apparent in closely divided cases, where five Supreme Court justices thought a particular law could not be reconciled with the text of the Constitution, and was thus invalid, and four thought it was valid. In such cases one group of humans had made the law—the legislators who had drafted and enacted it—and another group had "unmade" it—the five justices who concluded that it was unconstitutional. To equate the process of constitutional interpretation with the discovery of preexisting legal principles made no sense in such cases, for had one of the justices who found the law unconstitutional changed his view, the meaning of the Constitution would have been different. The above arguments were crystallized in a 1927 book by Howard Lee McBain, a professor at Columbia Law School. The title of McBain's book was *The Living Constitution.* Its purpose was to demonstrate that "judges are men . . . made of human stuff like the rest of us and sharing with us the common limitations and frailties of human nature," and that "[l]aws are man-made, man-executed, man-interpreted." The distinction between a government of laws and a government of men was "absurd" to McBain. "Laws," he maintained, "live only because men live and only to the extent that men will to have them live. Apart from men a government of laws is a thing inert, . . . a thing that has no existence outside the realm of imagination." Thus, the Constitution could not be seen as "handed down on Mount Sinai by the Lord God of Hosts," but by "human means." All governments, "whatever their form," McBain believed, were the equivalent of "those who hold the throttle of power at the moment."[42]

The different views expressed by Beck and McBain with respect to the nature of the Constitution, and the distinction between a government of laws and one of men, revealed them to be participants in the same jurisprudential debate that had accompanied the American Law Institute's publication of the first Restatements of common law subjects. Beck was insisting on a distinction between the authority of sources of law and that of officials charged with the interpretation of those sources. He took the Constitution to be a collection of fundamental principles whose authority could not be altered by interpreters of those principles. The role of the interpreters was to discern the existence of the principles and to apply them to new cases that were the product of changed conditions. Their authority to perform those functions was derived from their judicial offices and from their legal knowledge. It was not the equivalent of the authority of their sources, and thus judicial applications of constitutional principles to new cases were not the equivalent of the principles themselves.

The associated beliefs that the Constitution did not change with time, but that its principles could be adapted to changing conditions, were consistent with this posited separation between the authority of sources of law and that of officials charged with interpreting the meaning of those sources in particular cases. Constitutional interpretation, for those who shared Beck's perspective, was a process in which judges reaffirmed the integrity of essentialist constitutional principles by demonstrating their applicability to novel disputes. In Beck's version of constitutional adaptivity the essential meaning of constitutional principles did not change: it was simply extended to govern disputes to which those principles had hitherto not been applied. Although judges had the authority to apply principles to novel situations and thus extend, and reaffirm, their meaning, they did not have the authority to modify the principles themselves. Beck's metaphor of the Constitution as a floating dock, adjusting to changing tides without losing its essential moorings, captured the view of constitutional adaptivity held by those who insisted on a fundamental distinction between the authority of American sources of laws and that of their interpreters.

In contrast, McBain's "living Constitution" theory of constitutional interpretation, like the views expressed by Realist critics of the first Restatement volumes, denied the intelligibility of that distinction. The authority of constitutional principles, McBain asserted, was no more or less than the authority of those officials who had been given the power to interpret those principles. Three conclusions for constitutional interpretation followed from that assertion. First, the meaning of constitutional language and principles was found in the judicial interpretations of those principles and in no other sources because such sources did not exist. Second, since human interpreters were responsible for determining the meaning of the Constitution, that meaning could change with time. Humans were capable of disagreement, prone to error, and fated to live for only a limited duration, so that one set of constitutional interpreters would necessarily be replaced with other sets who might reject their predecessors' conclusions. Third, given those conclusions about the locus of constitutional authority and the inevitability of human-directed constitutional change, constitutional adaptivity was best described as a process in which human interpreters altered the meaning of the Constitution to make it responsive to changed social conditions.

The alternative jurisprudential perspectives held by Beck and McBain had thus produced two irreconcilable views about constitutional adaptivity. Those views, in turn, reflected two equally irreconcilable theories of the nature of legal authority and of the role of judges in constitutional interpretation. As the Supreme Court considered the constitutionality of novel governmental experiments in the redistribution of economic benefits and the regulation of economic activity in the 1930s, the contrasting views were to surface in opinions addressing the Constitution's capacity to change with time.

Those opinions revealed that some justices on the Court that first considered New Deal legislation had retained the traditional conception of constitutional adaptivity endorsed by Beck, and continued to believe in a meaningful separation between the authority of fundamental legal principles and the authority of judges charged with the duty of applying those principles to new cases. They also revealed that other judges on the Court were beginning to subscribe to an alternative conception of constitutional adaptivity. Those judges, at the same time, were beginning to wrestle with the implications of that conception for their role as constitutional interpreters. They were beginning to think about the implications of a stance of guardian review should no meaningful distinction exist between the authority of sources of law and that of judges as interpreters of those sources. They were beginning to think about the countermajoritarian implications of lawmaking by judges in a democratic society.

The first of the New Deal era opinions in which irreconcilable theories of constitutional adaptivity surfaced was *Home Building & Loan Association v. Blaisdell*,[43] decided in 1934. The depressed economic conditions of the 1930s had resulted in a number of homeowners being unable to meet mortgage payments on their houses, with the result that many were threatened with foreclosure. Minnesota responded to this situation by passing "emergency" legislation that enabled courts to postpone deadlines for mortgage redemption. A homeowner's deadline was extended under the statute, and the mortgagor sued to compel foreclosure, arguing that the statute was unconstitutional under the Contracts Clause of the Constitution,[44] which provides that "[n]o State shall . . . impair the obligation of contracts."[45]

The Contracts Clause of the Constitution had been inserted to respond to the precise situation present in *Blaisdell*, where a legislature intervened to protect debtors against creditors. Prior to the framing of the Constitution debtor relief laws, which postponed the time for payment of debts or altered the currency they could be paid in, had been common in the states. Some of the framers felt that this situation was deleterious to commercial development; others were sympathetic to the interests of creditors; and many were fearful of the unknown consequences of governmental intervention in the economic transactions of individuals. There was widespread agreement that the Constitution should curb the opportunities of state legislatures to interfere with private contractual arrangements.[46]

In the course of the Court's development of Contracts Clause jurisprudence it became clear that although debtor relief laws were invalid, the states retained power to vitiate certain contractual agreements on grounds of public policy, such as those involving transactions to participate in illegal activity.[47] Despite this concession, the Contracts Clause remained an important barrier to legislative regulation as long as the sphere of state police powers remained relatively confined. But by the time of the *Blaisdell* decision the growth of legislative activity had resulted in the scope of the police power becoming a central question of early twentieth-century constitutional jurisprudence.

Hughes's opinion for a 5–4 majority of the Court, sustaining the Minnesota statute, proceeded on the assumption that Contracts Clause cases had now become analogous to police power due process cases, exercises in "harmonizing the constitutional prohibition with the necessary residuum of state power."[48] That statement itself was interesting because the Contracts Clause represented a much more explicit protection of private rights than the Due Process Clauses. Nonetheless, Hughes borrowed from due process analysis in outlining the Court's approach to Contracts Clause cases, which he described as an inquiry into "whether the legislation is addressed to a legitimate end and the measures taken are reasonable and appropriate to that end."[49]

Hughes then described the altered economic conditions, and altered perceptions about those conditions, that formed the context of "emergency" measures such as that adopted by Minnesota. "There has been," he maintained,

> a growing appreciation of public needs and of the necessity of finding ground for a rational compromise between individual rights and public welfare. The settlement and consequent contraction of the public domain, the pressure of a constantly increasing density of population, the interrelation of the activities of our people and the complexity of our economic interests, have inevitably led to an increased use of the organization of society in order to protect the very basis of individual opportunity. Where, in earlier days, it was thought that only the concerns of individuals or classes were involved, and that those of the State itself were touched only remotely, it has later been found that the fundamental interests of the State are directly affected, and that the question is no longer merely that of one party to a contract as against another, but of the use of reasonable means to safeguard the economic structure upon which the good of all depends.[50]

Hughes was intimating in the paragraph that the context of Contracts Clause challenges was important in determining their constitutional weight, and that part of that context included "a growing appreciation" of the effects of individual contractual relationships on the welfare of the general public. But what of the fact that the Contracts Clause was unambiguously designed to prevent the very legislative intervention being challenged in that case? However one sought to characterize the statute in *Blaisdell,* it was a debtor relief law, one by which the state was intervening to change the terms of preexisting contractual obligations.

Hughes was thus squarely confronted in *Blaisdell* between an interpretive theory of the Constitution that saw its provisions as having a fixed meaning, even though that meaning was capable of being applied to novel disputes, and an interpretive theory—the "living Constitution" theory—that treated the meaning of the Constitution as capable of radically changing with time. The framers had been conscious of the power of the states to impair contractual obligations through debtor relief laws, and had specifically prevented them from doing so. Upholding the Minnesota statute challenged in *Blais-*

dell could only mean that the Contracts Clause of the Constitution did not mean in 1934 what it had meant for the past 150 years.

Hughes attempted to evade this difficulty. He argued that

[i]t is no answer . . . to insist that what the provision of the Constitution meant to the vision of that day it must mean to the vision of our time. If by the statement that what the Constitution meant at the time of its adoption it means to-day, it is intended to say that the great clauses of the Constitution must be confined to the interpretation which the framers, with the conditions and outlook of their time, would have placed upon them, the statement carries its own refutation. It was to guard against such a narrow conception that Chief Justice Marshall uttered the memorable warning—"We must never forget that it is *a constitution* we are expounding—a constitution intend to endure for ages to come, and consequently, to be adapted to the various *crises* of human affairs."[51]

In the above paragraph Hughes, instead of contrasting two interpretive theories of the Constitution, acted as if they were two ways of expressing the same theory. But there was a significant difference in traditional constitutional jurisprudence as it existed in the 1920s and thirties between treating the Constitution's principles as enduring through adaptation to new conditions and treating those principles as changing in response to those conditions. Hughes was not merely suggesting in *Blaisdell* that the principle of insulating the terms of private contracts from governmental interference was being applied to circumstances in which the social impact of one set of contracts, mortgages providing for foreclosure on nonpayment, was wider than previously perceived. He was suggesting that the expanded social impact of mortgage foreclosures called for a modification of the principle itself. He was suggesting, in other words, that the Contracts Clause meant something different in the interdependent, depressed American economy of the 1930s from what it previously had meant.

Sutherland, dissenting in *Blaisdell*, had no difficulty identifying the novel character of Hughes's theory of constitutional interpretation. "A provision of the Constitution," he declared, "does not admit of two distinctly opposite interpretations. It does not mean one thing at one time and an entirely different thing at another time. If the contract impairment clause, when framed and adopted, meant that the terms of a contract for the payment of money could not be altered [by] a state statute enacted for the relief of hardly pressed debtors . . ., it is but to state the obvious to say that it means the same now."[52]

In Sutherland's comments one can see the fundamental incompatibility of the two theories of constitutional adaptivity being advanced in *Blaisdell*.

Sutherland's theory of adaptivity presupposed that since the meaning of the Constitution did not fundamentally change, then in circumstances where the framers of a constitutional provision had anticipated the very set of issues to which it was being applied, their views on the proper resolution of those issues necessarily governed. This meant that in such circumstances principles codified by past generations constrained the policymaking options of their successors.

In his dissent in *Blaisdell* Sutherland had argued that "[t]he defense of the Minnesota law [had been] made on grounds which were discountenanced by the makers of the Constitution," and under "facts and circumstances identical with those which brought it into existence." Such a defense could not possibly succeed if the essentialist principles of the Constitution were to remained fixed over time.[53] But for those who adopted Hughes's theory of constitutional interpretation in *Blaisdell,* the "facts and circumstances" of mortgage foreclosures in America of the 1930s were not identical to those at the time the Contracts Clause was framed. In light of the newly perceived social consequences of debt in a modern, interdependent, depressed economy, the principles embodied in the Contracts Clause had become a barrier against legislative efforts to alleviate some of the costs of economic depression. The Contracts Clause's "meaning"—that is, the social implications of its application by judges to cases such as *Blaisdell*—had changed. Judges were free to recognize and respond to those changes.

The theory of constitutional adaptivity that complemented the "living Constitution" construct was thought by its adherents to be a far more realistic approach to the application of constitutional provisions to changing social conditions than its traditional counterpart. But a recognition that judges, in interpreting the Constitution, might discover that the practical meaning of a constitutional provision had changed did not in itself provide a justification for concluding that the provision could be ignored. Even if one believed that the meaning of constitutional principles was, in reality, identical to the current interpretations of those principles by judges, it did not follow from that belief that judicial modification of the previous meaning of constitutional provisions was a legitimate practice, particularly in a society committed to democratic checks on lawmaking officials.

Judges from Marshall through Sutherland had sought to establish the legitimacy of judicial glosses on constitutional provisions by stressing the distinction between the sources of law and their official interpreters. In applying constitutional principles to legal disputes, they maintained, they were simply declaring the concrete meaning of preexisting authoritative sources, not creating law in the legislative sense. But cases such as *Blaisdell* did not seem to conform to that description of constitutional interpretation. When the Supreme Court declined to apply a constitutional provision to the very situation for which it had been designed, it appeared to be making new law. And if the justices were acting as creative lawmakers in such cases, the Constitution surely had become what the judges said it was, and no meaningful distinction between the authority of constitutional principles and the authority of their interpreters existed. But if that were so, the principal justification for judicial glossing of constitutional provisions had collapsed, and one confronted the prospect of unelected Supreme Court justices with life tenure making constitutional law on their own. The intellectual origins of what would later be called the countermajoritarian difficulty lay in that description of constitutional interpretation.[54]

Questions of judicial legitimacy, in a world in which judges were presumed to be a species of lawmakers, were to become central to discussions of constitutional interpretation in the three decades after *Blaisdell*. But it is anachronistic to assume that because a posture of guardian review, which had been premised on a distinction between the sources of law and its interpreters, became increasingly difficult to justify once that distinction collapsed, guardian review was quickly abandoned once the "living Constitution" view of constitutional adaptivity became orthodoxy. In fact, the model of guardian review, the Marshallian theory of constitutional adaptivity, and essentialist definitions of the principles embodied in constitutional provisions each persisted into the late 1930s. They represented one side of a jurisprudential debate about the meaning of constitutional provisions and the nature of constitutional interpretation, a debate that had major implications for the Court's posture of constitutional review. One can see evidence of that debate first in academic commentary in the 1930s, and then in the very cases most commonly identified with the "constitutional revolution."

Between the appearance of Beck's *The Constitution of the United States* and the mid-1930s the question of the proper role of the Constitution in American society was a recurrent subject of academic debate. Discussion centered on two issues: whether the Constitution, given the altered conditions of modern America, had become "obsolete," and, if so, what should be done about it. On one side of the debate were commentators such as Beck and Charles W. Pierson, who in a 1926 book, *Our Changing Constitution,* took note of "the drift toward centralization" that was occurring in governmental policy and expressed concern that in "moving forward with conscious power toward the achievement of their aims" the American people might give insufficient attention to the constitutional legitimacy of centralizing policies.

Pierson stressed the Constitution's capacity to adapt to change and insisted that experiments with centralization should have a proper constitutional basis, by which he meant a basis consistent with the traditional assumptions of republican government. He suggested the slogan "Back to the Constitution" as a rallying cry for those who desired renewed attention to its traditional role.[55]

On the other side were a variety of commentators who embraced one or another version of the "living Constitution" theory of constitutional adaptivity.[56] Some argued that the Constitution had become obsolescent in the 1930s and advocated amending its provisions or interpreting them out of existence.[57] Others found the ideological presuppositions on which many constitutional provisions appeared to be grounded inappropriately elitist or libertarian for a modern democratic society.[58]

In 1936 the American Academy of Political and Social Science thought that the debate over the proper role of the Constitution was sufficiently unresolved to devote a symposium on the topic. That symposium featured commentators who believed that the Constitution's greatest strength was its combination of permanent principles and adaptable language, and who worried about recent efforts to ignore its limitations on the power of the national government.[59] Other commentators in the symposium openly endorsed the "living Constitution" perspective, the celebrated historian Charles Beard writing that "[s]ince most of the words and phrases dealing with the powers and the limits of government are vague and must in practice be interpreted by human beings, it follows that the Constitution as practice is a living thing."[60]

The opposing viewpoints were summarized by one symposium participant, Johns Hopkins political science professor James Hart, as follows:

> Whoever would be consistent in his thinking about the Constitution must choose between two fundamentally different philosophies . . . The one assumes a dynamic universe in which new factors and hence new problems emerge. The other postulates a universe whose very changes take place in accordance with a few unchanging principles . . . From these two philosophies may be derived two sharply conflicting conceptions of the Constitution. In the one view it is a charter meant to endure for ages to come, and hence to be adapted to the circumstances and the dominant purposes of each succeeding generation. In the other view it is the enactment for all time of principles of fixed meaning and universal validity.[61]

Hart's characterizations of the "fundamentally different philosophies" of constitutional interpretation were doubtless influenced by his commitment to the "living Constitution" philosophy.[62] But Hart's characterizations nonetheless captured a fundamental difference between the interpretive perspectives dividing constitutional commentators in the 1930s.

The traditionalist perspective, which assumed a meaningful distinction between the authority of sources of law and that of their judicial interpreters, rested at bottom on a view of the universe in which humans could do little to alter the inevitable path of external forces. Principles of law and government, embodied in the Constitution, were themselves reflections of the inexorability of those forces. Although capable of adaptation to new circumstances, the principles were part of the essentialist order of things, so that their adaptability was evidence of their universality. The alternative "living Constitution" perspective emphasized human will, human power, and human creativity as the dominant causal agents in the universe, conceived of the Constitution as a document created by, and capable of modification by, human actors, and denied that constitutional principles retained an authority that was independent of their judicial application to concrete cases.[63] For those who held that perspective, cases in which constitutional language was being "adapted" to new situations invariably held out the possibility that judicial interpreters might, in response to altered conditions, change the meaning of the Constitution. Since that possibility always existed, it was inaccurate to think of the Constitution as an essentialist or universalist document.

Those who participated in debates about the nature of constitutional adaptivity in the 1930s were aware that adaptivity issues would figure prominently in cases raising constitutional challenges to state and federal legislation regulating economic activity.[64] If one held to the orthodox view of constitutional adaptivity, the meaning of provisions conferring specific powers on the federal government, or imposing specific restrictions on that government or the states, could not be altered by judges. The orthodox theory of adaptivity thus suggested that if constitutional principles limiting the capacity of the state or federal governments to regulate economic activity had already been discerned, they could be expected to govern cases challenging New Deal economic legislation. Examples of such principles were not confined to the Contracts Clause: they included two established judicial glosses on the Due Process Clauses and the Commerce Clause. One gloss defined "liberty" in the Due Process Clauses as including "liberty of contract," the right to bargain for goods and services on the terms one chose; another limited the range of the federal government's power to regulate economic activities under the Commerce Clause to activities that actually involved "commerce," as distinguished from related matters such as production or manufacturing, and to activities that had entered into the "stream" or "current" of interstate commerce, as distinguished from being primarily local. Such glosses had the status of established constitutional principles because they had been developed in the application of essentialist constitutional provisions to cases: they were examples of adaptivity as traditionally understood.

But *Blaisdell* had suggested that the Contracts Clause, an apparently unambiguous constitutional provision prohibiting states from impairing preexisting contractual obligations, could be "adapted" out of existence if enough of an economic emergency existed. Did that decision signal that the meaning of the two other constitutional provisions governing the regulation of economic activity could be comparably altered in the face of new conditions? That issue was at the heart of the "constitutional revolution" of the late 1930s and early 1940s.

West Coast Hotel v. Parrish, we have seen, has been identified as the very centerpiece of the constitutional revolution: the case, in which a majority of the Court abandoned the "liberty of contract" principle in police power due process cases, overruled its 1923 decision, *Adkins v. Children's Hospital,* striking down minimum wage legislation on liberty of contract grounds, and ushered in an era of judicial deference to legislative regulation of the industrial marketplace. But a comparison of the *Parrish* decision with *Adkins* reveals that the model of guardian review in police power cases was still in place on the Court in 1937. One has to look elsewhere to find the "revolutionary" character of the *Parrish* case.

All the opinions in *Adkins,* including Holmes's dissent, had treated the case as a familiar exercise of guardian review in police power due process cases. Congress had created a minimum wage board for the District of Columbia and delegated it power to establish minimum wages for women and minors employed within the District. The constitutional challenge to the statute employed a series of arguments characteristic of due process attacks on legislation based on the police powers.[65] The statute was said to have interfered with the "liberty" of employers and employees within the District to fix the terms of their employment contracts. Unlike a legitimate legislative use of the police power, the statute was not limited to businesses "affected with a public interest." It was not designed to protect persons engaged in a particularly hazardous occupation. It was not an effort to prevent fraud in the payment of wages. In short, it did not come within any of the established instances in which legislatures could exercise the police power to restrain freedom of contract.[66]

Sutherland's majority opinion, which struck down the statute, engaged in the orthodox guardian review exercise of placing the statute under review in one category rather than another so as to facilitate boundary pricking. Being an interference with "liberty of contract," and not having as its rationale one of the aforementioned bases for interfering with that liberty, it was an "arbitrary" interference with private rights rather than a "reasonable" exercise of public power. A reader of the opinion, noting the presumption against legislation invading "liberty," the instances in which that presumption could be overridden, and the failure of the legislation to represent any legitimate legislative interference, would have been provided with an intelligible road map of the constitutional boundary between the police power and private rights.

This dimension of Sutherland's opinion was unexceptional. But he also took pains to rehearse the justifications for guardian review itself. In reading the Due Process Clauses to preclude broadly based minimum wage legislation, Sutherland maintained, the Court was not "exercis[ing] . . . a substantive power to review and nullify acts of Congress."[67] No such substantive power existed. In reviewing the constitutionality of legislation judges were merely exercising the "power vested in courts to enable them to administer justice according to law." Judges had the authority "to ascertain and determine the law in a given case." It followed from such authority that if "by clear and indubitable demonstration a statute be opposed to the Constitution, we have no choice but to say so."[68] Judges were expected to discern the meaning of the Constitution in their applications of constitutional principles to cases. Although their "duty to declare and enforce the supreme law" was derived from their authority as designated interpreters of legal sources, the authority of the sources they interpreted came from the sources themselves. Judges exercised no independent will in the interpretive process.

It is apparent that Sutherland's conception of the role of judges in constitutional interpretation complemented the orthodox view of constitutional adaptivity. For Sutherland the "meaning" of the Constitution was sufficiently finite and universal that its principles were easily ascertainable; all judges did in interpreting the Constitution was to "declare and enforce the supreme law" by applying principles to cases. In police power due process cases in which a statute was challenged as infringing on constitutionally protected "liberties," the statute only passed constitutional muster if it was a reasonable exercise of the police power, and judges had, in the process of previous applications of due process principles, developed guidelines to determine its reasonableness. The guidelines had been derived from the principles themselves, so the interpretive exercise was straightforward police power boundary pricking and did not contain any "substantive" dimensions.

In denying that judges exercised any "substantive" powers in upholding due process challenges to police power legislation, Sutherland would seem to have ignored the extent to which boundary pricking in such cases was facilitated by judicial glosses on "liberty" in the Due Process Clauses, and the judicial creation of doctrinal formulas designed to clarify the analysis of recurrent issues. The doctrine that property "affected with a public interest" was subject to regulation under the police power, or the proposition that "liberty" in the Due Process Clauses embraced "liberty of contract," was helpful in drawing lines between private rights and public power, but they were not mentioned in the text of the Constitution.

But judicial glossing of the constitutional text to produce formulas that facilitated boundary pricking was not regarded, in the approach to constitutional interpretation reflected in Sutherland's *Adkins* opinion, as the equivalent of conflating authoritative sources of law with the "substantive" interpretations of those sources by judges. "Liberty of contract" was not a principle extracted from a plain reading of the Constitution's text. But it was a principle that could easily be derived from an ordinary reading of the term "liberty" in the Due Process Clauses. "Liberty" in the Due Process Clauses stood for something, but the Constitution did not say precisely what. It was the duty of judges to say precisely what "liberty" meant in concrete cases. Thus, glossing was required, and in deriving glosses judges could be mindful of the essentialist, fundamental character of constitutional principles. The judges who concluded that "liberty" included "liberty of contract" simply assumed that it *must necessarily* mean "liberty of contract" because the Constitution embodied foundational principles, and the liberty of private individuals to buy and sell their property on the terms they chose, without interference from the state, was a foundational principle of republican government in America.

Similarly, the obligation of governments to provide for the safety and to promote the health and morals of their citizens was equally a foundational principle of republican societies. Thus, some regulation of the activities of private individuals by the state—some exercise of police powers—was necessary, even though the Constitution had not spoken directly of those powers, unless elliptically in the Tenth Amendment. When police power regulations infringed on private "liberties," it was the duty of judges to maintain the boundary between public power and private rights. When private activity, in the form of a business, became sufficiently important to the general weal that its regulation appeared necessary to maintain the safety, or health, or moral fiber of the general citizenry, it was said to be "affected with a public interest." That judgment was not the idiosyncratic conclusion of individual judges. It was judicial recognition of the principle that government had an obligation to take care of its citizens when their collective interests were significantly affected by a particular enterprise.

For Sutherland and his contemporaries who subscribed to the interpretive canons of guardian review, there was nothing troubling about the fact that in the course of boundary pricking the category of constitutionally protected "liberties" in police power due process cases, or the category of businesses "affected with a public interest," might change. That form of constitutional adaptivity did not disturb the essentialist character of constitutional provisions and principles. But for advocates of the "living Constitution" perspective on constitutional adaptivity, judicial glossing and boundary pricking in police power jurisprudence appeared to be performing a function quite different from that implicitly ascribed to them by Sutherland's *Adkins* opinion. Sutherland's opinion had treated glosses and formulas as if they were finite guidelines a judge followed in police power cases. Interpretive critics of the opinion saw them as vessels into which ideological content could be poured. As such, they ceased to be mere guidelines in the process of applying constitutional principles to cases and became devices by which judges could interpret open-ended constitutional language to support their present convictions.

The "living Constitution" theory of constitutional interpretation thus treated judicial glossing of constitutional provisions as a far more creative and ideological exercise than Sutherland suggested. Holmes's dissenting opinion in *Adkins* treated judicial glossing in that fashion. Like Chief Justice William Howard Taft's dissent, Holmes engaged in orthodox police power due process analysis, but he declined to attach significant constitutional weight to the "liberty" that formed the basis of the challenge to minimum wage legislation.[69] In the process he hinted that judicial glosses and formulas in constitutional interpretation were ideologically derived, and argued that this fact made them difficult to justify in cases where the constitutional provisions being interpreted were broad and open-ended, such as "liberty" in the Due Process Clauses.

Nowhere in Holmes's *Adkins* dissent was there a suggestion that "liberty of contract" was a timeless principle of republican government. Instead, he described it as a creation of judges—a "dogma"—that resulted from the Due Process Clauses having "vague contours" that tempted judges to equate their own ideological predilections with constitutional principles. Such a posture was inappropriate because legislators, not judges, were charged with the responsibility of determining what was best for the public under the American system of government. If legislatures decided that minimum wage levels for women and children helped "remove conditions leading to ill health, immorality and the deterioration of the race," it was not for judges to second-guess them.[70] Although Holmes employed the orthodox guardian review analysis employed in police power cases in *Adkins,* his approach emphasized that when judges had themselves created constitutional "liberties" that had very little textual support, the boundary between public power and such "liberties" could extend rather far in the direction of legislative regulatory power.

In their enthusiasm for Holmes's attack on "liberty of contract" in his *Adkins* dissent, which they took to be an endorsement of the constitutionality of minimum wage and maximum hours legislation, acolytes of Holmes in the 1930s tended to ignore the fact that he had continued to employ a stance of traditional guardian review in the case.[71] And subsequent conventional accounts of the Court's early twentieth-century political economy decisions have also been far less interested in Holmes's posture of constitutional review in *Adkins* than in contrasting his critique of "liberty of contract" with the ideological overtones of Sutherland's majority opinion, which has been regularly characterized as an example of early twentieth-century judicial "laissez-faire" at its zenith.[72] But guardian review in economic due process cases was not only the stance adopted by all the judges who decided *Adkins;* it was the judicial stance employed by all the judges who decided *Parrish.*

Parrish tested the constitutionality of a Washington statute prescribing minimum wage levels for women and minors working in certain specified occupations within the state. A custodian, Elsie Parrish, brought suit against her employer, a hotel, to recover the difference between her wages and the minimum fixed by the state. She was awarded the amount of her claim, and the hotel appealed, citing *Adkins* and invoking the Fourteenth Amendment's Due Process Clause.

Hughes began his opinion for the Court by tracing a variety of cases in which statutes had restricted liberty because the business in question was "affected with a public interest" or because "health and safety, . . . peace and good order may be promoted through regulations designed to insure . . . freedom from oppression."[73] By the last phrase Hughes meant regulations striking at unequal bargaining power, in contexts where "proprietors lay down the rules and the laborers are practically constrained to obey them." In such circumstances, Hughes maintained, "self-interest is often an unsafe guide and the legislature may properly interpose its authority."[74]

Hughes then argued that legislative intervention in the employment of women, with the goal of correcting inequalities in wages brought about by inequalities in bargaining power, was particularly appropriate. Citing cases where the Court had permitted states to give special protection to female workers, Hughes noted that those cases "emphasized the need of protecting women against her oppression despite her possession of contractual rights." He took one such case, the Court's 1908 decision in *Muller v. Oregon,* to have concluded that because "there is that in [a woman's] disposition and habits of life which will operate against a full assertion of [her contractual] rights, some legislation to protect her seems necessary to secure a real equality of right."[75]

Moreover, Hughes suggested, there were public benefits in legislation placing women in an advantaged position. Because of "the performance of maternal functions," the physical well-being of women was "an object of public interest and care in order to preserve the strength and vigor of the race." Thus, minimum wage legislation, which was designed in part to prevent women from having to work long hours to earn a sufficient wage, was "not imposed solely for her benefit, but also largely for the benefit of us all."[76] This recital of standard reasons for sustaining police power legislation interfering with contractual liberties was thought by Hughes to be sufficient to sustain the legislation challenged in *Parrish*.

Notwithstanding the fact that Hughes's analysis in *Parrish* had been conducted in the conventional modes of guardian review in police power due process cases, he had twice signaled that the Court might consider adopting a more deferential posture toward police powers legislation. Both signals were noted by Sutherland, writing for the four dissenters in *Parrish;* Sutherland took the signals to be ominous developments.[77]

The first signal was Hughes's articulation of the standard of review in police power due process cases. Rather than speaking of "liberty of contract" in such cases as being "absolute and uncontrollable," Hughes defined it as "liberty in a social organization." He then suggested that a statute based on state police powers would conform to constitutional due process standards if it was "reasonable in relation to its subject and [was] adopted in the interests of the community."[78]

This standard of review meant that liberty of contract had ceased to be a fixed principle of republican government and become subject to the exigencies of changing political and economic conditions. It suggested that police power cases would no longer be considered against a backdrop of essentialist spheres and boundary lines. In such an analytical universe it was unlikely that many legislative judgments about the appropriate scope of regulatory legislation would be second-guessed because once a conceptual boundary had been stripped of its immanent significance, the consequences of its being blurred, or even dissolving, were less important.

Although this recharacterization of liberty of contract surely spelled the end of *Adkins* as a precedent with any weight, it was probably less provocative to Sutherland than the second of Hughes's signals in *Parrish*. That signal was directed at the external context of constitutional interpretation. In suggesting that *Adkins* did not definitively resolve the question being litigated in *Parrish*, Hughes pointed out some factors that "demand . . . on our part a re-examination of the *Adkins* case." He included among those factors "the economic conditions which have supervened, and in the light of which the reasonableness of the exercise of the protective power of the State must be considered, [which] make it not only appropriate, but we think imperative, that in deciding the present case the subject should receive fresh consideration."[79] Later in his opinion, Hughes referred to "the unparalleled demands for relief which arose during the recent period of depression and still continue to an alarming extent." Depressed economic conditions had accentuated the plight of "a class of workers who are in an unequal position with respect to bargaining power." Their vulnerability was "not only detrimental to their health and well being but cast . . . a direct burden for their support upon the community."[80] The clear import of these comments was that the meaning of constitutional principles was affected by their current social context.

Sutherland took Hughes's comments to be advancing an unorthodox, and disturbing, theory of constitutional adaptivity. "It is urged," he said in his *Parrish* dissent,

> that the question involved should now receive fresh consideration, among other reasons, because of "the economic conditions which have supervened"; but the meaning of the Constitution does not change with the ebb and flow of economic events. We frequently are told in more general words that the Constitution must be construed in light of the present. If by that it is meant that the Constitution is made up of living words that apply to every new condition which they include, the statement is quite true. But to say, if that be intended, that the words of the Constitution mean today what they did not mean when written—that is, they do not apply to a situation today to which they would have applied then—is to rob that instrument of the essential element which continues it in force.[81]

Sutherland was making the orthodox distinction between essentialist constitutional principles and the judicial application of those principles to changing conditions. As Sutherland put it, "What a court is to do . . . is *to declare the law as written,* leaving it to the people themselves to make such changes as new circumstances may require. The meaning of the constitution is fixed when it is adopted, and it is not different at any subsequent time."[82] Sutherland had stated the traditional meaning of adaptivity in constitutional interpretation. Judicial adaptation of fundamental principles to new cases might change the reach of the Constitution, but it did not change its meaning. Judges had authority to perform the former function but not the latter.

Because the authority of constitutional principles was separate from that of judges charged with the duty of applying them to cases, the role of the judge in Sutherland's version of adaptivity was not a creative one. As he put it in his *Parrish* dissent, "The suggestion that the only check upon the exercise of the judicial power . . . is the judge's own faculty of self-restraint is both ill considered and mischievous. Self-restraint belongs in the domain of will and not of

judgment. The check upon the judge is that imposed by . . . the Constitution
. . . [H]e has the duty to make up his own mind and adjudge accordingly."[83]

One can understand why a judge holding this conception of the role of the
judiciary in constitutional interpretation would have found Hughes's opinions in *Blaisdell* and *Parrish* particularly disturbing. In both cases the economic context in which a constitutional provision was to be applied had been
stressed. *Blaisdell*'s context had resulted in the Court's declining to enforce
the constitutional principle of governmental noninterference with preexisting contractual obligations because of a perceived economic "emergency."
In *Parrish* Hughes's opinion had attempted to build this contextual inquiry
into the methodology of constitutional review in due process cases. This
suggested to Sutherland that the meaning of "liberty" in the Due Process
Clauses might change "with the ebb and flow of economic events." It also
suggested that constitutional principles might not be treated as essentialist
and timeless; not only their meaning, but their very existence, would be dependent on judicial interpretations. The methodology proposed by Hughes
threatened not only to strip constitutional principles of their fundamental
character but to obliterate the distinction between the authority of sources of
law and that of their official interpreters.

Nonetheless, the interpretive signals of *Parrish* remained ambiguous because
Hughes's opinion could have been seen as simply another example of judicial
boundary pricking in cases involving private rights and the public welfare.
There were enough public welfare exceptions to the liberty of contract principle that finding one more—the public interest in protecting the health,
safety, and morals of female industrial laborers—might have amounted to just
another exercise in drawing boundary lines. Even Hughes's decision to overrule *Adkins* in *Parrish* did not necessarily signify diminished respect for the
liberty of contract principle because the *Adkins* court could simply have un-
derestimated the general public benefits of legislation designed to protect the
health of female workers. Hughes's comments about the economic context
of legislation could have been understood as part of the judicial obligation in
police power cases to discern public health or safety rationales on which a police power statute was based.

There was, however, a case in the period conventionally described as encompassing the "constitutional revolution" that clearly signified that the
Court was abandoning guardian review in at least one subset of political
economy cases and at the same time was endorsing the "living Constitution"
theory of constitutional adaptivity and its implications for the traditional sep-

aration of the authority of constitutional provisions from that of their judicial interpreters. An exchange of memoranda between Justice Robert Jackson, who authored the opinion in the case, and his law clerk, recently discovered in Jackson's papers by Barry Cushman, supports those conclusions.

The case was *Wickard v. Filburn*, which considered whether Congress's power under the Commerce Clause permitted it to invade the residuum of "private" and "local" economic activities to a hitherto unprecedented extent. Although confined to commerce power issues, *Wickard* can be seen as the culmination of, and at the same time a move beyond, parallel analytical trends in the Court's constitutional political economy cases from *Adkins* through *Blaisdell, Parrish,* and the early 1940s. The posture of constitutional review Jackson staked out for the Court in Commerce Clause cases was influenced by Hughes's opinions in *Blaisdell* and *Parrish* but was also far more revolutionary.

We have noted that guardian review required late nineteenth- and early twentieth-century judges to spend much of their energy developing analytical formulas that would aid in the application of constitutional principles to cases. Although the general purpose of those formulas, in the area of political economy, was to mark out the boundaries between federal and state powers and between public power and private rights, the formulas were also responsive to the discrete interpretive issues raised by a particular constitutional provision. Thus, formulas used in the interpretation of Contracts Clause cases employed different tests and standards from those employed in police power/due process cases or in Commerce Clause cases.

Nonetheless, the different formulas employed by the Court in early twentieth-century Contracts, Due Process, and Commerce Clause cases can be seen as grounded in common jurisprudential assumptions, which made them analytically analogous and permitted a degree of doctrinal radiation from one area to another. Doctrinal radiation was accentuated by the fact that in the period between *Adkins* and *Wickard v. Filburn* constitutional challenges to legislation regulating economic activity, whether they rested on the Contracts, Due Process, or Commerce Clauses, were based on essentialist definitions of the constitutional principles taken to be embodied in those provisions. In *Blaisdell* the principle was that of governmental noninterference with the contractual obligations of citizens; in the *Adkins/Parrish* sequence it was the freedom of individuals to bargain for goods and services on the terms they chose; in *Wickard v. Filburn,* which tested the reach of the federal government's commerce power, it was the reserved powers of the states and the people to exercise legal control over local productive activities.

In the use of interpretive formulas in early twentieth-century guardian review political economy cases, an issue had surfaced that was reflected in the objections Sutherland had made to Hughes's methodology in *Blaisdell* and *Parrish*. The issue was whether, in determining the applicability of constitutional principle embodied in a particular provision to a case challenging legislation on the basis of that provision, judges were required to stress the universalist character, or could emphasize the contextualist dimensions, of that principle. In his majority opinion in *Adkins*, and in his dissents in *Blaisdell* and *Parrish*, Sutherland, in applying the principles of liberty of contract and governmental noninterference with preexisting contractual obligations to new cases, treated the fact that the beneficiaries of legislation in *Adkins* and *Parrish* were women, or the fact that an economic "emergency" existed in *Blaisdell*, as largely irrelevant. His approach reinforced the universalist and essentialist character of the constitutional provisions being interpreted. In contrast, Hughes's majority opinions in *Blaisdell* and *Parrish* emphasized the dire economic conditions leading to a number of mortgage foreclosures and the effects on the general public of the special vulnerability of women as industrial laborers. His approach suggested that, at least in political economy cases, the meaning of constitutional provisions could not be separated from the social and economic context in which they were applied.

The contrasting approaches of Sutherland and Hughes demonstrated that the formulas associated with guardian review in political economy cases, although initially developed in a jurisprudential atmosphere in which the adaptation of constitutional principles to new circumstances was taken as reaffirming their essentialist and universalist character, could also be employed to contextualize the meaning of those principles, thereby opening up the possibility that they actually changed in response to time and circumstance. They also suggested that the contextual use of guardian review formulas in Contracts and Due Process Clause cases might radiate into the application of doctrinal formulas in Commerce Clause cases. Evidence suggests that that very phenomenon occurred in the Court's Commerce Clause decisions in the years between *Adkins* and *Wickard v. Filburn*.

In the period between the 1920s and the early 1940s doctrinal formulas associated with the interpretation of the Commerce Clause, such as whether an activity had entered the "current" or "stream" of interstate commerce, or whether it had "direct" or "indirect" effects on interstate commerce, became increasingly contextual, and essentialist definitions of commerce, as an activity distinct from production or manufacture, began to break down.[84] In the 1941 case of *United States v. Darby Lumber Co.*,[85] a unanimous Court applied the establishment by the Fair Labor Standards Act of 1938 of a wage floor for industries engaged in "production for interstate commerce" to the wages of workers in a lumberyard in Georgia. Previous Commerce Clause decisions had exempted from federal requirements wages in industries engaged in "manufacturing," as distinguished from "commerce." Chief Justice Stone's opinion for the Court in *Darby* abandoned those distinctions, as well as the "direct"/"indirect" distinction, for a test that permitted the federal government to regulate the wage levels of an activity if it had a "substantial effect" on interstate commerce. That test suggested that the Commerce Clause might provide a justification for federal regulation of a number of sectors of the American economy.

Hughes, whose opinion in the 1937 *Jones & Laughlin* case had employed traditional Commerce Clause formulas contextually to sustain a relatively broad application of federal commerce powers, only grudgingly joined Stone's *Darby* opinion. Hughes initially objected to the application of the commerce power to the hours and wages of workers in a local lumberyard, only "going along" with Stone's opinion when it became clear that there would be no dissenters. In the justices' conference on *Darby*, Hughes said that the Fair Labor Standards Act "reaches into the field of production" and as such threatened to put "our dual system of government . . . at an end." He had expressed similar sentiments in a letter to Stone.[86]

A year after *Darby* came the *Wickard* case. There the Court went even further, not only avoiding the use of any judicial formulas designed to determine the scope of the federal commerce power but concluding that Congress could regulate a particular industry or activity whenever it had a plausible economic reason for thinking that its regulation would have some substantial positive effects on interstate commerce. A striking feature of the *Wickard* opinion was the Court's assumption that future Commerce Clause cases could be seen as examples of the "living Constitution" theory of constitutional adaptivity, cases in which the meaning of that clause could be altered by judges to make it responsive to the exigencies of a modern economy.

Wickard was initially a troublesome case for the justices because they could not see any connection between the activities of Roscoe Filburn and interstate commerce. The Agricultural Adjustment Act of 1938 established marketing quotas for wheat production. Filburn, an Ohio farmer, planted twice the amount of wheat allotted to him by the quotas, retaining the excess for home consumption. After he was assessed a penalty, Filburn challenged the constitutionality of the AAA marketing quotas as applied to wheat grown for use at home.[87]

Although the *Darby* opinion had suggested that the Court's Commerce Clause jurisprudence was poised to abandon the categorical formulas of the early twentieth century, it was not clear what would be put in their place. Because the wheat for which Filburn had been penalized had neither been produced for nor shipped in interstate commerce, and yet Congress had sought to regulate its use in the Agricultural Adjustment Act of 1938, the case was treated as posing three options for the justices.[88] One was to employ traditional formulas and declare the Act unconstitutional as applied to the private consumption of wheat. Under this reasoning, Filburn's growing wheat for his private consumption would be "production," not "commerce," or, alternatively, an activity not designed for "interstate commerce." Accordingly, the effect of Filburn's use of that portion of his wheat on interstate commerce would be "indirect." After *Darby* it was patently clear that the Court would not exercise that option.

The second option was to sustain the Act by declaring that the production of wheat for home use had a "substantial effect" on interstate commerce, following language employed by Stone in *Darby* to characterize the activities of the local lumberyard. This option would have implicitly preserved some judicial power to make independent determinations, through the contextual application of formulas, of the scope of the commerce power in particular cases. Despite the advantages of that option, it posed one major difficulty for the Court. It was hard for the justices to see how one farmer's decision to produce more wheat for his own consumption had *any* effect on interstate commerce, let alone a substantial one. If all farmers acted as Filburn had, then the farming community might cease to become prospective buyers of each other's wheat, but there was no evidence that other farmers were inclined to follow Filburn's example, and most wheat that trafficked in interstate commerce was not sold to wheat farmers.

The third option was for the Court to treat Congress's decision to establish marketing quotas in the Agricultural Adjustment Act as evidence that it believed that the production of wheat for home use would have a substantial effect on interstate commerce. According to this line of reasoning, in establishing the quotas Congress apparently believed that if enough farmers produced wheat for their own consumption, the demand for wheat in interstate commerce would be reduced, and this would have a negative effect on the price of interstate wheat. A principal purpose of the Agricultural Adjustment Act had been to help depressed industries, such as the wheat industry, by supporting the prices of goods from those industries. Thus, one could conclude that Congress believed there was a substantial connection between supporting the price structure of the wheat industry and establishing federal marketing quotas for the production of wheat for home consumption. If the Court found that belief reasonable, it should sustain the legislation as an appropriate exercise of the commerce power.

Wickard was first argued before the Court in May 1942.[89] After that argument it was clear that although the justices believed that the marketing quotas amounted to a "regulation of commerce," they were hard-pressed to find that the application of the quotas to Roscoe Filburn amounted to an actual regulation of interstate commerce or a regulation of an activity that had a substantial effect on interstate commerce. Thus, penalizing Filburn for growing wheat for his own consumption seemed unconstitutional under any formula currently in use in Commerce Clause jurisprudence, including that adopted by the Court in *Darby.*

Barry Cushman has shown, through an investigation of internal Court papers related to the *Wickard* decision, that after the May 1942 argument, the justices discussed how more facts buttressing a finding that the regulation of wheat for home consumption had a substantial effect on interstate commerce might be obtained. An early draft of an opinion by Justice Robert Jackson favored remanding the case to a lower court to determine whether that substantial effect existed.[90] But that opinion was subsequently withdrawn, and a majority of the Court voted to have the case reargued in its next term.

It had become apparent in the Court's deliberations on *Wickard v. Filburn* that some justices were less interested in the details of the relationship between the production of wheat for home consumption and interstate commerce than they were in the question whether the Court should continue its traditional guardian role in Commerce Clause cases. An analogy from the Court's due process jurisprudence seemed to have affected their thinking. As we have seen, as police power/due process cases from the realm of political economy had been entertained by the Court in the years between *Adkins* and *Parrish,* bright lines between the public and private spheres of that realm had become dimmer, and Hughes's majority opinion in *Parrish* had hinted that judicial policing of boundaries in due process cases might be replaced by judicial deference to the rational judgments of legislatures. In their deliberations on *Wickard v. Filburn* some justices gave evidence of groping toward a similar posture for Commerce Clause cases.

As the Court was awaiting reargument in *Wickard v. Filburn,* Jackson exchanged letters with some other justices and his law clerk.[91] In those letters he articulated his growing conviction that drawing lines in Commerce Clause cases was no easier than in police power/due process cases. Just as there was no easily cabinable category of "liberties" immune from police power regulation or of businesses affected with a public interest, there was no easily cabinable definition of activities that were "intrastate" in character, bearing no relationship to interstate commerce. The questions in Commerce Clause cases, Jackson came to believe, were ultimately not legalistic ones but economic ones. "In such a state of affairs," he wrote to his law clerk in July 1942, "the determination of the limit of [Congress's power under the Commerce Clause] is not a matter of legal principle, but of personal opinion; not one of constitutional law, but one of economic policy."[92]

In successive memoranda on *Wickard* in the summer of 1942, Jackson gradually worked himself around to the position "that is within the commerce power which Congress desires to regulate." The facts of *Wickard* made it clear, Jackson wrote his law clerk, that if the Court sustained the Agricultural Adjustment Act of 1938 as applied to Roscoe Filburn, "I don't see how we can ever sustain states' rights again as against a Congressional exercise of the commerce power." Instead of using this conclusion as a basis for resurrecting the categories of Commerce Clause jurisprudence and invalidating the Act, Jackson began to think of using it as a basis for "[a] frank holding that the interstate commerce power has no limits except those which Congress sees fit to observe."[93] Having concluded that judicial interpretations of the Commerce Clause amounted to "personal opinion[s]" on "economic policy," he was prepared to abandon a posture of guardian review in commerce power cases.

In July 1942 Jackson outlined to his law clerk the basis of an opinion sustaining the application of the Act to Filburn. "Congress," he wrote,

> has seen fit to regulate small and casual wheat growers in the interest of large and specialized ones . . . Whether this is necessary, whether it is just, whether it is wise, is not for us to say . . . [W]e have no legal standards by which to set our judgment against the policy judgment of Congress . . . [The regulation of wheat grown for home consumption] is within the federal power to regulate interstate commerce, if for no better reason than the commerce clause is what the Congress says it is.[94]

The law clerk, stunned by the implications of Jackson's position, asked, "[Are] *all* the old formulae and tests junked? . . . Is the Court never to seek to preserve our 'dual system of government' by denying that the Commerce Power can reach to 'effects upon interstate commerce so indirect and remote that to embrace them, in view of our complex society, would effectively obliterate the distinction between what is national and what is local and create a completely centralized government'?"[95] Jackson had previously fashioned a response: "in order to be unconstitutional . . . the relation between interstate commerce and the regulated activity would have to be so absurd that it would be laughed out of Congress."[96]

In October 1942 the *Wickard* case was reargued, and in November of that year the Court handed down a unanimous opinion, authored by Jackson.[97] In sustaining the Agricultural Adjustment Act penalty against Filburn, Jackson announced that "questions of the power of Congress [under the Commerce Clause] are not to be decided by reference to any formula which would give controlling force to nomenclature such as 'production' and 'indirect.'" Such questions should focus on "the actual effects of the activity in question upon interstate commerce."[98] To clarify any doubts about the turn in the Court's Commerce Clause jurisprudence, he went on: "The Court's recognition of the relevance of the economic effects in the application of the Commerce Clause . . . has made the mechanical application of legal formulas no longer feasible."[99]

Jackson's opinion also made it plain that the "substantiality" of the effect of an activity on interstate commerce was not a matter for the Court to decide. He said of the *Wickard* case, "[t]his record leaves us in no doubt that Congress may properly have considered that wheat consumed on the farm where grown, if wholly outside the scheme of regulation, would have a substantial effect in defeating and obstructing its purpose to stimulate trade therein at increased prices." That "finding" was all that was necessary to sustain the statute.[100]

Doctrinal radiations from the police powers cases had unquestionably played some role in the transformation of the Court's posture in Commerce Clause cases. But *Wickard* was by no means a precise analog to *Parrish*. Hughes's opinion for the Court in *Parrish* had retained the formulas of police powers/due process jurisprudence, even though applying them contextually. His protests against the tenor of Stone's opinion in *Darby* suggested that he anticipated the continued existence of guardian review in Commerce Clauses. By 1942, with Hughes in retirement, Jackson's opinion for the Court in *Wickard* had completely destroyed the edifice of traditional Commerce Clause jurisprudence. It had explicitly stated that the reach of the commerce power would be determined by "economic effects" rather than "legal formulas."

The jurisprudential ramifications of *Wickard* for constitutional political economy cases were potentially immense. The role of the Court as a policer of the boundary between the "national" and "local" sectors of the realm of political economy had been abandoned and, by extension, the Court's guardian role in other political economy cases seemed to have been abandoned as well. The meaning of the Commerce Clause and, very possibly, the meaning of the Contracts Clause and the Due Process Clauses had been changed. By 1946 the last two developments were no longer mere possibilities: in the four years after *Wickard* not a single Contracts Clause or Due Process Clause challenge to federal or state legislation regulating economic activity had been entertained by the Court.

A new definition of constitutional adaptivity was in place on the Court, in which judges either changed the essentialist meaning of constitutional provisions through the increasingly contextual application of judicial formulas they had developed in their guardian role or, when even contextual applications would not suffice, abandoned the formulas and assumed a role of deference toward legislatures. The result was not only the triumph of the "living Constitution" theory of adaptivity but the disintegration of guardian review itself. The result was a constitutional revolution, one in which Supreme Court justices themselves had concluded that there was no intelligible distinction between the authority of legal sources and that of their designated interpreters.

The questions that have preoccupied this chapter are now in a position to be straightforwardly answered, and the significance of the Court-packing crisis can now be more accurately understood. What was the constitutional revolution ultimately about? Why did it happen when it did? What was the connection of the Court-packing crisis to it?

This chapter has drawn connections between three core elements of orthodox late nineteenth- and early twentieth-century constitutional jurisprudence: an essentialist conception of constitutional principles, as embodied in provisions of the Constitution's text; a theory of constitutional adaptivity in which the essentialist meaning of constitutional principles was reaffirmed in their application to new cases; and a stance of guardian review for judges in constitutional cases. We have seen that guardian review in political economy cases presupposed that the essentialist principles of the Constitution reinforced preordained boundaries between public power and private rights and between the nation and the states, and that judges would function as interpretive policers of those boundaries, developing glosses and formulas to aid them in their application of the relevant constitutional provisions to new cases. We have also seen that these ascribed functions of "pricking out" boundary lines and "adapting" constitutional principles to new cases were not treated as the equivalent of "lawmaking," as that term was employed in connection with the decisions of other branches of government.

The emergence of the "living Constitution" theory of constitutional interpretation in the 1920s and thirties, like the emergence of criticism of the jurisprudential assumptions of those involved with the Restatement project, was a signal that the interconnected premises that had given traditional constitutional jurisprudence its integrity were becoming contested. The debate between constitutional theorists such as Beck on the one hand and McBain on the other demonstrated that an assumed distinction between the sources and the authoritative interpreters of law, popularized as the distinction between a government of laws and that of men, was being treated by some commentators as unintelligible. And, just as in the case of the debate precipitated by the appearance of the first Restatements, modernist theories of legal authority and judicial interpretation eventually prevailed. By *Wickard v. Filburn* one can see evidence that those theories had been internalized by Supreme Court justices themselves.

The dangers of constitutional interpretation, at least in cases involving the realm of political economy, were radically relocated after *Wickard v. Filburn*. In orthodox constitutional political economy jurisprudence the principal dangers had been seen to flow from an insufficient policing by the judiciary of the public/private or federal/state boundaries, resulting in Congress or state legislatures undermining fundamental principles of republican government. After *Wickard* the principal dangers were seen to flow from the inappropriate substitution of one form of lawmaking—that engaged in by judges in the guise of constitutional interpretation—for another—that instituted by legislatures. In a world in which there was no meaningful separation of the authority of constitutional principles from the authority of those holding the power to say what those principles meant in cases before the Supreme Court, creative interpretations of the Constitution by judges amounted to lawmaking, and lawmaking by unelected judges raised problems of legitimacy in a democratic society. By the close of the Second World War the core dilemmas for American judges in constitutional cases centered not on boundary policing but on surmounting the countermajoritarian difficulty.

Thus, the central locus of the conventional account's constitutional revolution—political economy cases of the late 1930s and early 1940s that produced dramatic changes in the Court's Contracts Clause, economic due process, and Commerce Clause jurisprudence—was, fundamentally, an interpretive revolution, a revolution stemming from an altered juristic consciousness that eventually produced an altered view of the role of the judge in constitutional interpretation. Why did the revolution occur at that precise point in time? Here the Court-packing crisis can help clarify matters.

Suppose one were to think of the Court-packing plan, and the "crisis" it precipitated, as a symptom of jurisprudential change rather than as its cause. As a symptom of a crisis centering on the meaning of authoritative legal sources and the appropriate role for Supreme Court justices as constitutional interpreters, the Court-packing plan takes on considerable historical significance. It can be seen as a symbolic affirmation of the proposition that judges, in their role as constitutional interpreters, made law in the legislative sense. They made law because they were human beings; because debated constitutional issues were, at bottom, issues of politics; because the Constitution's text and essentialist principles gave no universal guidance to a changing world; and because change was inevitable and yet capable of being channeled by humans holding power and by the dictates of the democratic process. That same proposition, of course, had been endorsed by those endorsing the "living Constitution" view of constitutional adaptivity. And that same proposition was to undermine the integrity of guardian review.

The decade of the 1930s was a time when that proposition worked its way from the status of critique to something approaching orthodoxy. Its emergence was a product of a complex interaction of several factors, most visible of which were the economic and political dislocations and the epistemological unrest associated with the full-scale arrival of modernity in American civilization. The shock waves of modernity spawned the New Deal; they also spawned the widespread, but troubling, acceptance of the proposition that judges made law in constitutional interpretations as well as in common law decisions.

That proposition also has driven the conventional account of the constitutional revolution. If one assumes that judges are human and that judges make law in the guise of constitutional interpretation, the democratic remedy for inconvenient, politically unresonant, "obsolescent" constitutional decisions is to make the offending judges accountable. But Supreme Court justices are appointed for life. Accountability, in the straightforward political sense, can therefore only be obtained by forcing offending justices to retire or by balancing them with some new, politically resonant, colleagues. That is precisely what the Court-packing plan proposed. The plan failed in the short run because so stark a version of the proposition that Supreme Court justices were lawmakers in the legislative sense was not compatible with the deeply established image of the Constitution, and the members of the Court, as above conventional politics. But the proposition "succeeded" in the long run. Its success can be measured in the durability of the conventional account.

The Court-packing crisis explanation has been resonant because it so perfectly complements a view of Supreme Court justices as political actors who respond to the external pressures of changing social and economic conditions. But its resonance should not provide a basis for its plausibility. In fact, if one considers the multiple, complex factors that affect the decisions of humans holding high public office, and the particular set of constraints placed on a set of officials—Supreme Court justices—whose very identity is bound up in canons of impartiality and fidelity to the authority of law in America, the conventional explanation is vastly oversimple, and hence implausible.

Rather than seeing the constitutional revolution of the New Deal as a product of the Court-packing crisis, it is more profitable to think of the Court-packing crisis as a product of a constitutional revolution, one whose revolutionary character was far deeper and wider than any "switch in time."

By assuming that the Supreme Court of the United States could be "packed" with persons who would be sympathetic to the political goals of the Roosevelt administration, and who would translate that sympathy into constitutional doctrine, the proponents of Court-packing were taking as a given that America was a government of men, not laws. Theirs was a modernist, "living" view of constitutional interpretation and of the nature of legal authority. Their view of constitutional adaptivity was to prevail. And as winners, they have had a bastion of followers, so many that we have forgotten there was even a crisis of adaptivity.

III

The Creation of Triumphalist Narratives

We now may be in a position to appreciate the difficulty of getting disentangled from the historiographical underbrush of conventional narratives. Those narratives have identified the New Deal, and especially the Court-packing crisis it generated, as central causes of the emergence of a "revolution" in which the jurisprudence of a number of doctrinal areas of early twentieth-century constitutional law was transformed. In Part One I examined cases and commentary in those areas and some others, and concluded that the causal hypotheses posited by conventional narratives do not hold up; that their sample of constitutional cases has been inadequately thin; and that their readings of contested constitutional issues have been anachronistic and misleading.

But Part Two has resurrected the significance of the Court-packing plan as a symptom, rather than a cause, of an early twentieth-century revolution in constitutional jurisprudence, a revolution in which a traditional distinction between the will of the judge and the will of the law came to be seen as unintelligible, given modernist-inspired theories about the primacy of human will and power as causal agents in the universe. With the collapse of that distinction, claims that constitutional interpretations by judges were the equivalent of judicial findings and declarations of essential principles of law no longer resonated, and the "countermajoritarian difficulty" of a Supreme Court composed of unelected human political actors serving as the final arbiter of constitutional issues began to loom over discussions of the Court's interpretations.

Although neither the collapse of guardian review nor its ultimate replacement with bifurcated review can be associated with the Court-packing crisis in any precise chronological fashion, that crisis, and both those developments, can be associated with the triumph of modernist theories of the nature of law, the meaning of constitutional change, and the role of judges as constitutional interpreters. Modernist-inspired theories of law and judging can also be associated with each of the doctrinal transformations in areas of constitutional law that have been surveyed in Chapters 2 through 5. Doctrines facilitating executive discretion in foreign affairs, increasing the legal authority of administrative agencies staffed with experts, and expanding constitutional protection for free speech can each be seen as compatible with an enhanced appreciation of the importance of human agency in a modern industrial democracy.

If, therefore, the causal nexus between the Court-packing crisis and the constitutional revolution of the early twentieth century can be described as the inversion of its conventional description—the idea of Court-packing being derivative of the revolution rather than its cause—the question remains why the conventional narrative of early twentieth-century constitutional history has remained so durable and prominent.

Here we reach one of the most enduring side effects of the altered theories of causal attribution that accompanied the emergence of modernity in America. Once a behavioralist theory of judging in constitutional cases became entrenched, and once the Supreme Court itself began to act in a way consistent with that theory—experimenting with selectively deferential and heightened review as a way of responding to the countermajoritarian difficulty—it was as if those who had been observing developments in American constitutional law in the early years of the twentieth century underwent an epiphany. As a model of guardian review collapsed on the Court, and commentators characterized constitutional interpretation as another species of policymaking, judicial rhetoric in early twentieth-century constitutional opinions that appealed to essentialist constitutional principles, or insisted on separating "the law" from its interpreters, or claimed that the Constitution did not change over time, came to be seen as either otherworldly or disingenuous. Beginning in the 1930s, commentators increasingly sought to bypass such rhetoric in a search for what they regarded as more fundamental factors motivating judges in their interpretations of the Constitution, such as human temperament and political ideology.

The conventional account of early twentieth-century constitutional history has been constructed by narrators sharing a modernist sensibility. In Chapters 8 and 9 I explore two triumphalist narratives in that account, narratives that serve to reinforce the jurisprudential revolution in which the model of guardian review was replaced by that of bifurcated review in twentieth-century America. The narratives represent each of the tendencies I have associated with mid and late twentieth-century commentators. Chapter 8 focuses on the tendency of such commentators to engage in modernist readings of early twentieth-century guardian review cases. That tendency can be found in the narrative of "the rise and fall of substantive due process," which has been one of the centerpieces of the conventional account. Chapter 8 concludes that the narrative has produced a striking distortion of the meaning of the term "substantive due process" in early twentieth-century constitutional jurisprudence.

Chapter 9 then traces a narrative in which a behavioralist conception of judging has been combined with the normative criteria underlying bifurcated review to produce the canonization, and demonization, of certain early twentieth-century Supreme Court justices. Taken together, the two narratives have served to legitimize the jurisprudential revolution that took place in early twentieth-century constitutional law, while at the same time producing a distorted picture of doctrinal development and judicial performance in the years in which that revolution occurred. They thus help demonstrate the inadequacies of the conventional account of early twentieth-century constitutional history and at the same time help reveal the sources of its resonance.

8

The Myths of Substantive
Due Process

There is a story, told in nearly every treatment of early twentieth-century constitutional history for the past four decades,[1] about the judicial glossing of the term "liberty" in the Due Process Clauses as "liberty of contract," and the erection of "liberty of contract" as a constitutional barrier to state or federal redistributive legislation. In that story the "liberty of contract" cases are described as "substantive due process" cases, and an assumed understanding of the meaning of "substantive due process" accompanies that description.

According to the story, prior to the late nineteenth century "liberty" in the Due Process Clauses was commonly equated only with procedural protections against arbitrary or tyrannical governmental activity, such as protection against detention or incarceration without the benefit of some official legal proceeding. In the late nineteenth century, however, judges began to give "substantive" content to the Due Process Clauses in cases testing the constitutionality of redistributive legislation, so that the constitutional term "liberty" came to personify a sphere of private individual economic activity that was presumptively unreachable by the state. In one representative decision, the 1905 case of *Lochner v. New York*,[2] this "substantive" definition of liberty can be seen in clear relief. The Court majority in *Lochner*, in the course of invalidating a New York statute limiting the number of daily and weekly hours employees in the baking industry could work, equated "liberty" with "freedom of contract," a presumptively inalienable right on the part of workers and their employers in that industry to buy and sell employment services in the industrial marketplace on the terms they chose.

Judicial readings of liberty in the Due Process Clauses as "liberty of contract," the story continues, erected a constitutional barrier to most early twentieth-century state or federal legislation designed to regulate the practices of particular industries, including legislation directed at hours, wages, and working conditions. There were some exceptions to this general prohibition against legislative interference with market practices, such as when the industry was known to create health risks (mining) or when it employed particularly vulnerable classes of workers (women or children). But those exceptions were limited, with the result that the early twentieth-century American industrial marketplace remained a world of underpaid, overworked employees regularly exposing themselves to unhealthy and even dangerous working conditions.

Eventually a group of judges and commentators, responding to the negative side effects of unregulated industrial capitalism and to the flimsy constitutional basis of "substantive due process," launched an attack on liberty of contract as a barrier to legislation that sought to improve the social and economic conditions of industrial workers. They exposed "substantive" judicial readings of "liberty" in the Due Process Clauses as indefensible normative glosses on the Constitution by unelected, unaccountable judges. As it became apparent that "substantive due process" doctrines in cases testing the constitutionality of social welfare legislation were simply judicial devices to perpetuate "laissez-faire" attitudes toward economic activity, and as those attitudes became perceived as increasingly out of date in a modern industrialized society, the Court itself began to retreat from pouring substantive content into the Due Process Clauses, and legislation raising wage levels, reducing work hours, and improving working conditions received constitutional support. The 1937 case of *West Coast Hotel v. Parrish* illustrated the altered attitude. Eventually, after the late 1930s, the Court specifically repudiated the doctrine of substantive due process in cases involving legislative regulation of the economy.

The conventional time frame of the story is thus from 1905 to 1937, and the story's culmination in the *Parrish* decision provides another piece of evidence that the Court-packing crisis precipitated a constitutional revolution. Even though *Lochner* was not the first Court opinion glossing "liberty" in the Due Process Clauses as "liberty of contract,"[3] it initiates the story because two opinions from *Lochner* have been particularly beneficial to those telling it.

The first opinion is that of Justice Rufus Peckham for the majority in *Lochner*. Peckham described the New York statute that his opinion invalidated as "a mere meddlesome interference . . . with the rights of the individual," and noted that "[t]his interference on the part of legislatures of the several States with the ordinary trades and occupations of our people seems to be on the increase."[4] The Peckham opinion in *Lochner* has been characterized in the narrative as a judicial hymn to laissez-faire ideology. The other opinion, a dissent by Holmes that announced that "[t]his case is decided upon an economic theory which a large part of the country does not entertain," and suggested that "the Fourteenth Amendment does not enact Mr. Herbert Spencer's *Social Statics*,"[5] has been characterized as exposing the inappropriateness of reading normative judicial values into the Constitution.

There are a series of myths embedded in these characterizations, in related characterizations of the *Parrish* case, and in the story of the rise and fall of substantive due process itself. The myths spring from a modernist reading of the entire sequence of liberty of contract cases, a reading predicated on a behavioralist theory of judging and an estrangement from the starting assumptions of guardian review. In that reading judicial glosses on language in constitutional provisions inevitably have ideological dimensions because no essentialist or universalist interpretation of "liberty" is intelligible. Thus, the exercise that numerous early twentieth-century judges described themselves as engaging in when confronted with cases posing liberty of contract challenges to redistributive legislation—pricking out the boundary between the spheres of public power and private rights—was not an accurate statement of what those judges were actually doing. They were simply packing the constitutional term "liberty" with the assumptions of laissez-faire economic theory, giving a "substantive" meaning to the Due Process Clauses.

The conventional characterization of the Peckham and Holmes opinions in *Lochner* complements this perception of the Court's early twentieth-century liberty of contract cases. Peckham's characterization of the New York legislation as a "meddlesome interference" with individual rights is treated as evidence of his deep commitment to the sanctity of private economic transactions, and Holmes's remark about the Fourteenth Amendment not embodying the ideology of social Darwinism is taken as evidence that he had discerned the majority's bias. The Holmes opinion in *Lochner* plays a particularly large role in the conventional narrative of the "rise and fall of substantive due process": it is presented as illustrating an appropriately realistic perspective on all of the Court's early twentieth-century efforts to employ the "liberty of contract" gloss to invalidate redistributive legislation. Holmes is seen as having discerned that the *Lochner* majority, and the other majorities who engaged in that gloss, were giving a "substantive" reading of liberty in the Fourteenth Amendment that equated it with a particular economic ideology.

As a result the cases from *Lochner* to *Parrish* have been transformed into "substantive due process" cases. But not a single judge who decided liberty of contract cases or any other police power due process cases between 1905 and 1937—including Holmes—used the phrase "substantive due process" in those cases. That fact should not be surprising if one recalls the conceptual framework employed by the judges who decided the cases. Liberty of contract cases, and other cases in which liberty in the Fourteenth Amendment was the basis of a challenge to legislation grounded on police powers, were thought of as cases in which judges exercised their guardian review function of mapping out the boundary between public power and private rights. In such a framework it was expected that judges would make substantive glosses on the term "liberty": glossing was a necessary component of the process of judicial application of constitutional principles to concrete cases. Thus, the phrase "substantive due process" would have had no constitutional significance.

In mid and late twentieth-century constitutional law jurisprudence, by contrast, the term "substantive due process" does have constitutional significance. The term, as it appears in opinions, treatises, and casebooks, is used in two overlapping but distinguishable ways. It serves as an *analytical* encapsulation, serving to identify a line of constitutional decisions involving liberty-based due process challenges to legislation in which the thrust of the constitutional challenge is intended to have substantive, as distinguished from procedural, effects. For example, if there is a constitutional "liberty" on the part of each person in a marriage to make procreational choices with respect to potential offspring,[6] the Supreme Court's recognition of that liberty has the effect of rendering a federal or state statute that attempts to limit those choices substantively toothless: its policies cannot be enforced. In contrast, a successful liberty-based challenge to a state's policy of terminating the benefits of welfare recipients without a hearing means that the state can continue that policy if it affords affected persons constitutionally appropriate procedures.[7]

"Substantive due process" also serves as a *normative jurisprudential* category, signifying a particular attitude toward judicial review of constitutional provisions, such as "due process of law" in the Fifth and Fourteenth Amendments, that are seen as open-ended and hence susceptible to wide-ranging judicial glossing. If one believes that judicial review of such provisions should generally be limited because of the dangers of judicial encroachment into the domains of allegedly more accountable branches of government, "substantive" takes on the overtones of "judicially aggressive" or even "inappropriate." In modern constitutional commentary the designation "substantive due process," especially when applied to *Lochner*-type cases, often has a pejorative effect.

These two overlapping meanings of the term have played an important role in the emergence of myths about substantive due process in the conventional "rise and fall" narrative. Since the meanings give an inherent ambiguity to the term, calling a line of cases "substantive due process" cases invariably raises the normative stakes. The very encapsulation, even if it appears to be only for analytical convenience, necessarily directs one's attention to the normative issues raised by aggressive review of legislation under open-ended constitutional provisions. We will subsequently see how the overlapping meanings of "substantive due process" in commentary have contributed significantly to the emergence of the conventional "rise and fall of substantive due process" narrative, and how they have helped sustain the power of that narrative.

The emergence of the conventional rise and fall of substantive due process narrative was the product of three trends in early and mid-twentieth-century constitutional commentary. The first trend was a characterization of Holmes's dissents in liberty of contract cases as urging a more deferential role for the Court in all cases in which it reviewed regulatory or redistributive legislation. In this characterization Holmes's dissent in *Lochner* came to be seen as a general critique of guardian review, which it was not. The idea that the Court's cases from *Lochner* to *Parrish* represented inappropriate infusions of economic theories into constitutional provisions—that they were judicial affirmations of laissez-faire ideology—was related to the growing acceptance of Holmes's dissent as a critical symbol.

The second trend, which did not occur until after the *Parrish* case was decided, was the emergence in constitutional jurisprudence of an analytical separation between "procedural" and "substantive" due process cases. This development had nothing to do with liberty of contract cases. It was the result of the beginnings of selective judicial incorporation of the provisions of the Bill of Rights into the Due Process Clause of the Fourteenth Amendment, a development that had been given impetus by the *Gitlow* decision and was a regular concern of the Court by the late 1930s. By the 1940s constitutional law commentators were aware of that development and were attempting to reflect it in the analytical organization of casebooks and treatises, and the Court had begun to use the term "substantive due process" for the first time.

The last of the trends, which occurred in the early 1950s, was the reorganization of contemporary constitutional jurisprudence, and at the same time of early twentieth-century constitutional history, to emphasize themes that highlighted the replacement of guardian review with bifurcated review as the appropriate model of judicial interpretation in constitutional cases. That reorganization, for present purposes, had four noteworthy features. First was the aforementioned separation of cases involving judicial interpretations of the Due Process Clauses into "substantive" and "procedural" categories. The second was the conceptualization of cases in which the Court selectively incorporated provisions of the Bill of Rights into the Fourteenth Amendment as raising different analytical and jurisprudential issues from the *Lochner* line of cases. The third was the shrinking of "police power" cases from a general *analytical* category of constitutional cases to a limited *descriptive* subcategory of cases in which judges tended to defer to police power regulations.

The fourth was the fashioning of a historical narrative of the rise and fall of substantive due process in which the *Lochner* line of cases, not the incorporation cases, were identified as substantive due process cases. In that narrative the term "substantive due process" took on primarily normative implications, and the fact that the entire line of liberty of contract cases from *Lochner* through *Parrish* was decided as guardian review police power cases was ignored. I will be taking up each of the trends separately.

Revisionist scholarship in early twentieth-century constitutional history has spent more time with the line of cases from *Lochner* through *Parrish* than any of the other doctrinal areas explored in this book. A result of that work is that pejorative labels have been replaced with a more authentic sense of the jurisprudential categories and attitudes associated with early twentieth-century liberty of contract cases. One particular contribution of the revisionists will help us get a better sense of Holmes's dissent in *Lochner*.

As we have seen, police power due process cases such as liberty of contract cases were thought of as judicial applications of the boundary between public power and private rights. Revisionists have shown that a fundamental principle invoked to maintain that boundary was the principle that no legislature could enact "partial" legislation, legislation that imposed burdens or conferred benefits on one class of citizens rather than the citizenry as a whole. In such cases the role of judges under the Constitution was to determine whether the legislation in question was "partial," and therefore an illegitimate use of legislative power, or "general," and thus justifiable.[8]

When courts used the Due Process Clauses to strike down redistributive legislation in the late nineteenth and early twentieth centuries, they were thought of as doing so to prevent legislative tyranny or corruption. One example of such tyranny or corruption was legislation that violated the "anticlass" principle by failing to demonstrate that it was an appropriately "general" use of the police powers, as distinguished from an inappropriately "partial" one. That type of legislation amounted to the favoring of one class or interest above another or, more baldly, the taking of property from one class of citizens and giving it to another. "General" legislation based on the police powers, by contrast, regulated all citizens for the benefit of all citizens. Judicial classification of a particular legislative act as "partial" or "general" was a substantive exercise, but it was nonetheless a required exercise under the Constitution, since judges were the guardians of the individual liberties of citizens against tyranny or corruption.

Holmes's approach to redistributive legislation that was being challenged as a violation of the anticlass principle differed from that of all of his fellow judges in *Lochner*. He retained their working assumption that guardian review was the approved model of judicial interpretation in police power cases, a fact that his cryptic opinion-writing style and rhetorical flourishes sometimes made difficult to discern. But he did not begin an analysis of the boundary between public power and private rights from the same place as his colleagues. Holmes's strongly positivistic theories of sovereignty, plus the fatalistic deference toward majoritarian attitudes that he thought requisite in a democracy, made him feel that the scope of the police power was quite broad. As he put it in his *Lochner* dissent, "I think the word liberty in the Fourteenth Amendment is perverted when it is held to prevent the natural outcome of a dominant opinion, unless it can be said that a rational and fair man necessarily would admit that the statute proposed would infringe fundamental principles as they have been understood by our traditions and our law."[9] This was nothing more than a restatement of the obligation of judges exercising guardian review to identify fundamental principles embodied in constitutional provisions and apply them to cases, but it suggested that the anticlass principle would only be violated by the baldest legislative redistributions.

Nonetheless, Holmes intimated that he might have thought differently about the *Lochner* case had a particular ambiguity about it been clarified. The statute was defended as a legitimate exercise of the police power because it was designed to improve the condition of workers in bakeries, who had continual exposure to flour dust. Such a purpose was allegedly comparable to that of legislation limiting the hours of coal miners. The statute, however, was published in the general labor section of the New York laws, and Peckham, for the majority, expressed skepticism that it could be justified as a health measure, arguing that bakers were not an inherently susceptible class of workers and that a more general public health justification—that disabled bakers might be wards of the state—would apply to any occupation. On the other hand, Harlan, in dissent, took the health rationale as legitimate and voted to sustain the statute because of evidence that the lungs and bronchial tubes of bakers could be irritated by exposure to flour dust.

At the very end of his *Lochner* opinion, after suggesting that if the statute had infringed on "fundamental principles" it would have violated a constitutional liberty, Holmes added, "It does not need research to show that no such sweeping condemnation can be passed upon the statute before us. A reasonable man might think it a proper measure on the score of health. Men whom I certainly would not pronounce unreasonable would uphold it as a first instalment of a general regulation of the hours of work. Whether in this latter aspect it would be open to the charge of inequality I think it unnecessary to discuss."[10] It is not clear what Holmes meant by his last sentence. He might have meant that any "charge of inequality" that could have been leveled at general public health or safety statutes was not worth his time to discuss because such statutes were clearly constitutional. But it is more likely that he meant that the New York statute, viewed not as a specific health measure but as a general health and safety measure, might be constitutionally vulnerable because its application to a specific industry suggested it was "partial." Since the statute could be sustained as a specific health measure, however, it was unnecessary to discuss that issue.

Seen in this fashion, Holmes's dissent in *Lochner* looks like a conventional guardian review opinion with two distinctive features. One was that Holmes appeared to hold a broader conception of the scope of legitimate police power interferences with due process "liberties" than his colleagues. The other is that he seemed to have buttressed that latitudinarian view of police power legislation by two sorts of references that later generations of commentators would find resonant. One was to the "right of a majority to embody their opinions in law" in a democratic society. The other was to "convictions or prejudices," in the form of "particular economic theor[ies]," which might influence judges as they glossed constitutional provisions.

Those two sorts of references, with overtones of the "countermajoritarian difficulty" and behavioralist theories of judging, have tempted subsequent admirers of Holmes's dissent in *Lochner* to treat it as a fundamental critique of guardian review. But the dissent was, instead, a reaffirmation of the guardian review stance, coupled with a warning to judges not to confuse the sorts of "fundamental principles" that the term "liberty" in the Due Process Clauses embodied with their convictions that a particular piece of majoritarian legislation was foolish or partisan.

The warning was a product of Holmes's having concluded, after many years of being a judge, that judicial power to invalidate legislation that presumptively embodied the views of the majority should not be squandered on cases where the legislation only represented efforts to shift the costs of economic activity. By the time Holmes wrote his dissent in *Lochner* he had become fully resigned to legislative efforts to tinker with the distribution of wealth, even though he thought most of them futile. He was, consequently, skeptical of the "liberty of contract" gloss, having concluded that legislative interference with economic activity was predictable, unexceptionable, and often of only a transient effect. A passage from an unpublished draft of his opinion for the Court in *Keokee Consolidated Coke Co. v. Taylor*[11] shows his approach toward liberty of contract cases in sharp relief:

Whatever freedom of contract may be deduced from the word liberty in the Amendment, it is subject to restrictions in the interest of what the legislature conceived to be the general welfare . . . It is said that the power of duress has changed sides and is now with [organized labor]. But it if be admitted, as it certainly is established, that the legislature may interfere with theoretic in the interest of practical freedom, it would require a very clear case before a court could declare its judgment wrong and its enactment void.[12]

For Holmes the principle of economic freedom purportedly embodied in the liberty of contract was, in many contexts, an illusion. The economic freedom of individuals could be restricted by money, by power, or by politics, and a legislature, responding to any or all of those forces, could decide to protect the "practical" interests of public health or industrial efficiency at the expense of the "theoretic" freedoms embodied in the free labor ideal and the liberty of contract doctrine. As Holmes saw the judicial role in constitutional cases such as *Lochner*, it was not to discern whether legislation purportedly exercising police powers violated liberty in the abstract. Most legislation did. The judicial role was rather to discern whether such legislation really threatened fundamental constitutional principles, as where it amounted to a naked transfer of property or resources from A to B, in which case it would be a corrupt or arbitrary violation of the anticlass principle. That sort of legislation truly offended against constitutional liberty. Most redistributive legislation did not.

Thus, Holmes's standard of review in police power/due process cases was consistent with the orthodox guardian review model in that it required judges to evaluate the magnitude of particular legislative interferences with constitutionally protected liberties and to scrutinize the rationales offered in defense of the statutes under review. But since it confined judicial invalidation of police power legislation under the Due Process Clauses to blatant violations of foundational American traditions, it did not anticipate a high level of scrutiny in most cases challenging legislative redistributions.

Several of Holmes's colleagues on the Court in 1914 were provoked by the passage from his *Taylor* opinion quoted above. Their shared concern, expressed in different ways, was that Holmes's blithe acceptance of the ability of legislatures to "interfere with theoretic in the interest of practical freedom" would encourage a spate of regulatory legislation. Holmes, who was used to his fellow justices objecting when he called a spade a spade too openly, withdrew the passage.[13] But, by this time, Holmes's inference in his *Lochner* dissent that judges needed to get used to legislative tinkering with economic activity had come to be seen, by some enthusiastic supporters of his dissents in liberty of contract cases, as a broader criticism of the judicial practice of glossing constitutional provisions to invalidate majoritarian legislative policies.

Between 1905 and 1909 no analysis of the *Lochner* case in an American legal periodical described Holmes's dissent as a recognition of the counter-majoritarian dimensions of guardian review.[14] Most comments on the case treated it as a conventional exercise in guardian review, finding the central issue to be whether the New York statute could be justified as a paternalistic health measure, as in legislation affecting miners, or whether it amounted to an effort to buttress the economic status of employees in the baking industry, in which case it amounted to a violation of the anticlass principle.[15]

By 1909, however, Edward Corwin had described Holmes's dissent in *Lochner* as "cutting through the momentary question of policy to the deeper, though inarticulate, major premise underlying all preference for or against the popular view when it appears arrayed against private rights." Corwin's use of the phrases "inarticulate major premise" and "popular view" intimated that he thought the "deeper" issue raised by Holmes's dissent was whether the affinity or disaffinity of judges for the "popular view[s]" embodied in legislation should affect their conclusions about its constitutionality.

For Holmes's dissents in liberty of contract cases to be seen as charters for a new judicial stance toward redistributive legislation, it was necessary for early twentieth-century commentators to rethink the conception of governance in America on which the anticlass principle and other fundamental principles taken to be embodied in provisions of the Constitution were grounded. The liberties to own property, acquire it through economic transactions, improve it in the course of ownership, or enjoy the fruits of that ownership were inalienable, prepolitical rights. Legislation that took property from one citizen and gave it to another, or that otherwise fundamentally interfered with the possession, ownership, use, or enjoyment of private property, violated the essential obligation of republican government to secure the preexisting rights of its citizens, and was thus a demagogic overreaching by majorities of the limits on their powers. Liberty in the Due Process Clauses *had* to embody protection against governmental economic redistributions; otherwise the Constitution ceased to be a republican document.

Consider, in contrast, the conception of governance animating the following passage from a 1913 essay on redistributive legislation by Felix Frankfurter:

> The tremendous economic and social changes of the last fifty years have inevitably reacted upon the functions of the state. More and more gov-

ernment is conceived as the biggest organized social effort for dealing
with social problems . . . Growing democratic sympathies, justified by
the social message of modern scientists, demand to be translated into
legislation for economic betterment, based upon the conviction that
laws can make men better by affecting the conditions of living. We are
persuaded that evils are not inevitable, and that it is the business of
statesmanship to tackle them step by step, tentatively, experimentally.[16]

The world that Frankfurter portrayed was one marked by "tremendous economic and social changes," by "growing democratic sympathies," and by
"the social message of modern scientists." But it was the conviction that
these developments, taken together, meant that "government" should be the
prime mechanism for addressing social problems that distinguished Frankfurter's perspective.

Frankfurter had concluded that the onset of modernity required an expanded conception of government. Earlier generations of American legal and
social theorists had reacted to perceptions of economic, social, and scientific
transformations without concluding that government should be the primary
mechanism to respond to those changes.[17] Frankfurter's enthusiasm for governmental solutions was less a product of the novelty of the early twentieth-
century American environment than of an altered consciousness about the
power of human actors as causal agents.

For Frankfurter and his fellow "progressive" intellectuals "the social message of modern scientists" and "growing democratic sympathies" were both
evidence of a new confidence in the capacity of human beings to alter their
environment. Science had provided a new analytical key to the universe, one
that was founded not on divine will or other supernatural phenomena but on
empirical observations and deductions conducted by properly trained human
beings. The "social message of modern scientists" was that the same techniques employed to explain and to predict physical phenomena could be
applied to social phenomena. A mastery of such techniques gave humans
the power to control their own destiny. Thus, the social and economic policies of human actors—laws—could alter external conditions and "make men
better"; evils were no longer "inevitable."

One might contrast the set of interlocking epistemological assumptions reflected in Frankfurter's 1913 essay with the set on which the anticlass principle was founded. One of the reasons why protection for constitutional liberty
was embodied in the anticlass principle was that the possession, ownership,
and use of property were endemic to all human societies. The role of humans
as effective causal agents was not only limited by the omnipotence of external
forces in the universe; it was limited by the incapacity of humans to transcend

their own tendencies toward selfishness and corruption. The place of the courts as guardians of essentialist republican constitutional principles, confining the reach of governmental activity to those measures that benefited or burdened all members of the public equally, complemented those assumptions.

In Frankfurter's perspective constitutional liberty had been transformed from its orthodox version of protection from arbitrary or tyrannical governmental interference with prepolitical rights to a modern version in which enhanced economic opportunity would be abetted by affirmative governmental activity.[18] Once that shift in the conception of constitutional liberty had taken place, policing the boundary between the public and private spheres became a less vital task, and legislation conferring particular benefits on one class in society became less threatening to other classes. A law such as that tested in *Lochner* might be a "first instalment of a general regulation of the hours of work," but that "general regulation" had as its purpose the "betterment" of all classes in society. Thus, the increased encroachment of government on private activities through paternalistic legislation was not a cause for concern because those drafting the legislation were engaged in the purposive betterment of their fellow citizens along the lines of modern science and democratic theory.

Holmes's critique of the majority's posture in *Lochner* was also taken by commentators such as Frankfurter as more than a protest against the use of an inefficacious constitutional gloss in a line of cases. It was also taken as a revelation that judicial glossing of constitutional provisions produced a temptation for judges to equate those doctrines with particular economic policies, which raised serious questions of judicial accountability in a democratic society. Holmes's references to "economic theories" in *Lochner* had meant to raise this issue, and he continued to raise it in subsequent dissents in liberty of contract cases.[19] But he did not mean, in making such references, to suggest the abandonment of a role for judges as guardians of individual rights under the Constitution. He simply meant that the scope of protection for individual rights in police power cases was determined by the scope of the police power, and that in a democracy the range of the police power was extensive, with judicial invalidation of police power legislation being reserved for notorious violations of fundamental liberties.[20]

Holmes's "progressive" readers took Holmes to be saying something different in *Lochner*. They believed that he was pointing out that judges who opposed regulatory or redistributive legislation did so on the basis of their own economic biases, which took "liberty of contract" as a surrogate for "laissez faire." This reconfiguration of Holmes's position attributed to him the view that since judging, like other forms of governance, was human policymaking, unaccountable judges had no business substituting their policy preferences for those of more democratic institutions. Holmes's acolytes had come to see his *Lochner* dissent as an attack on any form of "substantive" judicial glossing.

By 1937, when the *Parrish* case was decided, the state of the Court's liberty of contract jurisprudence remained relatively unchanged from that when *Lochner* was decided, but commentary on the cases had taken a decided turn. In the years between *Lochner* and *Parrish* the Court's justices, with the exception of Holmes and sometimes Brandeis,[21] continued to prick out the boundaries between public power and private rights in liberty of contract cases. In the process they developed an additional justification for regulatory or redistributive legislation, what Justice Mahlon Pitney called "the interest of the public . . . in the prevention of pauperism, with its concomitants of vice and crime."[22] Although this rationale served to broaden slightly the scope of the police power to invade the sphere of protected private rights,[23] the Court stopped short of sustaining maximum hours or minimum wage legislation that could not be justified on public health grounds. In fact, in *Adkins v. Children's Hospital,* the Court concluded that after the Nineteenth Amendment to the Constitution, female industrial workers no longer needed special solicitude, and thus legislation requiring that they be paid minimum wage levels could not be justified on public health grounds.

Although Hughes's majority opinion in *Parrish* overruled *Adkins,* it employed the same guardian review framework, with its emphasis on pricking out constitutional boundaries, as Sutherland's dissenting opinion. As part of his justification for upholding the Washington minimum wage statute under review in *Parrish,* Hughes reviewed a line of police power cases in which the Court had concluded, as he put it, that due process liberties were subject to "reasonable regulations and prohibitions imposed in the interests of the community." He cited cases sustaining statutes limiting the hours of miners, forbidding the payment of seamen's wages in advance, enacting workmen's compensation laws, and prohibiting contracts that sought to limit the liability of employers for injuries to their employees. His conclusion that "the legislature has necessarily a wide field of discretion in order that there may be suitable protection of health and safety" was one that had been reached in a number of the Court's previous police power decisions.[24] Sutherland's dissent did not quarrel with that conclusion: he simply felt that minimum wage laws could not fairly be grounded on public health, safety, or moral concerns and were thus naked examples of "partial" legislation.

In short, as late as *Parrish,* and despite Holmes's *Lochner* dissent and his continued attacks on the "liberty of contract" gloss, cases testing liberty-based challenges to regulatory and redistributive legislation continued to be conceived as police power/due process cases in which judges exercised an interpretive role consistent with the model of guardian review. Further, not a single liberty of contract case had been characterized by any justice on the Court as involving substantive interpretations of the Due Process Clauses. In the same time period, however, one can see a different characterization of cases raising liberty-based due process challenges surfacing in commentary.

That characterization was not uniform nor was it widely advanced. Nonetheless, it discernibly surfaces in the 1920s. First, Frankfurter's view that the decisions by Court majorities in *Lochner* and *Adkins* had both reached substantively infelicitous results and represented an overreaching of the judicial function in constitutional cases continued to be articulated in some circles. A drumbeat of criticism of the Court's liberty of contract cases, first advanced by Frankfurter and others before World War I, mounted as the Court declared minimum wage legislation invalid.[25] Progressives characterized the Court's decisions in minimum wage cases as reflecting a deliberate and irresponsible judicial indifference to the efforts of legislative majorities to respond to the growing economic inequalities produced by industrial capitalism. The Court was repeatedly attacked by Frankfurter in *The New Republic*;[26] progressive disciples of Holmes, such as Harold Laski, complained to Holmes himself about the decisions;[27] and the National Consumers' League, with the cooperation of *The New Republic*, published a collection of articles denouncing *Adkins* and advocating minimum wage levels for industrial workers.[28]

In addition, scholarly commentators began to expand on one of the themes Holmes had first raised in *Lochner:* unreflective guardian review glosses of open-ended constitutional provisions could result in judges equating constitutional principles with particular economic theories. Some critics of the liberty of contract decisions began to suggest that the judicial majorities in those cases were not being unreflective; they were being willfully ideological. They were opposed to redistributive and regulatory legislation because they clung to a "laissez-faire" economic philosophy. Although this characterization of the *Lochner* line of cases as illustrations of judicial laissez-faire was more common after the late 1930s, it appeared as early as 1922.[29]

Finally, a development that at first blush appeared to have little to do with the primary quarrel between the Court and its progressive critics occurred after the Court's incorporation of the free speech provisions of the First Amendment into the Fourteenth Amendment's Due Process Clause in *Gitlow v. New York*. As we have seen in Chapter 5, Charles Warren, provoked by the possible implications of the *Gitlow* decision, wrote an article in the *Har-*

vard Law Review in which he attempted to show that the liberty of contract cases could be seen as of a piece with *Gitlow* and with other decisions in which Court majorities had glossed the Fourteenth Amendment's Due Process Clause to find "liberties" to choose the education of one's children. The liberty of contract decisions, *Gitlow*'s "incorporation" of Bill of Rights provisions into the Due Process Clause, and those "liberty of mind" cases, Warren suggested, all represented a "new conception of the 'liberty' of the individual."[30] He felt that a potential effect of this development might be an infringement on "the 'liberty' of the States," since the locus of protection for civil or economic rights might shift from state courts to the United States Supreme Court.[31]

Warren's concerns were not those of the progressives who had attacked the Court's liberty of contract decisions. He wanted to maintain "the 'liberty' of the State to control its own affairs and to regulate its own welfare and good order," which included the guaranteeing of "personal, civil, or property rights" by state constitutions and state courts. He was worried that "new liberty" decisions by the Court might result in the undue encroachment of the national government, via the Supreme Court, on state affairs. The imposition of "a new definition of 'liberty' applied to every State by the judicial branch of the National Government," he feared, might result in an inappropriate standardization of "legislation enacted by each state to meet local conditions and to regulate local relations."[32] Nowhere in Warren's article was there a suggestion that the Court's "new liberty" cases represented an illegitimate judicial usurpation of majoritarian policies.

But Warren's concern that the Court's "new liberty" cases might disturb a traditional balance of sovereign power between the national and state governments motivated him to emphasize the novelty of the judicial glosses on "liberty" that had surfaced in the early twentieth century. He rested that conclusion on four historically grounded claims. The first was that the original meaning of "liberty" in the Fifth Amendment's Due Process Clause was the equivalent of the meaning of that term in existing state constitutions at the time of the framing of the Constitution, "freedom from physical restraint of the person."[33] The second was that the Supreme Court, in an 1894 decision, had acknowledged that the Fourteenth Amendment conferred no new rights but only extended the protection of the Constitution over preexisting state rights.[34] The third was that the judicial gloss of "liberty" as "liberty of contract" had not accompanied either the passage of the Fifth or the Fourteenth Amendments: it had first been promulgated by the Court in 1897.[35] The fourth was that the Court's declaration of a "liberty of speech" in the Fourteenth Amendment's Due Process Clause was sudden and unprecedented. As Warren put it, in 1907, the Court expressly left the question undecided; in 1920 it stated that it did not consider it, or decide it, but simply conceded it for the purpose of the case; in 1922, it stated that the Federal Constitution "imposes upon the States no obligation to confer upon those within their jurisdiction either the right of speech or the right of silence." Yet, in 1925, it stated that "we may and do assume" that freedom of speech and the press is one of the "fundamental rights and liberties" protected by the Due Process Clause.[36]

Although Warren did not use the term "substantive due process" in his article, he provided a history that suggested that the Court's glosses on "liberty" in the Due Process Clauses had not been uniform over time; that "liberty of contract" had a relatively short doctrinal pedigree; and that the Court's interpretation of the Due Process Clauses had been, as he put it, "constantly expanding."[37] For commentators who were apprehensive about the last claim because they regarded the liberty of contract line of decisions as evidence of the Court majority's laissez-faire bias, Warren's history provided evidence that the original meaning of "due process" had been far more limited. By the 1930s commentators were anthologizing the conception of a "laissez-faire" Court[38] and adopting Warren's history as an authoritative demonstration that the Court had steadily expanded the meaning of "liberty" in the Due Process Clauses in the first two decades of the twentieth century.[39]

Meanwhile, constitutional law scholars in the 1930s were attempting to formulate analytical categories in their treaties and casebooks to make sense of the Court's various glosses on "liberty" in the Due Process Clauses. Their task was complicated by the fact that the Court began to expand its incorporation of Bill of Rights protections beyond those of free speech and freedom of the press. As this selective judicial incorporation of Bill of Rights guaranties progressed, Fourteenth Amendment "due process" came to include not only additional First Amendment rights, such as assembly,[40] but Sixth Amendment rights, such as the right to be informed of the nature of a criminal charge[41] or the right to be afforded counsel in a capital case.[42]

By the 1930s constitutional law casebooks and treatises had begun to analyze due process cases with these developments in mind. One response on the part of casebook editors was to separate the category of due process cases into, as one editor, Noel Dowling, put it, "Due Process As Affecting Matters of Procedure" and "Due Process As Affecting Matters of Substance."[43] In the former category they placed an older line of decisions in which the Due Process Clauses had been read to provide procedural safeguards, and added to that category some of the recent cases incorporating civil and criminal procedural rights against the states. In the latter category they placed liberty of contract cases, the cases in which the Court had identified a "liberty" to make educational choices, and cases in which First Amendment provisions had been incorporated in the Fourteenth Amendment's Due Process Clause. Having done this, they continued to treat all due process cases as subject to the sort of guardian review typically exercised in police power cases, anticipating that the judicial treatment of a liberty-based due process challenge would be the same whether *Lochner*-type liberties, liberties of the mind, or incorporated Bill of Rights provisions were involved.

By the 1940s further refinements in the classification of due process cases had taken place. The refinements reflected the fact that throughout that decade the Supreme Court continued to expand its incorporation of provisions of the Bill of Rights into the Fourteenth Amendment's Due Process Clause, while at the same time showing signs of retreating from aggressive review in *Lochner*-type cases. Casebook and treatise writers began to identify a category variously called "Civil and Political Rights" or "Political and Public Rights," and to separate that category from "Due Process" cases. One writer, who in a 1932 edition of a casebook had distinguished "Restrictions on Governmental Regulation of Private Economic Interests" from "Restrictions on Government Control over Private Non-Economic Interests," but had treated both lines of cases as susceptible to standard police power analysis, decided, in his 1948 edition, to place cases involved with "Protection of Civil and Political Rights" in a different category from "Due Process" cases involving "Regulation of Economic Activities."[44]

As early as 1941 one commentator had taken an additional step, creating a separate category for cases involving the "Bill of Rights of the Federal Constitution." He described that category as reflecting a "broadening of the concept of liberty to include fundamental rights under due process,"[45] and subdivided cases into various Bill of Rights "liberties," ranging from freedom of speech and the press to various criminal procedure protections. At the same time he retained a "Police Power" category of cases, with several subdivisions: *Lochner*-type cases were placed in the subcategory of "Regulatory Control of Industrial Relations." This left him a truncated "Due Process" category, which consisted of cases that would be thought of today as involving challenges to the actions of governmental bodies on the ground that officials exercised discretion without any controlling standards.[46] Although the creation of an entirely separate category for incorporated rights cases was atypical, by the close of the 1940s the "Due Process of Law" category had become more identified with procedural due process cases, and incorporated, noneconomic "liberty" cases, now described as "Political and Civil Rights" cases or the equivalent, had been separated from *Lochner*-type cases. The "Police Power" category, although retained, typically contained only economic activity cases.[47]

These developments reflect several implicit judgments by commentators. First, they had sensed that incorporated due process rights appeared to be in a different analytical category from the due process liberties the Court had identified in the *Lochner* line of cases or in the "liberty of mind" cases that did not rest on Bill of Rights provisions. The Court had itself identified incorporated due process rights as "fundamental" and "essential to a system of ordered liberty," so the identification of a particular provision as eligible for incorporation against the states seemed to suggest that the "liberty" it protected was presumptively entitled to considerable weight when allegedly infringed by a state statute. Second, commentators in the 1940s were well aware that the Court was retreating from vigorous affirmations of the liberty of contract principle, and at the same time, in its incorporation decisions, was demonstrating enhanced support for noneconomic civil and political rights. The only incorporated Bill of Rights provision that protected liberties to engage in economic activity was the Just Compensation Clause of the Fifth Amendment, which the Court had incorporated against the states in 1897.[48] Since then all of the provisions incorporated into "due process" had protected activity that was not associated with economic transactions.

Finally, commentators were becoming aware of the implications of these developments for the term "due process of law." Of the three types of due process "liberties" that Warren's 1926 article and the 1930s casebooks had anticipated would be treated comparably in constitutional challenges entertained by the Court, one type, *Lochner*-style "liberties of contract," seemed to be diminishing in constitutional importance, and another type, nonincorporated "liberties of mind," now appeared to be subsumed in the cases incorporating First Amendment provisions against the state, which were increasing in constitutional importance. Moreover, not all incorporated due process cases were the result of challenges to police power legislation; some of them were the products of claims that the absence of protections for criminal defendants in a state's criminal justice system constituted denials of "due process."

While casebook editors were struggling to derive an organizational framework to accommodate the differing types of due process cases, no clear distinction between "substantive" and "procedural" due process cases had yet emerged. The term "substantive due process" appeared in four cases between 1935 and 1946, once in an argument by counsel in a Supreme Court case and three times in lower federal court opinions. But on each occasion it was employed to describe a claim based on inadequate procedural protections, such as the absence of a notice or a hearing in a case involving a civil or criminal penalty. None of the cases in which the term appeared was a "liberty" challenge to a police power statute.[49]

By the early 1950s the term "substantive due process" had been employed twice in Supreme Court opinions, and in both instances the cases involved challenges based on incorporated Bill of Rights provisions. The term was used to distinguish Bill of Rights challenges that were grounded on provisions conferring procedural safeguards from those grounded on provisions that imposed substantive limitations on legislation. Thus, in his dissent in *Republic Natural Gas v. Oklahoma*,[50] Justice Wiley Rutledge noted that due process challenges based on "procedure" were distinct from those based on "judicially adopted rules of substantive law," and in his concurrence in *Beauharnais v. Illinois*,[51] Justice Stanley Reed described a free speech challenge to the constitutionality of an Illinois group libel statute, resting on the incorporation of First Amendment provisions against the states through the Fourteenth Amendment, as a "substantive due process" challenge.

By 1950 the casebook editor Noel Dowling had recognized that the incorporation of Bill of Rights protections into the Fourteenth Amendment had resulted in a variety of different types of due process challenges being available, and that one way to distinguish those challenges was to note that some had "procedural" and some had "substantive" effects. As early as the 1937 edition of his casebook, we have seen, Dowling had divided due process cases into "matters affecting procedure" and "matters affecting substance." In his 1950 edition he rephrased that division as "procedural due process" and "substantive due process." He also subdivided "substantive" due process cases into cases involving "Regulation of Economic Affairs" and cases involving "Freedom of Speech, Press, and Assembly."[52]

This was a familiar 1940s division, reflecting the different types of constitutional "liberties" Warren had identified in 1926. But Dowling felt it reflected more than subject matter. In an introductory note to the freedom of speech, press, and assembly cases he said that "[t]he title, 'substantive due process,' is somewhat arbitrary, but in the present stage of the development of constitutional law . . . it comprehends most of the questions considered in the cases in this section, and it helps us to emphasize the distinction . . . in the judicial methods used in liberty of mind cases, on the one hand, and economic affairs cases, on the other."[53]

Dowling had recognized that in both *Lochner*-type police power cases and certain incorporated Bill of Rights cases successful liberty-based challenges had the effect of invalidating state legislation. They were cases in which due process challenges had "substantive" rather than "procedural" effects. He had also noticed that the "judicial methods" employed by the Court in the 1940s were different in the two sets of cases. By separating *Lochner* and other liberty of contract cases from incorporated Bill of Rights cases raising freedom of speech, press, and assembly issues, Dowling was not only underscoring the difference between "liberty of contract," a judicial gloss, and "liberty of speech," a textually protected, incorporated right; he was emphasizing the Court's increasing tendency to uphold the latter set of "substantive due process" challenges but not to uphold the former set.

Dowling's conclusion that different types of due process cases were eliciting different judicial treatment was shared by many other commentators in the 1950s. With that recognition the grounds for the conventional narrative of the rise and fall of substantive due process were laid. Casebook editors in the 1950s began to adopt a new organizational framework for presenting the three types of due process cases that Warren's article and earlier casebook and treatise editions had lumped together.

In that new organizational framework a category of "Constitutional Requirements of Fair Procedure"[54] or the equivalent[55] was created, in which the incorporation cases affording procedural safeguards in state proceedings were placed. This left a residual category of "Constitutional Safeguards of Substantive Rights"[56] or the equivalent,[57] in which all the other due process cases, which had previously been identified as police power cases, were grouped. That category was itself divided into "Freedom of Enterprise" cases[58] or the equivalent[59] and "Freedom of Expression" cases.[60] The category of "Police Power" cases virtually disappeared, with the term "police power" primarily being relegated to the casebook index.[61]

The casebook editors' subdivision of the residual category of due process cases, now identified as "substantive due process" cases, was accompanied by comments suggesting that the "freedom of enterprise" cases, which included the entire line of liberty of contract cases, were not analytically comparable to the "freedom of expression" cases, either with respect to judicial methodology or with respect to the governing standard of constitutional review. As one editor put it,

> In his study of the case materials . . . the student should observe the degree of judicial protection accorded freedom of expression . . . as an implied fundamental right of a substantive character limiting the states under the Fourteenth Amendment, and compare the judicial protection accorded economic rights . . . in the interpretation of the implied substantive liberties secured by the Due Process Clauses of the Fourteenth and Fifth Amendments . . . Do the judicial tests and techniques evident

in the freedom of expression cases, as compared with the judicial tests and techniques employed in the cases dealing with economic rights, indicate that the substantive rights in the freedom of expression category stand on a higher level than the substantive economic liberties?[62]

This new organizational framework for due process cases conveyed some clear messages. Most modern due process cases, the framework suggested, were not properly seen as police power guardian review cases. They were either "procedural due process" cases or "substantive due process" cases. Procedural due process cases and the "freedom of expression" variety of substantive due process cases were incorporated Bill of Rights cases. The central judicial inquiry in those cases was not where the boundary between private rights and public power lay but whether a particular Bill of Rights provision was sufficiently "fundamental" to be incorporated within the Fourteenth Amendment's Due Process Clause. As for the remaining substantive due process cases, only the liberty of contract cases appeared to be governed by the methodologies of police power guardian review. The other "liberty" cases that had been decided prior to *Gitlow* were increasingly seen as "liberty of mind" or "liberty of worship" cases, which made them appear analogous to incorporated First Amendment cases.

These developments had the effect of isolating the liberty of contract line of cases. The new conceptualization suggested that there were *no* due process cases in which current judges pricked out the boundary between the police power and private rights. There were, instead, two different lines of incorporated Bill of Rights cases and a line of economic activity cases in which the Court now adopted a deferential standard toward regulatory and redistributive legislation. In none of the cases did the Court appear to be engaging in the same sort of glossing of "liberty" that it had undertaken in the liberty of contract cases. That glossing had already been characterized by commentators as a judicial endorsement of the economic philosophy of laissez-faire. The new conceptualization implied that no comparable judicial glossing was taking place in the incorporation due process cases. Although judges were deciding whether the rights protected by a particular provision of the Bill of Rights were sufficiently "fundamental" to require that provision's incorporation, that inquiry did not tempt them to equate "liberty" with a particular economic philosophy.

Thus, the only true substantive due process cases, this organization suggested, were *Lochner*-type cases, and those cases were no longer properly described as police power cases because the modern Court had demonstrated that it was disinclined to guard the boundary between public power and private rights when regulatory or redistributive legislation was challenged. Once the category of substantive due process cases had become limited to economic liberty cases, the conventional "rise and fall" narrative was in a position to be launched.

That narrative would rest on the blending together of two elements. One, in place since the 1930s, was the characterization of the *Lochner* line of cases as exercises in the judicial glossing of constitutional provisions to conform with the assumptions of laissez-faire economics. The other was the isolation of those cases from all other due process cases in casebook reorganizations in the 1940s and 1950s. The blending of these elements invested the term "substantive due process" with its familiar dual meaning in late twentieth-century constitutional jurisprudence. "Substantive due process" stood for a technique by which judges poured content into indeterminate constitutional provisions, and it also illustrated the illegitimacy of such an exercise in a democratic society.

The attribution of this dual character to substantive due process cases was reinforced by the other features of the reorganization of constitutional law casebooks in the late 1940s. The disappearance of "police power" as a general analytical category conveyed the message that economic liberty cases were no longer to be seen as unexceptionable exercises in boundary pricking. The separation of *Lochner*-type cases from incorporated substantive rights cases, and the recognition of different judicial attitudes and techniques in "free enterprise" and "freedom of expression" cases, suggested that the "substantive" judicial inquiries in incorporation cases were of a different order from those in liberty of contract cases because incorporation cases involved the interpretation of textually grounded liberties rather than judicially created liberties. And the contrast presented between the Court's continuing development of substantive criteria for selectively incorporating Bill of Rights provisions and its disinclination to uphold challenges based on economic "liberties" reinforced the pejorative characterization of substantive due process as a technique, now abandoned as illegitimate, in which the Court had read "liberty" as the equivalent of the laissez-faire principle of "liberty of contract." This characterization was to dominate the rise and fall narrative.

One can see that narrative taking shape in works in the 1950s. In an article in the *Minnesota Law Review* in 1950,[63] Monrad Paulsen set out to show what he called the "persistence of substantive due process in the states." What Paulsen meant by "substantive due process" was, exclusively, the *Lochner* line of cases. He began his article with a short history of the Court's police power/due process decisions between 1890 and 1937:[64]

By giving broad scope to these vague expressions of the Fourteenth Amendment, the judiciary seized the power to nullify legislative enactments because the judges found them vicious or silly. "Liberty" was found to include freedom to contract and to engage in business. Interference with this freedom was in accordance with "due process" only if the interference bore, in the eyes of the judges, some relation to public health, safety or welfare. Few legal doctrines have been subjected to more bitter criticism than this testing of regulatory legislation by the due process clause . . . It has been charged that the doctrine of substantive due process has been the means whereby conservative judges have read classical economic theory into the Constitution. [Here Paulsen inserts a footnote citation to Holmes's dissent in *Lochner*.] The doctrine is seen as a violation of sound democratic procedures in that it permits judges to substitute their judgment as to political policy for that of the legislature . . . These criticisms have not failed to influence the Supreme Court in recent years . . . It is significant that since 1937 the Court has not declared a statute regulating economic affairs to be a violation of due process . . . [T]he invalidation by reason of the due process clause of state laws seems . . . to be a matter of history.[65]

In the excerpt from Paulsen one can see all of the central characteristics of the conventional narrative of the rise and fall of substantive due process. He applied the term "substantive due process" to the *Lochner* line of cases, not to the cases incorporating noneconomic substantive rights against the states, nor to the pre-*Gitlow* "liberty of mind" cases. He treated the substantive reading given to "liberty" in the *Lochner* line of cases as not grounded in the constitutional text but rather as evidence that a given Court majority found regulatory legislation "vicious or silly." He associated the majority's attitude with a "conservative" ideology rooted in "classical economic theory." He cited Holmes's suggestion in *Lochner* that the case had been decided on an "economic theory." He pointed out the "countermajoritarian difficulty" presented by "substantive" judicial readings of the Due Process Clauses that invalidated majoritarian policies. He noted that "substantive due process" had been roundly criticized, and he concluded by suggesting that the Court had abandoned the doctrine.

In a 1959 constitutional law casebook intended for undergraduates and graduate students in political science, Rocco J. Tresolini combined the new conceptualization of due process cases with an extended version of Paulsen's narrative. Tresolini presented a chapter entitled "The Fourteenth Amendment and Economic Regulation," which contained the liberty of contract cases from *Lochner* through *Parrish*. He also included a section devoted to

"Individual Rights," which consisted of an introductory portion on the technique of incorporation and three chapters, one on "Freedom of Religion," a second on "Freedom of Speech, Press, & Assembly," and a third on "Criminal Procedure Cases." He eliminated "police power" as an analytical category, mentioning the term only as an index entry keyed to his discussion of economic regulation cases.[66] This organization of due process cases produced an even more marked methodological isolation of the *Lochner* line of cases than had been achieved in earlier 1950s casebooks. By introducing "individual rights" cases with an essay on judicial incorporation, and by including both "procedural" and "substantive" incorporated rights cases in that chapter, Tresolini implied that the salient methodological feature of modern "individual rights" cases was that they involved judicial applications of specific textual guaranties of the Bill of Rights against the states, as distinguished from judicial glosses on open-ended constitutional provisions. They were, in short, not "substantive due process" cases at all.

To clinch that point, Tresolini introduced his chapter on "The Fourteenth Amendment and Economic Regulation" by telling a seven-page version of Paulsen's history.[67] The first heading of Tresolini's introduction was "The Rise of Substance Due Process";[68] its final heading was "The Decline of Substantive Due Process."[69] The text between those headings discussed *Lochner*, *Adkins*, *Parrish*, and other "substantive due process" cases, characterizing Court majorities who upheld liberty of contract challenges as "conservative" and dedicated to "laissez-faire" economics. None of the cases were described as "police power" cases. Tresolini ended his narrative with the sentence, "In our time the importance of the due process clause is to be found in other areas. It is now used primarily to limit legislation affecting individual liberties."[70] He did not suggest, however, that such a usage amounted to "substantive due process." That term was reserved for the liberty of contract decisions.

By the 1950s, then, the rise and fall narrative had taken on the elements of a morality play. Substantive due process cases had been placed in a historical episode that ended with the "decline" of the approach. The generally deferential stance of the Court toward legislation regulating economic activity after the early 1940s, coupled with the increasing number of incorporated rights cases, was taken as evidence that the Due Process Clauses were now being used appropriately, as the basis for judicial application against the states of Bill of Rights provisions protecting civil liberties rather than as the basis for judicial invalidation of legislation that offended the gospel of laissez-faire. The *Parrish* decision, in this scenario, became a doubly enlightened farewell to "substantive due process," being both a judicial recognition of the antiquated state of laissez-faire economics and a judicial acquiescence in majoritarian policymaking in a democracy. The fact that *Parrish* had actually been conceptualized by the judges who decided it as a boundary-pricking police power case, identical in form to *Lochner*, played no part in the narrative.

In contemporary constitutional law casebooks, versions of the above history remain firmly in place. The methodology of judicial incorporation of Bill of Rights provisions is not described as a version of substantive due process but receives independent analysis, and cases involving established incorporated rights, such as free speech cases or religion clause cases, are treated as if they do not implicate the Due Process Clause at all. Substantive due process cases are divided into two classes, "economic" due process cases and cases, since the 1970s, in which the Court has concluded that some noneconomic "liberties" that are not singled out in the Bill of Rights deserve a measure of constitutional protection.[71] The rise and fall narrative persists, encompassing only the *Lochner* line of cases; "police power" is employed to describe a species of eminent domain cases rather than as a general analytical category; and, to the extent that "substantive due process" is treated as a currently viable constitutional doctrine, its context does not include any economic liberty cases.[72] The consequence of this organization is not only to retain the rise and fall narrative as a morality play but to underscore the replacement of guardian review with bifurcated review. Even the sorts of substantive judicial glosses on liberty that proved to be anathema in the economic context, the organization suggests, are permissible so long as they are employed in the service of protection for noneconomic rights.

It remains to make sense of how this remarkable distortion of the conceptual apparatus employed by all the justices who decided *Lochner*, including Holmes, could have taken place. The conventional account of the rise and fall of substantive due process has been created by persons of respectable scholarly standing, and the account has endured for many years and has only very recently begun to be questioned. Nonetheless, it remains the case that the conventional account has utterly failed to see *Lochner*-type police power cases as those cases were seen by the judges who decided them, and has imposed a label on those cases that is wildly anachronistic. Why did this happen?

An understanding of the creation of the myths of early twentieth-century substantive due process begins with a recognition of Holmes's jurisprudential isolation in the sequence of cases beginning with *Lochner*, and the eventual elevation of his posture, in slightly misunderstood form, to mainstream jurisprudential status. One can best understand those two phenomena by focusing on the consciousness that distanced Holmes from his colleagues (excepting Brandeis) on the Fuller, White, and Taft Courts, that affected his methodology in police power/due process cases, and that made him a resonant judicial figure for succeeding generations.

Holmes began police power cases by adopting the orthodox methodology of his judicial colleagues, that of searching for the boundary between permissible legislative restrictions and impermissible legislative usurpations. He assumed, as they did, that the Constitution protected the fundamental liberties of American citizens from being infringed by government. But he also assumed, in contrast to nearly all of his colleagues, that the "liberty of contract" late nineteenth-century judges and commentators had extracted in their interpretations of the Due Process Clauses was nothing but a "dogma." He did not believe that property or liberty was always an inviolate right, incapable of being restricted by government in the interest of public health or safety. Nor did he think that the right to contract was in that category. On the contrary, he believed that human beings holding power regularly restricted liberties and would continue to do so. Although he believed that humans had comparatively little power to affect fundamental economic laws, he expected legislative majorities to try to do so, and did not think, in most cases, that the Constitution stood in their way.[73]

Holmes could not see any theoretical limits on the power of government, which was after all nothing but the aggregate policies of human powerholders. There were practical limits—other humans would revolt and displace powerholders if their acts were intolerably tyrannical or arbitrary—but those limits could not be fixed in advance. It was thus an illusion to talk of "liberty of contract," or other "liberties," as if they were unassailable timeless principles. They were what a current majority deemed them to be. The same could be said of the "police power," the "public interest," and other judicial formulas ostensibly designed to mark out the limits of governmental interference with private activity.

Since Holmes believed that the scope of the police power or the boundary between "public" and "private" activity was in the great bulk of cases simply a question of historical circumstance and majoritarian will, he found judicial readings of the Due Process Clauses that held up "liberty of contract" as a barrier to legislative regulation inappropriate. Such readings sought to erect a definition of the scope of the police power as allegedly timeless, natural, and externally derived. This was not the case, Holmes thought: the boundary between which sets of activities were "public" and which sets remained "private" would change with time, circumstance, and human intervention. Even in *Pennsylvania Coal Co. v. Mahon,* where he thought that the limits of the police power had been reached, Holmes acknowledged that each instance would "depend . . . on the particular facts."[74]

No one else on the *Lochner* Court, and no one else who participated in the decision in *Adkins,* held so modernist a view of police power cases. For the rest of Holmes's judicial colleagues in those cases, limits on the reach of public power, and limits on the capacity of legislatures to favor one class of persons at the expense of another, were foundational principles of republican constitutional government in America. Those principles were foundational, in part, because the inherent tendencies of humans in power toward tyranny and corruption were self-evident, making the vigilant defense of "liberty" essential. They were also foundational because many governmental efforts to modify the inexorable course of the laws of nature or economics were bound to be futile.

Thus, for Holmes's judicial contemporaries to embrace the idea that all legislation was "general" because all individual transactions bore some connection to the public welfare—or the corresponding idea that all activity was "public" if it was thought to have a sufficient impact on the majority of the people—would have been to abandon those foundational principles. To abandon them was to embrace the terrifying prospect that the forces of modernity could combine to transform their understanding of governance in America.

In contrast, those who approved of Holmes's approach to liberty of contract cases found it "natural" and compelling because they shared Holmes's accommodations to modernity. For the most part they were not Holmes's chronological contemporaries. They had experienced some of the shock waves of a modernizing world: the democratization of American political culture, global war, economic depression in an advanced industrial capitalist society, the increasing momentum of scientific and technological innovation. They were less inclined than their predecessors to believe in the omnipotence of external forces as causal agents. They believed that they could make over their experience to mandate "progress," and that they could use law in that process. They did not think of principles of constitutional and common law as timeless and essentialist but as human-crafted and thus malleable.

So when they came to positions of power and influence as legislators and judges during the 1930s, they began to abandon the anticlass principle in police power cases and the foundationalist republican premises driving that principle. Then, in the capacity of commentators, they looked back on the actions of early twentieth-century judges and wondered why they had invested concepts such as "liberty of contract" with so much constitutional weight. Their modernist sensibilities dictated that they would take "liberty of contract" as nothing but a human-created ideological dogma, whose presuppositions were oblivious to modern economic conditions and equally oblivious to the capacity of government to increase the economic opportunities of citizens in a democratic society. So they labeled judges whose invocation of "liberty of contract" revealed their belief in the foundational principles of orthodox police power jurisprudence as captives of a "laissez-faire" ideology. Eventually, they labeled foundationalist interpretations of the Due Process Clause in police power cases as "substantive" and constructed the "rise and fall" narrative.

The collective disaffinity with liberty of contract cases, and affinity with incorporated rights cases, which animated the construction of the rise and fall narrative, were intuitive and largely unself-conscious. Those who erroneously labeled the *Lochner* line of police power decisions "substantive due process" cases, and who, at the same time, declined to attach that label to decisions extending the class of incorporated Bill of Rights provisions, thought they knew what the two sets of cases truly embodied. The *Lochner* cases were illegitimate, countermajoritarian glosses in the service of laissez-faire. The incorporated rights cases were symbols of the importance of protecting noneconomic civil liberties in an antitotalitarian modern society. Since guardian review was now illegitimate in a constitutional order dominated by the countermajoritarian difficulty—a state of affairs revealed by the disappearance of police power as an analytical category—a new conceptualization of constitutional law and a new narrative of early twentieth-century constitutional history were necessary to signal the emergence of the model of bifurcated review.

In order to achieve that goal, it was necessary to cleanse cases demonstrating enhanced judicial solicitude for noneconomic rights of the taint of the *Lochner* line of cases. This was accomplished by denying that the incorporated rights cases of the 1940s and 1950s were substantive due process cases, despite their initially having been recognized as such. It was also accomplished by asserting that the *Lochner* line of cases were substantive due process cases, a label that, although meaningless as a description of the actual framework in which those cases were decided, was evocative for those who believed in bifurcated review. The result was a triumphalist narrative in which the Court came to recognize the evils of "substantive due process," rededicated itself to the protection of civil rights, and abandoned its guardian review posture toward constitutional interpretation. The result has also been the creation of some enduring myths about substantive due process cases in the early twentieth century.

9

The Canonization and Demonization of Judges

When the adaptivity debates of the 1920s and 1930s were eventually resolved on the side of those who embraced the concept of a "living Constitution," bifurcated review emerged as an alternative to guardian review, and behavioralist theories of judging became orthodoxy, persons who had directly experienced the years of early twentieth-century jurisprudential ferment, or were mindful of the legacies of those years, sought to make sense of their immediate past. They began to construct the narratives of early twentieth-century constitutional history that make up the conventional account being revised in this study. Among the most vivid of those narratives were those featuring the attachment of ideological labels to the performance of certain early twentieth-century Supreme Court justices. The labels have served as the basis for elevating the reputations of some justices and lowering the reputations of others: the narratives have consisted of a collective effort in canonization and demonization.

Narratives of judicial canonization and demonization can be thought of as triumphalist at three levels. At their most explicit level, they have evaluated judicial performance in accordance with the extent of a judge's support for the expansion of the regulatory and redistributive power of the federal and state governments. The labels "progressive" and "liberal" have been attached to judges whose decisions helped engineer the triumph of constitutional doctrines facilitating the emergence of expanded government; those of "conservative" and "reactionary" to judges who opposed those doctrines. Since expansionist government became an established presence in mid and late twentieth-century America, judges who supported it in the early twentieth century could be characterized as visionaries, and those who resisted it as defenders of an obsolescent structure of governance.

Narratives evaluating judicial performance on the basis of a judge's support for or antipathy toward expanded government were common in the 1930s,

269

when most of the central contested issues of constitutional jurisprudence involved challenges to legislation regulating economic activity or redistributing economic burdens and benefits. As time passed, however, the evaluative labels employed to canonize and demonize early twentieth-century judges took on another dimension, and in so doing narratives of canonization and demonization revealed themselves as triumphalist at a deeper level. Instead of merely signaling a judicial attitude toward expanded governmental regulation, the labels "progressive," "liberal," "conservative," and "reactionary" also came to signify a judicial attitude toward the protection of certain noneconomic rights—primarily those of free expression—against legislative efforts to restrict those rights. At this level of the labeling process, judicial "progressives" and "liberals" were those who combined deference to redistributive and regulatory legislation with a vigilant stance toward legislation restricting rights of expression, whereas judicial "conservatives" and "reactionaries" were those who failed to exhibit either, or both, of those stances.

In the labeling process the characterization of a judge's performance as "liberal" or "conservative" was not just a surrogate for an attitude toward expanded government but for an attitude toward bifurcated review. Moreover, the labels, in their extended sense, began to be attached during the 1940s and 1950s, when bifurcated review assumed a position of orthodoxy. Thus, the labels served to identify particular judges either as pioneering figures in an early twentieth-century "revolution" in constitutional interpretation, or figures who failed to grasp the incompatibility of guardian review with behavioralist theories of judging. The triumphalist dimensions of this more extensive labeling were more expansive. "Progressive" and "liberal" judges had not merely taken positions on political issues that were vindicated over time; they had embraced a reconfiguration of their own role as constitutional interpreters that was necessary for effective judging in a modern democratic society. In contrast, "conservative" and "reactionary" judges had failed to adapt their interpretive stance to the imperatives of modernity.

The dual inquiry that this expanded version of ideological labeling required commentators to undertake—they needed to evaluate a judge's performance reviewing legislation restricting freedom of expression as well as legislation restricting economic activity—produced two sets of complications. One was that the performances of most early twentieth-century Supreme Court justices, if measured by the judge's stance of review toward economic activity cases and freedom of expression cases, were not easily replicated in the standard evaluative labels. Some justices insisted on stringent review of all legislation; others adopted a universally deferential stance. When the labels "liberal" and "conservative" expanded to convey attitudes toward judicial review, they proved more difficult to apply to judicial performances across a range of cases.

That difficulty was accentuated by the second, more fundamental, complication that arose when the labels were applied to early twentieth-century judges. The labels presupposed that the stance of bifurcated review could be treated as an alternative—indeed, over time, as a superior alternative—to guardian review. But, as we have seen, bifurcated review did not emerge as an orthodoxy on the Supreme Court until the 1940s. This meant that any characterization of the review postures of judges who served on the Court during the first three decades of the twentieth century would, of necessity, be based on decisions and opinions in which guardian review was the controlling interpretive stance. If early twentieth-century judges were to be identified as "progressives," "liberals," "conservatives," or "reactionaries" on the basis of whether they embraced or resisted bifurcated review, only a judge who anticipated a posture that had not yet fully emerged could qualify for the label of "progressive" or "liberal." Moreover, judges who subscribed to the orthodox guardian review stance of their time appeared as "conservatives" or "reactionaries" merely because their successors had abandoned that stance.

In short, using the labels "progressive," "liberal," "conservative," and "reactionary" as surrogates for enlightened or unenlightened attitudes toward guardian and bifurcated review assured that when those labels were applied to early twentieth-century judges, the labeling process would not only be triumphalist but anachronistic. As we will see, however, this did not deter those who canonized and demonized early twentieth-century justices. Those narrators repeatedly used ideological labels to signify not only judicial attitudes toward expanded governmental regulation of the realm of political economy but attitudes toward the protection of freedom of expression. They also used those labels to signify whether a judge had understood, or ignored, his obligation to ground his approach toward constitutional challenges to legislation on the principles of democratic theory.

There was a third level at which the canonization and demonization narratives were triumphalist, a level that can be seen as far less explicit, but potentially more far-reaching, than the others. The canonization and demonization narratives proceeded from an assumption that applying conventional ideological labels to the performance of Supreme Court justices—characterizing them as "liberals" or "conservatives"—was a useful way of capturing their identity as public officials. Most mid and late twentieth-century commentary on Supreme Court justices has been grounded on that assumption. But the premise that a commentator could disengage a justice's judicial performance from the collective performance of the Court on which he served did not itself surface until the twentieth century. Nor did the accompanying premise that the jurisprudential tendencies of a justice could be rendered intelligibly through conventional political labels. Both premises were dependent on the triumph of a behavioralist theory of judging.

This claim about the narratives of canonization and demonization may be misunderstood. Judges were perceived as eminently capable of partisanship—indeed, as incapable of not being partisan—at the time of the Constitution's founding.[1] Particular decisions of the Court were characterized as partisan, and judges prominently associated with those decisions were similarly characterized. Nonetheless, characterizations of the *general* performance of individual Supreme Court justices in ideological terms did not exist in commentary during the nineteenth century. In fact, very few discussions of the performance of individual members of the Court, such as doctrinally centered reviews of the opinions of a justice in a particular line of cases, can be identified prior to the twentieth century. The first justice to elicit this form of treatment was Holmes, and, as we shall see, the commentary on Holmes was not duplicated for any other Supreme Court justice prior to the early 1930s.

The absence of commentary on the personal jurisprudential tendencies of members of the Court can be seen as a predictable side effect of the model of guardian review and the jurisprudential assumptions on which it was grounded. Although the process of glossing and application might result in boundary lines being drawn in one place rather than another, so that the impact of a constitutional provision might vary from case to case, the exercises were not themselves taken as ideologically determined despite the partisan implications of results the Court reached. Indeed, guardian review permitted judicial glossing and formula promulgation precisely because the distinction between the will of the law and the will of the judge was widely understood.

Thus, in late nineteenth- and early twentieth-century commentary it was perfectly appropriate to criticize the techniques of glossing and application that had produced outcomes in particular cases as evidence of deficient learning or ability in a justice or justices. But it was assumed that in the great majority of cases the particular "wills" of judges—their partisan tendencies as individuals—had not played an important part in the process by which legal principles were discerned and applied to cases.[2]

The surfacing of commentary that not only emphasized the ideological orientation of judges, but assumed that ideology could serve as a defining characteristic of a judge's performance, thus illustrated the emergence in the 1930s of a different conception of the nature of judging. A behavioralist theory of judging has grounded narratives canonizing and demonizing the performances of early twentieth-century Supreme Court justices. Since that theory has been taken by most mid and late twentieth-century students of the Court to be accurate and unexceptionable, the attachment of ideological labels to judicial performance has been taken as informative. The use of such labels has served to validate the superiority of an approach to constitutional interpretation that no longer posits any meaningful distinction between the will of the law and the will of the judge.

A good deal has followed, therefore, from the surfacing in the 1930s of narratives that began the process of canonizing and demonizing certain twentieth-century Supreme Court justices. We now turn to the composition of some of those narratives, as they have been perpetuated from the early years of the century until the very recent past.

I have examined two groups of early twentieth-century justices as subjects in canonization and demonization narratives. One group consists of justices whose decisions in constitutional cases were given ideological labels such as "progressive," "liberal," or, eventually, "modern," and who were, as a result, canonized. The prominent members of this group were Justices Holmes and Brandeis. The other group consists of justices whose decisions were characterized as "conservative," "reactionary," or "old-fashioned," and who were thus revealed to be opponents of the "constitutional revolution" and accordingly demonized. The most visible members of that group were Justices Van Devanter, McReynolds, Sutherland, and Butler, who came to be lumped together, by the 1950s, as the "Four Horsemen of Reaction."

Narratives of canonization and demonization began with the discovery of Holmes as a "progressive" judge. By Holmes's death in 1935 a characterization of him as "progressive" had become well established, with one commentator stating in 1929 that "no judge who has ever sat upon the bench has ever been more progressive in his attitude,"[3] and another describing him as "the idol of progressives who believed that America must evolve and change."[4] Felix Frankfurter, whose laudatory essay in a Festschrift celebrating Holmes's seventy-fifth birthday in 1916 had launched the canonization process,[5] had set forth a litmus test for "progressive" judges. Holmes had "thr[own] the weight of his authority on the side of social readjustments through legislation,"[6] and had criticized arid constitutional formulas, such as "liberty of contract," which sought to block laws designed to alleviate the costs of unregulated industrial capitalism.

Those who first celebrated Holmes as a "progressive" were members of a generation of early twentieth-century intellectuals, of whom Frankfurter and Harold Laski were the most visible and for whom *The New Republic* was a policy organ. The attractiveness of Holmes for this group of commentators lay in his "modern" attitudes as a judge and jurist. They appreciated Holmes's impatience with categorical and formulaic reasoning in constitutional jurisprudence; his concession that judges were not remote from the realm of policy; and his fatalistic deference to majoritarian power.

Between the First World War and the early 1930s "progressive" commentators acted as publicists for Holmes. Frankfurter commemorated "twenty years of Mr. Justice Holmes's constitutional opinions" in the *Harvard Law Review*.[7] Laski arranged for the publication in 1920 of *Collected Legal Papers*, a book made up of several of Holmes's previously published essays.[8] Meanwhile, *The New Republic*, which as early as 1915 had described Holmes's dissent in *Lochner* as "classic,"[9] began to emphasize another of his "progressive" characteristics: his capacity to transcend the prejudices of his "Puritan" (by which they meant upper-class Bostonian) background. Philip Littell, in a *New Republic* column, described Holmes as "a Puritan whom doubt had civilized,"[10] and Elizabeth Sergeant, in an article, called him a member of "the natural Puritan aristocracy."[11]

By the late 1920s and 1930s Holmes had come to be pictured as "an aristocrat with a genuine interest in the welfare of the common man."[12] Those holding that image of Holmes pointed not only to his political economy opinions, in which he demonstrated his support for peaceful strikes and boycotts or his tolerance of legislation designed to improve the conditions of industrial laborers, but his free speech opinions, in which he exhibited a willingness to give constitutional protection to the speech of anarchists, syndicalists, and pacifists.

Holmes's transcendence of his class was central to his image as a "great liberal,"[13] a designation applied to him with increased frequency at the end of his career.[14] Silas Bent, his first biographer, characterized Holmes in 1932 as having "freed himself from the group loyalties and prejudices . . . which are a heritage of those reared in the security of the genteel tradition."[15] Three years later Morris Cohen attributed to him "the true liberal attitude that enabled him to rise above his hereditary class prejudices,"[16] and Adolf Berle, in an article entitled "Justice Holmes: Liberal," described his most "glorious . . . achievement" as "transcending the bounds of his apparent emotional security."[17]

By the 1940s Holmes's canonization had been largely accomplished. His reputation ran into some difficulties with commentators who associated his positivistic pronouncements with potential support for totalitarianism,[18] but his awkwardness did not prevent his appeal from moving beyond the legal profession to popular culture at large. The emergence of Holmes as a personage who evoked broad popular interest can be seen in the appearance of two books in the 1940s that were designed to make Holmes's life and work accessible to a general audience.

The first of the books, *The Mind and Faith of Justice Holmes* (1943), was an edition of Holmes's writings by the political scientist Max Lerner. *The Mind and Faith of Justice Holmes* had a heavy emphasis on constitutional law and was obviously intended for a lay audience.

Both journalists and reviewers with legal training were delighted with the exposure to Holmes made possible by Lerner's collection. Writing in *The Nation*, I. F. Stone said that Lerner had "performed a service for American literature" by introducing the public to "a supremely civilized man, a judge, thinker, and artist of the first rank." [19] Charles Clark, the dean of Yale Law School, suggested that if "many of our brilliant young men still cherish a belief in idealism as a proper motivating force for a public career and law as an assisting means," then "we owe . . . a large measure of gratitude to that wise, witty and eloquent aristocrat who dared to desert his class to express these thoughts."[20]

The appearance of Lerner's collection confirmed for reviewers that, as Chicago law professor Max Rheinstein put it, "Holmes is on the way of becoming one of the great representative figures of his nation, . . . a type of man which has so far been rare in American history."[21] Rheinstein's comments suggest that the canonization of Holmes had reached a stage where his admirers had become not simply reputation-makers but defenders of the reputation they had helped to create. This can be seen in the indignant reactions of some reviewers to the second major book on Holmes published in the 1940s that was designed for a lay audience.

The book was Catherine Drinker Bowen's *Yankee from Olympus*, which appeared in 1944. Bowen was a popular writer without legal training. Her book virtually ignored Holmes's careers as a judge and a legal scholar, was unabashedly centered on his family life and personal relationships, and was in many places an openly fictional portrait. In addition to relying on unattributed sources, Bowen dramatized events, repeated gossip, and invented dialogue for her characters. *Yankee from Olympus* deeply offended some reviewers.

Edmund Wilson's review in *The New Yorker* called *Yankee from Olympus* "an impertinence" in its attribution of prosaic and banal thoughts to Holmes. "We are . . . rather surprised," Wilson said, when "we are taken by Mrs. Bowen inside [the] mind . . . [of a] fastidious and cultivated . . . intellectual . . . and presented with a stream of consciousness almost invariably colorless and obvious."[22] Other reviewers chimed in. Max Lerner found that Bowen's book was "blurred where [Holmes] was sharp and soft where he was unsentimental," and it was "sometimes evasive of difficulties in the personality of a man whose injunction was always to strike for the jugular."[23] Matthew Fitzsimons was harsher still, concluding that Bowen was "completely vague about the origin and development of [Holmes's] philosophy," devoted "many pages to a sketch of American history that is not always relevant or accurately presented," and suffered "frequent lapses into breathless, school-girl mannerisms."[24]

The reaction to *Yankee from Olympus* demonstrated that a community of persons, some of whom had themselves contributed to the broadening of Holmes's popular appeal, had become apprehensive about the distortions in his image that might follow from his becoming a cultural figure. But despite their reaction to Bowen's work, it became a best-seller and contributed to the widening of Holmes's popular appeal. By the 1950s Holmes had been the subject of a Broadway play and a movie.[25] It was to be another decade before scholarly assessments of him began a full-scale reassessment of the "progressive" and "liberal" stereotypes that had accompanied his canonization.[26]

The next candidate for canonization was Louis Brandeis, whose canonization process produced a judicial image comparable to that of Holmes. But there was a feature of Brandeis's canonization that distinguishes it from Holmes's and underscores the time-bound dimension of canonization and demonization narratives. The discovery of Holmes as a progressive and a liberal took place in a world in which commentary on Supreme Court justices as individuals was still virtually nonexistent, being limited to their nominations to the Court, retirements, or deaths. Between 1902, the year of Holmes's Supreme Court nomination, and 1931, when Brandeis turned seventy-five, the *only* justice whose individual performance elicited commentary in legal or popular journals was Holmes.

Even the singling out of Holmes was an exception that proved the rule. A good deal of the commentary on Holmes was prompted by celebratory events in his life, such as his seventy-fifth birthday, his twentieth year on the Court, his ninetieth birthday, or by the appearance of works by or about him. Holmes was nearly unique among his judicial contemporaries in having produced a corpus of extrajudicial work to which commentators could refer, and was conspicuous in being a gifted and accessible writer. His intellectual positions were thus easier to discover—if not necessarily to comprehend—than those of the average early twentieth-century Supreme Court justice.

The process of canonizing Brandeis did not begin until he had been on the Court for fifteen years, and surfaced alongside the beginnings of a general tendency to label Supreme Court justices in ideological terms.[27] The absence of commentary on Brandeis as an individual justice is particularly suggestive because perceptions about his ideological orientation had contributed to the controversy that surrounded his nomination to the Court in 1916. Unlike Holmes, who did not have a discernibly ideological reputation when appointed to the Court in 1902, Brandeis had been identified as holding strongly "progressive" views at the time he was nominated.

The characterization of Brandeis as a "progressive" was accurate. He had written an article the year of his nomination[28] in which he had suggested that American law "had not kept pace with the rapid development of our political, economic, and social ideals." In 1914 he had published two books justifying government regulation of business practices and the banking industry,[29] and he had participated in the drafting of Wilson administration legislation creating the Federal Trade Commission and the Federal Reserve Bank. The visibility of his views contributed to the Senate's delaying his confirmation for over three months, at a time when most Court nominations were routinely confirmed without any public input. His public views also provided the basis for support of his nomination: during his confirmation proceedings *The New Republic* consistently endorsed him as the model of a progressive judge.[30]

Given Brandeis's discernibly ideological orientation and his tendency to take "progressive" or "liberal" positions in visible constitutional cases in the years between 1916 and 1931—he regularly voted to sustain wages and hours legislation against liberty of contract challenges and identified himself as generally inclined to support free speech claims—it is striking that during the same years in which Holmes's canonization was under way, not a single piece of commentary in legal or lay journals focused on the individual contributions of Brandeis as a Supreme Court justice. He was the subject of only three lay periodical articles in that entire period, none of which discussed his judicial opinions.[31]

The absence of commentary on so tempting a subject as Brandeis, for at least fifteen years after his appointment, thus confirms the general disinclination of those who paid close attention to Supreme Court decisions during the first two decades of the twentieth century to single out individual justices for treatment. But beginning in the 1930s, commentary on Brandeis became extensive, and his canonization began. The process had some parallels with that of Holmes. Ideological labels were applied to Brandeis, and some of those distorted his positions. A paradigmatic opinion served as the touchstone for forging Brandeis's judicial image. For Holmes that opinion had been his *Lochner* dissent; for Brandeis it was his 1932 dissent in *New State Ice Co. v. Liebmann*.[32] And canonizers invested in their subject, resulting in defenders of Brandeis's reputation deflecting criticism of him for many years after his death in 1941.

There were two differences in emphasis between narratives canonizing Holmes and those eulogizing Brandeis, reflected in the use of the *Lochner* and *Liebmann* dissents as embodiments of the two justices' judicial tendencies. Holmes's *Lochner* dissent had devoted most of its attention to criticizing indiscriminate judicial glossing of constitutional provisions, of which the "liberty of contract" principle was an example. His discussion of the actual legislation being challenged in *Lochner* had been offhand and cursory: it was enough for him that the legislators might have viewed it as a health measure or a first installment in regulating the hours of work. Brandeis's *Liebmann* dissent, also a product of a liberty of contract challenge to redistributive legislation, provided a much more detailed treatment of the policy justifications for the legislation being challenged.

In using opinions such as *Lochner* as the basis for describing Holmes as a "progressive" or a "liberal," commentators were not suggesting that his judicial performance merited those labels because he had advanced reasons why regulatory and redistributive legislation was efficacious. His progressive or liberal stance reflected, instead, an enlightened tolerance for majoritarian policies, whether or not he thought they made sense. The fashioning of Brandeis's image as a progressive or liberal, in contrast, rested more heavily on passages in Brandeis's opinions in which he advanced policy reasons in support of an expanded regulatory role for government. That feature of Brandeis's opinions resulted in his canonizers attaching two additional labels to his judicial performance. He was characterized as a "modern" judge, who understood that modernity required an increased role for government, and as a "prophet," who had anticipated the policies of the New Deal before they came into existence.

The *New York Times,* having shifted its posture on Brandeis from the time of his nomination,[33] was at the forefront of favorable commentary on his judicial work in the early 1930s. It found Brandeis's dissent in *New State Ice Co. v. Liebmann* sufficiently important to merit front-page treatment. That case involved a suit by the New State Ice Company, an Oklahoma manufacturer of ice, against Liebmann, who had sought to build a competing ice plant without first obtaining a certificate of "public convenience and necessity" from the state. The New State Ice Company had obtained such a certificate before building its plant at the cost of $500,000. When it sued to prevent Liebmann from erecting his plant without the approval of the state, Liebmann defended on the ground that he had a "liberty" under the Due Process Clause to engage in a common calling. A majority of the Court, in an opinion written by Sutherland, agreed with Liebmann, concluding that the business of ice manufacturing was not "affected with a public interest," and thus the state could not attach conditions to the entry of ice manufacturing companies into the market.

Brandeis had strongly held views on the issues he thought raised by the *Liebmann* case. He believed that states should be permitted room to act as "laboratories," experimenting with solutions to social ills. He thought that attaching conditions to the entry of producers into markets was an appropriate response to one of the root causes of the weakness of the American economy in the 1930s, an imbalance between production and consumption that had resulted in a surplus of goods and correspondingly depressed prices.[34] "The people of the United States are now confronted with an emergency more serious than war," he declared in his *Liebmann* dissent. "Economists are searching for the cause of this disorder and are reexamining the bases of our industrial structure . . . All agree that irregularity in employment . . . cannot be overcome unless production and consumption are more neatly balanced."[35]

Brandeis then emphasized the value of permitting state experimentation with the economy:

> There must be power in the States and the nation to remould through experimentation our economic practices and institutions to meet changing economic and social needs . . . It is one of the happy incidents of the Federal system that a single courageous State may . . . serve as a laboratory; and try novel social and economic experiments without risk to the rest of the country . . . If we would guide by the light of reason, we must let our minds be bold.[36]

Brandeis's *Liebmann* dissent was to serve as the origins of his image, developed throughout the 1930s, as "Isaiah," the prophetic visionary who had foreseen the coming of the New Deal and economic regulation.[37] In fact, the dissent was characteristic of views he had developed several years earlier, views that put him in the mainstream of Wilson progressives. He was enthusiastic about legislative "experimentation" with the economy on the state level, believing that economies of scale were more likely to be realized and that "the public interest" could be more easily discerned. He thought that states should intervene to prevent the uneven distribution of wealth and purchasing power.[38] He injected these views into his *Liebmann* dissent by attributing them to "economists," "many persons," and "some thoughtful men."

None of the views demonstrated that Brandeis would be a supporter of the New Deal. He may have agreed with critics of "unbridled competition" about the causes of the economic disorder of the 1930s, but he did not believe the remedy was to have the federal government emerge as a regulatory force in the nation's economy. However "prophetic" he may have been about economic difficulties, he was not sympathetic toward the Roosevelt administration's experiments at responding to those difficulties through federal legislation implemented by federal administrative agencies. He joined Court majority opinions striking down such legislation in the *Panama Refining* and *Schechter* cases.

The *Liebmann* dissent nonetheless revealed two facets of Brandeis's judicial perspective that endeared him to many commentators in the 1930s. One was his tendency to see legal issues as bottomed in social and economic realities, as exemplified by his finding the views of economists relevant in an inquiry into the constitutionality of a state-required "public convenience and necessity" certificate in the ice industry. For Brandeis a policy of "correct[ing] the evils of technological unemployment and excess productive capacity" was self-evidently sensible, and the Constitution should not be read as preventing its implementation. The *Times* had been correct, in an article on Brandeis in 1931, in suggesting that Brandeis's Constitution was a "garment" rather than an "iron strait-jacket."[39]

Brandeis also revealed himself in *Liebmann* as a judge who believed in the capacity of humans to alter purportedly inexorable external forces in a nation's history. If "evils" embedded in the structure of American industry created economic difficulties, those evils could be corrected. In a passage in *Liebmann* Brandeis had made clear his belief in the causative powers of human agency: "[T]he advances in the exact sciences and the achievements of invention remind us that the seemingly impossible sometimes appears. There are many men now living who were in the habit of using the age-old expression: 'It is impossible as flying.' The discoveries in the physical sciences, the triumphs of invention, attest the value of the process of trial and error. These advances have been due, in large measure, to experimentation."[40]

Appreciative commentators found a constitutional blueprint for the New Deal in Brandeis's *Liebmann* dissent. In 1936 the New York *Times,* in the course of calling Brandeis "a vigorous defender of many New Deal measures and social experimentation," traced that perspective to *Liebmann*. After quoting from Brandeis's dissent, the *Times* observed that "[t]his opinion, in 1932, was often recalled in the days that followed, when many New Deal measures were falling before the power of the Court."[41] On the same day, R. L. Duffus wrote a feature in the *Times* on Brandeis at eighty. Duffus spoke of Brandeis's "method" as a judge, which he described as "that of a fearless, objective investigator, with an extraordinary gift for collecting and analyzing masses of data." Brandeis's major influence on the Court, Duffus believed, was that "he [had] forced even conservative judges off the ground of abstract theory and on to the basis of tangible, present-day fact."[42]

Of all the comments describing Brandeis in the 1930s, two were most explicit in associating him with a modernist consciousness. The first appeared in 1931 from Alpheus Mason, then an assistant professor of politics at Princeton. Mason's article in the *University of Pennsylvania Law Review,* entitled "Mr. Justice Brandeis: A Student of Social and Economic Science,"[43] concluded that Brandeis, more than any current judge, demonstrated a "sympathetic appreciation of the economic and social life of today and its bearing on the problem of government."[44] As a lawyer Brandeis had "piled facts upon facts, having to do with labor, fatigue, health, economic productivity, and so forth, all for the purpose of showing the urgent social need for the legislation he was supporting." As a judge he "has continued his researches in the realm of the social sciences and has himself made investigations similar to those which he undertook formerly as counsel." Brandeis, for Mason, was "essentially a social scientist."[45]

The second comment was by Max Lerner, writing in 1939, the year of Brandeis's retirement. In a tribute essay, Lerner brought together many of the elements of Brandeis's idealized image as a modern judge. For Lerner, Brandeis had "led the phalanxes that have brought the economic emphasis into legal thought." He had seen "the constitutional phrase and legal doctrine" as "part of the living context of . . . history and economic fact." He had combined a "belief in the life of reason" with "a concrete and massive knowledge" and "enormous social inventiveness." In short, Brandeis had "set . . . currents . . . in motion."[46]

At the time of Brandeis's death in October 1941, his reputation as a judge whose contributions seemed peculiarly suited to the modern age was firmly in place. Legal figures from Chief Justice Hughes to Zechariah Chafee referred to his "prophetic vision" and his knowledge of "the commercial and industrial facts underlying [Supreme Court cases]."[47] Newspapers, from the *Chicago Daily Times* to the *Denver Rocky Mountain News*,[48] identified him as "the spiritual father of the New Deal"[49] and a pioneer in unearthing "economic and sociological facts" that illuminated the decision of legal issues.[50] He appeared, in those tributes, as the archetypal modern judge.

The attribution of a modernist jurisprudential consciousness to Brandeis was not entirely accurate. To be sure, he believed that legal principles and doctrines were malleable and contextual rather than universalist and essential, and he was convinced that humans had the capacity to shape their destiny and make their future an improvement on their past.[51] He therefore held a robust view of the Constitution's capacity to change with time, and felt that most regulatory and redistributive legislation was constitutionally legitimate. Moreover, as we have seen, he was one of the first twentieth-century judges to explicitly link enhanced constitutional protection for free speech to democratic theory.

But one of Brandeis's deepest convictions made him reluctant to embrace judicial decisions that significantly altered the boundaries between enumerated national and reserved state powers erected by orthodox late nineteenth-century jurisprudence. Despite his belief in the capacity for human-generated progress, he believed that individual humans had a limited capacity to surmount their inherent passions, prejudices, and frailties. In particular, he felt that the limited ability of humans to master the large enterprises of modernity required small units of social and economic organization to further efficiency and protect human freedom.[52]

Thus, Brandeis was presumptively skeptical of large institutions, including the federal government, and presumptively supportive of the states as laboratories for paternalistic experiments in small-unit management. This meant that he was instinctively attracted to federalism challenges to the exercise of regulatory power by the national government. For this reason he might well have been reluctant to support the Court's increased deference to congressional legislation extending the range of the national government's commerce power. Even though Brandeis felt that governmental regulation of the economy was necessary and often beneficial, he preferred it to take place at the state level.[53]

Unlike that of Holmes, Brandeis's image did not fluctuate significantly in the decades after his death. By the 1960s commentators had begun to assume a more detached posture toward Holmes and to point out some of the difficulties in describing Holmes as a "progressive" or "liberal."[54] A similar trend did not take place in the literature on Brandeis. Instead, canonizers continued to emphasize Brandeis's "modern" and "prophetic" qualities by fashioning an image of Brandeis as a judge who had internalized the countermajoritarian difficulty. According to this line of commentary, Brandeis set aside his strongly held views on public issues as a judge, refusing to substitute his judgments for those of more democratic institutions. He was seen, in the vocabulary of the 1950s and 1960s, as an apostle of "judicial self-restraint," invalidating legislation only when it offended democratic principles.

Developing that image required some selectivity on the part of commentators. One example came in 1957 when Alexander Bickel demonstrated, in *The Unpublished Opinions of Mr. Justice Brandeis,* that on several occasions Brandeis had been prepared to suppress dissenting or concurring opinions in exchange for concessions in language in a majority opinion.[55] The general portrait of Brandeis that emerged from Bickel's study was that of a consummate strategist who readily discerned the political implications of constitutional cases that came before the Court and who sought to maximize his chances to infuse his ideological views into opinions. That portrait of Brandeis was not emphasized by reviewers of Bickel's work. Although some reviewers wondered about the propriety of Bickel's revealing information about the Supreme Court's internal deliberations, none suggested that the disclosure of Brandeis's strategizing affected his reputation.[56]

Another example came in 1967, when Louis Jaffe raised the question whether Brandeis was a judicial "activist," and concluded that Brandeis, "by common consent . . . among the greatest of Supreme Court judges," had not "transcend[ed] the proper limits upon the exercise of judicial power."[57] The question of the appropriate scope of judicial policymaking, in the service of constitutional interpretation, had become a burning issue in constitutional commentary during the years of the Warren Court: a number of scholars maintained that a series of "activist" Warren Court decisions affecting race relations, religion in the public schools, and the reapportionment of state legislatures had been insufficiently mindful of the countermajoritarian difficulty.[58] Brandeis, according to Jaffe, could not be described as an "activist" in the Warren Court sense. He "had firm, deeply felt convictions on most of the social, economic, and political issues of the day," but he "was neither eager to exercise power nor wholly without question as to the efficacy and propriety of judicial power in a democratic system."[59]

The furious reaction engendered by political scientist Bruce Murphy's 1982 book, *The Brandeis/Frankfurter Connection,* can also be traced to this characterization of Brandeis as a judge who understood "the proper limits upon the exercise of judicial power" under a model of bifurcated review. Murphy's book was centered on claims that while Brandeis was on the Supreme Court he had hired Frankfurter, then a Harvard law professor, to engage in lobbying efforts on behalf of causes Brandeis championed. Murphy's claims tarnished Brandeis's image as an appropriately "restrained" judge.

The most influential of the critical reviews of Murphy's book came from Yale law professor Robert Cover, who was at the time working on a history of the Supreme Court covering a portion of Brandeis's tenure.[60] Cover argued that Murphy's most serious charge, Brandeis's creation of a secret fund to finance Frankfurter's lobbying efforts on behalf of causes the two men supported, was based on insubstantial evidence. Murphy's claim, Cover suggested, rested on correspondence between the two men that could be read simply as documentation of Brandeis's support for Frankfurter's public interest activities.[61]

In criticizing Murphy, Cover made it clear where he stood on Brandeis. He called him one of "the greatest American judges of this century," "a prophetic figure with commitment to the quest for justice in an imperfect world," a "great justice who intended no violence to his role on the Court." He credited Brandeis's "extraordinary influence in the Second New Deal" to "his intellectual vision and his moral authority." "Above all," Cover concluded, "Brandeis never perverted justice—never *misused his judicial power.*"[62] Several subsequent critical reviews of *The Brandeis/Frankfurter Connection* agreed with Cover's critique.[63]

Those who canonized Brandeis as an apostle of judicial self-restraint only described one feature of his calculus as a judge. Through his impressive formulations of the precepts of judicial self-restraint, Brandeis was able to convey a sense that although his judicial decisionmaking could not be constrained by some essentialist conception of "law," it could be constrained by the recognition of his countermajoritarian role. That message served to respond to the selective character of bifurcated review by calling for judges to internalize its groundings in democratic theory through self-imposed limitations on their lawmaking powers. But the ultimate basis of Brandeis's decisionmaking remained his set of convictions about public policy, and when canons of judicial self-restraint clashed with the deepest of those convictions, he ignored them.[64]

A full appreciation of Brandeis as a "modern" judge would thus emphasize the separate, but related, insights that he drew from experiencing the collapse of the jurisprudential assumptions that had nurtured guardian review. At bottom, judges engaging in constitutional interpretation were a species of policymakers and theoretically had ample room to write their public policy agendas into constitutional law. But the vulnerable status of judges as policymakers in a democracy, and the evidence of judicial overzealousness in the glossing of constitutional provisions, required that judges communicate their awareness of the dangers of judicial usurpation. Developing a laundry list of doctrines and maxims of judicial self-limitation, which had the effect of avoiding full-blown decisions of constitutional issues where they could be avoided, was a way of communicating that awareness.[65] Doctrines of self-limitation were particularly appealing to a judicial strategist such as Brandeis because the decision to invoke, or not to invoke them, rested with the judge.

This view of Brandeis as a "modern" judge was not present in the line of commentary that emphasized his status as an apostle of self-restraint, but it may be surfacing in late twentieth-century commentary that has exhibited a revived appreciation of Brandeis as an activist judge who employed self-limitation techniques pragmatically. In 1987, for example, Samuel Krislov noted that "[t]he onrush of Brandeisia . . . reflects a growing conviction that he is the most significant architect of the modern Court," that he is a "magnet for those who seek social reform," and that he was "hardly a judicial recluse."[66] Brandeis was described as a pragmatist as early as 1941;[67] in 1995 he was rediscovered as one.[68]

Alongside the process by which Holmes and Brandeis were canonized evolved another process of judicial image-making that, until very recently, has received almost no attention. This was the creation of collective images for four justices who identified themselves as constitutional opponents of New Deal legislation in the mid-1930s. Unlike the processes by which Holmes and Brandeis were canonized, the process by which Justices Willis Van Devanter, James McReynolds, George Sutherland, and Pierce Butler became demonized as the "Four Horsemen of Reaction" emerged suddenly, established its dominant images as it emerged, and retained those images, without significant alteration, for several decades. Van Devanter, McReynolds, Sutherland, and Butler had no discernible public images as justices prior to the 1930s. By the 1940s they had been regularly pictured as a "conservative" bloc on the Court. By the 1950s they had become "the Four Horsemen." In the conventional account of early twentieth-century constitutional history they are still given that label.[69]

The ideological labels of "progressive" and "liberal" for Holmes, and of "progressive," "liberal," "modern," and "prophet" for Brandeis, had been based on narrow evaluative criteria and on a relatively small sampling of decisions. The criteria and sampling base of the process that attached labels to the Four Horsemen were narrower still.

Between 1910 (the year Van Devanter was appointed to the Court) and the mid-1930s, the only sustained attention to any of the four justices was at the time of their Court nominations. After 1935, when coverage of the personalities and ideological orientations of individual justices on the Court expanded, the label "conservative" was attached to each of them. By the time of their respective retirements or deaths, which took place between 1937 and 1946, the labels "conservative" or "reactionary," based almost exclusively on their constitutional opposition to some New Deal legislation, had become synonymous with their public images. As noted, by the 1950s they had been dubbed the Four Horsemen of Reaction. The demonization process culminated in a series of surveys, beginning in 1972, in which academic commentators rated the performance of the justices who have served on the Supreme Court.[70] In those surveys all the Horsemen, save Sutherland, received the lowest performance rating.

The dearth of coverage on Van Devanter, McReynolds, Sutherland, and Butler between 1910 and the early 1930s paralleled that of Brandeis in those years. Not a single law journal devoted space to a treatment of their individual jurisprudence. Nor did any nonlegal periodical. Newspaper comments were limited almost exclusively to stories at the time of their nominations to the Court, and these included only scattered ideological characterizations.

Eventually, as we have seen, law journals did feature some treatments of Brandeis's constitutional decisions in the 1930s, as they had occasionally done with Holmes in the previous two decades. But not only were there no law journal articles on Van Devanter, McReynolds, Sutherland, and Butler for the entire duration of their judicial careers, there were no discussions of them in law reviews as a jurisprudential bloc on the Court. The first source of labels and stereotypes for the four justices was the popular press, and the labels attached to them were not subjected to any evaluation, on the basis of wider sampling or closer reading of their opinions, by specialists. The subsequent perpetuation, in scholarly as well as in popular literature, of images of Van Devanter, McReynolds, Sutherland, and Butler has not been based on any additional sampling or detailed analysis of their opinions. Their demonization has continued to rest on journalistic characterizations made on the basis of a handful of constitutional decisions in the 1930s.

To illustrate the emergence of those characterizations, and their contrast with the attenuated coverage of Van Devanter, McReynolds, Sutherland, and Butler in the preceding two decades, I have surveyed the *New York Times* from 1910, when Van Devanter was nominated to the Court, to 1941, when McReynolds, the last of the "Four Horsemen," retired. The *Times* coverage was chosen as illustrative for several reasons. It was one of a handful of newspapers that covered the Supreme Court with any regularity during the period. Its conspicuous endorsement of journalistic norms of factual accuracy and objectivity placed pressure on its correspondents to limit the partisan dimensions of their reportage. It was generally regarded as the dominant American newspaper during the period, and other papers regularly relied on coverage that first appeared in the *Times*. And its editorial policies, which shifted from a moderate Republican to a liberal Democratic stance in the early 1930s, paralleled those of a number of other elite American newspapers in the same time span.[71] Even if one were to discount all the above reasons for focusing on the *Times*, its coverage of the "Four Horsemen" between 1935 and 1941 remains the largest single source of popular or specialized commentary about those justices during the time period in question.

The *Times*'s account of Van Devanter's nomination noted that "while many insurgents [in the Republican Party] are inclined to regard [Van Devanter] in a friendly way, several of them feel that certain decisions must be carefully scrutinized before his nomination is allowed to pass to confirmation." The reference to "certain decisions" was based on the fact that Van Devanter, who was on the United States Court of Appeals for the Eighth Judicial Circuit at the time of his appointment, had been a member of a three-judge panel that upheld an antitrust prosecution of the Standard Oil Company under the Sherman Antitrust Act.[72] This had "caused some comment," the *Times* noted, "on the ground that it looked like 'stacking' the Supreme Court against Standard Oil."[73] That was the sum total of the *Times*'s comments on Van Devanter as an individual for the next twenty-five years.

The *Times* was slightly more interested in McReynolds, who had been attorney general under Wilson before being nominated to the Court on August 18, 1914. Three weeks before the nomination it reported that McReynolds was the leading candidate for a vacancy on the Court, caused by the death of Horace Lurton on July 12. That report made no characterizations of McReynolds, save his "not [being] a wealthy man by any means," being "fond of society," and being a bachelor. The relevance of those comments was a report that McReynolds might not be inclined to accept the appointment because "the emoluments to him in . . . the private practice of law . . . would be substantial."[74]

After McReynolds officially received the nomination, the *Times* wrote an unenthusiastic editorial, suggesting that he had been undistinguished before becoming attorney general and excessive in his trust-busting zeal. It hoped that in his new position "Mr. McReynolds will come within the radiance of the light of reason."[75] With one minor exception,[76] that was the last comment the *Times* made about McReynolds until the mid-1930s.

The *Times*'s treatment of George Sutherland's nomination suggested that the paper regarded him as in a different category from the average nominee to the Supreme Court. On September 10, 1922, four days after the Senate had unanimously affirmed Sutherland's nomination,[77] the *Times* devoted three full pages to a profile of the new justice.

The article stressed Sutherland's "high qualifications" for the Court, referring to his reputation as "one of the country's foremost authorities on the Constitution," his presidency of the American Bar Association, and his Blumenthal Lectures at Columbia. It did not engage in any direct ideological characterizations of Sutherland, although it did attribute characterizations of him to others. In one example it mentioned that Sutherland had "frequently been called a 'reactionary' and a 'standpatter,'" but noted that in a speech Sutherland had said, "I am no standpatter. I am not in favor of standing still. Of course we must advance, but we must at our peril distinguish between real progress and what amounts to a mere manifestation of the speed mania."[78]

The *Times*'s treatment of Pierce Butler was more consistent with its general inattentiveness to the individual justices who served on the Supreme Court between 1910 and the 1930s. Butler, who had spent his entire professional career as a lawyer in Saint Paul, Minnesota, was virtually unknown to the press at the time of his nomination in 1922: the *New York World* said that "[n]o man has probably ever been appointed to the United States Supreme Court about whom the general public knew less."[79] When Butler's nomination was announced, the *Times* reported that he was a railroad lawyer, a Democrat, and a Catholic, "one of those lawyers whose natural bent is the study of legal principles and whose devotion to the profession has screened him from wide public fame." The *Times* predicted, accurately, that Butler's longtime representation of the railroad industry, particularly in rate valuation cases, would result in progressive Republican Senator Robert La Follette opposing his nomination. It regarded Butler's political affiliation as a testament to the broad-mindedness of President Harding, and his religious affiliation as an instructive rejoinder to bigotry.[80]

Although both *The Nation* and *The New Republic* wrote editorials opposing Butler's nomination,[81] and La Follette made a lengthy speech in opposition in the Senate, the nomination was easily confirmed.[82] The *Times* reacted by criticizing the "continual bleating" of "Mr. LaFollette and the others, along with our omniscient 'intellectuals,'" who "don't want Judges with a judicial mind."[83] Previously it had run an article that had made light of the opposition to Butler, suggesting that "the assertion of a radical group that Butler has been attorney for public service corporations . . . does not appear to carry weight with those who know the varied nature of his law practice," and that "the most being said by those opposing Mr. Butler is that 'a more progressive man should be placed on the high tribunal.'"[84]

In summary, the *Times*'s coverage of the Four Horsemen at the time of their nominations was attenuated, and, in the case of Van Devanter and McReynolds, devoid of any ideological characterizations. By the time Sutherland and Butler were nominated, the *Times* had reported some opposition to them in "progressive" circles, and in Butler's case had weighed in against that opposition. Although the differences in the coverage suggest that public perceptions of Supreme Court justices as political actors were becoming more commonplace in the 1920s,[85] the labels "conservative" or "reactionary" had not been consistently attached to any of the Horsemen, in the *Times* or elsewhere, by the opening of the 1930s. Nor had the Horsemen been identified as a judicial bloc.

By 1934 a dramatic change had taken place in the treatment of the Court and its justices in the *Times*. There were several related features of the new treatment. First, the Court was identified as an institution whose forthcoming decisions were likely to have important short-run consequences for the general public. It was expected to pass on the constitutionality of a number of New Deal legislative measures, and commentators began to speculate on the outcomes of forthcoming challenges.

The *Times*'s interest in the Court, however, ranged well beyond speculation about its forthcoming decisions in cases challenging New Deal legislation. For the first time since Van Devanter had been appointed to the Court in 1910, the *Times* exhibited a sustained interest in the justices as individuals, running articles in which the postures of individual justices were characterized in conventional political labels. In the process Van Devanter, McReynolds, Sutherland, and Butler began to be identified as a bloc, and eventually as a "conservative" bloc. The sample on which those labels were based consisted exclusively of Court responses to regulatory legislation initiated by the Roosevelt administration or analogous state legislation affecting economic activity.

One can see these characteristics of the *Times*'s new approach to the Court and its justices in Mildred Adams's February 18, 1934 article in the magazine section of the *Times*, "Nine Men the Nation Watches Intently."[86] Adams noted early in her article that "[c]ertainly the court has been very much in the public consciousness ever since it became apparent that the validity of certain laws governing the New Deal was to be tested here." As two examples of recent Court decisions foreshadowing that prospect, Adams listed "[t]he close decision upholding the Minnesota mortgage moratorium" and the pending "New York milk-rate case," which "tests another joint in the New Deal's armor." Her references to *Home Building & Loan Association v. Blaisdell*[87] and *Nebbia v. New York*[88] as "New Deal" cases signaled that both state and federal legislation restricting economic activity had been identified with the social philosophy of the Roosevelt administration. The fact that the legislation in *Blaisdell* and *Nebbia* had been challenged on constitutional grounds, Adams felt, had raised "some obscure fear" in the American people, "lest their power to enact and maintain legislation be taken away from them" by the Court.

Adams suggested that enhanced public awareness of the Court might tempt those who could not "ask a justice what he is going to do" in a given case to attempt to find out "what kind of a person he is."[89] This prompted her to inquire about "the extraordinary group of Americans" who sat on the Court in 1934. She searched for "classifications which may be set up for the easier looking at" the Justices. One "tempting" classification was "[t]he common grouping of them as conservative and liberal." Adams admitted that the terms "conservative" and "liberal" were "easy and satisfactory pigeon-holes" that "once accepted make it no longer necessary to do any thinking."[90] But she continued to employ the "conservative" and "liberal" labels for the balance of her article.

Adams noted that Van Devanter, McReynolds, Sutherland, and Butler had dissented "[i]n the Minnesota mortgage moratorium case." The majority had taken "the more liberal view." The four dissenters in *Blaisdell* were "commonly believed to be always conservative." Adams felt that the labels amounted to "popular beliefs" about the justices. She admitted that the labeling "[was] sound only so long as one does not inquire into it too closely."[91] Yet from 1934 through the early 1940s the *Times* consistently featured articles that labeled justices "conservatives" and "liberals," identified the Four Horsemen as a "conservative" bloc on the Court, and derived the labels from decisions rendered in constitutional challenges to "New Deal" legislation regulating economic activity.

Initially, *Times* articles classifying the Four Horsemen as "conservatives" also emphasized the fact that they had been on the losing side of divided decisions. But by April 1935, R. L. Duffus noted in the *Times* that, in addition to *Blaisdell* and *Nebbia,* the Court had decided *Panama Refining Co. v. Ryan,* in which New Deal legislation had been struck down and the "conservatives" had been joined in the majority by all the other justices except Cardozo. With so many cases challenging New Deal legislation pending, Duffus felt that "[t]he divergent legal and economic philosophies of the Supreme bench are bound to be closely interwoven with the entire history of this generation." He added that it was "certain . . . [t]hat the Supreme Court . . . does represent two opposing philosophies."[92]

Duffus presented a more refined set of labels for the justices than had previously appeared in the *Times*. He concluded that the terms "conservative" and "progressive" were "two fairly accurate" ways of rendering "the existing differences of attitude in the court." By "progressive" Duffus meant one who believed "that the law must not always be a reluctant marcher at the tail of the progression" of social change but "[s]ometimes it must lead." "Progressive" judges saw the Court as "near to being a continuing constitutional convention." In contrast, "conservative" justices held "a more nearly static, less frankly evolutionary conception of the law," and held a "structural" conception of the Constitution, one that could "be made to collapse . . . if its keystone and supporting girders are weakened." Duffus suggested that the "progressive" position was now dominant on the Court.[93]

In Duffus's account of the two "legal and economic philosophies" he found on the Court in 1935 one sees the beginnings of a characterization of Van Devanter, McReynolds, Sutherland, and Butler that would not only label their jurisprudence and group them into a "conservative" bloc, but would stigmatize them as individuals resisting the forces of history and progress. Duffus had given a fair characterization of the Four Horsemen's constitutional jurisprudence. They did believe—Sutherland had explicitly said as much in one of the speeches quoted by the *Times* on his appointment to the Court—that the Constitution was a "structure" of timeless principles, and attendant interpretive categories, whose fundamental precepts could not be abandoned lest it collapse. But in 1935 it was premature to conclude that "conservative" interpreters would now be in a permanent minority on the Court. And although the criteria for labeling a justice "progressive" or "conservative" were to widen to encompass philosophies of constitutional adaptivity and attitudes toward judicial review, the context for the labels was still a handful of cases that had originated in 1934.

The *Times*'s next use of labels for justices of the Court came in January 1936. By then it was clear that Duffus's confidence that a "progressive" mode of interpretation was dominant on the Court would have to be revised, at least if the basis for labeling justices was their decisions in cases testing the constitutionality of federal legislation regulating economic activity. When the *Times* examined such cases, it noted that the Court had struck down "New Deal" legislation on constitutional grounds in five of six cases decided in the 1934 and 1935 Terms. The article was precipitated by *United States v. Butler*,[94] invalidating the Agricultural Adjustment Act as an unauthorized extension of the commerce power into purely "local" transactions. The *Times*, after listing the previous cases in which New Deal legislation had been struck down (two of which were 9–0 decisions, one 8–1, and a fourth 6–3), advanced the following characterization of the Court's justices: "With Justices Van Devanter, McReynolds, Sutherland and Butler listed in the conservative bloc of the court, and Justices Brandeis, Stone, and Cardozo in the liberal section, Chief Justice Hughes and Justice Roberts have been the more or less unpredictable factors . . . With this showing of the court's attitude on past cases, New Dealers were fearful tonight as to the fate of their other ideas, soon to be decided by the justices."[95]

An interesting feature of the characterization was that of all the justices surveyed, only one, Cardozo, had found more New Deal measures constitutional than unconstitutional, and six justices had found at least four of the six measures unconstitutional. Nonetheless, Hughes and Roberts, probably because they had authored the *Blaisdell* and *Nebbia* decisions, were treated as "unpredictable factors" rather than as members of "the conservative bloc of the court."

By the spring of 1936 the line of commentary in the *Times* emphasizing the human dimensions of Supreme Court judging began to dovetail with the line of commentary claiming that the Court appeared to contain a majority of justices determined to resist the New Deal. Articles began to recast the labels of "progressive" or "liberal" and "conservative" to include judicial attitudes toward the efficacy of governmental activity itself. This had the effect of hardening the images of Van Devanter, McReynolds, Sutherland, and Butler as members of a conservative bloc.

In March 1936 Arthur Krock wrote an article in the *New York Times Magazine* entitled "Nine Judges—and Nine Men, Too."[96] This was the fourth article on the justices of the Court as individuals that had appeared in the *Times* within a two-year span, but Krock, noting that "[l]ately the judicial system has itself been on trial," concluded that it was a particularly appropriate time to consider "the influences that play upon [a judge] personally" and "whether an opinion, completely emancipated from predilection, is ever possible." He concluded that "[b]ecause a judge has come to a position where, with four of his brethren, he can overturn an act of Congress, passed by whatever majority and signed by the President of the United States with warm approval, he does not cease to be a man with opinions, convictions, prejudices, and a definite political philosophy."[97]

Krock's article maintained that the resistance of judicial "conservatives" to expanded governmental regulation of the economy was in the face of a popular mandate. If a majority of the American people had elected a Democratic president and a Democratic Congress, and those entities had produced regulatory legislation that Congress enthusiastically passed and Roosevelt enthusiastically signed, why should the people tolerate that legislation being invalidated by nine men who had not been elected by anyone? Why, especially, should the public tolerate the Court's striking down majoritarian legislation if justices were simply human beings with their own "predilections" and political agendas? Krock had linked judicial "conservatism" to insensitivity to the countermajoritarian difficulty.

At the height of the controversy engendered by the Court's resistance to "New Deal" legislation in the 1934 and 1935 Terms a book appeared that combined stereotyped labeling of the justices with the claim that Supreme Court judging was, at bottom, an exercise in human whimsy. In so doing, the book extended the demonization of Van Devanter, McReynolds, Sutherland, and Butler to a larger popular audience.

The book was *The Nine Old Men*, written by Drew Pearson with the assistance of Robert Allen.[98] Pearson was one of the pioneers of a style of journalism, symbolized by his syndicated "Washington Merry-Go Round" column, which featured undocumented "inside" information about political figures, allegedly based on confidential sources. *The Nine Old Men* was constructed along those lines. Pearson filled his text with unattributed stories about the justices and their careers, each consistent with stereotyped profiles. To this he added a potted history of the Supreme Court whose prominent themes were the consistent involvement of the Court and its members in politics and the tendency of the Court to resist popularly mandated social and economic change.

Pearson never explained why he chose to characterize the Court and its members as "nine old men," a phrase he applied to all the justices, who in 1936 ranged from sixty-one to seventy-nine years of age. But the phrase perfectly captured the themes he most wished to emphasize. "Nine" stood for the remarkably small size of the institution that assumed power to invalidate legislation passed by members of Congress and allegedly representing the views of millions of constituents; "old" embodied the Court's outmoded attitudes toward New Deal legislation; "men" reminded his audience that judges were humans wielding political power. For Pearson the Court's invalidation of "progressive" legislation in the 1934 and 1935 Terms had provoked a political confrontation between "opposing social and economic philosophies . . . between the doctrine of omnipotent intransigeance and the thesis that no nation or people can stand still."[99]

Pearson's treatment of Van Devanter, McReynolds, Sutherland, and Butler in *The Nine Old Men* amounted to a series of caricatures in keeping with his central themes. Van Devanter was a "fanatical reactionary" who was "relentless in his denunciation [of] . . . the New Deal."[100] McReynolds was "unalterably opposed to progress" and was "the unalterable enemy of the underdog."[101] Sutherland was "extremely conservative," the "chief opinion writer for the conservative majority."[102] Butler was "the chief brain and mainspring of the court reactionaries," who "has set himself the task of keeping the conservative wing of the Court intact, keeping it always one vote ahead of the distrusted and unqualified liberals."[103]

As an accurate or searching characterization of the Supreme Court and its justices as they passed on the constitutionality of New Deal legislation in the mid-1930s, *The Nine Old Men* was a strikingly inadequate effort. Much of the gossip Pearson reported about the justices was garbled or implausible, and his caricatured portraits of the Court's personnel amounted to strings of adjectives. But *The Nine Old Men* managed to collect in one place a series of vivid characterizations of Van Devanter, McReynolds, Sutherland, and Butler that, when coupled with their consistent constitutional opposition to governmental regulation of the economy in the 1934 and 1935 Terms, offered some resonant labels for the public. The labels may have been gratuitous overstatements, based on an alarmingly limited sample of decisions. But at the time Van Devanter, McReynolds, Sutherland, and Butler left the Court, in the years between 1937 and 1941, they had become established characterizations.

By the late 1930s, Court majorities had upheld a state minimum wage law for women, a revised version of the federal legislation governing farm bankruptcies, the National Labor Relations Act, and the Social Security Act,[104] and coverage of the Court in the *Times,* although continuing to employ the conventionally stereotyped labels, suggested that a majority of the Court had begun to recognize its countermajoritarian status and act accordingly.[105] This suggestion subtly shifted the implications of the Four Horsemen's labels of conservatives or reactionaries: instead of the labels symbolizing the capacity of justices to resist popular mandates, they came to signal the obsolescence of their views. One can see this shift taking place in the late 1930s. When Van Devanter retired in 1937, the *Times* commented on his "prominence among the four conservative justices who had made the Supreme Court a constant challenge to New Deal acts." Although the *Times*'s own survey of decisions for the 1936 Term had indicated that Van Devanter had "stood with the Roosevelt forces nine times and against them three times," it characterized him as "[a]lways a conservative" and "a thorn in the administration's side when it came to decisions on New Deal measures."[106] On Van Devanter's death in 1941 the *Times*'s obituary described him as "the court's most ardent defender of property rights" and "its most consistently conservative member" during his tenure,[107] and an editorial characterized him as "a persistent and gallant defender of an older order."[108]

In May 1937 Delbert Clark profiled McReynolds in the *New York Times Magazine,* describing him as "Spokesman for the Conservatives." "Through all the eventful history of the Roosevelt administration," Clark wrote, "the lank, sharp-featured Kentuckian, now 75 years old, has consistently and passionately opposed every one of its major acts of reform whenever they have come before the Supreme Court for adjudication. The New Deal is abhorrent to him as a lawyer, as a judge and as an individual." In Clark's view McReynolds's "impassioned extemporaneous addresses from the bench, with which he frequently supplements his written opinions, have combined with his acknowledged leadership to fix him in the public mind as the great exponent of the conservative point of view on the court."[109] On McReynolds's death in 1946, the *Times* pictured him as one of "the nine old men of the Supreme Court" and as, in the last years of his tenure, "the sole—and ineffective—bulwark against an expanding Federal program." In an accompanying editorial, the *Times* said that when McReynolds retired from the Court in 1941 he was the last of the "dwindling ranks of conservatives" who "stood immovable on the rock of 'the written Constitution,' resisting the New Deal and all its works." "With the election of President Roosevelt," the *Times* asserted, "it was clear that times and attitudes were changing, but Justice McReynolds refused to shift with the wind."[110]

When Sutherland retired from the Court in the middle of the 1937 Term, the *Times* declared that the retirement "leaves the Supreme Court in control of liberals, with every likelihood . . . that the New Deal program will be vindicated in all respects."[111] At the time of Sutherland's death in 1942 he had become a "frequent defen[der] of the status quo" and an "unswerving . . . fundamentalist" in his jurisprudence. His 1938 retirement, the *Times* obituary noted, had "made the liberalization of the court complete."[112]

In November 1939 Butler died of complications from a bladder infection. In an article on the Court vacancy his death caused, and in a second article on his performance as a justice, the *Times* sought to place Butler and his "conservative" colleagues in historical perspective. Butler's death left "only one stalwart conservative" on the Court, and gave Roosevelt "an opportunity . . . to assure a Court majority composed of men sympathetic to his ideas on social and economic progress."[113] Although "the legal philosophy that was to run through [Butler's] opinions represented in the Twenties the views of the majority," by the 1930s "a world disaster had brought the necessity for "change [in the law]." Butler and his fellow ultraconservatives "conscientiously resisted change." He and they "lacked that 'insight into social values' and that 'suppleness of adaptation to changing social needs'" that Justice Cardozo had identified as "qualities befitting the great judge." Consequently, the "'great generalities' of the Constitution were not redefined" by Butler or the others, and thus he "was not a great judge." The most one could say of Butler, and by extension the other Horsemen, was that "it takes a brave man to keep on year after year reiterating unpopular convictions."[114]

By Butler's death the demonization of him and his "fundamentalist" colleagues was entrenched. A series of sketchy associations had created their public images, and the identification of their jurisprudential positions with a perspective that was passing into oblivion had served to demonize the images. From mainstream, unremarkable figures in the 1920s they had emerged, primarily on the basis of two terms' worth of constitutional decisions, as part of a "reactionary majority" standing in the way of New Deal social policies. By the time of their retirements and deaths commentary implied that Van Devanter, McReynolds, Butler, and Sutherland had been "reactionaries" for the entire duration of their respective tenures.

This last characterization of the four justices, if one takes into account the general corpus of their constitutional opinions, was grossly inaccurate. The conventional meanings of the labels "conservative" or "reactionary" in narratives of canonization and demonization fail to capture the Four Horsemen's stance across even a moderate sample of cases.

Van Devanter, McReynolds, Sutherland, and Butler took separate positions toward constitutional issues as frequently as they voted as a bloc, and on the majority of instances in which they voted as a bloc they were joined by at least one, and often all, of the other justices who served with them. They repeatedly upheld police powers legislation against due process and Contracts Clause challenges.[115] They regularly sustained the taxing and spending powers of the state and federal governments.[116] They voted to sustain several New Deal statutes regulating economic activity.[117] They consistently upheld the powers of administrative agencies against constitutional challenges.[118] And they demonstrated considerable solicitude for civil rights and civil liberties, of both the incorporated and the preincorporated variety.[119] In short, a comprehensive treatment of the constitutional decisions of each of the Four Horsemen could produce a fair amount of supportive evidence for labeling them "progressives" or "liberals." Their collective characterization as "conservatives," "reactionaries," and a "reactionary bloc" in conventional accounts has rested on a handful of visible cases in the 1930s. It has also been a product of the awareness of mid and late twentieth-century commentators that Van Devanter, McReynolds, Sutherland, and Butler subscribed to the starting assumptions of orthodox early twentieth-century constitutional jurisprudence. But so did the vast majority of the other justices with whom the Four Horsemen served during their tenures.

It remained, to complete the demonization process, for Van Devanter, McReynolds, Sutherland, and Butler to be given a collective label that symbolized their obsolescence. This was supplied by Fred Rodell of the Yale law faculty in his 1955 book, *Nine Men*. Rodell's book was in some respects a sequel to *The Nine Old Men*, relying on some of Pearson's unattributed anecdotes or characterizations of justices,[120] adopting Pearson's view that the members of the Supreme Court were first and foremost human beings and political actors,[121] and sharing Pearson's support for the New Deal and inclination to see constitutional rhetoric as a smoke screen for social and economic biases.[122] It was also designed to appeal to a popular audience: written, as Rodell said in his foreword, "so that any halfway literate non-lawyer can understand it."[123] Rodell's posture was that of a self-described "liberal" who had witnessed the passing of the anti-New Deal Court and "the first time in Court history . . . when liberalism . . . was promoted from a vehicle of eloquent dissent to an instrument of actual judicial power—when views that had been fine and brave and outvoted five or fifty years before became taken-for-granted truths."[124]

Rodell's characterizations of Van Devanter and his three "ultraconservative" colleagues were thus made with a sense that they had been on the losing side. He was able to associate the four justices with a recurrent motif of American constitutional history. "Especially in times of crisis and change," Rodell claimed,

> a reluctant and backward-looking Supreme Court, dominated by a man or group of men who owe their power to a repudiated President or party, can create at least friction, at most chaos, in the running of a nation . . . [I]n the 1930s, a high bench top-heavy with the Four Horsemen of the Old Deal brought the Court, as an institution, to one of its lowest ebbs and greatest crises when it flouted the nation's voters by vetoing much of Franklin Roosevelt's New Deal . . . [A]s so often in our history, a majority of the Justices were behind the political times.[125]

The first characterization of Van Devanter, McReynolds, Sutherland, and Butler as "the Four Horsemen" had been made in a passage whose purpose was to cement their reputations as symbolic adherents of an outmoded judicial philosophy.

Rodell did not explain the origins of his "Four Horsemen" epithet. He said that after the group had been identified as constitutional opponents of Roosevelt administration policies "New Dealers were soon to dub [them] the Four Horsemen of Reaction." He did not specify which "New Dealers," or when the dubbing took place.[126] And if the "Four Horsemen" label was in common usage, it did not appear in any published commentary on the Court in the 1930s.

In 1931 and 1936, however, Learned Hand was reported as having privately described the four justices as, respectively, "the mastiffs" and "the Battalion of Death." Both those descriptions reached the ears of Felix Frankfurter and Justice Harlan Fiske Stone.[127] In the years before his appointment to the Court in 1939 Frankfurter was a consummate Court-watcher, and before he became chief justice in 1941 Stone was not loath to gossip about his colleagues: a snide comment he made about Hughes had found its way into one of Pearson's "Merry-Go-Round" columns in 1932.[128] Thus, a collective characterization of Van Devanter, McReynolds, Sutherland, and Butler was circulating among a group of persons who devoted their attention, in the late 1930s, to supporting the New Deal and criticizing the Court. Rodell, who had been on the Yale law school faculty since the early 1930s,[129] would have had access to those persons.

So the likeliest explanation for the appearance of the "Four Horsemen" label is that Fred Rodell, with his penchant for colorful, informal language, his background as a Court watcher, his indebtedness to *The Nine Old Men,* and his contacts with persons who would have been inclined to caricature Van Devanter and the others as a bloc of reactionaries, summoned up the label from the "universal filing cabinet"[130] of a memory that stretched back for at least twenty years. Regardless of its origins, the phrase was too good to resist in a book designed to portray Supreme Court justices as "powerful, irresponsible, and human."[131] It has also been too good to resist for commentators ever since. So have its overtones, which suggest that by labeling Van Devanter, McReynolds, Sutherland, and Butler the "Four Horsemen" one can also relegate them to a place in the conventional account of early twentieth-century constitutional history, that of "expounders of the perfect symmetry and unity of a jurisprudence whose time had passed."[132]

The label has also stigmatized the careers of the "Four Horsemen." In a 1970 survey of sixty-five law school deans and professors of law, history, and political science, each of whom was identified as an "expert" in American constitutional law, ninety-six Supreme Court justices, from John Jay through Thurgood Marshall, were ranked.[133] Those polled were asked to classify an individual justice as "great," "near-great," "average," "below average," or a "failure." Twelve justices, including four from the Court that confronted New Deal legislation in the 1930s, were ranked as "great." After John Marshall, rated "great" by all sixty-five participants, Brandeis, with sixty-two "great" designations, and Holmes, with sixty-one, led the category. In contrast Van Devanter, McReynolds, and Butler were each included among the eight "failures." Sutherland was given a "near great" rating.[134]

The survey was taken at a time when the overwhelming number of persons holding faculty positions in American academic life would have been sympathetic toward the objectives of the New Deal, and most of the persons polled would have described themselves as political "liberals' rather than "conservatives."[135] The "failure" category may well have been affected by those facts, since, when compared with the other categories, it revealed itself to be a slot into which participants placed justices with whom they were sufficiently familiar to have garnered negative impressions.[136]

There was another common thread linking the "failures." All were seen as insufficiently mindful of the criteria for enlightened judging associated with a model of bifurcated review. Fred M. Vinson, Harold H. Burton, Sherman Minton, and Charles Whittaker were perceived, not entirely accurately, as generally unsympathetic to civil liberties claims.[137] James F. Byrnes, who served only one term on the Court, was a native of South Carolina who, as governor of that state, resisted racial integration in the 1950s. The other members of the "failures" category were three of the Four Horsemen.

Given the relatively anonymous status of the Four Horsemen until the mid-1930s, and given the fact that all of them had retired from the Court by 1941, it is striking that they generated such marked reactions from a group of Court-watching academics in 1970. This suggests that their demonized images had become an embedded part of legal academic culture between the 1930s and the end of the 1960s. Only a handful of the participants in the survey had been members of academic faculties during the time that the Court first confronted New Deal legislation;[138] the great percentage were products of subsequent generations. Their perceptions of Van Devanter, McReynolds, Sutherland, and Butler were primarily derived from those justices' particularly well-constructed historical images. The images had begun to solidify in the late 1930s and were still resonant, not only in the 1950s when Rodell gave them their collective label, but as the 1970s opened. Those images are still solidly in place. They are likely to remain in place until the conventional account of twentieth-century American constitutional history is revised. Until then Rodell's "Four Horsemen of Reaction" will retain their demonic status.

The evaluative criteria that generated the canonization of Holmes and Brandeis and the demonization of the Four Horsemen have also formed the starting points of the conventional account of twentieth-century American constitutional history. Those criteria can best be understood as emanating from a mixture of explicit and tacit premises about the role of the Constitution, and of judges who interpret it, in American life.

The most explicit of the premises is reflected in the concept of a "living Constitution," an adaptive document that responds to changing social and economic conditions through altered judicial interpretations of its central textual provisions. The Constitution, for Pearson, Rodell, and their successor contributors to the conventional account, has been "what the judges say it is."[139]

This explicit premise has emanated from two tacit premises. One is that humans who hold power are not fundamentally constrained by unalterable external phenomena in the universe. Humans have the capacity to control their experience and to alter their environment. Although their experiences and environments are constantly changing, they can contribute, positively or negatively, to that process.

The other tacit premise is that judges are no different from other humans in their powers and in their limitations. In particular, judges do not lose their status as humans by being given power to advance interpretations of the Constitution or other authoritative legal sources. They are different from other humans only in being given that authoritative interpretive power.

Since neither the Constitution itself, nor the status of judges as designated interpreters of that document, can be said to represent fundamental constraints on the power of judges to adapt the Constitution to changing external conditions, some other constraints need to be derived to prevent judicial interpretations of the Constitution from being the equivalent of tyranny or arbitrariness. The only viable constraints are those related to human activity itself: political and ideological constraints. Judges must demonstrate that their interpretations conform, as far as possible, to the current political goals and ideological foundations of American society. Otherwise judges, unlike legislators or members of the executive, are not just powerful and human but, in Rodell's terms, powerful, irresponsible, and human, since they have no accountability to the mass of citizens in a democracy.

The conventional account of early twentieth-century constitutional history has been constructed on the assumption that the posture of the Four Horsemen, and all other judges who subscribed to an essentialist view of the Constitution and a role for themselves as constitutional guardians, was so fundamentally defective in its understanding of constitutional interpretation, and of the nature of judging, that it can be dismissed as "outmoded" and "reactionary." With this assumption in place, the account has ranged through areas of early twentieth-century constitutional law, characterizing decisions and opinions in terms of the evaluative criteria that follow from "the living Constitution" theory of adaptivity and the necessity for judges to internalize the constraints that follow from their countermajoritarian status.

In this process of selective ranging, the conventional account has largely ignored the fact that *none* of its evaluative criteria were taken to be an appropriate basis for assessing the role of Supreme Court justices as constitutional interpreters in the first three decades of the twentieth century. Some justices, and some commentators, had adopted a modernist view of causal attribution in the universe, a fluid conception of constitutional provisions, and a creative theory of constitutional interpretation in the first two decades of that period. Most had not. By the fourth decade most justices and commentators can be described as jurisprudential modernists, and the "living Constitution" theory of constitutional adaptivity had become a mainstream interpretive stance.

Jurisprudential modernism, embodied in the assumptions about constitutional interpretation and the role of Supreme Court justices that animated the replacement of guardian review by bifurcated review, has been so dominant an orthodoxy in the discourse of mid and late twentieth-century constitutional decisionmaking and commentary that the orthodox jurisprudence that it supplanted, reflected in the Four Horsemen's view of constitutional adaptivity, has been caricatured and "lost." The result has not only been to produce a series of triumphalist narratives that reinforce the displacement of guardian review by bifurcated review and recenter the task of constitutional interpretation on the countermajoritarian difficulty. It has also been to misconceive the nature of a period of great jurisprudential ferment in American law, one in which fundamentally antipathetic conceptions of the nature of law, the meaning of authoritative legal sources, and the role of the judge as a constitutional interpreter were in collision.

Ultimately the canonization of Holmes and Brandeis and the demonization of the "Four Horsemen" illustrate jurisprudential modernism's powerful grip on the generations of commentators who have treated the New Deal as a symbol of modern constitutional governance in America. If one takes the emergence of expansive government to be an inevitable product of the interaction of human agency and modernity, the "revolution" in which bifurcated review displaced guardian review can be seen as the culmination of a progressive truth that was first revealed in Holmes's *Lochner* dissent, refined in the political economy cases and preferred position cases of the 1940s, and has shaped constitutional decisionmaking ever since. It then only remains to tell the story, in the form of triumphalist narratives, of how that truth came to be revealed.

If, however, one steps past the narratives of canonization and demonization, disengages oneself from the myths of substantive due process, and attempts to recreate the constitutional universe of the early twentieth century as it was understood by participants in that world, that universe appears far more contested and its history more complicated. In the process the New Deal begins to lose some of its symbolic power as a formative constitutional event, appearing more as a historical episode than as a source of universal inspiration. The New Deal and the "constitutional revolution" begin to be cabined in time.

10

Cabining the New Deal in Time

It is time to collect the argumentative threads of this study and to underscore their implications for the history of early twentieth-century constitutional jurisprudence. It is also time to speculate on why the New Deal, as a political and constitutional symbol, has occupied so important a place in the lives of twentieth-century scholars and other Americans. Finally, it is time to achieve some distance on the New Deal in its symbolic role.

At the outset of this work I claimed that the conventional account of early twentieth-century American constitutional history is inaccurate. I suggested that its inaccuracies have primarily resulted from a set of anachronistic readings of the constitutional jurisprudence of the period. At this point we are in a position to discern the common feature that links those anachronistic readings, the tendency of conventional narratives to advance a monolithic interpretation of changes in early twentieth-century constitutional law.

The monolithic quality of conventional narratives has been produced by their obsession with two themes, the Court-packing crisis and the countermajoritarian difficulty. I have chosen to expose this feature of the narratives by first detailing their inaccuracies, then demonstrating a connection between those inaccuracies and anachronistic interpretations of early twentieth-century sources, and then connecting those interpretations to a particular view of law, judging, and constitutional interpretation to which conventional narrators have subscribed. That view, which I have labeled behavioralist, assumes that judges are a species of political actors, constitutional interpretation an exercise in infusing the ideological views of interpreters into provisions of the Constitution, and the distinction between the will of the judge and the will of the law a specious one.

A behavioralist theory of law and judging has served to center early twentieth-century constitutional history around the themes of the Court-packing crisis and the countermajoritarian difficulty. Because they have subscribed to that theory, contributors to the conventional account have anticipated that early twentieth-century Supreme Court justices, being a species of political actors, would respond to external political pressures on their institution, and that their response would take the form of altered interpretations of the Constitution. Those expectations have served to elevate the introduction of the Court-packing plan to causal significance in producing a judicially created "revolution" in early twentieth-century constitutional jurisprudence. A behavioralist theory of law and judging has also helped commentators draw the principal jurisprudential lesson of the Court-packing crisis: the resistance of "conservative" or "reactionary" judges to popularly mandated New Deal legislation exposed the countermajoritarian status of the Court, eventually chastening its members and attitudes and resulting in the replacement of guardian review with bifurcated review.

The outstanding characteristic of the conventional account of early twentieth-century American constitutional history, however, has neither been its inaccuracy nor its tendency to advance monolithic explanations for constitutional change. It has been its remarkable durability as accepted historical wisdom. Given the account's descriptive and analytical vulnerability, its longstanding stature among twentieth-century constitutional historians and legal scholars is particularly intriguing. In searching for explanations of the conventional account's prominence, I became aware of the significant investment its contributors have made in the New Deal as a transformative constitutional event. Although that investment could be seen simply as a product of the ideological orientation of most mid and late twentieth-century constitutional commentators—the majority of whom have seen themselves as "liberals," sympathetic to New Deal policies and hostile to constitutional opposition to those policies—such an explanation did not fully capture the instinctive sense among commentators that the New Deal was a special episode in twentieth-century constitutional governance. That instinctive sense seemed more satisfactorily explained at the level of epistemology.

I have sought to extract the epistemological underpinnings of the conventional account by determining the symbolic role occupied by the New Deal in conventional narratives of early twentieth-century constitutional history, and asking why it had been assigned that role. I found that in several narratives of early twentieth-century constitutional change the New Deal played the same role, that of creating pressure on the judiciary to produce an altered corpus of constitutional law that would facilitate the emergence of a new realm of American governance.

"New Deal" policies were described in the narratives as dramatic breaks with the immediate past. In the domestic arena they were characterized as ushering in an expanded role for the states, and especially for the federal government, as regulators of the economy and distributors of economic benefits throughout the population. They were also described as creating a phalanx of federal administrative agencies to implement the goals of affirmative, regulatory government. In foreign affairs, they were associated with an aggressive, creative role for the executive branch in the formation of foreign policy.

Judges were characterized in the narratives as initially resisting, but eventually endorsing, these "New Deal" innovations in governance. In the process they were seen as assuming a new posture toward their function as constitutional interpreters. Judges would construe the Constitution as permitting a great deal of legislative and administrative autonomy in the sphere of domestic economic regulation and redistribution, and a great deal of federal executive autonomy in foreign affairs, but would insist that the Constitution required significant judicial scrutiny of legislation infringing on certain specified civil rights and liberties, those deemed foundational to a modern democratic society. In assuming this posture the judiciary in the New Deal period abandoned its traditional function as guardians of the essentialist principles of the Constitution.

The narratives have also supplied a common explanation for why the New Deal eventually produced those transformations in the corpus of constitutional law and in the posture of the judiciary toward constitutional review. The New Deal innovations in governance that spawned constitutional challenges were pragmatic responses to modernity. The domestic political and economic crises of the 1930s, and their international counterparts, required greater governmental intervention in the industrial marketplace and a more flexible foreign policymaking apparatus. Eventually the Supreme Court recognized that its failure to grant New Deal innovations constitutional legitimacy would expose its members as holding outmoded, and countermajoritarian, theories of governance. So, over time, the Court changed its constitutional jurisprudence to accommodate the New Deal's governmental apparatus. It needed some help in doing so—not only persistent criticism but a reminder of its vulnerability to the more majoritarian branches in the form of a threat to change its composition. But by Roosevelt's death it had become a "New Deal Court."

In retrospect, the most surprising feature of the New Deal's ascribed role in conventional narratives is that so many scholars have treated that role as unproblematic, even obvious. For, as we have seen, causal connections between New Deal initiatives and *any* of the major transformations in early twentieth-century constitutional domestic or foreign relations jurisprudence have been difficult to draw. The principle of executive discretion in constitutional foreign affairs jurisprudence had surfaced before the First World War and was largely in place on the Supreme Court before the Court-packing plan was launched. Judicial review of the decisions of federal administrative agencies on constitutional grounds was actually heightened between the 1930s and 1946. The disintegration of guardian review was in process before the 1930s, and bifurcated review did not fully replace guardian review until the end of the 1940s. The Court-packing crisis was more of a symptom than a cause of the early twentieth-century "constitutional revolution."

Thus, the symbolic role of the New Deal in conventional narratives of early twentieth-century constitutional jurisprudence does not serve to reinforce the accuracy of those narratives' historical claims; quite the opposite. Instead, it serves to reinforce the epistemological resonance of the narratives. The New Deal and the Court-packing crisis figure prominently in the narratives because they are vivid modernist symbols: illustrations of the capacity of humans holding power to develop new theories in governance in the face of modernity. The central tale of the conventional account of early twentieth-century American constitutional history, that of the New Deal, the Court-packing crisis, and the "constitutional revolution," has been an archetypal triumphalist narrative.

My effort to dislodge the conventional account from its position of current stature has required more than a series of attempts to portray early twentieth-century constitutional transformations in a more accurate and less anachronistic fashion. I have also felt the obligation to offer an alternative to the monolithic interpretation of early twentieth-century constitutional change advanced in the conventional account. And since my alternative explanation minimizes the significance of the New Deal in precipitating any "constitutional revolution," I have thought it necessary to explore why so many commentators have accorded the New Deal that significance. This has resulted not only in a historicization of the conventional account of early twentieth-century constitutional history but of the New Deal itself. At this point I want to identify some of the implications of my reassessment of the relationship between the Constitution and the New Deal.

I have argued that if a number of areas of early twentieth-century constitutional law covered in narratives of the conventional account are reexamined, and supplemented by the investigation of some additional areas, a quite different picture of American constitutional jurisprudence in the first four decades of the twentieth century emerges. If one then projects the altered historical impressions generated by that exercise back upon the conventional account, the starting presuppositions of that account come into sharper relief. One can list a series of ascribed characteristics of early twentieth-century constitutional jurisprudence that are prominent in the conventional account, each of which is partially contradicted by evidence and all of which contribute to the account's monolithic quality.

The most concrete characteristic of the account is its descriptive and normative investment in bifurcated constitutional review. The account takes for granted that the first four decades of early twentieth-century constitutional history witnessed the emergence of bifurcated review as an approved judicial stance. The triumph of bifurcated review lends another dimension to the struggles between judicial "progressives" or "liberals" and judicial "conservatives" or "reactionaries" that are emphasized in conventional narratives: the labels are intended to evoke a judge's attitude toward constitutional review as well as his general political inclinations. Characterizing a judge as "conservative" or "reactionary" thus becomes the equivalent of describing his perspective as "obsolete."

More detailed investigation reveals that the shift from guardian to bifurcated review was a gradual and irregular phenomenon, and one not easily correlated to political ideologies. Deferential judicial review in cases involving economic activity did not become entrenched as a mainstream position until the early 1940s. At no time previous to that, despite a vigorous modernist critique of orthodox guardian review by commentators, had the position captured a majority of the justices who sat on the Supreme Court. Moreover, aggressive judicial review in cases involving noneconomic civil rights and liberties was not a departure from guardian review. The major change in the Court's posture in those cases between the 1920s and the early 1940s was not its review stance but its tendency to treat liberties associated with freedom of expression as eligible for greater constitutional protection, a tendency exhibited by both "conservative" and "liberal" justices. By the end of the Second World War a rationale for aggressive review of free speech or freedom of religion claims had been articulated, the idea that those claims occupied a constitutionally "preferred position." But that rationale was not consistently invoked by a majority of the Court, and the remaining areas of *Carolene Products* heightened scrutiny remained undeveloped.

In short, the dominant posture of constitutional review adopted by the Court from the 1950s onward, with its supine "rational basis" review of most forms of economic legislation, and its development of "tiers" of heightened scrutiny for claims based on freedom of expression or based on various forms of discrimination, was not the dominant posture of the New Deal period. By treating late twentieth-century bifurcated review as already established in that period, conventional narratives have been able to characterize the positions of some early twentieth-century justices as "obsolescent," and others as prescient, through the use of anachronistic criteria.

The conventional account's investment in bifurcated review has not simply produced anachronistic readings of early twentieth-century constitutional decisions or indiscriminate labeling of the positions of justices. It has resulted in the confining to oblivion of a number of legal arguments and propositions that were seriously entertained by participants in early twentieth-century constitutional jurisprudence. The arguments and propositions that conventional narratives have "lost" have been those based on orthodox late nineteenth- and early twentieth-century conceptions of the nature of law and judging.

The central difference between guardian and bifurcated review, as we have seen, is the idea that judges, being countermajoritarian officials, should defer to majoritarian policymakers except when majoritarian policies are themselves inconsistent with democratic theory. Those who have invested in the conventional account have established bifurcated review as a necessary corollary to behavioralist theories of law and judging, and to the modern and democratic character of twentieth-century American society, through a series of interrelated propositions. Judges are political actors, exhibiting creativity in their interpretations of the Constitution. The vast majority of the significant provisions of the constitutional text have no fixed or finite meaning. Therefore, the only fundamental lodestar in constitutional interpretation is conformity to the principles of democratic theory, which requires deference in many cases, as well as aggressive scrutiny, against a backdrop of normal deference, in a few. Given the causal significance of human powerholding in modern societies, the only way to check potential tyranny or arbitrariness in judges is to make them accountable to a political philosophy that treats all human contributions as potentially deserving of equal concern and respect. Thus, judicial creativity is not checked by the Constitution, "the law," or any permanent metaprinciples undergirding those entities, but by conformity to the foundational values of democratic theory.

Narrators sharing those starting propositions have tended to exhibit no sympathy for the posture of guardian review or for methodologies or techniques of constitutional interpretation employed by judges who subscribed to that posture. From the perspective of conventional narrators, those methodologies presupposed that the provisions of the Constitution embodied universalist, essentialist principles that judges merely applied to cases. That presupposition misconceived the nature of law and judging. Hence when conventional narrators have encountered early twentieth-century judicial opinions that posited the existence of essentialist constitutional checks on official decisionmaking, they have tended to treat those opinions as rhetorical obfuscations or examples of ineptitude.

The result has been a failure to appreciate the stature of arguments in early twentieth-century opinions and commentary that were premised on essentialist readings of constitutional provisions. This has produced in the area of foreign affairs a failure to grasp the degree to which the discretion of the federal executive was taken to be constrained by both enumerated and reserved constitutional powers. It has had the effect in the area of administrative law of minimizing the importance of orthodox separation of powers principles in defining that field. It has caused the great majority of mid and late twentieth-century historians and constitutional law scholars to ignore the "living Constitution" debate of the 1920s, and to fail to appreciate the relationship of the "Formalist"/"Realist" debate in common law jurisprudence to that controversy. It has resulted in the area of due process in an inability to understand the methodology of early twentieth-century police powers jurisprudence and the meaning of "substantive due process" itself. And, of course, this failure to appreciate the stature of constitutional arguments predicated on a meaningful separation between the will of the law and the will of the judge has reinforced a fixation with the political culture of the New Deal, embodied in the Court-packing crisis, as a phenomenon of great constitutional significance.

Thus, the conventional account of early twentieth-century American constitutional law and jurisprudence has been an exercise in "winners' history": one that not only proceeds from unexpressed starting assumptions but reinforces those assumptions in its findings. The source of the account's durability, I have suggested, does not lie in its political tilt, or its monolithic central hypothesis, but in the widespread acceptance of its starting presuppositions about law and judging.

At those levels the claims of the conventional account seem most powerful, and one can appreciate its continued resonance for mid and late twentieth-century Americans. Even if the account's narratives can be shown to have generated some caricatured labels of early twentieth-century judges, or some inaccurate or simplistic descriptions of constitutional issues, and even if its monolithic emphasis has resulted in some of its conclusions being based on egregiously inadequate data, the account can still implicitly claim to rest on a fundamentally sound theory of the nature of law, judging, and constitutional interpretation, and, consequently, to have made the appropriate historical evaluations of those early twentieth-century judges and commentators who clung to an alternative, misguided theory.

If the central source of the conventional account's resonance can be said to lie in the widely assumed veracity of its starting assumptions about law and judging, one can see how the New Deal would readily assume in that account the status of a defining moment in twentieth-century constitutional history. The New Deal coincided with the period when a behavioralist theory of law, judging, and constitutional interpretation first became orthodoxy in American jurisprudence. Examples of a purported connection between the New Deal and the triumph of modernist conceptions of law and judging are easily supplied. The New Deal period produced a defiant claim by a popular president that the Supreme Court was nothing but a group of nine old men. It witnessed the Court's own belated recognition that the Constitution was a living document, and a resultant revolution in the constitutional jurisprudence of political economy that legitimated the welfare state. Its proliferation of administrative agencies eventually resulted in functional definitions of governmental powers once thought essentialist. The expanded degree of executive discretion accompanying the legitimation of domestic agencies complemented and fueled the growth of executive discretion in foreign affairs. All of those developments can be seen as reflecting the triumph of a behavioralist theory of constitutional governance, one in which human officials in power altered the meaning of the Constitution to ensure that its principles responded to the imperatives of a modern democratic society. All of them can be seen as taking place in the New Deal period.

But the flip side of the New Deal's resonance as a defining moment in modernist constitutional governance has been the relative inability of those who have invested in it to imagine a world in which legal actors could approach their experience without holding to behavioralist theories of law, judging, and constitutional interpretation. We have seen that conventional narratives have claimed far too much for the New Deal's accomplishments. The critique that eventually undermined the guardian role for judges in police power balancing cases had been articulated as early as 1905, well before the New Deal political and economic reconfigurations were under way. Nor did the New Deal have much to do with the abandonment of "substantive due process." If one emphasizes the linguistic and conceptual dimensions of that characterization, there were no substantive due process cases to abandon; if one treats "substantive due process" as a normative comment on a posture of constitutional review, the guardian role of judges in political economy cases was not decisively abandoned until the mid-1940s.

Similar chronological and analytical difficulties abound for other claims of a close correspondence between the New Deal and major shifts in twentieth-century constitutional jurisprudence. The central jurisprudential debates that were eventually resolved in the interpretive revolution that transformed Due Process and Commerce Clause cases, and in the modernist attack on the first set of Restatements, were under way in the 1920s. The transformation of constitutional foreign affairs jurisprudence was well under way before the New Deal came into being. The genesis of administrative law owed as much to orthodox constitutional attacks on the agency form as it did to newer extraconstitutional justifications for agency government. Neither of the

twentieth-century judges who have been canonized in the conventional account can, on examination, be claimed as prominent supporters of the New
Deal. None of the Four Horsemen invariably voted to invalidate New Deal
legislation.

The New Deal, in sum, was a particularized moment in time that coincided,
in the realm of constitutional jurisprudence, with the triumph of modernist
conceptions of law and judging that have had wide ramifications. Among
those ramifications have been the construction of a defective, but exceptionally resonant, account of early twentieth-century constitutional history. The
significance conventionally attributed to the New Deal in that account needs
to reconsidered, and the symbolic place of the New Deal in twentieth-century constitutional jurisprudence needs to be understood in a different way.

The New Deal had its own parochial flavor and its own discrete constitutional issues, which can be seen as distinct from, and not in themselves more
significant than, the constitutional issues that were central to the 1920s or to
the 1950s. In this sense the transformative status accorded to constitutional
developments that took place in the New Deal period—the monolithic description of a "constitutional revolution" centering around the Court-packing crisis—needs to be abandoned. As an external precipitating force for massive constitutional change, the New Deal needs to be cabined in time, and
the tendency of narrators to see its particular constitutional issues as being
foreshadowed in earlier decades needs to be resisted.

But the special importance of the New Deal as the midpoint of a crisis
in early twentieth-century American jurisprudence needs to be appreciated.
This study has argued that the crisis was underway by the early 1920s and not
fully resolved until after the Second World War, so neither its surfacing nor its
resolution can be attributed solely to developments in the New Deal period.
Nonetheless, the existence in the 1930s of other crises related to the emergence of modernity, signaled by the appearance of new models of social relations, political participation, and economic organization, cannot be ignored.[1]
In my view the transformations in American social relations, politics, and economics that contemporaries observed to be taking place in the New Deal period can most profitably be seen as responses to modernity that paralleled the
jurisprudential responses I have described in this study.

In trying to peel away the layers of normative investment in the New Deal
that have so affected the shape and form of the conventional account one
keeps coming up against this sense that the decade of the 1930s was a special
historical moment. That sense lies at the foundation of the conventional ac-

count, and can be seen as the primary source of its continued resonance and durability. But it is not necessary to abandon that sense in order to reject the conventional account's narratives of early twentieth-century constitutional history. It is only necessary to reduce the historiographical and normative significance of the New Deal as a formative event in modernist constitutional governance.

If one believes that the eventual resolutions of the parallel crises of modernity that helped to define American culture in the 1930s have produced permanent features of our twentieth, and twenty-first, century constitutional polity, investing in the New Deal becomes an affirmation of a late twentieth-century collection of essentialist metapolitical and constitutional principles. Once one makes that affirmation, it is almost inevitable that, in surveying the constitutional history that took place before the crises of modernity were resolved, one will see doctrinal and jurisprudential issues in the terms of that resolution. The new essentialist principles of the resolution become touchstones for assessing those issues, and the decisions and opinions of constitutional actors are stripped of their historical context.

Investment in the New Deal as the defining event in twentieth-century modernist constitutional governance thus results in an indiscriminate projection of the New Deal, as symbol, backward and forward from its time frame. Instead of being an episode that took place in a particular, limited time period, it becomes an inspirational example for twentieth-century governance. Instead of being a period with its time-bound constitutional issues, it becomes a period when new essentialist constitutional principles are grasped. Its shadow dominates narratives of constitutional history in the years prior to its existence, and the triumphalist narratives of those who have been inspired by it continue to be fashioned sixty years after it first surfaced.

The relationship between the Constitution and the New Deal becomes, in these projections, the center of twentieth-century constitutional history. But the relationship between the Constitution and the New Deal should only take on that centrality if the New Deal experiments in modernist constitutional governance are assumed to have become permanent features of our polity and thus to amount to essentialist constitutional truths. The details of twentieth-century constitutional history demonstrate that such beliefs cannot be maintained. Theories of government, models of politics, economics, and social organization, postures of constitutional review, and assumptions about the nature of law or judging have radically changed over the course of the century. Modernist-inspired, post–New Deal essentialism in constitutional jurisprudence is still essentialism.

A reassessment of the relationship between the Constitution and the New Deal requires that we make every effort to resist the projection of the New

Deal, as a symbolic episode in modernist constitutional governance, backward and forward in time. To engage in the former set of projections will result in a continuation of the inaccurate and monolithic historical narratives of early twentieth-century constitutional law that I have been seeking to revise. To engage in the latter set of projections is to perpetuate a disabling nostalgia for an idealized model of constitutional governance. My focus in this book has been on the difficulties inherent in a backward projection of the New Deal as a formative constitutional episode. There is a great deal more work that can be done in recovering a more accurate picture of early twentieth-century constitutional law and jurisprudence, and I hope others may be encouraged by my example. But the more serious consequences of idealizing the New Deal are those that follow from its forward projection. We can no longer afford to employ the New Deal as a standard for measuring the effectiveness of current political and constitutional theories. The New Deal needs to be cabined in its own time.

Notes | Index

Notes

Introduction

1. The "Court-packing plan" of 1937, as it is commonly called, was embodied in a provision in the Judiciary Reform Act of 1937, a proposed bill to reorganize the federal judiciary submitted to Congress by President Roosevelt on February 5 of that year. The provision allowed the president to nominate an additional justice to the Supreme Court if any justice sitting on that Court remained in office for six months after his seventieth birthday. When the bill was submitted by Roosevelt to Congress, six of the sitting justices were over seventy, so had the "Court-packing" provision of the bill become law, and none of those justices retired, Roosevelt would have had six appointments to the Court. Although the Judiciary Reform Act, 50 Stat. 751 (1937), was eventually passed by Congress, the "Court-packing" provision failed to be reported out from the Judiciary Committees of the House and Senate. For more detail on the circumstances under which the plan failed to gain congressional endorsement, see Barry Cushman, *Rethinking the New Deal Court: The Structure of a Constitutional Revolution,* 11–25 (1998).

2. Katie Loucheim, ed., *The Making of the New Deal: The Insiders Speak* (1984). The New Deal lawyers interviewed by Loucheim, in addition to Corcoran, Fortas, Hiss, and Pritchard, were Kenneth Crawford, Thomas H. Eliot, Thomas I. Emerson, Henry Hamill Fowler, Milton Freeman, Paul Freund, Gerhard Gesell, Arthur Goldschmidt, Thornton Greene, Paul M. Herzog, Charles A. Horsky, Milton Katz, Charles A. Kaufman, David A. Morse, Joseph Rauh, Jr., David Riesman, Robert L. Stern, Telford Taylor, Frank Watson, and Herbert Wechsler.

3. See "Felix Frankfurter, the Old Boy Network, and the New Deal," 39 *Arkansas Law Review* 400 (1986); "Recapturing New Deal Lawyers," 102 *Harvard Law Review* 489 (1988); and "Revisiting the New Deal Legal Generation," 17 *Capital University Law Review* 37 (1989), in G. Edward White, *Intervention and Detachment: Essays in Legal History and Jurisprudence,* 132–203 (1994).

4. My own work has been part of the conventional account. In the first edition of *The American Judicial Tradition,* for example, I characterized constitutional differences among Supreme Court justices in the mid-1930s as turning on the degree to which an individual judge was sympathetic or unsympathetic to the New Deal. I also suggested that Justice Owen Roberts had "reacted to the

Court-packing controversy by voting differently in two nearly indistinguishable cases," invalidating legislation regulating economic activity in the earlier case, and then, after the Court-packing crisis had surfaced, sustaining comparable legislation in the later one. G. Edward White, *The American Judicial Tradition: Profiles of Leading American Judges,* 177, 178 (1st ed., 1976). I repeated the same characterization in the second edition, which appeared in 1988.

5. See Dorothy Ross, "Introduction," in Dorothy Ross, ed., *Modernist Impulses in the Human Sciences,* 8 (1994).

6. For a compilation of sources claiming that modernity can be traced back to the emergence of the nation-state in the Reformation period, and that modernist consciousness incorporates a variety of attitudes in addition to a theory of human-centered causal agency, see Stephen M. Feldman, *American Legal Thought from Premodernism to Postmodernism* 15–28 (2000).

7. Compare Gordon S. Wood, *The Radicalism of the American Revolution,* 6–7 (1992), which treats American republican theory in the framing period as modernist-inspired but unaccompanied by modernity. For an extension of Wood's formulation to the Civil War years, see Jurgen Heideking, "The Pattern of American Nationalism from the Revolution to the Civil War," 129 *Daedalus* 219–245 (2000).

J. G. A. Pocock's *The Machiavellian Moment* (1975) identified the tendency of American constitutional republicanism at the framing of the Constitution, and beyond, to take a "millennial" form, one which anticipated a long-standing period of future time in which "first principles" of morality and justice would be reasserted as barriers to social and institutional decay. In "Historical Consciousness in Nineteenth-Century America," 89 *American Historical Review* 909–928 (1984), and subsequently in *The Origins of American Social Science* (1991), Dorothy Ross reconfigured Pocock's insight, suggesting that the millennial tendency of early nineteenth-century American constitutional thought was part of a more general "prehistoricist" attitude toward cultural change over time. In *The Marshall Court and Cultural Change* (1988), I sought to make more detailed and explicit links between a prehistoricist conception of change over time and early American constitutional jurisprudence. By "prehistoricist" Ross and I both meant a conception of historical change as merely the successive unfolding of preordained, fundamental cycles of birth, maturity, and decay rather than, as she put it, "a realm of human construction, propelled ever forward in time by the cumulative effects of human action, and taking new qualitative forms." Ross, *The Origins of American Social Science,* 3.

In both *The Origins of American Social Science* and in "Modernism Reconsidered," her introductory essay in *Modernist Impulses,* Ross stressed the links between modernity and historicist conceptions of cultural change. In that essay she associated modernity, at least in America, with the late nineteenth century rather than the Enlightenment, and in another essay in *Modernist Impulses* she suggested that only by the early twentieth century had American social scientists developed fully historicist visions. See Ross, "Modernist Social Science in the Land of the New/Old," in *Modernist Impulses,* 171–189.

For a continuation of the current scholarly debate over the terms millenialism and exceptionalism, and over the appropriate chronological boundaries of modernity in nineteenth- and twentieth-century America, see Thomas L. Haskell, "Taking Exception to Exceptionalism," 28 *Reviews in American History* 151–166 (2000), reviewing Daniel T. Rodgers, *Atlantic Crossings: Social Politics in a Progressive Age* (1998).

8. The generalizations I am making in the next several paragraphs rest on a variety of historical sources, some of which deserve singling out at this juncture. On the significance of class as a category, see Martin J. Burke, *The Conundrum of Class* (1995). On the persistence of republicanism as a mainstream American political ideology into the twentieth century, and the gradual merger of republican ideals with more "democratic," participatory ones in the Progressive movement, see Frank Tariello, Jr., *The Reconstruction of American Political Ideology 1865–1917* (1982). On the persistence of an older model of economic relationships into the twentieth century, and the simultaneous emergence of challenges to that model, compare volume 3 of Joseph Dorfman's *The Economic Mind in American Civilization* (5 vols., 1946–1959) with Morton Keller, *Regulating a New Economy* (1990). On the continued prominence of explanatory theories of higher learning centered in the natural sciences, and the challenge to those theories from the late nineteenth-century developments in the social sciences, see Thomas Haskell, *The Emergence of Professional Social Science* (1977) and Ross, *The Origins of American Social Science.* On the chronology of modernism in America, see Daniel Joseph Singal, *The War Within: From Victorian to Modernist Thought in the South, 1919–1945* (1982).

9. For documentation of the transformation from class-centered to individual or group-centered aspirational social models among residents of New York City in the early twentieth century, see William E. Nelson, "The Legalist Reformation: Law, Politics, and Ideology in New York, 1920–1980" (unpublished manuscript, 1999).

10. Two excellent general accounts of the related, but distinguishable, appeals of the Progressive movement and the New Deal are David Kennedy, *Over Here* (1980) and Alan Brinkley, *The End of Reform* (1995). For closer analyses of the relationship of Progressivism to the New Deal, compare Otis Graham, *An Encore for Reform: The Old Progressives and the New Deal* (1967) with Eldon J. Eisenach, *The Lost Promise of Progressivism* (1994).

11. The classic study here is Ellis Hawley, *The New Deal and the Problem of Monopoly* (1966). See also Keller, *Regulating a New Economy.*

1. The Conventional Account

1. Typically cited are Panama Refining Co. v. Ryan, 293 U.S. 388 (1935), invalidating a section of the National Industrial Recovery Act (NIRA) on the grounds that it represented an unconstitutional delegation of power from Congress to the executive; Railroad Retirement Board v. Alton Railway Co., 295 U.S. 330 (1935), invalidating an effort on the part of Congress to establish a pension system for railroad workers as an unauthorized use of the commerce power; Schechter Poultry Corp. v. United States, 295 U.S. 495 (1935), invalidating ad-

ditional sections of the NIRA on delegation grounds; Louisville Joint Stock Land Bank v. Radford, 295 U.S. 555 (1935), holding the Frazier-Lemke Federal Farm Bankruptcy Act an unconstitutional infringement on the due process liberties of creditors; United States v. Butler, 297 U.S. 1 (1936), invalidating the Agricultural Adjustment Administration's efforts to regulate agricultural production as an unauthorized use of the commerce power; Carter v. Carter Coal Co., 298 U.S. 238 (1936), invalidating a federal statute seeking to establish minimum wage levels and collective bargaining in the mining industry on commerce power and delegation grounds; and Morehead v. New York ex rel. Tipaldo, 298 U.S. 587 (1936), invalidating a New York state minimum wage law for women as an infringement of "liberty of contract" under the Fourteenth Amendment's Due Process Clause.

Typically ignored, in this characterization of the Court's response to state and federal regulation between 1934 and 1937, are Home Building & Loan Association v. Blaisdell, 290 U.S. 398 (1934), sustaining a Minnesota statute establishing a moratorium on the enforcement of mortgage payments in the face of a challenge that the law violated the clause in the Constitution prohibiting states from impairing the obligation of contracts; Nebbia v. New York, 291 U.S. 503 (1934), permitting New York to regulate prices in the milk industry even though the state had not established that the milk industry was a business "affected with a public interest"; Ashwander v. Tennessee Valley Authority, 297 U.S. 288 (1936), upholding the constitutionality of a public authority created by the federal government to produce electricity as an appropriate exercise of federal power over navigable waters; and St. Joseph Stockyards Co. v. United States, 298 U.S. 38 (1936), sustaining the constitutionality of rate regulation of an industry by a federal agency if Congress had provided that agency with sufficiently clear guidelines.

2. The most commonly cited cases are West Coast Hotel v. Parrish, 300 U.S. 379 (1937), upholding a Washington state law fixing minimum wages for women against a liberty of contract challenge; Wright v. Vinton Branch, 300 U.S. 440 (1937), unanimously sustaining a revised Frazier-Lemke Bankruptcy Act with a provision for staying, rather than completely discharging, creditors' claims; National Labor Relations Board v. Jones & Laughlin Steel Corp., 301 U.S. 1 (1937), upholding the National Labor Relations Act of 1935, which provided for collective bargaining in industries engaged in interstate commerce; Stewart Machine Co. v. Davis 301 U.S. 548 (1937), and Helvering v. Davis, 301 U.S. 619 (1937), upholding the Social Security Act of 1935, whose unemployment compensation provisions were similar to those struck down in the Alton case; Mulford v. Smith, 7 U.S. 38 (1939), upholding a redrafted version of the Agricultural Adjustment Act; Sunshine Coal v. Adkins, 310 U.S. 381 (1940), upholding a revised version of the Bituminous Coal Conservation Act on the grounds that Congress could employ the commerce power to regulate wages in the coal mining industry; and United States v. Darby, 312 U.S. 100 (1941), and Wickard v. Filburn, 317 U.S. 111 (1942), dramatically extending the reach of the federal government's power to regulate "local" industries or activities.

3. See William E. Leuchtenburg, *The Supreme Court Reborn: The Constitutional*

Revolution in the Age of Roosevelt, 115–119 (1995). Leuchtenburg suggests that Corwin's correspondence in December 1936 with Attorney General Homer S. Cummings influenced Cummings to consider a proposal in which an additional justice could be appointed to the Court if one of its sitting justices reached the age of seventy and declined to resign. That idea, according to correspondence in Corwin's papers, originated with Arthur Holcombe, a professor of government at Harvard, who proposed it to Corwin in a December 7, 1936 letter. The letter is quoted by Leuchtenburg, 117.

4. Corwin used the phrase "switch in time that saved nine" in a letter to Homer S. Cummings, May 19, 1937, Edward S. Corwin Papers, Princeton University, quoted in William E. Leuchtenburg, "FDR's Court-Packing Plan: A Second Life, A Second Death," 1985 *Duke Law Journal* 673. See also Michael Ariens, "A Thrice-Told Tale: Or Felix the Cat," 107 *Harvard Law Review* 620, 623 (1994), examining a variety of claims to authorship of the phrase and concluding that Corwin is the most likely author.

5. See Alsop and Catledge, *The 168 Days,* 141; Benjamin F. Wright, *The Growth of American Constitutional Law,* 200–202, 205, 222.

6. See Edward S. Corwin, *Court over Constitution,* 127 (1938); Corwin, *Constitutional Revolution, Ltd.,* 74–75 (1942).

7. See, e.g., Louis Henkin, "The Treaty Makers and the Law Makers: The Niagara Reservation," 56 *Columbia Law Review* 1151 (1956); Henkin, "The Treaty Makers and the Law Makers: The Law of the Land and Foreign Relations," 107 University of Pennsylvania Law Review 903 (1959). These articles, and several more Henkin wrote in the 1960s, would culminate in his massively influential book, *Foreign Affairs and the Constitution* (1972).

8. If the "New Deal period" is defined broadly, to parallel the central time frame of this study, the relevant Supreme Court justices, with their years of service, would be, in chronological order, Oliver Wendell Holmes (1902–1932), Willis Van De Vanter (1910–1937), Charles Evans Hughes (1910–1916, 1930–1941), James C. McReynolds (1914–1941), Louis D. Brandeis (1916–1939), William Howard Taft (1921–1930), George Sutherland (1922–1938), Pierce Butler (1922–1939), Edward T. Sanford (1923–1930), Harlan Fiske Stone (1925–1946), Owen Roberts (1930–1945), Benjamin N. Cardozo (1932–1938), Hugo L. Black (1937–1971), Stanley F. Reed (1938–1957), Felix Frankfurter (1939–1962), William O. Douglas (1939–1975), Frank Murphy (1940–1949), James F. Byrnes (1941–1942), Robert H. Jackson (1941–1954), and Wiley B. Rutledge (1943–1949). For the tenures of other Supreme Court justices discussed in this work, see Kermit L. Hall, ed., *The Oxford Companion to the Supreme Court of the United States* (1992).

9. William F. Swindler, *Court and Constitution in the Twentieth Century: The Old Legality, 1889–1932* (1969) and *The New Legality, 1932–1968* (1970).

10. In his preface to *The Supreme Court Reborn* Leuchtenburg noted that he began his project on the Court-packing plan in 1962 (p. vii). That volume contains updated versions of essays written between 1966 and 1994. It does not include Leuchtenburg's most detailed defense of the mainstream position on the Court-packing/constitutional revolution tale, "Franklin D. Roosevelt's Supreme

Court 'Packing' Plan: A Second Life, a Second Death," 1985 *Duke Law Journal* 673.

11. In *The Supreme Court Reborn* Leuchtenburg included an essay, "The Constitutional Revolution of 1937," defending the significance of the Court-packing episode. The essay contained footnote references to work written as late as 1994. After summarizing several arguments by "commentators [inclined to] deny that there was a Constitutional Revolution in 1937 or to insist that the conception be severely qualified," Leuchtenburg concluded that "[t]hese objections . . . fall short of raising a formidable challenge to the conception of a Constitutional Revolution." He presented no new evidence in support of that conclusion. Leuchtenburg, *The Supreme Court Reborn*, 230–231.

12. 4 *Historian* 286 (1978).

13. 59 *Washington Law Review* 273 (1984).

14. 61 *Journal of American History* 970 (1975).

15. 53 *Business History Review* 304 (1979).

16. 1984 *Yearbook of the Supreme Court Historical Society* 20.

17. 3 *Law and History Review* 293 (1985).

18. 1985 *Wisconsin Law Review* 767.

19. 1983 *Yearbook of the Supreme Court Historical Society* 53.

20. 142 *University of Pennsylvania Law Review* 1891 (1994).

21. Colin Gordon, "Rethinking the New Deal," 98 *Columbia Law Review* 2029, 2033, 2036–37 (1998).

22. See, for example, the comments of Leuchtenburg on Cushman's conclusions in *The Supreme Court Reborn*, 318–319.

23. For a succinct but comprehensively documented account of the "historical turn" in legal scholarship these developments spawned, see Laura Kalman, *The Strange Career of Legal Liberalism*, 132–162 (1996).

24. 198 U.S. 45 (1905).

25. 298 U.S. 587 (1936).

26. 300 U.S. 379 (1937).

27. 84 *Columbia Law Review* 1689 (1984).

28. 38 *Stanford Law Review* 29 (1985).

29. 87 *Columbia Law Review* 873 (1987).

30. Such arguments had surfaced in the 1980s. See, e.g., Bernard Siegan, *Economic Liberties and the Constitution* (1980); Richard Epstein, *Takings* (1985).

31. Cass R. Sunstein, "Free Speech Now," 59 *University of Chicago Law Review* 255 (1992).

32. See, for example, the account of the history of the *Lochner* line of cases in Geoffrey R. Stone, Louis M. Seidman, Cass R. Sunstein, and Mark V. Tushnet, *Constitutional Law*, 813–842 (3rd ed., 1996), which retains the descriptive categories of the original and mainstream versions of the conventional account, while at the same time injecting public choice theory into the analysis of the cases being considered.

33. Compare Cass R. Sunstein and Lawrence Lessig, "The President and the Administration," 94 *Columbia Law Review* 1, 93 (1994) with Cass R. Sunstein, "The Idea of a Useable Past," 95 *Columbia Law Review* 601 (1995).

34. In Ackerman's most recent formulation, "[t]his country's Constitution focuses with special intensity on the rare moments when transformative movements earn broad and deep support for their initiatives." Bruce Ackerman, *We the People: Transformations*, 4–5 (1998).
35. Id., 7.
36. A fair amount of *We the People: Transformations* is therefore devoted toward elaborations of Ackerman's argument that a certain form of transformative constitutional change can be treated as the equivalent of an amendment of the Constitution. Ackerman's portrait of the New Deal period as one of major changes in constitutional jurisprudence serves to buttress those arguments, but the question of their cogency is not my concern here. My focus is the image of New Deal constitutional jurisprudence that Ackerman presents.
37. See Gordon, "Rethinking the New Deal," 2048–50, for a detailed criticism of the thin chronological base of Ackerman's description of early twentieth-century constitutional change.
38. See Laura Kalman, *Legal Realism at Yale, 1927–1960* (1986); Laura Kalman, *Abe Fortas* (1990); Laura Kalman, *The Strange Career of Legal Liberalism* (1996).
39. Kalman, *The Strange Career of Legal Liberalism*, 348–351 (note 70). Kalman's endorsement of Ackerman was arguably all the more effective because of the careful and balanced way she treated the work of other scholars, on a variety of topics, throughout her book.
40. Laura Kalman, "Law, Politics, and the New Deal(s)," 108 *Yale Law Journal* 101 (1999).
41. Id., 126, 142.
42. Ackerman, *Transformations*, 290–291.
43. Kalman, "Law, Politics, and the New Deal(s)," 103.
44. Id., 125–126.
45. Id., 122.

2. The Transformation of the Constitutional Jurisprudence of Foreign Relations

1. United States v. Belmont, 301 U.S. 324, 332 (1937).
2. The myth of jurisprudential continuity has facilitated the purposes of several groups of twentieth-century scholars. Some have been interested in de-emphasizing federalism limits on the national government's foreign relations powers. See Louis Henkin, *Foreign Affairs and the United States Constitution*, 185–194 (2d ed., 1996); Harold H. Koh, *The National Security Constitution* (1990). Others have been concerned with establishing the constitutional interchangeability of treaties and executive agreements. See, e.g., a line of work stretching from Myers McDougal and Asher Lans, "Treaties and Congressional-Executive or Presidential Agreements: Interchangeable Instruments of National Policy," 54 *Yale Law Journal* 182, 534 (1945), to Bruce Ackerman and David Golove, "Is NAFTA Constitutional?" 108 *Harvard Law Review* 799 (1995). Still others, writing in the genres of diplomatic history and political science, have perpet-

uated the myth in the context of establishing a "realistic" theory of foreign policymaking that emphasizes distinctions between the national government's possession of broad foreign relations powers and its cautious exercise of those powers. See, e.g., Hans J. Morgenthau, *In Defense of the National Interest: A Critical Examination of American Foreign Policy* (1951); George Kennan, *American Diplomacy, 1900–1950* (1951); Norman A. Graebner, *Ideas and Diplomacy: Readings in the Intellectual Tradition of American Foreign Policy* (1964). For a powerful critique of the historical foundations of the last line of scholarship, see Fareed Zakaria, *From Wealth to Power: The Unusual Origins of America's World Role* (1998). Although Zakaria's chronological focus is earlier than that of this chapter, his arguments tend to reinforce its conclusions.

3. Much of the recent work has been precipitated by current constitutional foreign relations controversies, which have tended to make its historical inquiries purposive and selective. Nonetheless, this work has brought a series of early twentieth-century constitutional foreign affairs decisions and accompanying commentary into focus for the first time in many years. See, e.g., Ackerman and Golove, "Is NAFTA Constitutional?"; Laurence H. Tribe, "Taking Text and Structure Seriously: Reflections on Free-Form Method in Constitutional Interpretation," 108 *Harvard Law Review* 1221 (1995); Curtis A. Bradley and Jack L. Goldsmith, "Customary International Law as Federal Common Law: A Critique of the Modern Position," 110 *Harvard Law Review* 815 (1997); Jack L. Goldsmith, "Federal Courts, Foreign Affairs, and Federalism," 83 *Virginia Law Review* 1617 (1997); Curtis A. Bradley, "The Treaty Power and American Federalism," 97 *Michigan Law Review* 390 (1998). The Bradley and Goldsmith article has precipitated some further commentary: see Gerald L. Neuman, "Sense and Nonsense about Customary International Law: A Response to Professors Bradley and Goldsmith," 66 *Fordham Law Review* 371 (1997); Harold Koh, "Is International Law Really State Law?," 111 *Harvard Law Review* 1824 (1998).

4. U.S. Const., Art. I, sect. 10, cl. 2; Art. II, sect. 2, cl. 2; Art. VI, sect. 2.

5. Art. II, sect. 2, cl. 2.

6. Art. I, sect. 10, cl. 2.

7. Art. VI, sect. 2.

8. Art. I, sect. 10, cl. 3.

9. See Chief Justice William Howard Taft's comments in his dissent in the 1923 domestic police powers case, Adkins v. Children's Hospital of the District of Columbia, 261 U.S. 525, 562: "The boundary of the police power beyond which its exercise becomes an invasion of the guaranty of liberty under the Fifth and Fourteenth Amendments is not easy to mark. Our court has been laboriously engaged in pricking out a line in successive cases."

10. The "republican government" example is from Luther v. Borden, 7 How. 1 (1849). For an early example of the political question category in a foreign affairs case, see Foster v. Neilson, 2 Pet. 253 (1829).

11. See Oliver P. Field, "The Doctrine of Political Questions in the Federal Courts," 8 *Minnesota Law Review* 485 (1924).

12. Jones v. United States, 137 U.S. 202, 212–213 (1890).

13. The Sapphire, 11 Wall. 164 (1870).

14. Doe v. Braden, 16 How. 635 (1853).
15. The Three Friends, 116 U.S. 1, 63 (1897).
16. The Prize Cases, 2 Black 635 (1862).
17. The Protector, 12 Wall. 700 (1871).
18. See The Paquete Habana, 175 U.S. 677 (1900), affirming that proposition, which had been stated as early as 30 Hogsheads of Sugar v. Boyle, 9 Cranch 191, 198 (1815). Foreign sovereign immunity cases provide an illustration: nineteenth-century courts deferred to executive findings of "fact" as to whether a foreign government was officially sovereign but did not treat that finding as resolving the question of whether a sovereign was immune in a given case. That question was generally decided on the basis of international maritime law or domestic common law. See a long line of cases stretching from The Schooner Exchange v. McFadden, 7 Cranch 116 (1812), to Underhill v. Hernandez, 168 U.S. 250 (1897). For a fuller discussion of the dramatic changes in early twentieth-century foreign sovereign immunity jurisprudence, see G. Edward White, "The Transformation of the Constitutional Regime of Foreign Relations," 85 *Virginia Law Review* 1, 134–145 (1999).
19. 143 U.S. 649 (1892).
20. Id. at 681. The term "unconstitutional delegation of powers," as used in late nineteenth-century jurisprudence, was employed somewhat more loosely than it would come to be in cases in the 1920s and 1930s. It could signify the inappropriate exercise of power by one branch of government at the expense of another, based on a bright-line conception of the functions of the branches of government and a strict reading of the constitutionally enumerated powers of the various branches. Under this interpretation of what came to be called the nondelegation doctrine, the McKinley Tariff Act appeared to allow the executive to enter into commercial "treaties" or pass tariff legislation without submitting its actions to Congress for ratification.
21. Id. at 683.
22. 2 Stat. 528 (1809); 2 Stat. 605 (1810).
23. See 143 U.S. at 700, citing 26 Stat. 567.
24. Id. at 699–700.
25. John Bassett Moore, "Treaties and Executive Agreements," 20 *Political Science Quarterly* 385 (1905). Moore's article was prompted by a vigorous debate in the Senate over the nature and scope of the foreign affairs power prompted by an agreement between President Theodore Roosevelt and the government of Santo Domingo that the Senate attempted to amend to the form of a "treaty." Id., 386–388.
26. U.S. Const., Art. II, sect. 2, para. 1. Between 1882 and 1896 various presidents allowed Mexican troops to enter the borders of the United States in pursuit of Indians. Those agreements, which did not rest on treaties or on the consent of the Senate, were sustained in Tucker v. Alexandroff, 183 U.S. 424, 434–435 (1902), on the ground that "the power to give such permission without legislative assent was probably assumed to exist from the authority of the President as Commander-in-Chief."
27. See Moore, "Treaties and Executive Agreements," 397–398. An example was an

1899 agreement between the American Secretary of State John Hay and the British interim charge d'affaires that established a provisional boundary between Alaska and Canada. That agreement eventually led to a formal treaty in 1903. Id., 398.

28. See the discussion in Ackerman and Golove, "Is NAFTA Constitutional?" 826, suggesting that as late as 1931 international postal agreements were regarded by the State Department's treaty adviser as "business arrangements between offices of transport rather than agreements between governments in the ordinary sense." (Quoting 1 Hunter Miller, ed., *Treaties and Other International Acts of the United States of America*, 7 (2 vols., 1931).)

29. Moore, "Treaties and Executive Agreements," 403.

30. Id., 408.

31. Id., 417.

32. Id., 388.

33. Id., 392.

34. These included the Taft-Katsura Agreement of 1905, the "Gentlemen's Agreement" of 1907, the Root-Takahira Agreement of 1908, and the Lansing-Ishii Agreement of 1917. See Ackerman and Golove, "Is NAFTA Constitutional?" 818.

35. See the state statutes and cases cited in 1 John Bassett Moore, *A Treatise on Extradition and Interstate Rendition*, 53–71 (2 vols., 1891). This practice was periodically contested on constitutional grounds. Id., 70.

36. Gerald L. Neuman has shown that federal regulation of immigration did not take place until 1875; prior to that a number of states had laws restricting the migration of aliens within their borders. Neuman, "The Lost Century of American Immigration Law (1776–1875)," 93 *Columbia Law Review* 1833 (1993). Even after the federal government passed immigration legislation in 1875, states continued to pass laws discriminating against aliens or regulating their conduct in various respects, and as late as the years between 1915 and 1927 the Supreme Court sustained some of that legislation in the face of constitutional challenges. See, e.g., Heim v. McCall, 239 U.S. 175 (1915) (New York); Frick v. Webb, 263 U.S. 326 (1923) (California); Porterfield v. Webb, 263 U.S. 225 (1923) (California); Ohio ex rel. Clarke v. Deckebach, 274 U.S. 392 (1927) (Ohio).

37. An example was the state of New York's 1895 declaration that it would discriminate against German-owned insurance companies doing business within the state because of the restrictions placed by Prussia on New York-based insurance companies doing business within that nation. See Dennis James Palumbo, "The States and American Foreign Relations," 48–50 (unpublished Ph.D. diss., University of Chicago, 1960). For additional examples of late nineteenth- and early twentieth-century state laws or practices directed toward the realm of foreign policy, see id., 50–88.

38. See the commentary on state efforts to discriminate against aliens between 1907 and 1924, collected in Goldsmith, "Federal Courts, Foreign Affairs, and Federalism," 1655 n.162. None of these commentators assumed that a power in the national government to make treaties affecting the rights of foreign aliens within the United States precluded the states from exercising any powers with respect

to foreign aliens. On the contrary, they assumed that in the absence of specific treaty coverage the states could exercise foreign affairs powers.

39. U.S. Const., Art. I , sect. 10, cl. 3.

40. The opinions most regularly cited were those of Justice Henry Baldwin in Holmes v. Jennison, 14 Pet. 616 (1840), Justice Peter Daniel in The License Cases, 5 How. 504, 613 (1847), Chief Justice Roger Taney in The Passenger Cases, 7 How. 283, 466 (1849), and Taney in Prevost v. Greneaux, 19 How. 1 (1856). In the last case the Court sustained a Louisiana law imposing a tax on property in the state inherited by a citizen of France, despite the presence of an 1853 treaty between the United States and France providing for a reciprocal right of inheritance of the citizens of one country in the territory of the other on the same terms as the citizens of that country itself. Louisiana citizens did not pay a succession tax on property they inherited in the state. The operation of the treaty was expressly limited, however, "to the States of the Union whose laws permit it." Id. at 7.

41. See Ware v. Hylton, 3 Dall. 199 (1796); Hauenstein v. Lynham, 100 U.S. 483 (1879); and Geofroy v. Riggs, 133 U.S. 258 (1890).

42. Colloquially speaking, the "Chinese Exclusion Cases" have referred only to two cases, Chae Chan Ping v. United States, 130 U.S. 581 (1889), "the First Chinese Exclusion Case," and Fong Yue Ting v. United States, 149 U.S. 698 (1893), "the Second Chinese Exclusion Case." These were the cases in which the Court specifically rested its rationale for sustaining exclusionist congressional legislation in the face of the 1868 treaty on an "inherent" power in the national government to exclude aliens. See *Chae Chan Ping*, 130 U.S. at 604–609; *Fong Yue Ting*, 149 U.S. at 711–713.

43. The decisions, in addition to *Chae Chan Ping* and *Fong Yue Ting*, were Chew Heong v. United States, 112 U.S. 536 (1884); United States v. Jung Ah Lung, 124 U.S. 621 (1888); Wan Shing v. United States, 140 U.S. 424 (1890); Nishimura Ekiu v. United States, 142 U.S. 651 (1891); In re Lau ow Bew, 141 U.S. 583 (1891), subsequently decided as Lau ow Bew v. United States, 144 U.S. 47 (1892); Lem Moon Sing v. United States, 158 U.S. 538 (1895); Wong Wing v. United States, 163 U.S. 228 (1896); United States v. Wong Kim Ark, 169 U.S. 649 (1898); and United States v. Mrs. Gue Lin, 1176 U.S. 459 (1900). As the names of the original defendants in these cases reveal, not all of the "Chinese Exclusion Cases" involved aliens of Chinese descent.

44. *Fong Yue Ting*, 149 U.S. at 711. Three late nineteenth-century domestic cases, Ex parte Yarbrough, 110 U.S. 651 (1884), Logan v. United States, 144 U.S. 263 (1892), and In re Quarles and Butler, 158 U.S. 532 (1895), also contained some language consistent with the idea of "inherent" sovereign powers that could be constitutionally exercised. But these cases were distinctly exceptional.

45. Kansas v. Colorado, 206 U.S. 46, 89 (1907), in which Justice David Brewer, for the Court, said that "the proposition that there are legislative powers affecting the nation as a whole which belong to, although not expressed in the grant of powers, is in direct conflict with the doctrine that this a government of enumerated powers."

46. Compare Charles Henry Butler, 2 *The Treaty-Making Power of the United States,*

111–112 (2 vols., 1902), indicating that a power to exclude aliens resided in "the United States, in its national capacity, and by virtue of its attributes of sovereignty," with 1 Westel W. Willoughby, *The Constitutional Law of the United States,* 69, 455 (2 vols., 1910), stating that "an examination of the cases in which . . . dicta . . . might seem to indicate the acceptance by the Supreme Court of the doctrine of sovereign powers . . . discloses . . . that in each instance they were *obiter*."

47. The term "Insular Cases" is also a colloquialism, referring to eleven cases decided by the Court between 1901 and 1905. The first five of those cases, DeLima v. Bidwell, 182 U.S. 1, Dooley v. United States, 182 U.S. 222, Armstrong v. United States, 182 U.S. 243, Downes v. Bidwell, 182 U.S. 244, and Dooley v. United States, 183 U.S. 151, were all decided in 1901, and all involved the legal status of tariffs imposed on goods in transit between the United States and Puerto Rico. Two other cases, also decided in 1901, reinforced the holdings of the first five cases and extended their application to the Philippines. Goetze v. United States, 182 U.S. 221; Fourteen Diamond Rings v. United States, 183 U.S. 176. The remaining four cases, decided between 1903 and 1905, dealt with the application of criminal procedure provisions in the Bill of Rights to courts in Hawaii, the Philippines, and Alaska. Hawaii v. Mankichi, 190 U.S. 197 (1903); Kepner v. United States, 195 U.S. 100 (1904) (the Philippines); Dorr v. United States, 195 U.S. 138 (1904) (the Philippines); and Rasmussen v. United States, 197 U.S. 516 (1905) (Alaska).

48. U.S. Const., Art. IV, sect. 3, para. 2.

49. Downes v. Bidwell, 182 U.S. 244.

50. Hawaii v. Mankichi, 190 U.S. 197.

51. Dorr v. United States, 195 U.S. 138.

52. See 1 Willoughby, *Constitutional Law of the United States,* 411, 430–436.

53. Examples include Willoughby, *Constitutional Law of the United States;* Edward S. Corwin, *The President's Control of Foreign Relations* (1917); and Charles C. Hyde, *International Law Chiefly as Interpreted and Applied by the United States* (1922).

54. Quincy Wright, *The Control of American Foreign Relations,* 233 (1922).

55. Id., 233, 236.

56. Id., 235.

57. See id., 236–246, discussing postal agreements, modi vivendi, the ratification of armistices, protocols, and agreements settling pecuniary claims.

58. Id., 246–247.

59. Id., 261–262.

60. Id., xii. Wright's discussion of "constitutional limitations upon the foreign relations power" occupied over fifty pages, of which about a third were devoted to "states' rights" limitations. See id., 71–128.

61. Id., 75.

62. U.S. Const., Art. IV, sect. 4.

63. Id.

64. Id.

65. U.S. Const., Art. I, sect. 9, cls. 4–6; Art. I., sect. 8, cl. 1.

66. Wright, *The Control of American Foreign Relations*, 86.
67. For background on Sutherland's early life and career, see Alan E. Gray, "Biographical Sketch of George Sutherland," George Sutherland Papers, U.S. Supreme Court Library; Joel Francis Paschal, *Mr. Justice Sutherland*, 2–26 (1951); and Hadley Arkes, *The Return of George Sutherland: Restoring a Jurisprudence of Natural Rights*, 39–50 (1994). The Gray sketch is by one of Sutherland's law clerks during his tenure on the Supreme Court, which lasted from 1922 to his retirement in 1938. Gray reported that Sutherland had read over the sketch for accuracy. See Paschal, *Mr. Justice Sutherland*, 4.
68. Sen. Doc. 417, 61st Cong., 2d Sess. (1909).
69. George Sutherland, "The Internal and External Powers of the National Government," 191 *North American Review* 373 (1910).
70. 299 U.S. 304 (1936).
71. 301 U.S. 324 (1937).
72. I do not mean to suggest that Sutherland was invariably opposed to New Deal legislation on constitutional grounds. For an extensive analysis of Sutherland's voting record, which points out the thin doctrinal base on which most generalizations about his domestic constitutional jurisprudence have rested, see Barry Cushman, "The Secret Lives of the Four Horsemen," 83 *Virginia Law Review* 559 (1997).
73. Sutherland, "Internal and External Powers," 374.
74. Id., 383–386.
75. Id., 387–388.
76. Sutherland had attended Campbell's course, "The Jurisprudence of the United States," at the University of Michigan Law School in the 1882 academic year. See Paschal, *Mr. Justice Sutherland*, 15–20.
77. Van Husan v. Kanouse, 13 Mich. 303, 313–314 (1864).
78. See 44 Cong. Rec. 248–264, 2506 (1909).
79. Sutherland, "Internal and External Powers," 388.
80. The distinction between what Sutherland called "extra-constitutional" and "unconstitutional" sovereign powers was first made in Sutherland, "Internal and External Powers," 384.
81. Id., 378–379.
82. Id., 376–377.
83. Id., 376.
84. Id., 381. Emphasis in original.
85. Id., 382.
86. Sutherland quoted language from the Legal Tender Cases, 12 Wall. 457 (1870), in which two justices referred to powers in the national government "which grew out of . . . sovereignty" or were "inherent and implied, . . . generally considered to belong to every government as such." The *Legal Tender Cases* involved the constitutionality of legislation making paper currency the equivalent of specie.
87. Justice Gray in Jones v. United States, 137 U.S. at 212, referred to "the law of nations, recognized by all civilized states" as justifying the acquisition of territory by discovery and occupation.

88. *Nishimura Ekiu*, 142 U.S. at 659.
89. *Fong Yue Ting*, 149 U.S. 698.
90. United States v. Kagama, 118 U.S. 375, 380 (1886), in which Justice Miller referred to the "right of exclusive sovereignty which must exist in the National government."
91. Sutherland, "Internal and External Powers," 384.
92. Id., 389. Emphasis in original.
93. The lectures were published by Columbia University Press in 1919 as *Constitutional Power and World Affairs*. Paschal, *Mr. Justice Sutherland*, 104.
94. These powers included the power to acquire territories and to confer upon territories and their inhabitants a status consistent with the discretion of Congress. Sutherland made it clear that in his view the Constitution did not "follow the flag," and even any procedural "rights" accorded the inhabitants of territories were a function of their "fundamental personal character," which the Constitution had recognized but not created. He thus signaled the lessons he had drawn from the *Insular Cases*. Sutherland, *Constitutional Power and World Affairs*, 68–69.
95. Id. at 47.
96. Id.
97. Id. at 155, 154.
98. Id. at 155–156.
99. Missouri v. Holland, 252 U.S. 416, 433 (1920).
100. The migratory bird treaty was recorded as Convention with Great Britain for the Protection of Migratory Birds, 39 Stat. 1702 (1916). The enabling legislation was 40 Stat. 755 (July 3, 1918). The statute forbade the hunting, killing, or subsequent sale and shipment of certain species of migratory birds, those covered by the treaty, except as allowed by regulations to be established by the secretary of agriculture.
101. For a discussion of the early efforts in Congress that led to protective federal migratory bird legislation in 1913, see Charles A. Lofgren, *"Government from Reflection and Choice": Constitutional Essays on War, Foreign Relations, and Federalism*, 117–119 (1986).
102. For references to remarks by individual supporters and opponents on the problematic constitutional status of legislation being debated in Congress in 1911, 1912, and 1913, see id., 118–119, citing volumes 47, 48, and 49 of the Congressional Record.
103. See, e.g., Geer v. Connecticut, 161 U.S. 519 (1896); The Abby Dodge, 223 U.S. 166 (1912).
104. For details, see White, "The Transformation of the Constitutional Regime of Foreign Relations," 65.
105. Quoted in 51 Cong. Rec. 8349 (May 9, 1914). Root's comment was actually made in January 1913 but omitted from the published record of Senate proceedings in volume 49 of the Congressional Record. See Lofgren, *"Government from Reflection and Choice,"* 121.
106. 50 Cong. Rec. 2339–40 (July 7, 1913).
107. Between 1913 and June 1918, when the 1913 enabling legislation was in effect,

the Department of Agriculture reported 1,132 violations of the act but only prosecuted 29 of them. A 1918 enabling act and its regulations went into effect on July 31, 1918; in the first year of its operation the Department of Agriculture reported 110 convictions. See *Annual Reports of the Department of Agriculture*, 274 (1919).

108. Missouri v. Holland, 258 Fed. 479, 481, 483–485 (W. D. Mo. 1919).

109. 252 U.S. at 433.

110. Id.

111. This had come in the remaining portion of the last sentence in the first excerpted passage (see page 55), which had concluded, "and it is not lightly to be assumed that, in matters requiring national action, 'a power which must belong to and somewhere reside in every civilized government,' is not to be found." 252 U.S. at 433. A fair reading of the entire sentence could have concluded that Holmes was saying that the treaty power had subject matter limitations but was inherent.

112. In a commentary on Missouri v. Holland, Thomas Reed Powell recognized this hint of Holmes's. As Powell put it, "It is to be noted that the decision is placed on grounds which would not necessarily support treaties with foreign powers regulating conditions of labor, as now proposed in some quarters, and yet that hints are thrown out which would lend sanction to such a treaty. Even if the existence of a national interest of considerable magnitude is accepted as a prerequisite, well-established canons of judicial action would make this question a political one, on which the courts would accept the judgment of the political departments of the government. Mr. Justice Holmes made it clear that lack of precedent sets no constitutional obstacle in the way of novel exertions of the treaty-making power." Powell, "The Supreme Court and the Constitution, 1919–1920," 35 *Political Science Quarterly* 411, 417 (1920).

113. 252 U.S. at 433–434.

114. 1 Butler, *The Treaty-Making Power*, 5: "[A]cts of Congress enforcing [treaty] stipulations which, in the absence of [such] stipulations, would be unconstitutional as infringing upon the powers reserved to the States, are constitutional, and can be enforced, even though they may conflict with State laws or provisions of State constitutions."

115. 1 Willoughby, *Constitutional Law of the United States*, 505: "The author is convinced that the *obiter* doctrine that the reserved rights of the States may never be infringed upon by the treaty-making power will sooner or later be frankly repudiated by the Supreme Court. In its place will be definitely stated the doctrine that in all that properly relates to matters of international rights and obligations, . . . the United States possesses all the powers of a constitutionally centralized sovereign State; and, therefore, that when the necessity from the international standpoint arises the treaty power may be exercised, even though thereby the rights ordinarily reserved to the States are invaded."

116. Edward Corwin, *National Supremacy: Treaty Power vs. State Power*, v–vi (1913).

117. George Sutherland, *Constitutional Power and World Affairs* (1919): "When we come to consider that . . . the full exercise of the [treaty] power necessarily devolves upon the general government as the only possible agency, and that in its

legitimate exercise the certainty of an occasional collision with state affairs must have been foreseen, the claim for the supremacy of the police powers of the state must be disallowed, unless we are willing to charge the framers of the Constitution with the folly of conferring a power so incompletely that its exercise in many important and, perhaps in some vital, particulars may be precluded altogether. The matter, after all, is quite simple." At this point Sutherland cited the Supremacy Clause.

118. Edward Corwin, "Constitutional Law in 1919–1920, II," 15 *American Political Science Review* 52, 53–54 (1920); Thomas Reed Powell, "Constitutional Law in 1919–1920," 19 *Michigan Law Review* 1, 11–13 (1920). See also Powell, "The Supreme Court and the Constitution, 1919–1920," a briefer version of his *Michigan Law Review* article.

119. Note, "The Treaty-Making Power under the United States Constitution—The Federal Migratory Birds Act," 33 *Harvard Law Review* 281 (1919); Note, "Constitutional Law: Encroachment by Treaty upon the Reserved Powers of the States," 8 *California Law Review* 177 (1920); Note, "The Power to Make Treaties," 20 *Columbia Law Review* 692 (1920); Note, "Treaty-Making Power as Support for Federal Legislation," 29 *Yale Law Journal* 445 (1920).

120. L. L. Thompson, "State Sovereignty and the Treaty-Making Power," 11 *California Law Review* 242, 247–251 (1923).

121. Note, "Constitutional Law: The Treaty Making Power and the Constitution," 6 *Cornell Law Quarterly* 91 (1920); Note, "The Treaty Power and the Tenth Amendment," 68 *University of Pennsylvania Law Review* 160 (1920).

122. Henry St. George Tucker, *Limitations on the Treaty-Making Power under the Constitution of the United States* (1915).

123. Wright, *The Control of American Foreign Relations*, 89.

124. Kansas v. Colorado, 206 U.S. 46.

125. Wright, *The Control of American Foreign Relations*, 87–89.

126. Id., 93.

127. See Melvyn P. Leffler, *The Elusive Quest: America's Pursuit of European Stability and French Security, 1919–1933* (1979).

3. The Triumph of Executive Discretion in Foreign Relations

1. "The Question of Current Recognition," 32 *Current History* 1065 (September 1930), quoted in E. C. Buehler et al., *Selected Articles on Recognition of Soviet Russia*, 238, 241 (1941). The quotation from Bainbridge Colby is at 241.

2. An illustration can be found in Senator William E. Borah's speech in the Senate on March 3, 1931, reprinted in Buehler, *Selected Articles on Recognition of Soviet Russia*, 252–270.

3. The letters between Roosevelt and Litvinov, each bearing the date November 16, 1933, are set forth in 28 *American Journal of International Law* 1, 2–11 (Supplement, 1934). Collectively, the letters, five by Roosevelt, six by Litvinov, and a joint statement, are known as the Litvinov Agreement.

4. The contribution of the New York state courts in shaping doctrinal issues in recognition cases can be gleaned from Louis L. Jaffe's *Judicial Aspects of Foreign Relations*, 124–232 (1933).

5. Examples of such cases were Sokoloff v. National City Bank of New York, 239 N.Y. 158 (1924); Fred S. James & Co. v. Second Russian Insurance Co., 239 N.Y. 248 (1925); Russian Reinsurance Co. v. Stoddard, 240 N.Y. 149 (1925); First Russian Insurance Co. v. Beha, 240 N.Y. 601 (1925); and Petrogradsky Mejdunarodny Kommerchesky Bank v. National City Bank of New York, 253 N.Y. 23 (1930).

6. An example was Salminoff & Co. v. Standard Oil Co., 262 N.Y. 220 (1933), which sought to reconcile several of the cases cited above.

7. 262 N.Y. at 226.

8. Russian Reinsurance Co. v. Stoddard, 240 N.Y. at 158.

9. For examples, see Thomas Baty, "So-called de Facto Recognition," 31 *Yale Law Journal* 469 (1921); Edwin Borchard, "Can an Unrecognized Government Sue?" 31 *Yale Law Journal* 534 (1922); Edwin Dickinson, "The Unrecognized Government of State in English and American Law," 22 *Michigan Law Review* 29, 118 (1923); Louis Connick, "The Effect of Soviet Decrees in American Courts," 34 *Yale Law Journal* 499 (1925); and Manley Hudson, "Recognition and Multipartite Treaties," 23 *American Journal of International Law* 126 (1929). Later summaries include Dickinson, "Recognition Cases 1925–1930," 25 *American Journal of International Law* 214 (1931), and Borchard, "The Unrecognized Government in American Courts," 26 *American Journal of International Law* 261 (1932).

10. See, e.g., Connick, "Effect of Soviet Decrees in American Courts"; Dickinson, "Recognition Cases 1925–1930"; and Borchard, "The Unrecognized Government in American Courts."

11. Jaffe, *Judicial Aspects of Foreign Relations,* 233.

12. Id.

13. Roosevelt to Kalinin, October 10, 1933, quoted in Chandler P. Anderson, "Recognition of Russia," 28 *American Journal of International Law* 90, 95 (1934).

14. Kalinin to Roosevelt, October 17, 1933, quoted in id., 95.

15. The assignment claims provision of the Litvinov Agreement is set forth in 28 *American Journal of International Law* 10 (Supplement, 1934).

16. See Chandler P. Anderson, "Assignment of Claims by the Russian Government to the United States," 28 *American Journal of International Law* 545, 546 (1934).

17. For more discussion of the background to the joint resolution and presidential arms sales proclamation that lead to the *Curtiss-Wright* case, see Charles A. Lofgren, "*United States v. Curtiss-Wright Export Corporation:* A Historical Reassessment," 83 *Yale Law Journal* 1 (1973).

18. 48 Stat. 811 (1934).

19. 48 Stat. 1744 (1934).

20. United States v. Curtiss-Wright Export Corp., 14 F. Supp. 230, 232 (S.D.N.Y. 1936).

21. Id. at 240 (on rehearing).

22. United States v. Curtiss-Wright Export Corp., 299 U.S. 304, 314 (1936).

23. For more detail on these agreements, see Bruce Ackerman and David Golove, "Is NAFTA Constitutional?" 108 *Harvard Law Review* 799, 845–846 (1995).

24. Silver Agreement of 1933, July 22, 1933, E.A.S. No. 63; Gold Reserve Act of 1934, 48 Stat. 334 (1936).

25. Wheat Agreement of 1933, 141 L.N.T.S. 71.

26. Act of June 12, 1934, 48 Stat. 943.

27. See Ackerman and Golove, "Is NAFTA Constitutional?" 847–849, citing 78 Cong. Rec. 9008–11, 9014, 9683–84 (1934).

28. See 78 Cong. Rec. 9007–08 (remarks of Senator Borah) and 10,214 (remarks of Senator Austin).

29. Ackerman and Golove, "Is NAFTA Constitutional?" 850, citing 78 Cong. Rec. 10,395 (1934).

30. Panama Refining Co. v. Ryan, 293 U.S. 388 (1935); Schechter Poultry Corp. v. United States, 295 U.S. 495 (1935); Carter v. Carter Coal Co., 298 U.S. 235 (1936).

31. 298 U.S. at 295. As we will see, the context of Sutherland's sentence did not make it clear that he had delegation issues as well as commerce power issues in mind, but his opinion in *Curtiss-Wright* would reveal that he did.

32. The relationship of orthodox separation of powers jurisprudence to the proliferation of federal administrative agencies in the years between 1933 and 1937 is discussed in Chapter 4.

33. Emphasis in original. Sutherland stated that he was refuting the proposition that "the power of the federal government inherently extends to purposes affecting the nation as a whole with which the states severally cannot deal." 298 U.S. at 291. His criticism of an inherent "federal police power" was interesting in that the government had attempted to justify the legislation challenged in *Carter v. Carter Coal* solely on commerce power grounds. See id. at 289. This evidence, taken together with Sutherland's earlier writings on the foreign affairs power and his sentence alluding to the "inherent power of [the federal] government as to the external affairs of the nation," suggests that he may have concluded that the nondelegation doctrine was only relevant to domestic affairs well before the Court decided *Curtiss-Wright*.

34. 298 U.S. at 295.

35. "Mr. Justice McReynolds does not agree. He is of opinion that the court below reached the right conclusion and its judgment ought to be affirmed." 299 U.S. at 333. Since the district court had sustained a demurrer on the unconstitutional delegation argument, the only conclusion reversed by Sutherland's opinion, McReynolds obviously thought that the joint resolution and proclamation had been an invalid delegation. But what else he "[did] not agree" with in Sutherland's opinion was not clear.

36. 299 U.S. at 313.

37. Both *Panama Refining* and *Schechter* were cited in the Curtiss-Wright Corporation's brief. 299 U.S. at 308.

38. Id. at 315.

39. Id. at 316.

40. Id. at 316–318.

41. David M. Levitan, "The Foreign Relations Power: An Analysis of Mr. Justice Sutherland's Theory," 55 *Yale Law Journal* 467, 476 (1946).

42. 299 U.S. at 320.
43. Id.
44. Id.
45. Id.
46. Id.
47. Id. at 321–322.
48. Id. at 322.
49. Id. at 324.
50. Id. at 328–329.
51. Id. at 320.
52. Paul Murphy, "Time to Reclaim: The Current Challenge of American Constitutional History," 69 *American Historical Review* 64, 76 (1963). For similar assessments, see Charles Lofgren, *"Government from Reflection and Choice": Constitutional Essays on War, Foreign Relations, and Federalism* (1955); and Levitan, "The Foreign Relations Power."
53. See, e.g., Comment, 36 *Columbia Law Review* 1162 (1936); Comment, 50 *Harvard Law Review* 691 (1937); Comment, 25 *Georgetown Law Journal* 738 (1937); Comment, 6 *Fordham Law Review* 303 (1937); Comment, 1 *Maryland Law Review* 167 (1937); Comment, 6 *Brooklyn Law Review* 382 (1937); Comment, 11 *Temple Law Quarterly* 418 (1937); and James W. Garner, "Editorial Discretion in the Conduct of Foreign Relations," 31 *American Journal of International Law* 289 (1937).
54. E.g., Comment, 36 *Columbia Law Review,* 1163–64; Comment, 50 *Harvard Law Review,* 692; Comment, 25 *Georgetown Law Journal,* 739–740; Comment, 6 *Fordham Law Review,* 303–305; Comment, 1 *Maryland Law Review,* 170–171.
55. E.g., Comment, 6 *Fordham Law Review,* 306; Comment, 11 *Temple Law Quarterly,* 419–421.
56. E.g., Comment, 25 *Georgetown Law Journal,* 739; Comment, 6 *Fordham Law Review,* 305.
57. E.g., Comment, 6 *Fordham Law Review,* 304; Comment, 6 *Brooklyn Law Review,* 383 ("[I]n its recognition of the President's superiority in conducting foreign affairs, the Court's decision may be compared to judicial approval of necessary delegation on a broad standard to boards expert in their field.").
58. Comment, 11 *Temple Law Quarterly,* 420.
59. Comment, 25 *Georgetown Law Journal,* 740.
60. Garner, "Editorial Discretion in the Conduct of Foreign Relations," 289.
61. Compare Garner, "Editorial Discretion in the Conduct of Foreign Relations," 290–292 with George Sutherland, *Constitutional Power and World Affairs,* 36–45, 124–25 (1919), and *Curtiss-Wright,* 299 U.S. at 317–324.
62. Garner, "Editorial Discretion in the Conduct of Foreign Relations," 293.
63. Ackerman and Golove identify Garner as a supporter of the agendas of the Roosevelt administration in "Is NAFTA Constitutional?" 826–827.
64. 301 U.S. 324 (1937).
65. Edwin Borchard, "Confiscations, Extraterritorial and Domestic," 31 *American Journal of International Law* 675, 676 (1937).

66. 85 F.2d 542 (1936).

67. Hughes, Butler, McReynolds, Roberts, and Van Devanter. If conventional ideological stereotypes of the judges sitting on the Court in 1937 are employed, this meant that three determined opponents of the New Deal, often described, together with Sutherland, as the "Four Horsemen," and two "swing justices" joined Sutherland's opinion dramatically extending the foreign relations powers of the federal executive branch. Three other justices conventionally identified as supporters of the New Deal, Brandeis, Cardozo, and Stone, declined to join the opinion.

68. Underhill v. Hernandez, 168 U.S. 350 (1897), reaffirmed in Oetjen v. Central Leather Co., 246 U.S. 297 (1918). The act of state doctrine is not a principle of international law but an American jurisprudential creation. Under international law no sovereign has any obligation to respect the acts of another sovereign in its own courts; the question is entirely a matter of discretion. See the discussion in Quincy Wright, *The Control of American Foreign Relations*, 161–174 (1922).

69. 301 U.S. at 330.

70. Id. at 330–331.

71. Id. at 331–332.

72. Id. at 332.

73. Id.

74. Id.

75. Borchard, "Confiscations, Extraterritorial and Domestic," 678. In a subsequent New York case involving the disposition of confiscated Russian assets affected by the Litvinov Agreement, the State Department indicated its intent to make at least some funds it recovered as a result of the assignment provisions in the Litvinov Agreement available to American private claimants against the Soviet Union. See Moscow Fire Insurance Co. v. Bank of New York & Trust Co., 280 N.Y. 286 (1939). The *Moscow Fire* case will subsequently be discussed.

76. 301 U.S. at 331, 334, 336. Stone concluded, however, that New York did not have a discernible policy on the disposition of assets where a New York debtor was questioning the title to a claim of a creditor acquired by a confiscatory decree of the Soviet government. He thought the situation would have been different if New York creditors of confiscated Russian corporations with assets in the state had sued. Id. at 336.

77. For two examples of this chronology, see William F. Swindler, *Court and Constitution in the Twentieth Century: The New Legality 1932–1968*, 28–115 (1970); William E. Leuchtenburg, *The Supreme Court Reborn: The Constitutional Revolution in the Age of Roosevelt*, 213–236 (1995).

78. 300 U.S. 379 (1937).

79. 301 U.S. 1 (1937).

80. Philip C. Jessup, "The Litvinoff Assignment and the Belmont Case," 31 *American Journal of International Law* 481, 482 (1937).

81. Id., 483–484.

82. Note, "Effect of Executive Agreement on the Status of Confiscation Decrees," 47 *Yale Law Journal* 292, 293–294 (1937).

83. Stefan A. Riesenfeld, "The Power of Congress and the President in International Relations," 25 *California Law Review* 643, 673 (1937).
84. Id., 674.
85. Id.
86. Harry Willmer Jones, "The President, Congress, and Foreign Relations," 29 *California Law Review* 567, 574 (1941).
87. Among the sources Jones cited were Edward S. Corwin, *The President's Control of Foreign Relations* (1917); Edward S. Corwin, *The President: Office and Powers* (1940); Sutherland, *Constitutional Power and World Affairs;* and Sutherland's arguments on behalf of executive discretion in foreign affairs in *Curtiss-Wright.* See Jones, "The President, Congress, and Foreign Relations," 568–571.
88. Id., 567–573.
89. Id., 572, 582–583.
90. Jones's article, which appeared in the July 1941 issue of the *California Law Review,* was based on an address he had made to the Los Angeles Bar Association on April 24, 1941.
91. 315 U.S. 203 (1942).
92. Douglas's opinion was treated as the "opinion of the Court," and there were only two dissenters, Stone and Owen Roberts. But Robert Jackson and Stanley Reed did not participate, probably because as attorney general and solicitor general they had been involved in litigation related to *Moscow Fire* or to *Pink.* The remaining justices were Hugo Black, James Byrnes, Felix Frankfurter, and Frank Murphy. Frankfurter wrote some separate "observations" after Douglas's opinion, which were not given a formal label but were surely not a dissent. If one were inclined to treat Frankfurter's "observations" as a concurrence, the *Pink* opinion's language arguably had the support of only four justices.
93. The majority opinion in *Belmont* only decided that the United States had a cause of action against the Belmont bank, which it treated as a custodian of the assets to the Petrograd Metal Works. Sutherland stated that the decision did not prevent directors or stockholders of the Metal Works from making claims against the assets, and Stone's concurrence agreed. See 301 U.S. at 332–333, 337.
94. 280 N.Y. 286 (1939).
95. Id. at 309. The decision was 4–3, with Judge Irving Lehman writing for the majority.
96. The New York Court of Appeals decision was handed down on April 11, 1939. On September 2 the United States filed a petition for certiorari, and the Supreme Court granted that petition on October 23. 3 Transcript of Record, United States v. Moscow Fire Insurance Co., 2041 (1940).
97. The New York Court of Appeals had concluded that the Litvinov Agreement did not apply to the extraterritorial assets of Russian insurance companies in New York. This conclusion suggested that there might be no federal question in the *Moscow Fire* case because the Court of Appeals had decided it on an independent state ground. The Supreme Court's 1938 decision in Erie Railroad Co. v. Tompkins, 304 U.S. 64, had intimated that federal courts could no longer make independent judgments on common law issues decided by state courts on state

law grounds. The extensive briefs filed before the Supreme Court in *Moscow Fire* argued both the federal question issue and the issue of whether *Erie* should be limited to domestic common law cases. Compare Brief for the United States in 3 Transcript of Record, at 26–46, with Brief for Respondent Paul Luck as Sole Surviving Director of Moscow Fire Insurance Co., id. at 41–59.

98. 309 U.S. 624 (1940).

99. See Matter of People (First Russian Insurance Co.), 255 N.Y. 415 (1931); United States v. Pink, 284 N.Y. 555 (1940).

100. United States v. Bank of New York & Trust Co., 296 U.S. 436 (1936). The theory of the dismissal was that the Litvinov Agreement did not terminate state proceedings already in existence before its promulgation. Thus, the federal courts could not take control over the fund awaiting distribution in a state court. Id. at 479, 480.

101. The developments are set forth in Douglas's opinion in *Pink*, 315 U.S. at 214–215.

102. In connection with the *Moscow Fire* case, the United States had asked the Soviet Union, through diplomatic channels, for a certification that its 1918 nationalization decree affecting the property of Russian insurance companies was intended to apply to property situated outside the territorial limits of the Soviet Union. A certification to that effect by the People's Commissariat for Justice of the Soviet Union was produced and introduced as evidence in *Moscow Fire* but never made part of the official record of that case. Douglas found the certification "conclusive so far as the intended extraterritorial effect of the Russian decree is concerned." 315 U.S. at 220. There was not one shred of language in the nationalization decree itself, which Douglas set forth in *Pink*, suggesting that it was to have an extraterritorial effect. See id. at 219.

103. For support for these propositions, see, on the extraterritorial invalidity of confiscatory decrees in international law, Borchard, "Confiscations, Extraterritorial and Domestic," 675–676; on the hostility of American common law to such decrees, United States v. Percheman, 7 Pet. 51 (1833), Greenwood v. Freight Co., 105 U.S. 13 (1881), and a line of New York cases cited in United States v. Director of Manhattan Co., 276 N.Y. 396, 403 (1938); and on the negative implications for extraterritorial confiscatory decrees of the Fifth Amendment's Just Compensation Clause, Willard B. Cowles, *Treaties and Constitutional Law: Property Interference and Due Process of Law*, 75–88 (1941).

104. 315 U.S. at 219.

105. Id. at 227.

106. A Note in the *Yale Law Journal* on the New York Court of Appeals' decision in *Moscow Fire* had previously made this point. Note, "Extraterritorial Effect of Confiscatory Decrees," 49 *Yale Law Journal* 324, 328 (1939).

107. As noted, the State Department had only declared an intention to make funds recovered under the Litvinov Agreement "available, in whole or in part," to Americans who could establish bona fide claims against the Soviets. See Brief for the United States in 3 Transcript of Record, United States v. Moscow Fire Insurance Co., 46.

108. U.S. Const., Amend. V.

109. 315 U.S. at 228.

110. Id. at 229–230.

111. Id. at 233–234.

112. Id. at 577–578.

113. For a sample, see Philip Jessup, "The Litvinov Assignment and the Pink Case," 36 *American Journal of International Law* 282 (1942); Note, "Effect of Soviet Recognition upon Russian Confiscatory Decrees," 51 *Yale Law Journal* 848 (1942); Edward D. Re, "The Extraterritorial Effect of Confiscatory Decrees," 17 *St. John's Law Review* 20 (1942); and Lewis A. McGowan, Jr., "The Pink Case, the Recognition of Russia, and the Litvinov Assignment," 30 *Georgetown Law Journal* 663 (1942).

114. Edwin Borchard, "Extraterritorial Confiscations," 36 *American Journal of International Law* 275 (1942).

115. Edwin Borchard, "Shall the Executive Agreement Replace the Treaty?" 38 *American Journal of International Law* 637, 642–643 (1944).

116. The transformation extended into the area of foreign sovereign immunity jurisprudence, where, in a series of decisions between the 1920s and 1945, the Court abandoned the traditional view that executive determinations of the sovereign status of a foreign nation had no effect on the adjudication of cases in which that nation claimed immunity from suit. This gave way to a posture of considerable deference toward executive "suggestions" with respect to the immunity issue. For the details, see G. Edward White, "The Transformation of the Constitutional Regime of Foreign Relations," 85 *Virginia Law Review* 1, 134–145 (1999).

4. The Emergence of Agency Government and the Creation of Administrative Law

1. For examples, see James M. Landis, *The Administrative Process* (1938); Robert E. Cushman, *The Independent Regulatory Commissions* (1941); Robert H. Jackson, *The Struggle for Judicial Supremacy* (1941).

2. The two most influential examples of mainstream narratives were Louis L. Jaffe's *Judicial Control of Administrative Action* (1965) and Kenneth Culp Davis's *Discretionary Justice* (1969). Both took the administrative agency as an established feature of American government, including brief histories of the emergence of administrative agencies in the late nineteenth and twentieth centuries.

3. For examples, see Steven Skowronek, *Building a New American State: The Expansion of National Administrative Capacities, 1877–1920* (1982); Morton Horwitz, *The Transformation of American Law, 1870–1960*, 213–246 (1992); Eldon J. Eisenach, *The Lost Promise of Progressivism* (1994).

4. See Skowronek, *Building a New American State*, 289–292; Horwitz, *The Transformation of American Law*, 222–225; Eisenach, *The Lost Promise of Progressivism*, 259–266.

5. See, e.g., Thomas Cooley, *Constitutional Law*, 137 (2d ed., 1891).

6. This shorthand version of the doctrine that legislative powers may not be delegated appears in contemporary constitutional law treatises and casebooks. See, e.g., Geoffrey Stone et al., *Constitutional Law,* 426 (3rd ed., 1996).

7. Examples of late nineteenth-century commentary reflecting the constitutionally alien status of agencies include Appleton Morgan, "The Political Control of Railways: Is It Compensation?" 34 *Popular Science Monthly* 455 (1888); Aldace Walker, "Operation of the Interstate Commerce Law," 11 *Forum* 524 (1891); Henry C. Adams, "A Decade of Federal Railway Regulation," 81 *Atlantic Monthly* 433 (1898). These commentators suggested that the greatest impact the ICC was likely to have was as a moral force, since it could not actually exercise any independent governmental powers. See, e.g., Walker, "Operation of the Interstate Commerce Law," 524; Adams, "A Decade of Federal Railway Regulation," 433.

8. Chief Justice William Howard Taft, "Proceedings on the Death of Chief Justice White," 257 U.S. xxv–xxvi (1922).

9. The ICC also believed, initially, that when it had determined that a particular rate was not "just and reasonable" it could establish an alternative rate that it felt met that standard. It proceeded to do so for a decade after its creation until the Supreme Court decided, in Interstate Commerce Commission v. Cincinnati, New Orleans & Texas Pacific Railway Co., 167 U.S. 479 (1897), that the ICC had no authority to fix rates itself.

10. For additional examples of arguments tracking those made in the sources cited in note 7, see Cushman, *The Independent Regulatory Commissions,* 58–60.

11. Id., 46–47.

12. Id., 46, referring to views expressed in the hearings and debates, noted at 46–47.

13. See the discussions of Karl Pearson's *The Grammar of Science,* which went through three editions between 1892 and 1911, by David Hollinger, Theodore Porter, and Dorothy Ross in Dorothy Ross, ed., *Modernist Impulses in the Human Sciences,* 51–52, 143–151, 176–178 (1994).

14. By the 1920s the ICC had been joined by the Federal Reserve Board, the Federal Trade Commission, a federal maritime commission, and an ex officio federal power commission. For the details of the creation of those agencies, and the Supreme Court's grudging tolerance of them, see Cushman, *The Independent Regulatory Commissions,* 146–160, 177–213, 228–232, 275–278.

15. Act of June 29, 1906, 34 Stat. 584. The ICC's rate-setting powers were extended to include a power to set "reasonable" railroad rates prospectively, but prospective rates could only be set after a formal complaint by persons who had been adversely affected by "unreasonable" rates.

16. A summary of those objections had been provided by Richard Olney in a 1905 article, "Some Legal Aspects of Railroad Rate-Making by Congress," 181 *North American Review* 486 (1905).

17. Testimony in Hearings before the Senate Committee on Interstate Commerce, 58th Cong., 3rd Sess., vol. IV, 2893. Prouty was subsequently to summarize his views in an article in the *American Lawyer.* See Charles A. Prouty, "A Funda-

mental Defect in the Act to Regulate Commerce," 15 *American Lawyer* 515 (1907).

18. 40 Cong. Rec. 2086 (1906).
19. Id. at 2191.
20. Id. at 1972.
21. Id. at 5134.
22. Id. at 3118.
23. Id. at 4977.
24. See the discussions in 51 Cong. Rec. 11,092–13,048 (1914) (Federal Trade Commission); 59 Cong. Rec. 235–259 (1920) (Federal Power Commission). For examples of extraconstitutional arguments supporting the agencies by individual participants, see Cushman, *The Independent Regulatory Commissions,* 179–181, 190–191 (Federal Trade Commission), 280–281 (Federal Power Commission).

    For examples of academic commentary recognizing and attempting to deflect objections to agencies on separation of powers and delegation grounds, see Edward Martin, "The Lines of Demarcation between Legislative, Executive, and Judicial Functions," 47 *American Law Review* 715 (1913); Stephen A. Foster, "The Delegation of Legislative Power to Administrative Officers," 7 *Illinois Law Review* 397 (1913); Ernst Freund, "The Substitution of Rule for Discretion in Public Law," 9 *American Political Science Review* 666 (1915); Charles W. Needham, "Judicial Determinations by Administrative Commissions," 10 *American Political Science Review* 235 (1916).

    For examples of academic commentary emphasizing, in addition to the above arguments, the efficiency and expertise of agencies as contrasted with traditional governing institutions, see Thomas Reed Powell, "Separation of Powers: Administrative Exercise of Legislative and Judicial Power," 27 *Political Science Quarterly* 215 (1912); Jasper Y. Brinton, "Some Powers and Problems of the Federal Administrative," 61 *University of Pennsylvania Law Review* 136 (1913).

25. See 51 Cong. Rec. (Federal Trade Commission); 59 Cong. Rec. (Federal Power Commission). For examples of objections by individual participants, see Cushman, *The Independent Regulatory Commissions,* 206–213 (Federal Trade Commission), 281–283 (Federal Power Commission). Two examples of academic commentary illustrating that orthodox constitutional objections to federal agencies retained their power in the 1920s are Frederick Green, "Separation of Governmental Powers," 29 *Yale Law Journal* 369 (1920); Nathan Isaacs, "Judicial Review of Administrative Findings," 30 *Yale Law Journal* 781 (1921).

26. For a sense that the growth of administrative agencies was in part a product of judicial tolerance, based on the option of due process review, see Cuthbert Pound, "The Judicial Power," 35 *Harvard Law Review* 787 (1922). This is not to say that the scope of procedural due process review was consistently applied between 1906 and the 1920s. See Alexander Bickel and Benno Schmidt, Jr., *The Judiciary and Responsible Government, 1910–21,* 664 (1984).

27. Elihu Root, "Public Service by the Bar," 41 *American Bar Association Reports* 355, 368–369 (1916).

28. Charles Evans Hughes, "Some Aspects of the Development of American Law," 39 *Proceedings of the New York State Bar Association* 266, 269–270 (1916).

29. George Sutherland, "Private Rights and Governmental Control," 42 *American Bar Association Reports* 197, 201–206 (1917).

30. See, e.g., Frank J. Goodnow, *Comparative Administrative Law* (1893); Ernst Freund, "The Law of the Administration in America," 9 *Political Science Quarterly* 419 (1893); Bruce Wyman, *Principles of Administrative Law* (1903); Frank J. Goodnow, *The Principles of the Administrative Law of the United States* (1905). For a discussion of the orientation of these sources, see William C. Chase, *The American Law School and the Rise of Administrative Government*, 60–75 (1982).

31. See, e.g., Roscoe Pound, "The Causes of Popular Dissatisfaction with the Administration of Justice," 40 *American Law Review* 729 (1906); Pound, "Executive Justice," 46 *American Law Register* 144 (1907); Pound, "Justice According to Law," 13 *Columbia Law Review* 696 (1913), and 14 *Columbia Law Review* 1, 116 (1914). As late as 1924 Pound was still prepared to assert that "the rise of administrative justice" was one of the "natural results of the evolution . . . from a predominantly rural agricultural society to a predominantly urban industrial society." Pound, "The Growth of Administrative Justice," 2 *Wisconsin Law Review* 321, 330–331 (1924).

32. Felix Frankfurter, "The Task of Administrative Law," 75 *University of Pennsylvania Law Review* 614 (1927). Frankfurter's essay also appeared as a foreword to the first published volume in the Harvard Studies in Administrative Law series, Edwin Wilhite Patterson's *The Insurance Commissioner in the United States* (1927).

33. Frankfurter, "The Task of Administrative Law," 615.

34. Id., 618.

35. Id., 619–620, 621.

36. The other volumes were Patterson, *The Insurance Commissioner*, and four volumes that appeared in 1933: Harold M. Stephens, *Administrative Tribunals and the Rules of Evidence* (vol. 3); John Willis, *The Parliamentary Power of English Government* (vol. 4); Carl McFarland, *Judicial Control of the Federal Trade Commission* (vol. 5); and Louis L. Jaffe, *Judicial Aspects of Foreign Relations* (vol. 6), discussed in Chapter 3. All were S.J.D. dissertations supervised in significant part by Frankfurter.

37. John Dickinson, *Administrative Justice and the Supremacy of Law in the United States*, vii–viii (1927).

38. Dickinson's survey was of cases reviewing agency decisions rather than of "the processes, . . . practices, [or] determining factors" that led to those decisions. He analyzed federal and state public utility regulation cases, cases where agency regulations based on state police powers had been challenged on constitutional grounds, and a miscellany of cases where "the government is a direct party in interest," such as public lands cases, pension cases, and revenue cases. See id., 251–306.

39. Id., 234.

40. Felix Frankfurter and James M. Landis, "Power of Congress over Procedure in

Criminal Contempts in 'Inferior' Federal Courts—A Study in Separation of Powers," 37 *Harvard Law Review* 1010 (1924).

41. Id., 1012–14, 1016 (emphasis in original).

42. At the time of the first edition Davison was an S.J.D student at Harvard Law School; by the second edition, which appeared in 1935, he was an assistant professor of law at George Washington.

43. Felix Frankfurter and J. Forrester Davison, *Cases and Materials on Administrative Law,* v (2d ed., 1935). The second edition contained a verbatim reprinting of the preface to the first edition.

44. Based on order of footnote appearance in the 1924 Frankfurter and Landis article, the cases were Wayman v. Southard, 10 Wheat. 1 (1825), 364 in the 1932 edition of Frankfurter and Davison, *Administrative Law;* Cary v. Curtis, 3 How. 236 (1845), 56; The Brig Aurora, 7 Cranch 382 (1813), 464; Field v. Clark, 143 U.S. 649 (1892), 469; Intermountain Rate Cases, 234 U.S. 476 (1914), 780; Brown v. Walker, 161 U.S. 591 (1896), 181; The Laura, 114 U.S. 411 (1885), 177; Interstate Commerce Commission v. Brimson, 154 U.S. 447 (1894), 722; Buttfield v. Stranahan, 192 U.S. 470 (1904), 494; Union Bridge v. United States, 204 U.S. 364 (1907), 414; Sinking-Fund Cases, 99 U.S. 700 (1878), 37; Michaelson v. United States, 291 F. 940 (7th Cir. 1923), 386.

45. Felix Frankfurter, "Introduction," 18 *Iowa Law Review* 129 (1933).

46. Maurice H. Merrill, "Three Possible Approaches to the Study of Administrative Law," id., 228; Oliver P. Field, "The Study of Administrative Law: A Review and Proposal," id., 233; Paul L. Sayre, "A Common Law of Administrative Powers," id., 241.

47. Edwin W. Patterson, "Legislative Regulation and the Unwritten Law," id., 193.

48. Edwin Borchard, "French Administrative Law," id., 134–135.

49. Field, "The Study of Administrative Law," 241, 242–243.

50. Gerald C. Henderson, *The Federal Trade Commission,* 98 (1924). Examples were Interstate Commerce Commission v. Delaware, Lackawanna & Western Railroad, 220 U.S. 235 (1911); Interstate Commerce Commission v. Union Pacific Railroad, 222 U.S. 541 (1912), and a line of cases stretching from Texas Pacific Railway v. Abilene Cotton Oil Co., 204 U.S. 426 (1907), to Director General v. Viscose Co., 254 U.S. 498 (1921). See the discussions in 2 I. L. Sharfman, *The Interstate Commerce Commission,* 385–393 (2 vols., 1931), and Alexander M. Bickel and Benno C. Schmidt, Jr., *The Judiciary and Responsible Government, 1910–1921,* 650–653 (1984).

51. Federal Trade Commission v. Gratz, 253 U.S. 421 (1920), vacating a cease and desist order by the Commission as unsupported by the evidence.

52. Henderson, *The Federal Trade Commission,* 97–98.

53. Procter & Gamble v. United States, 225 U.S. 282 (1912).

54. See, e.g., Edward Hines Yellow Pine v. United States, 263 U.S. 143 (1923).

55. Bi-Metallic Co. v. Colorado, 239 U.S. 441 (1915).

56. 2 Sharfman, *Interstate Commerce Commission,* 424.

57. For background to the passage of the NIRA and its constitutional defense, see Peter H. Irons, *The New Deal Lawyers,* 17–54 (1982).

58. Section 9(c) of the National Industrial Recovery Act, 48 Stat. 195 (1933).

59. 293 U.S. 389 (1935). Ryan was one of the officials of the Petroleum Agency Board charged with enforcing the Interior Department's regulations.

60. See Irons, *New Deal Lawyers*, 48–54.

61. 293 U.S. at 415.

62. Id. at 417.

63. Id. at 421.

64. Id. at 430.

65. Id. at 432.

66. Public Law No. 14, 74th Cong., 1st Sess. (1935).

67. 295 U.S. 495 (1935).

68. The Court's conclusions on delegation were more significant than its conclusions on the Commerce Clause argument because the industry in *Schechter*, a good candidate to be brought into court because there was strong evidence of its failure to conform to the NIRA codes, was more "local" in its orientation than many of the other industries to which those codes applied.

69. 295 U.S. at 530.

70. Id. at 531.

71. Id. at 533.

72. Id. at 537.

73. 298 U.S. 238 (1936).

74. Philip Levy, one of the lawyers who drafted the Wagner Act, which created the National Labor Relations Board, thought of it as resembling a "full blown, full fledged judicial agency like the Federal Trade Commission." Levy's comments were part of an oral history in the Cornell University Labor-Management History Project. They are quoted in Irons, *New Deal Lawyers*, 228.

75. Irons, id., 252–253, citing NLRB lawyers.

76. See National Labor Relations Board v. Jones & Laughlin Steel Corp., 301 U.S. 1; National Labor Relations Board v. Fruehauf Trailer Co., 301 U.S. 49; National Labor Relations Board v. Friedman-Harry Marks Clothing, 301 U.S. 58; Associated Press v. National Labor Relations Board, 301 U.S. 103 (1937). In the first three of the cases the justices were divided 5 to 4 on the issue of whether the National Labor Relations Board was seeking to regulate labor practices pertaining to "commerce" or "manufacture," but in the *Associated Press* case, where there was no dispute that the communication of news was across state lines, the justices were unanimous on the commerce power issue. In none of the cases was there any suggestion that Congress's delegation of power to the NLRB exceeded constitutional limits.

77. J. Forrester Davison, "Administration and Judicial Self-Limitation," 4 *George Washington Law Review* 291, 299 (1936).

78. Id., 296–297.

79. Charles Grove Haines, "Judicial Review of Acts of Congress and the Need for Constitutional Reform," 45 *Yale Law Journal* 816, 835 (1936).

80. Reuben Oppenheimer, "The Supreme Court and Administrative Law," 37 *Columbia Law Review* 1, 41 (1937).

81. Id., 14.

82. Id., 21.

83. Id., 25.
84. See, e.g., Horwitz, *The Transformation of American Law, 1870–1960*, 213–216.
85. James M. Landis, *The Administrative Process*, 5, 7–8 (1938).
86. Id., 99.
87. Id., 98–101.
88. Id., 152.
89. St. Joseph Stockyards Co. v. United States, 298 U.S. 38, 84 (1936).
90. Landis, *The Administrative Process*, 124.
91. For a recognition of this implicit acknowledgment, and evidence that at least some of Landis's academic colleagues remained unreconstructed opponents of agency government in the late 1930s, see George K. Gardiner's book review of *The Administrative Process*, 52 *Harvard Law Review* 336 (1938).
92. My analysis of the antiagency rhetoric and legislation that took place in the years between 1933 and the passage of the Administrative Procedure Act in 1946 has benefited from Reuel E. Schiller, "Policy Ideals and Judicial Action: Expertise, Group Pluralism, and Participatory Democracy in Intellectual Thought and Legal Decision-Making, 1932–1970," 380–425 (Ph.D. diss., University of Virginia, 1997); and George B. Sheperd, "Fierce Compromise: The Administrative Procedure Act Emerges from New Deal Politics," 90 *Northwestern Law Review* 1557 (1996).
93. For details on the 1933 Logan bill, see Sheperd, "Fierce Compromise," 1566–69.
94. See, e.g., "Report of the Special Committee on Administrative Law," 1933 *A.B.A. Annual Report* 409 (1933); "Report of the Special Committee on Administrative Law," 1934 *A.B.A. Annual Report* 544, 549 (1934).
95. Sheperd, "Fierce Compromise," 1569–98.
96. National Labor Relations Board v. Jones & Laughlin Steel Corp., 301 U.S. 1 (1937) (upholding the Wagner Act creating the National Labor Relations Board); Stewart Machine Co. v. Davis, 301 U.S. 548 (1937), and Helvering v. Davis, id., 619 (upholding the Social Security Act).
97. See Sheperd, "Fierce Compromise," 1581–82.
98. [Roscoe Pound,] "Report of the Special Committee on Administrative Law," 1938 *A.B.A. Annual Report* 331, 343 (1938).
99. The original bill was first presented in "Report of the Special Committee on Administrative Law," 1937 *A.B.A. Annual Report* 789, 846–850 (1937). Most of the differences between that bill and the Walter-Logan Act were technical rather than substantive. For a comparison of the ABA Committee's 1937 draft bill and the Walter-Logan Act, see James M. Landis, "Crucial Issues in Administrative Law," 53 *Harvard Law Review* 1077, 1083–87 (1940).
100. For a description of the membership of the Committee, which originally included twelve members, eight of whom were sympathetic to New Deal policies, see Sheperd, "Fierce Compromise," 1595.
101. Final Report of the Attorney General's Committee on Administrative Procedure (1941).
102. Id., 195–202. See the discussion in Sheperd, "Fierce Compromise," 1632–33.
103. Final Report of the Attorney General's Committee, 228–232.

104. Id., 226–227.
105. Id., 246.
106. Among the favorable reviews were four in the *Columbia Law Review* by Forrester Davison, John Foster Dulles, Abe Feller, and Felix Frankfurter. J. Forrester Davison, "Administrative Technique—the Report on Administrative Procedure," 41 *Columbia Law Review* 628 (1941); John Foster Dulles, "The Effect in Practice of the Attorney General's Report on Administrative Procedure," id., 617; A. H. Feller, "Administrative Law Investigation Comes of Age," id., 589; Felix Frankfurter, "The Final Report of the Attorney General's Committee on Administrative Procedure," id., 585. See also Louis L. Jaffe, "The Report of the Attorney General's Committee on Administrative Procedure," 8 *University of Chicago Law Review* 401 (1941); Edward Jennings, "The Report of the Attorney General's Committee on Administrative Procedure," 19 *Texas Law Review* 436 (1941); and Gilbert Montague, "Reform of Administrative Procedure," 40 *Michigan Law Review* 501 (1942).

　　For the *Journal of the American Bar Association*'s lukewarm endorsement of the Committee's report, see Editorial, "Great Issues as to Administrative Procedure," 27 *A.B.A. Journal* 95 (1941).

107. See "Report of the Special Committee on Administrative Law," 1941 *A.B.A. Annual Report* 401–403, 454 (1941).
108. The bill was introduced by Senator Pat McCarran and Representative Hatton Summers, the respective chairmen of the Senate and House Judiciary Committees. It had been drafted by the ABA's Special Committee on Administrative Law, chaired by Carl F. McFarland. The bill, in its Senate and House versions, was referred to as S. 2030 and H.R. 5081. See 78th Cong., 2d Sess. (1944). See the discussion in Sheperd, "Fierce Compromise," 1649–52.
109. "Report of the Special Committee on Administrative Law," 1944 *A.B.A. Annual Report* 472 (1994); Sheperd, "Fierce Compromise," 1649.
110. Sheperd, "Fierce Compromise," 1654–62.
111. Id., 1666–74. During the two years between 1944 and 1946, most of the modifications to the bill had been in the form of private negotiations between the ABA, agency representatives, and the Roosevelt and Truman administrations, in the course of which each group sought to construct legislative histories for the bill in order to influence subsequent judicial interpretation. The Attorney General's Office served as a liaison between agencies and the Senate and House committees drafting the bill, and eventually issued a *Manual on the Administrative Procedure Act* (1947), which offered its own legislative history. For more discussion of that manual, see below.
112. See, for example, the statement by Attorney General Tom C. Clark, in "Administrative Procedure Act: Legislative History," at 230 (Congressional Record, 1946).
113. Pat McCarran, "Improving 'Administrative Justice': Hearings and Evidence; Scope of Judicial Review," 323 *A.B.A. Journal* 827, 893 (1946).
114. Walter Gellhorn, *Federal Administrative Proceedings*, 43 (1941).
115. Id.

116. Paul R. Verkeuil, "The Emerging Concept of Administrative Procedure," 78 *Columbia Law Review* 258 (1978). Verkeuil thanked Gellhorn for "[i]nvaluable criticism and encouragement" in his acknowledgments. Id., 258.
117. Id., 269.
118. Id.
119. Id., 273.
120. Id., 270–271.
121. Id., 275–276.
122. Id., 277–278.
123. *Attorney General's Manual on the Administrative Procedure Act* (1947).
124. See Tom C. Clark in id., 6.
125. Clark in id., 5.
126. See, for example, the following comments in the *Manual*'s discussion of Section 10 of the APA, which contains the provisions affecting judicial review of agency decisions. "The intended result of the introductory clause . . . is to restate the existing law as to the area of reviewable agency action" (*Manual*, 94). "Section 10(b) does not purport to change existing venue requirements for judicial review." Id., 98. "So interpreted, [Section 10(b)] restates existing law." Id., 99. "The provisions of this subsection [10(c)] are said to 'involve no departure from the usual and well understood rule of procedure in this field.'" Id., 101.
127. Steadman v. Securities and Exchange Commission, 450 U.S. 91, 102–103 n.22 (1981); Bowen v. Georgetown University Hospital, 488 U.S. 204, 218 (1988). See Sheperd, "Fierce Compromise," 1682–83.
128. Walter Gellhorn, "The Administrative Procedure Act: The Beginnings," 72 *Virginia Law Review* 219, 232 (1986).
129. Id.
130. Kenneth Culp Davis and Walter Gellhorn, "Present at the Creation: Regulatory Reform before 1946," 38 *Administrative Law Review* 511, 516 (remarks of Walter Gellhorn) (1986).
131. Id., 515 (remarks of Gellhorn).
132. 1 Kenneth Culp Davis, *Administrative Law Treatise*, 29 (4 vols., 1958).
133. Davis and Gellhorn, "Present at the Creation," 525 (remarks of Kenneth Culp Davis).
134. 1 Davis, *Administrative Law*, 30.

5. The Emergence of Free Speech

1. See, e.g., Paul L. Murphy, *The Constitution in Crisis Times 1918–1969*, 172–175 (1972); William E. Leuchtenburg, *The Supreme Court Reborn: The Constitutional Revolution in the Age of Roosevelt*, 234–235 (1995).
2. As one casebook puts it, the modern stance of bifurcated review starts with a "presumption of constitutionality" for all legislation on the ground that it represents the wishes of majorities in a democratic society, but reverses that presumption in three instances: "when legislation restricts rights to free political communication and political processes"; "when legislation singles out for disadvantage

minorities who lack political power"; and "when legislation impinges on a right of an individual citizen listed in the constitutional document." Walter F. Murphy et al., *American Constitutional Interpretation*, 474 (1986).

3. 304 U.S. 144 (1938).

4. Id. at 152.

5. Murphy, *American Constitutional Interpretation*, 473.

6. Leuchtenburg, *The Supreme Court Reborn*, 235.

7. See, e.g., Howard Gillman, "Preferred Freedoms: The Progressive Expansion of State Power and the Rise of Modern Civil Liberties Jurisprudence," 47 *Political Research Quarterly* 623 (1994).

8. For a more detailed analysis of the topics covered in this chapter, see G. Edward White, "The First Amendment Comes of Age," 95 *Michigan Law Review* 299 (1996).

9. 165 U.S. 275 (1897).

10. 4 William Blackstone, *Commentaries on the Law of England* (4 vols., 1769).

11. Patterson v. Colorado, 205 U.S. 454 (1907).

12. See, e.g., Fox v. Washington, 236 U.S. 273 (1912), where Holmes, for the Court, again conceptualized a free speech case as a police power case and read "bad tendency" broadly.

13. Gitlow v. New York, 268 U.S. 652 (1925).

14. The most extensive treatment of late nineteenth- and early twentieth-century libertarian free speech commentary is David M. Rabban, *Free Speech in Its Forgotten Years* (1997). See also Mark A. Graber, *Transforming Free Speech: The Ambiguous Legacy of Civil Libertarianism*, 51–67 (1991).

15. Espionage Act of 1917, 40 Stat. 217 (1954) (revised version), and Sedition Act of 1918, 40 Stat. 553 (1919).

16. 249 U.S. 47 (1919).

17. 250 U.S. 616 (1919).

18. 249 U.S. at 52.

19. 250 U.S. at 627.

20. Chafee's commentary began with a *New Republic* article, "Freedom of Speech," which appeared in the November 16, 1918 issue, p. 66. He then published a virtually identical law journal article, "Freedom of Speech in War Time," 32 *Harvard Law Review* 932 (1919). In 1920 his book *Freedom of Speech* appeared, and in 1941 Chafee published a revised version, *Freedom of Speech in the United States*. A useful biography of Chafee is Donald L. Smith, *Zechariah Chafee, Jr.: Defender of Liberty and Law* (1986).

21. The terms *progressive* and *Progressive*, as applied to early twentieth-century legal commentators, can be a source of confusion. As employed here, the term *progressive* is used to characterize commentators who described themselves as "progressives," by which they meant a circle of persons with a reformist jurisprudential and political agenda. The term *Progressive* is used to characterize supporters of the national Progressive Party, which ran candidates for the presidency in 1912, 1916, 1920, and 1924. Not all progressives were Progressives in the time frame of this study.

22. See Graber, *Transforming Free Speech*, 77–86.

23. See Eldon J. Eisenach, *The Lost Promise of Progressivism*, 193–195 (1994); Robert H. Wiebe, *Self-Rule: A Cultural History of American Democracy*, 162–165 (1995).

24. For examples of the policies, see generally Robert H. Wiebe, *The Search for Order, 1877–1920* (1977).

25. Id. at 38.

26. 244 F. 535 (S.D.N.Y. 1917). Hand held in that case that only speech that constituted a "direct incitement to violent resistance" could be constitutionally suppressed. Id. at 540. Chafee dedicated the 1920 edition of *Freedom of Speech* to Hand.

27. Chafee, *Freedom of Speech*, 25–32.

28. See G. Edward White, *Justice Oliver Wendell Holmes: Law and the Inner Self*, 418–420 (1993), discussing Holmes's use of "bad tendency" language and analysis in two Espionage Act cases following *Schenck*.

29. 32 *Harvard Law Review* 932 (1919). As noted earlier, Chafee had published an earlier version of this article, then titled "Freedom of Speech," in the November 16, 1918 issue of *The New Republic*.

30. Chafee, "Freedom of Speech in War Time," 967. In *Freedom of Speech*, 89, Chafee made the identical statement.

31. 250 U.S. at 616.

32. E.g., his definitions of "truth" as "the prevailing can't helps of the majority" or "the majority vote of that nation that can lick all others." Holmes to Harold Laski, January 11, 1929, Oliver Wendell Holmes Papers, microfilm edition (1985), quoted in White, *Justice Oliver Wendell Holmes*, 435; Holmes to Learned Hand, June 24, 1918, Holmes Papers, quoted in id.

33. 250 U.S. at 628, 629.

34. For an argument that Holmes held no consistent theory of free speech throughout his judicial career but rather issued a series of rhetorical formulations, not necessarily consistent with one another, that demonstrated an increasingly speech-protective emphasis in his jurisprudence, see White, *Justice Oliver Wendell Holmes*, 410–454.

35. See Abrams v. United States, 250 U.S. 616 (1919); Gitlow v. New York, 268 U.S. 652 (1925); Whitney v. California, 274 U.S. 257 (1927); Fiske v. Kansas, 274 U.S. 257 (1927). In *Fiske* the Court unanimously invalidated a conviction under the Kansas Criminal Syndicalism Act for soliciting members of a local branch of the International Workers of the World. It used the same bad tendency test as had been employed in *Gitlow* and *Whitney* and treated the free speech claim within conventional police power analysis.

36. See United States ex rel. Milwaukee Social Democratic Publishing Co. v. Burleson, 255 U.S. 407, 426 (1921); *Gitlow*, 268 U.S. at 672–673; United States v. Schwimmer, 279 U.S. 644, 654–655 (1929).

37. N.Y. Penal Law sect. 161 (Matthew Bender, 1909).

38. The California statute prohibited any person from organizing or knowingly becoming a member of any organization advocating "the commission of crime, sabotage, or unlawful acts of force and violence or unlawful methods of terrorism as a means of accomplishing a change in industrial ownership or control, or

effecting any political change." See 274 U.S. at 359–360, quoting Criminal Syndicalism Act, ch. 188, sect. 1, 1919 Cal. Stat. 281. On its face the platform of the Communist Labor Party, which advocated industrial revolts and strikes, clearly came within the statute. For general background on the *Whitney* case, see Vincent Blasi, "The First Amendment and the Ideal of Civic Courage," 29 *William & Mary Law Review* 653 (1988).

39. *Whitney,* 274 U.S. at 379.

40. Id. at 375–376.

41. Id. at 374. Later in his concurrence Brandeis suggested that the standard should be a very speech-protective reading of the phrase "clear and present danger," permitting legislative repressions of speech only when the speech posed "imminent danger" creating "the probability of serious injury to the state." Id. at 378.

42. Id. at 377.

43. Id. at 374.

44. In the majority opinion Justice Sanford only said that "[f]or present purposes we may and do assume that freedom of speech and of the press—which are protected by the First Amendment from abridgment by Congress—are among the fundamental personal rights and 'liberties' protected by the due process clause of the Fourteenth Amendment from impairment by the States." *Gitlow,* 268 U.S. at 666. Holmes, in his dissent, said that "[t]he general principle of free speech, it seems to me, must be taken to be included in the Fourteenth Amendment, in view of the scope that has been given to the word 'liberty' as there used." Id. at 672.

45. See, for example, the opinions by Justice Joseph McKenna and Brandeis in Gilbert v. Minnesota, 254 U.S. 325 (1920), in which a Minnesota statute preventing interference with enlistment in the armed services was attacked as inconsistent with free speech. McKenna's opinion assumed that a right of free speech could apply against state statutes but concluded that it could be restricted in the interests of public safety. Brandeis, in dissent, said that "I have difficulty in believing that the liberty guaranteed by the Constitution [in the Fourteenth Amendment,] which has been held to protect against state denial the right . . . to contract . . . does not include liberty to teach . . . the doctrine of pacifism . . . I cannot believe that the liberty guaranteed by the Fourteenth Amendment includes only liberty to acquire and to enjoy property." Id. at 343.

46. Prudential Insurance Co. v. Cheeck, 259 U.S. 530, 543 (1922). The opinion of the Court was written by Justice Mahlon Pitney.

47. Meyer v. Nebraska, 262 U.S. 390 (1923).

48. Pierce v. Society of Sisters, 268 U.S. 510 (1925).

49. For example, in two 1931 cases, O'Gorman v. Hartford Insurance Co., 282 U.S. 251 (1931), and Near v. Minnesota, 283 U.S. 697 (1931), Holmes and Brandeis joined Chief Justice Hughes and Justices Roberts and Stone in sustaining a New Jersey statute regulating the fees paid to local insurance agents by out-of-state insurance companies in the face of a "liberty of contract" challenge, and joined the same majority in invalidating a Minnesota statute that allowed subsequent issues of a newspaper whose contents had been found to be defama-

tory to be enjoined. The majority opinions in both cases employed police power analysis.

50. In an article commenting on *Gitlow,* the lawyer and scholar Charles Warren suggested that the majority's denotation of freedom of speech as "among the fundamental personal rights and 'liberties' protected by the due process clause of the Fourteenth Amendment" would lead to an equation of textually protected status with "fundamentality," and eventually result in "every one of the rights contained in the Bill of Rights [being] included within the definition of 'liberty'" in police power due process cases. Charles Warren, "The New 'Liberty' under the Fourteenth Amendment," 39 *Harvard Law Review* 431, 432, 460 (1926).

51. See, in addition to Near v. Minnesota, 283 U.S. 697 (1931): Stromberg v. California, 283 U.S. 359 (1931), invalidating a state statute providing criminal punishment for any person who expressed "opposition to government" by displaying "any flag, badge, banner, or device" (the display in question was a red flag); Grosjean v. American Press Co., 297 U.S. 233 (1936), striking down the Louisiana statute taxing the advertising revenues of papers beyond a certain circulation; and De Jonge v. Oregon, 299 U.S. 353 (1937), invalidating the application of a criminal syndicalist statute, similar to that in *Whitney,* to a peaceful rally conducted by a person who was a member of the Communist Party.

52. *Near; Grosjean.*

53. Hamilton v. Regents of the University of California, 293 U.S. 245 (1934).

54. *De Jonge.*

55. In the 1932 case of Powell v. Alabama, 287 U.S. 45, the Court incorporated the Sixth Amendment's provision for the assistance of counsel in a criminal case. In Chicago, Burlington & Quincy R.R. v. Chicago, 166 U.S. 226 (1897), it had incorporated the Fifth Amendment's provision against the taking of property without just compensation.

56. 302 U.S. 319 (1937).

57. Id. at 324, 327.

58. See, e.g., Robert McKay, "The Preference for Freedom," 34 *New York University Law Review* 1184 (1959); Leonard W. Levy, "Preferred Freedoms," in Leonard W. Levy et al., eds., 3 *Encyclopedia of the American Constitution,* 1439 (4 vols., 1986).

59. 302 U.S. at 327, citing Warren, "The New 'Liberty' under the Fourteenth Amendment," 431.

60. 302 U.S. at 325–326.

61. 310 U.S. 585 (1940).

62. 319 U.S. 624 (1943).

63. 308 U.S. 147, 160 (1939).

64. Id. at 161.

65. Id.

66. *Gobitis,* 310 U.S. at 599.

67. Id. at 606–607.

68. Between 1938 and 1946 the Court considered six such cases. See Lovell v.

Griffin, 303 U.S. 444 (1938); Schneider v. Irvington, 308 U.S. 147 (1939); Jones v. Opelika, 316 U.S. 584 (1942); Murdock v. Pennsylvania, 319 U.S. 105 (1942); Prince v. Massachusetts, 321 U.S. 158 (1944); and Marsh v. Alabama, 326 U.S. 501 (1946). Of these cases all but *Lovell* produced rhetoric identifying free speech rights as occupying a "preferred position."

69. 316 U.S. 584 (1942).

70. Id. at 608.

71. Id. at 623.

72. Id. at 624.

73. 319 U.S. 105 (1943). Frankfurter protested against the Court's grant of certiorari in *Murdock,* which was a virtually identical case to Jones v. Opelika. See H. N. Hirsch, *The Enigma of Felix Frankfurter,* 166 (1981).

74. 319 U.S. at 115.

75. West Virginia State Board of Education v. Barnette, 319 U.S. 624 (1943).

76. Id. at 641.

77. Id. at 638.

78. Id. at 639.

79. Id. at 648. Frankfurter's comment that rights deriving from the Fifth Amendment's Just Compensation Clause had "the same constitutional dignity" as First Amendment rights was not accidental, since that provision had also been incorporated against the states.

80. Felix Frankfurter to Harlan Fiske Stone, April 27, 1938, Harlan Fiske Stone Papers, Library of Congress, quoted in Murphy et al., *American Constitutional Interpretation,* 490.

81. Felix Frankfurter, *Mr. Justice Holmes and the Supreme Court,* 49–51 (1938).

82. Felix Frankfurter to Harlan Fiske Stone, May 27, 1940, Harlan Fiske Stone Papers, Library of Congress, quoted in Hirsch, *The Enigma of Felix Frankfurter,* 151.

83. See American Federation of Labor v. Swing, 312 U.S. 321, 325 (1941).

84. Frankfurter to Stone, May 27, 1938.

85. For evidence that the flag-salute cases were a pivotal episode in Frankfurter's tenure on the Supreme Court, see Hirsch, *The Enigma of Felix Frankfurter,* 176–177, 211.

86. 336 U.S. 77 (1949).

87. Id. at 88.

88. Id. at 90.

89. Id.

90. Id. at 95.

91. Frankfurter, *Mr. Justice Holmes and the Supreme Court,* 49.

92. See United States v. Rumely, 345 U.S. 41, 56 (1953).

93. Alexander Meiklejohn, *Free Speech and Its Relation to Self-Government,* ix (1948).

94. Id., 1–2.

95. Id.

96. See id., 37–39.

97. See Zechariah Chafee, Jr., "Book Review," 62 *Harvard Law Review* 891, 892 (1949); Lee Bollinger, *The Tolerant Society*, 149–151 (1986).
98. Meiklejohn, *Free Speech*, 38–39.
99. See Valentine v. Chrestensen, 316 U.S. 52 (1942).
100. See Chaplinsky v. New Hampshire, 315 U.S. 568 (1942).
101. See id. at 568.
102. See Barber v. Time Inc., 159 S.W. 2d 291 (Mo. 1942).
103. Meiklejohn, *Free Speech*, 22–25.
104. Several of the categories of unprotected speech that remained after the "preferred position" cases, and that Meiklejohn believed should remain without protection, have been given a measure of constitutional protection by Supreme Court decisions between the 1960s and the present. For details, see White, "The First Amendment Comes of Age," 358–372.
105. This posture on the part of the Court in the 1940s should not be equated with the "toothless" review standard it subsequently endorsed in cases such as Williamson v. Lee Optical, 348 U.S. 483 (1955). For a fuller discussion of the governing standards of deferential review in existence on the Court in the late 1930s, which a majority of the Court's justices subscribed to in the 1940s, see Barry Cushman, "Lost Fidelities," 41 *William & Mary Law Review* 95, 129–145 (1999).
106. See Michael J. Klarman, "*Brown*, Racial Change, and the Civil Rights Movement," 80 *Virginia Law Review* 7, 26–27 (1994).
107. Justices Cardozo and Reed took no part in the decision; Chief Justice Hughes and Justices Brandeis and Roberts joined Stone's entire opinion; Justice Black joined Stone's opinion except for the portion in which the quoted passage and its accompanying footnote occurred; Justice Butler concurred in the result; and Justice McReynolds dissented. This meant that although Stone's opinion in *Carolene Products* was technically an opinion of the Court, a minority of the justices on the Court at the time endorsed its celebrated footnote 4.
108. 304 U.S. at 152–153, note 4.
109. 283 U.S. 359 (1931).
110. 303 U.S. 444 (1938).
111. The previously uncited cases in the footnote are, in the order they appeared: Nixon v. Herndon, 273 U.S. 536 (1927); Nixon v. Condon, 286 U.S. 73 (1932); Herndon v. Lowry, 301 U.S. 242 (1937); Bartels v. Iowa, 262 U.S. 404 (1923); and Farrington v. Tokushige, 273 U.S. 248 (1927). In addition, in the omitted portion of the excerpt, Stone cited McCulloch v. Maryland, 17 U.S. (4 Wheat.) 316 (1819), and South Carolina v. Barnwell Bros. 303 U.S. 177 (1935).

6. The Restatement Project and the Crisis of Early Twentieth-Century Jurisprudence

1. The term "common law" refers to the collective body of judicial decisions in distinctive private law fields, such as property, contracts, or torts, whose governing

rules and principles are primarily handed down by courts, as distinguished from some other source of legal authority. Some private law fields currently governed primarily by statutes, such as the fields of secured transactions or criminal law, would not be included, even though at some point in their history they were principally governed by court decisions. Constitutional law is not considered a "common law" subject, even though a great many of its governing doctrines are promulgated by courts, because those doctrines are treated as interpretations of the text of an independent authoritative source, the Constitution.

2. See, e.g., Thomas C. Grey, "Langdell's Orthodoxy," 45 *University of Pittsburgh Law Review* 1 (1984); William P. LaPiana, *Logic and Experience: The Origin of Modern American Legal Education* (1994); Laura Kalman, *Legal Realism at Yale, 1927–1960* (1986); John Henry Schlegel, "Langdell's Legacy," 36 *Stanford Law Review* 1517 (1984); John W. Johnson, *American Legal Culture, 1908–1940*, 52–72 (1981).

3. An exception is Mark Tushnet and Louis Michael Seidman, *Remnants of Belief: Contemporary Constitutional Issues*, 31–37 (1996).

4. Roscoe Pound, one of the most prominent critics of "liberty of contract," stated that the judicial application of the doctrine to modern industrial enterprise, without any attention to the actual conditions of employment, amounted to "mechanical jurisprudence." See Roscoe Pound, "Mechanical Jurisprudence," 8 *Columbia Law Review* 605 (1908); Pound, "Liberty of Contract," 18 *Yale Law Journal* 454 (1909).

5. See William Twining, *Karl Llewellyn and the Realist Movement*, 275–276 (1973); and Robert Stevens, *Law School: Legal Education in America from the 1850s to the 1980s*, 133–135 (1983). This interpretation has been perpetuated in sources such as Kalman, *Legal Realism at Yale*, 14, and Neil Duxbury, *Patterns of American Jurisprudence*, 24, 59–60 (1995).

6. See, e.g., N. E. H. Hull, "Restatement and Reform: A New Perspective on the Origins of the American Law Institute," 8 *Law and History Review* 55 (1990); Hull, "Vital Schools of Jurisprudence: Roscoe Pound, Wesley Newcomb Hohfeld, and the Promotion of an Academic Jurisprudential Agenda, 1910–1919," 45 *Journal of Legal Education* 235 (1995).

7. The term "black letter law" reflects a distinction between those portions of legal texts in which authoritative syntheses of legal rules or doctrines are promulgated, and those portions in which potential complexities or ambiguities in those rules and doctrines are explored. The latter portions are typically referred to as "commentary," to signal the reader that the discussions are dealing with unsettled issues. In some legal texts the typeface employed in the portions setting forth synthetic general rules differs from that employed in the portions commenting on those rules. This convention has sometimes resulted in syntheses of rules being set in more prominent typefaces, or "black letter."

8. C. C. Langdell, "Harvard Celebration Speeches," 3 *Law Quarterly Review* 123, 124 (1887). This comment tracked positions Langdell had taken as early as 1871. See C. C. Langdell, *A Selection of Cases on the Law of Contracts*, vii (1871).

9. See M. H. Hoeflich, "Law and Geometry: Legal Science from Leibniz to Langdell," 30 *American Journal of Legal History* 95 (1986).

10. See G. Edward White, *The Marshall Court and Cultural Change*, 144–155, 361–362 (1988); R. Kent Newmyer, *Supreme Court Justice Joseph Story: Statesman of the Old Republic*, 44–45, 68 (1985); LaPiana, *Logic and Experience*, 54.

11. See Grey, "Langdell's Orthodoxy," 15, 20, 24. Stephen Siegel's article, "Joel Bishop's Orthodoxy," 13 *Law and History Review* 215 (1995), has shown that it was possible for Langdell's contemporaries to retain religious-based conceptions of law as a "science."

12. Langdell, *A Selection of Cases on the Law of Contracts*, vii.

13. Id., iv.

14. Id., vii.

15. Grey, "Langdell's Orthodoxy," 8–9, 42–47; Siegel, "Joel Bishop's Orthodoxy," 222–225. I have suggested that Langdell and many of his Harvard Law School colleagues can be seen as embodying a "Brahmin gentry" perspective on late nineteenth-century issues of political economy. See G. Edward White, "Revisiting James Bradley Thayer," 88 *Northwestern University Law Review* 28 (1993).

16. My attribution of views to the "founders" of the ALI comes from a collective statement, probably written by William Draper Lewis, the Institute's first director, in 1 *Proceedings of the American Law Institute* 68 (1923).

17. Id. at 66. This apparent paradox was a common thread in late nineteenth-century commentary. Judges were seen as handing down illustrations of legal principles without explicitly articulating the principles, which were revealed by "jurisconsults." Instead of the process being taken as evidence of the creativity of either the judges or the commentator jurisconsults, it was taken as evidence of the essential nature of the principles and the learning of those who revealed them. See Siegel, "Joel Bishop's Orthodoxy," 223–224.

18. 1 *Proceedings of the American Law Institute*, 70.

19. Id., 73.

20. Id., 74.

21. Id., 70.

22. Id., 6.

23. Id., 70.

24. Id., 77.

25. Id.

26. Id., 78.

27. Id.

28. Id.

29. Id., 82.

30. For an example of that alternative reading, see Joseph W. Bingham, "What Is the Law?" 11 *Michigan Law Review* 1, 109 (1912). I do not mean to suggest that such a reading occupied "mainstream" status in early twentieth-century jurisprudential discourse. On the contrary, it was regarded as distinctly beyond the fringe. See John Henry Schlegel, "Between the Harvard Founders and the American Legal Realists," 35 *Journal of Legal Education* 311 (1985).

31. Treatise writing had continued in the late nineteenth and early twentieth centuries, and by the early 1920s such volumes as Joseph Beale's *Conflict of Laws*

(1916), Samuel Williston's *Contracts* (1920), and John Wigmore's *Evidence* (1923) had appeared.

32. See Hull, "Restatement and Reform," 79, 83–85.
33. See the remarks of John W. Davis in 1 *Proceedings of the American Law Institute*, 42.
34. A number of scholars have made this general point in different ways. Compare Twining, *Karl Llewellyn and the Realist Movement*, 274–276, with John Henry Schlegel, *American Legal Realism and Empirical Social Science*, 25–57 (1995), and Kalman, *Legal Realism at Yale*, 10–20.
35. Jeremiah Smith, "Legal Cause in Actions of Tort," 24 *Harvard Law Review* 303, 315 (1912).
36. Wesley Newcomb Hohfeld, "Some Fundamental Conceptions as Applied in Judicial Reasoning," 23 *Yale Law Journal* 16 (1913), 26 *Yale Law Journal* 710 (1917). The fullest statement of Hohfeld's views, published after Hohfeld's sudden death from influenza in 1919, is Walter Wheeler Cook's edition of Hohfeld's work, *Fundamental Legal Conceptions as Applied in Judicial Reasoning and Other Legal Essays* (1919).
37. See the discussion in Cook, ed., *Fundamental Legal Conceptions*, 5.
38. George R. Farnum, "Terminology and the American Law Institute," 13 *Boston University Law Review* 203, 204, 208 (1933).
39. William Draper Lewis, 7 *Proceedings of the American Law Institute* 209 (1930), quoted in Farnum, "Terminology and the American Law Institute," 208.
40. Harry Bigelow, in 7 *Proceedings of the American Law Institute*, 207, quoted in id., 210.
41. Farnum, id., 212, 210.
42. Id., 213.
43. Id., 214–215.
44. Id., 216.
45. Id.
46. Id., 217.
47. See Hull, "Vital Schools of Jurisprudence," 256–263.
48. Arthur Corbin, "The Restatement of the Common Law by the American Law Institute," 15 *Iowa Law Review* 19 (1930), quoted in Farnum, "Terminology and the American Law Institute," 217–218.
49. See Charles Clark, "The Restatement of the Law of Contracts," 42 *Yale Law Journal* 643, 649–652 (1933).
50. Karl Llewellyn, "A Realistic Jurisprudence—The Next Step," 30 *Columbia Law Review* 431 (1930); Llewellyn, "Some Realism about Realism—Responding to Dean Pound," 44 *Harvard Law Review* 1222 (1931). In the latter article, Llewellyn stated that Frank should have been listed as a joint author, and "the paper could not have been written without his help." Id., 1222.
51. Llewellyn, "Some Realism about Realism," 1237.
52. Jerome Frank, *Law and the Modern Mind*, 147 (1930).
53. Myers McDougal, "Book Review [of Volumes 1 and 2 of the Restatement of Property]," 32 *Illinois Law Review* 509, 510, 513 (1937).
54. Id., 513.

55. McDougal was referring to the Restatements of Contracts, Conflict of Laws, Torts, and Property, all of which had appeared in print between 1932 and 1937. Critical reviews of those Restatements are subsequently discussed.

56. Clark, "The Restatement of the Law of Contracts," 42 *Yale Law Journal* 643, 653, 655.

57. Leon Green, "The Torts Restatement," 29 *Illinois Law Review* 582, 584–585, 592 (1935).

58. Joseph Beale, 14 *Proceedings of the Association of American Law Schools* 38 (1914), quoted in Ernest G. Lorenzen and Raymond J. Heilman, "The Restatement of the Conflict of Laws," 83 *University of Pennsylvania Law Review* 555, 556 (1935).

59. Walter Wheeler Cook, "The Logical and Legal Bases of the Conflict of Laws," 33 *Yale Law Journal* 457, 459 (1924), quoted in Lorenzen and Heilman, "The Restatement of the Conflict of Laws," 558.

60. Edward S. Robinson, *Law and the Lawyers*, 36 (1935).

61. Id.

62. Herbert F. Goodrich, "Institute Bards and Yale Reviewers," 84 *University of Pennsylvania Law Review* 449, 452–453, 454 (1936).

63. Thurman Arnold, "Institute Priests and Yale Observers—A Reply to Dean Goodrich," 84 *University of Pennsylvania Law Review* 811, 813 (1936).

64. Id., 813, 816.

65. Id., 817.

66. Id., 823.

67. Id., 823–824.

7. The Constitutional Revolution as a Crisis in Adaptivity

1. Morehead v. New York ex rel. Tipaldo, 298 U.S. 587 (1936).

2. West Coast Hotel v. Parrish, 300 U.S. 379 (1937).

3. 298 U.S. 238 (1936).

4. 301 U.S. 1 (1937).

5. 295 U.S. 330 (1935).

6. 297 U.S. 1 (1936).

7. 301 U.S. 548 (1937).

8. 301 U.S. 619 (1937).

9. 295 U.S. 495 (1935).

10. 312 U.S. 100 (1941).

11. 317 U.S. 111 (1942).

12. 261 U.S. 525 (1923).

13. 290 U.S. 398 (1934).

14. William E. Leuchtenburg, *The Supreme Court Reborn: The Constitutional Revolution in the Age of Roosevelt*, 236 (1995).

15. 291 U.S. 502 (1934), sustaining the constitutionality of a New York statute regulating the price of milk.

16. See Barry Cushman, *Rethinking the New Deal Court: The Structure of a Constitutional Revolution*, 11–32 (1998).

17. See id., 209–225.

18. In the 1936 Term the Court was composed of Chief Justice Hughes and Associate Justices Van Devanter, McReynolds, Brandeis, Sutherland, Butler, Stone, Roberts, and Cardozo. By the 1940 Term only Hughes, McReynolds, Stone, and Roberts remained. By the 1941 Term only Stone and Roberts remained. All the new appointees—Justices Black, Reed, Douglas, Frankfurter, Murphy, Jackson, and Byrnes—were, of course, nominated by Roosevelt.

19. In almost any version of the conventional account one finds this "switch" portrayed by the waggish expression, "the switch in time that saved nine," or a closely equivalent phrase. For a recent effort to locate the origins of the phrase, see Michael Ariens, "A Thrice-Told Tale: Or, Felix the Cat," 107 *Harvard Law Review* 620, 623 note 11 (1994), concluding that the first use of the phrase came in a letter from Edward S. Corwin to Homer Cummings, May 19, 1937, in Homer Cummings Papers, Princeton University.

20. Perhaps the most influential version of this critique of Roberts, because of its widespread use as a graduate and undergraduate text, has been Robert McCloskey, *The American Supreme Court*, 175, 224 (1960). The most detailed version is J. W. Chambers, "The Big Switch: Justice Roberts and the Minimum-Wage Cases," 10 *Labor History* 44 (1969). For additional examples, see Cushman, *Rethinking the New Deal Court*, 243.

21. For an overview of Cushman's argument, see *Rethinking the New Deal Court*, 5–7.

22. Id., 92–104. Cushman also suggests that Chief Justice Hughes, who dissented in *Tipaldo*, was reluctant to use that case as an occasion to overrule *Adkins*. Id., 101–103.

23. Cushman relies in part on a memorandum written by Roberts on November 9, 1945, and included in a tribute to Roberts on his death by Felix Frankfurter, "Mr. Justice Roberts," 104 *University of Pennsylvania Law Review* 311, 314–315 (1955). The authenticity of the memorandum and its accuracy have been the subjects of considerable dispute. Compare Ariens, "A Thrice-Told Tale," with Richard D. Friedman, "A Reaffirmation: The Authenticity of the Roberts Memorandum, or Felix the Non-Forger," 142 *University of Pennsylvania Law Review* 1985 (1995). Cushman accepts the memorandum as authentic and largely accurate. He suggests that the *Tipaldo/Parrish* sequence should be taken as demonstrating that a majority of the Court—including Roberts—was prepared to abandon a strong reading of economic "liberty" in police power due process cases before the Court-packing plan was even conceived. Cushman, *Rethinking the New Deal Court*, 104–105, 243.

24. Cushman singles out Hughes, Roberts, and Cardozo, appointed to the Court by President Herbert Hoover between 1930 and 1932 to replace Chief Justice William Howard Taft, Associate Justice Edward Sanford, and Holmes. Cushman, *Rethinking the New Deal Court*, 225.

25. The phrase "living Constitution" has become so commonplace in late twentieth-century constitutional discourse that its comparatively recent historical origins may be overlooked. As far as I can determine, the phrase was used for the first time in Arthur W. Machen, Jr.'s article, "The Elasticity of the Constitution," 14 *Harvard Law Review* 200, 205 (1900). Machen's use of the term,

however, was in the context of an argument for what I call the traditional or essentialist meaning of adaptivity. I am indebted to Professor Eric Segall for calling Machen's article to my attention.

In my exploration of the historical origins of the phrase I profited from an unpublished paper by Howard Gillman, "The Problem of Political Development for Constitutional Theory: The Collapse of Foundationalist Constitutionalism and the Origins of the Concept of the Living Constitution," presented to the Western Political Science Association in April 1995. I am indebted to Professor Gillman for first drawing my attention to several of the sources I discuss in connection with the debate over the meaning of constitutional adaptivity in the 1920s and 1930s. His essay represents the first sustained effort, so far as I am aware, to connect the debate to the constitutional revolution.

I also profited from Michael Kammen's discussion of some of the sources associated with the "living Constitution" debate in *A Machine That Would Go of Itself: The Constitution in American Culture,* 219–254 (1986). For a more detailed discussion of sources related to the topics discussed in this chapter, see G. Edward White, "The Constitutional Revolution as a Crisis in Adaptivity," 48 *Hastings Law Journal* 867 (1997).

26. McCulloch v. Maryland, 4 Wheat. 316, 415 (1816).
27. For a discussion of Marshall's interpretive assumptions, see G. Edward White, *The American Judicial Tradition: Profiles of Leading American Judges,* 21–22 (1988 ed.).
28. Osborne v. Bank, 9 Wheat. 738, 866 (1824).
29. Justice David Brewer, "The Movement of Coercion," 1893 address before the New York State Bar Association, quoted in White, *The American Judicial Tradition,* 145.
30. The most celebrated version of this line of comments has been Charles Evans Hughes's 1907 statement, "We live under a Constitution, but the Constitution is what the judges say it is." Hughes, address, Elmira, New York, May 3, 1907, in Charles Evans Hughes, *Addresses and Papers,* 139 (1908). Despite the frequency with which Hughes's statement has been quoted as evidence of a behavioralist view of judging, it can also be read as saying that since the Constitution is a largely general and open-ended document, judges are charged with the duty of declaring the precise meaning of constitutional principles in legal disputes requiring the application of those principles.
31. Quoted in *New York Times,* February 28, 1934, p. 14.
32. 44 *Reports of the New York State Bar Association* 263 (1934).
33. Morton Keller, *In Defense of Yesterday: James M. Beck and the Politics of Conservatism,* 157–159 (1958).
34. James M. Beck, *The Constitution of the United States,* 151–152 (1922).
35. Quoted in Keller, *In Defense of Yesterday,* 158–159.
36. Borah to Beck, December 4, 1924, Beck Papers, quoted in id., 159.
37. See, e.g., Thomas Reed Powell, "The Judiciability of Minimum Wage Legislation," 37 *Harvard Law Review* 545 (1924).
38. Thomas Reed Powell, "Constitutional Interpretation and Misinterpretation," 33 *New Republic* 297, 298 (February 7, 1923).
39. Thomas Reed Powell, "Constitutional Metaphors," 41 *New Republic* 314 (Feb-

ruary 11, 1925). This review provoked Fred Rodell, a Yale law professor who generated his own reputation for vitriolically amusing reviews, to call it "my favorite review of all time." Rodell to Powell, June 1936, quoted in Kammen, *A Machine That Would Go of Itself,* 249.

40. See Boygue Jean, "American Government," *The Nation,* April 11, 1923, pp. 436–437; William MacDonald, "Mr Beck Draws an Indictment against a Whole People," *New York Times,* August 3, 1924, p. 3; Keller, *In Defense of Yesterday,* 296, noting additional negative reviews of Beck's *The Constitution of the United States* in the *New York Evening Post,* March 14, 1923, the *New York Call,* September 2, 1923, and the *New York Tribune,* December 18, 1923.

41. The quoted phrase is from Karl Llewellyn in an August 11, 1936 letter to Edward Corwin, Corwin Papers, Princeton University Library, quoted in Kammen, *A Machine That Would Go of Itself,* 249.

42. Howard Lee McBain, *The Living Constitution,* 2–3, 272 (1927).

43. 290 U.S. 398 (1934).

44. Id. at 415–416, 418–419.

45. U.S. Constitution, Art. 1, sect. 10.

46. See Benjamin F. Wright, Jr., *The Contract Clause of the Constitution,* 4–5 (1938).

47. See, e.g., Stone v. Mississippi, 101 U.S. 814, 818–819 (1880), upholding a state law that invalidated corporate charters authorizing lotteries; Manigault v. Springs, 199 U.S. 473 (1905), upholding a state law that invalidated a contract pertaining to the damming of a navigable stream.

48. *Blaisdell,* 290 U.S. at 435.

49. Id. at 438.

50. Id. at 442.

51. Id. at 442–443 (emphasis in original).

52. Id. at 448–449.

53. Id. at 472.

54. The phrase was first used by Alexander Bickel in *The Least Dangerous Branch,* 1 (1960). For an effort to derive a long historical pedigree for the concept of a "countermajoritarian" difficulty, see Barry Freidman, "The History of the Countermajoritarian Difficulty, Part I: The Road to Judicial Supremacy," 73 *New York University Law Review* 333 (1998).

55. Charles W. Pierson, *Our Changing Constitution,* 143–144, 151 (1926).

56. Gillman, "The Problem of Political Development," and Kammen, *A Machine That Would Go of Itself,* 248–254, offer different interpretations of a number of the sources discussed in the next few pages.

57. E.g., Henry Hazlitt, "Our Obsolete Constitution," *The Nation,* February 4, 1931, pp. 124–125.

58. See Kammen, *A Machine That Would Go of Itself,* ascribing such views to Charles Beard, Vernon Parrington, Carl Becker, and J. Allen Smith.

59. For examples, see David Prescott Barrows, "The Constitution as an Element of Stability in American Life," 185 *Annals of the American Academy of Political and Social Science* 1 (May 1936); Walter F. Dodd, "The Powers of the National Government," id., 65; William J. Donovan, "The Constitution as the Guardian

of Property Rights," id., 145; William L. Ransom, "The Rights Reserved to the States and the People," id., 170.

60. Charles Beard, "The Living Constitution," id., 29, 31. For additional articles in the symposium adopting Beard's perspective, see Edward S. Corwin, "Curbing the Court," id., 45; James Hart, "A Unified Economy and States' Rights," id., 102; W. Y. Elliot, "Getting a New Constitution," id., 115; Francis W. Coker, "Property Rights as Obstacles to Progress," id., 133.

61. James Hart, "A Unified Economy and States' Rights," id., 102–103.

62. "When it is faced with precedents," Hart suggested, "[the Court] may override them . . . In view of the radically changed conditions, the Court could at any time shift its whole position by a simple appeal to what may be called the logic of new situations." Hart, "A United Economy and States' Rights," 105.

63. As Beard put it, "it seems utterly impossible to construct any mental picture of the Constitution that does not include the human personnel engaged in formulating and discharging functions under its provisions . . . [T]he Constitution . . . is what living men and women think it is." Beard, "The Living Constitution," 31, 34.

64. Of the twenty-one articles collected in the American Academy of Political and Social Science's 1936 symposium, sixteen addressed the prospective regulation of economic activity by states and the federal government.

65. Technically, the challenge to the congressional legislation at issue in *Adkins* involved the Fifth Amendment's rather than the Fourteenth Amendment's Due Process Clause. The legislation under attack in *Adkins* was assumed to be grounded on police powers because Congress was treated as having special responsibilities toward the residents of the District of Columbia, akin to those that states had toward their residents. Among those responsibilities was that of protecting the morals, safety, and health of those who resided in the District. See 261 U.S. at 528–538 (arguments of Felix Frankfurter, for the Children's Hospital, and Wade Ellis, for the petitioners challenging the statute).

66. Id. at 536–538.

67. Id. at 544.

68. Id.

69. Taft concluded that the legislation in question, although it infringed on "liberty of contract," could be justified under the police powers. His opinion worked within the established doctrinal categories of police powers jurisprudence, and accepted the established role of judges as "pricking out the boundary" between private rights and the sphere of public governance in the realm of political economy. 261 U.S. at 562. His opinion also came close to conceding that judicial formulas in police power due process cases reflected commonly held assumptions about political economy. Id. at 565.

70. Id. at 567–568.

71. See, for example, the comments of Holmes's most vocal and arguably influential acolyte in the late 1920s and 1930s, Felix Frankfurter, in "Mr. Justice Holmes and the Constitution," 41 *Harvard Law Review* 121 (1927), and *Mr. Justice Holmes and the Supreme Court* (1938). For an effort to associate Holmes's interpretive posture in cases such as *Adkins* with the jurisprudential assumptions of

the Realist movement, see Karl N. Llewellyn, "Holmes," 35 *Columbia Law Review* 485 (1935).

72. See, e.g., Leuchtenburg, *The Supreme Court Reborn,* 164–166.
73. West Coast Hotel v. Parrish, 300 U.S. at 393.
74. Id. at 394.
75. Id. at 394–395 (citing Muller v. Oregon, 208 U.S. 412 (1980).)
76. Id.
77. See id. at 400–414.
78. Id. at 391.
79. Id. at 390.
80. Id. at 399.
81. Id. at 402–403.
82. Id. at 404.
83. Id. at 402.
84. For details, see Cushman, *Rethinking the New Deal Court,* 141–153, 155–171.
85. 312 U.S. 100 (1941).
86. See Conference Notes, William O. Douglas Papers, Library of Congress; Conference Notes, Frank Murphy Papers, University of Michigan Library; Opinion draft of *Darby,* February 3, 1941, Harlan Fiske Stone Papers, Library of Congress; Hughes to Stone, January 27, 1941, Stone Papers. Cushman discusses the same sources in *Rethinking the New Deal Court,* 209.
87. Wickard v. Filburn, 317 U.S. 111, 113–116 (1942). The named respondent in the case was Claude Wickard, the secretary of the Department of Agriculture.
88. The options were set forth by Justice Robert Jackson in a memorandum to his law clerk, written on June 19, 1942. "Memorandum for Mr. Costelloe, Re: *Wickard* Case," Robert Jackson Papers, Library of Congress. Cushman makes extensive use of this memorandum and another Jackson wrote to his law clerk on July 10, 1942. See Cushman, *Rethinking the New Deal Court,* 216–219.
89. *Wickard,* 317 U.S. at 111.
90. The details of the internal Court deliberations on *Wickard,* set forth in the next several paragraphs, are taken from Cushman's more complete account in *Rethinking the New Deal Court,* 212–224.
91. These documents are in the Robert Jackson Papers in the Library of Congress.
92. Jackson, "Memorandum for Mr. Costelloe, Re: *Wickard* Case," July 10, 1942, p. 15, Robert Jackson Papers, Library of Congress. For more detail on this memorandum, see Cushman, *Rethinking the New Deal Court,* 216–219.
93. Jackson, "Memorandum to Mr. Costelloe, Re: *Wickard,*" June 19, 1942, p. 6. See the discussion in Cushman, *Rethinking the New Deal Court,* 218.
94. Jackson, "Memorandum for Mr. Costelloe, Re: *Wickard,*" July 10, 1942, p. 20. See the discussion in Cushman, *Rethinking the New Deal Court,* 218.
95. "Memorandum, AAA," p. 1, Jackson Papers. The author of the memorandum was not named but was clearly written by Jackson's law clerk. It is quoted in Cushman, *Rethinking the New Deal Court,* 304.
96. Jackson, "Memorandum for Mr. Costelloe, Re: *Wickard,*" June 19, 1942, p. 20.
97. *Wickard,* 317 U.S. at 113.
98. Id. at 120.

99. Id.
100. Id. at 128–129.

8. The Myths of Substantive Due Process

1. The strongest evidence of this story's familiarity and conventional acceptance is that it has been told in recent encyclopedias of constitutional law and constitutional history. See Laurence H. Tribe, "Substantive Due Process of Law," in 4 Leonard W. Levy et al., *Encyclopedia of the American Constitution, 1796–1802* (4 vols., 1986); Donald G. Nieman, "The Fourteenth Amendment Receives Its First Judicial Construction," Fred D. Ragan, "'Mere Meddlesome Interferences': The Apogee of Substantive Due Process," and C. Herman Pritchett, "The Chambermaid's Revenge," in John W. Johnson, ed., *Historic U.S. Court Cases 1690–1990: An Encyclopedia*, 252–260, 269–277, 279–283 (1992).
2. 198 U.S. 45 (1905).
3. That opinion is generally acknowledged to be Allgeyer v. Louisiana, 165 U.S. 578 (1897), where a judicial definition of "liberty" in the Fourteenth Amendment as embracing "the right of the citizen to be free in the enjoyment of all of his faculties" was employed to invalidate a Louisiana statute preventing Louisiana residents from entering into contracts with out-of-state insurance companies.
4. 198 U.S. at 57, 64.
5. Id. at 75, 76.
6. Griswold v. Connecticut, 381 U.S. 479 (1965). Justice William O. Douglas's opinion for the Court in *Griswold* took the position that the Court was not invalidating the Connecticut birth control statute through a "substantive" reading of "liberty" in the Fourteenth Amendment's Due Process Clause. "[W]e decline this invitation," he announced, "as we did in *West Coast Hotel v. Parrish*." Id. at 481–482. Eight years later, in Roe v. Wade, however, the Court admitted that the "liberty" to procreate or to choose to have an abortion was grounded in the Due Process Clauses, and its recognition could make a statute substantively invalid. Roe v. Wade, 410 U.S. 113, 168 (1973).
7. See, e.g., Goldberg v. Kelly, 397 U.S. 254 (1970).
8. Beginning with Charles W. McCurdy's "Justice Field and the Jurisprudence of Government-Business Relations: Some Parameters of Laissez-Faire Constitutionalism," 61 *Journal of American History* 970 (1975), a number of historical works in the last three decades, especially since the mid-1980s, have begun to recreate the categories and formulas of the guardian review model of police powers/due process jurisprudence. Examples of revisionist work include Michael Les Benedict, "Laissez-Faire and Liberty: A Re-Evaluation of the Meaning and Origins of Laissez-Faire Constitutionalism," 3 *Law and History Review* 293 (1985); William Forbath, "The Ambiguities of Free Labor: Labor and Law in the Gilded Age," 1985 *Wisconsin Law Review* 767 (1985); and three books, Morton Horwitz, *The Transformation of American Law 1870–1960*, 19–31 (1992); Owen Fiss, *Troubled Beginnings of the Modern State, 1888–1910*, 156–160 (1993); and Howard Gillman, *The Constitution Besieged: The Rise and De-*

mise of Lochner Era Police Powers Jurisprudence, 61–145 (1993). A particularly succinct overview of revisionist scholarship as it affects the liberty of contract line of cases is McCurdy, "The Liberty of Contract Regime in American Law," in Harry Scheiber, ed., *The State and Freedom of Contract,* 161–197 (1998).

9. *Lochner,* 198 U.S. at 76.

10. Id.

11. 234 U.S. 224 (1914).

12. Draft of opinion of the Court, Keokee Consolidated Coke Co. v. Taylor, in Oliver Wendell Holmes Papers, microfilm edition (1985), University of Virginia School of Law. I am indebted to Charles McCurdy for first calling this draft opinion to my attention. The *Taylor* draft opinion is also cited in Alexander M. Bickel and Benno C. Schmidt, Jr., *The Judiciary and Responsible Government,* 297–298 (1984).

13. See Bickel and Schmidt, *The Judiciary and Responsible Government,* 298.

14. Holmes's old friend Frederick Pollock did note, in a 1905 article in the *Law Quarterly Review,* a British journal, that "we are much inclined to agree with Mr. Justice Holmes" that it was "no business of the Supreme Court of the United States to dogmatize on social or economic theories." Pollock added, however, that "English lawyers are perhaps naturally prejudiced in favor of the competence of legislators." He assumed that the legislation under review in *Lochner* was an appropriate public health measure. So although it is possible to take his comments as evidence that some readers of Holmes's *Lochner* dissent saw it as a general attack on guardian review, it is equally possible to take them as only suggesting that Holmes was correct in agreeing with the legislature that the statute was a "general" public health measure rather than "partial" class legislation. See Pollock, "The New York Labor Law and the Fourteenth Amendment," 21 *Law Quarterly Review* 211, 212 (1905).

15. For example, Ernst Freund's 1905 comment, "Limitation of Hours of Labor and the Federal Supreme Court," 17 *Green Bag* 411 (1905), did not distinguish between the dissents of Holmes and Harlan, taking them both to have suggested that *Lochner* involved "an issue of judgment," and that the Court should have followed the New York state courts, which "had approved the judgment of the legislature." Freund pointed out that the statute in *Lochner* had been justified on health grounds, and that had it been justified as "a measure for the social and economic advancement of bakers' employees [it] would doubtless have been open to the objection of being partial or class legislation." Id. at 412, 416. See also Jefferson B. Browne, "The Super-Constitution," 54 *American Law Review* 321, 342 (1920), noting, in the course of discussing *Lochner,* that "legislation in favor of a class is as obnoxious as legislation against a class . . . there must be no special law for a particular person or a particular class."

16. *The Survey,* January 1913, at 3, reprinted in Felix Frankfurter, *Law and Politics,* 4 (Archibald MacLeish and Edward S. Pritchard, eds., 1962).

17. See G. Edward White, *The Marshall Court and Cultural Change,* 5–10 (1988).

18. For additional evidence of this modern conception of liberty, see Richard T. Ely, *Studies in Evolution of Industrial Society,* 400–403 (1903), in which Ely defined "true liberty" as "the expression of the positive powers of the individual," and

argued that its protection required state action to regulate "nominally free contract."

19. Tyson & Brother v. Banton, 273 U.S. 418, 446 (1927).

20. One example, for Holmes, was when a legislature blatantly took property from one class of citizens and gave it to another. See his opinion in Pennsylvania Coal Co. v. Mahon, 260 U.S. 399 (1922), invalidating a Pennsylvania statute forbidding the mining of anthracite coal under public buildings, public thoroughfares, and private homes.

21. In some liberty of contract decisions Brandeis did not merely protest against the indiscriminate judicial application of the constitutional principles embodied in "liberty" to legislation redistributing the costs and benefits or particular economic transactions, he sought to demonstrate the efficacy of the legislation being challenged, sometimes by the use of empirical data. See, e.g., Adams v. Tanner, 244 U.S. 590 (1917); Truax v. Corrigan, 257 U.S. 312, 354 (1922) (dissent); Burns Baking Co. v. Bryan, 264 U.S. 504, 517 (1924) (dissent).

22. New York Central R.R. Co. v. White, 243 U.S. 188, 207 (1917).

23. See the discussion and cases cited in McCurdy, "The Liberty of Contract Regime in American Law," 184–189.

24. West Coast Hotel v. Parrish, 300 U.S. 379, 393 (1937).

25. Other examples of pre-World War I criticism of liberty of contract by progressives include Roscoe Pound, "Liberty of Contract," 18 *Yale Law Journal* 454 (1909), and Learned Hand, "Due Process of Law and the Eight-Hour Day," 21 *Harvard Law Review* 495 (1908). Two years after *Adkins,* in Murphy v. Sardell, 269 U.S. 530 (1925), a unanimous Court summarily affirmed the holding of a lower federal court that the decision in *Adkins* also meant that state minimum wage statutes, such as the Arizona statute at issue, were unconstitutional. Holmes concurred in the *Murphy* decision.

26. See [Felix Frankfurter,] "The Same Mr. Taft," *The New Republic,* January 18, 1922; [Felix Frankfurter], "The Red Terror of Judicial Reform," *The New Republic,* October 1, 1924.

27. "What an intolerable Court you have just now," Laski wrote to Holmes after the *Adkins* decision. Harold Laski to Oliver Wendell Holmes, Jr., April 13, 1923, in 1 Mark DeWolfe Howe, ed., *Holmes-Laski Letters,* 493 (2 vols., 1953).

28. The National Consumers' League, *The Supreme Court and Minimum Wage Legislation* (1925).

29. See, e.g., Robert E. Cushman, "The Social and Economic Interpretation of the Fourteenth Amendment," 20 *Michigan Law Review* 737 (1922).

30. Charles Warren, "The New 'Liberty' under the Fourteenth Amendment," 39 *Harvard Law Review* 431, 432 (1926).

31. Id. at 432.

32. Id. at 464–465.

33. Id. at 433–445; the quoted language is at 440.

34. Id. at 440–445, citing Mobile & Ohio R.R. v. Tennessee, 153 U.S. 486, 506 (1894).

35. Id. at 445–449, citing Allgeyer v. Louisiana, 165 U.S. 578 (1897).

36. Id. at 458.

37. Id. at 431.
38. See Robert E. Cushman, "Due Process of Law," in 5 *Encyclopedia of the Social Sciences,* 265, 266 (1931), an encapsulation and updating of his *Michigan Law Review* article.
39. See Walton H. Hamilton, "The Path of Due Process of Law," in Conyers Read, ed., *The Constitution Reconsidered,* 167 (1938).
40. DeJonge v. Oregon, 299 U.S. 353 (1937).
41. Connally v. General Construction Co., 269 U.S. 385 (1926).
42. Powell v. Alabama, 287 U.S. 45 (1932). This line of cases was not always treated by the Court as resting on "incorporation." Sometimes the "liberties" protected by the Court were forthrightly associated, as in *Powell,* with "due process" itself.
43. Noel T. Dowling, *Cases on Constitutional Law,* xiv, xv (1937 ed.). See also Dudley O. McGovney, *Cases on Constitutional Law,* viii (2d ed., 1935), distinguishing between "Due Process . . . As a Standard of Validity of Modes of Law Enforcement" and "As a Standard of Validity of the Substance or Purpose of Legislation," and Lawrence B. Evans, *Cases on American Constitutional Law,* xiii–xiv (1938), distinguishing between "Due Process in Relation to Procedure" and "Due Process in Relation to the Police Power." Despite Evans's organization, he did not suggest that "procedural" due process cases required a different judicial approach from "police power" due process cases: the purpose of his distinction was to highlight the consequences of a successful liberty-based challenge.

 For a comparable treatment of due process cases in a constitutional law treatise from the same time period, see Hugh Willis, *Constitutional Law of the United States,* vii–viii (1936), distinguishing between "Due Process as a Matter of Procedure" and "Due Process as a Matter of Substance," but sweeping "liberty of contract," "liberty of mind," and First Amendment incorporated due process cases into the latter category, while treating all due process cases as susceptible to standard guardian review analysis.
44. Compare Henry Rottschaefer, *Cases on Constitutional Law,* vii, viii (1932), with Henry Rottschaefer, *Cases and Materials on Constitutional Law,* vii (2d ed., 1948).
45. Robert Maurer, *Cases on Constitutional Law,* 327 (1941).
46. Id., xiii, xiv, xvi, xvii.
47. See Samuel Weaver, *Constitutional Law and Its Administration,* xv, xvi, xvii (1946), confining "Due Process of Law" to procedure cases, creating a category of "Political and Public Rights" in which noneconomic incorporated rights cases were placed, and retaining a "Police Power" category that included *Lochner*-type cases. For a comparable treatment, see Walter Dodd, *Cases on Constitutional Law,* xx, xxi (4th ed., 1949).
48. Chicago, Burlington & Quincy Railroad v. Chicago, 166 U.S. 226 (1897).
49. See the argument for the petitioner in Schechter Poultry Corp. v. United States, 295 U.S. 495, 501–503 (1935), and the lower federal court decisions in National Broadcasting Co. v. Federal Communications Commission, 132 F.2d 545, 549–550 (D.C. Cir. 1942), Ochikubo v. Bonsteel, 60 F. Supp. 916, 923 (S.D. Cal. 1945), and United States v. General Petroleum of California, 73 F. Supp. 225, 252 (S.D. Cal. 1946).

50. 334 U.S. 62, 90 (1948).
51. 343 U.S. 250, 277 (1952).
52. Noel T. Dowling, Cases on Constitutional Law, xviii–xix (4th ed., 1950).
53. Id., 925.
54. 2 Paul Freund et al., *Constitutional Law: Cases and Materials*, vi (2 vols., 1954).
55. Paul G. Kauper described this category as "Procedural Limitations in Criminal Cases and in Civil Proceedings," in his *Constitutional Law*, xiii–xiv (1954).
56. 2 Freund, *Constitutional Law*, ix.
57. Kauper called this category "Substantive Rights." Kauper, *Constitutional Law*, xiv.
58. Kauper, *Constitutional Law*, xiv; Ray Forrester, *Constitutional Law: Cases and Materials*, xix (1959).
59. Edward Barrett described this category as "Due Process: Business and Economic Relationships." Barrett, *Constitutional Law: Cases and Materials*, xxi–xxii (1959).
60. Kauper, *Constitutional Law*, xv; Forrester, *Constitutional Law*, xxxii.
61. See, e.g., Barrett, *Constitutional Law*, 1222. A few 1950s casebook editions retained "police power" as a descriptive subject matter category, using it in the discussion of cases that would today be treated as Takings Clause cases or eminent domain cases. See, e.g., 2 Freund, *Constitutional Law*, 1199–1212; Forrester, *Constitutional Law*, 789–797.
62. See, e.g., Kauper, *Constitutional Law*, 890.
63. Monrad G. Paulsen, "The Persistence of Substantive Due Process in the States," 34 *Minnesota Law Review* 91 (1950).
64. Paulsen cited Walton Hamilton's "The Path of Due Process of Law" as "the best telling of the history." Paulsen, "The Persistence of Substantive Due Process in the States," 92.
65. Id., 92–93.
66. Rosco J. Tresolini, *American Constitutional Law*, xvii, xviii (1959).
67. Id., 315–322.
68. Id., 315.
69. Id., 321.
70. Id., 322.
71. Examples are the line of abortion rights cases stretching from Roe v. Wade, 410 U.S. 113 (1973), to Planned Parenthood of Southeastern Pennsylvania v. Casey, 505 U.S. 833 (1992); Moore v. City of East Cleveland, 431 U.S. 494 (1977), finding that "liberty" in the Due Process Clauses encompasses freedom of personal choice in the composition of families; and Cruzan v. Director, Missouri Department of Health, 457 U.S. 261 (1990), finding a constitutionally protected "liberty" to refuse unwanted livesaving medical treatment.
72. See, e.g., Walter F. Murphy et al., *American Constitutional Interpretation*, 98–100, 772–73, 1083–84 (separating incorporation cases from other due process cases); 940–946 (the "rise and fall" narrative); 1147–54 (confining contemporary substantive due process cases to privacy or family relations) (1986). See also Geoffrey Stone et al., *Constitutional Law*, 804–813 (separating incorporation cases); 813–842 (the "rise and fall" narrative, characterized as including "economic substantive due process" cases); 1660–63 (identifying the term "police

power" with specific eminent domain cases); 940–1048 (characterizing substantive due process cases related to privacy, personhood, or family relations as "modern substantive due process" cases) (3rd ed., 1996).
73. For a fuller discussion, see G. Edward White, *Justice Oliver Wendell Holmes: Law and the Inner Self,* 391–396 (1993).
74. 260 U.S. at 413.

9. The Canonization and Demonization of Judges

1. See the discussion in G. Edward White, *The Marshall Court and Cultural Change,* 195–200 (1988).
2. An illustrative example can be found in comments on the Supreme Court's sequence of legal tender decisions, Hepburn v. Griswold, 75 U.S. (8 Wall.) 603 (1870), and Legal Tender Cases, 79 U.S. (12 Wall.) 457 (1871), in which a newly constituted Court flatly overruled a decision it had handed down one year before. The sequence was explained by contemporary journals directed at the general public as being influenced by partisan considerations. *Harper's Weekly,* in an 1871 comment on the sequence, noted that it was "sorry to add . . . that except for certain political hopes and expectations that opinion would probably not have been rendered." *Harper's* was referring to the presidential ambitions of Chief Justice Salmon P. Chase, who had written the majority opinion of the Court in *Hepburn. Harper's Weekly,* May 20, 1871, p. 450. Nonetheless, James Bradley Thayer's discussion of the cases, in an 1887 issue of the *Harvard Law Review,* was confined entirely to legal issues. James Bradley Thayer, "Legal Tender," 1 *Harvard Law Review* 73 (1887).
3. Charles Carpenter, "Oliver Wendell Holmes, Jurist," 8 *Oregon Law Review* 269, 270 (1929). Readers seeking more detail on the creation of images for Holmes and Brandeis should consult G. Edward White, "The Canonization of Holmes and Brandeis," 70 *New York University Law Review* 576 (1995).
4. Irving Villard, "Issues and Men: The Great Judge," 140 *Nation* 323 (1935).
5. Felix Frankfurter, "The Constitutional Opinions of Mr. Justice Holmes," 29 *Harvard Law Review* 683 (1916).
6. Felix Frankfurter, *Mr. Justice Holmes and the Supreme Court,* 43–44 (1938).
7. Felix Frankfurter, "Twenty Years of Mr. Justice Holmes's Constitutional Opinions," 36 *Harvard Law Review* 909 (1923).
8. O. W. Holmes, *Collected Legal Papers* (1920). For a discussion of Laski's role in the appearance of the book, see G. Edward White, *Justice Oliver Wendell Holmes: Law and the Inner Self,* 365–366 (1993).
9. Editorial, *New Republic,* December 11, 1915, p. 132. The editorial may well have been written by Frankfurter.
10. Philip Littell, "Books and Things," *New Republic,* May 29, 1915, p. 100.
11. Elizabeth Sergeant, "Oliver Wendell Holmes," *New Republic,* December 8, 1926, pp. 59, 60, 63–64.
12. James Pollard, "Justice Holmes, Champion of the Common Man," *New York Times,* December 1, 1929, sect. 4, p. 4.
13. Carpenter, "Oliver Wendell Holmes, Jurist," 270.

14. See, e.g., *New York Times,* January 13, 1932, sect. 1, p. 3 ("liberal and lovable philosopher"); *New York Times,* March 6, 1935, sect. 1, p. 1 ("chief liberal of [the] supreme bench for 29 years").

15. Silas Bent, *Justice Oliver Wendell Holmes,* 72 (1932).

16. Morris Cohen, "Justice Holmes," *New Republic,* April 3, 1935, pp. 206–207.

17. Adolf Berle, "Justice Holmes: Liberal," 24 *Survey Graphic* 178 (1935).

18. For the details of that controversy, which stretched into the early 1950s, see G. Edward White, *Patterns of American Legal Thought,* 211–216 (1978).

19. I. F. Stone, "Justice Holmes," *Nation,* July 17, 1943, p. 76.

20. Charles E. Clark, "Mr. Justice Holmes," *New Republic,* June 28, 1943, p. 868.

21. Max Rheinstein, "Book Review," 29 *Virginia Law Review* 1074, 1076–77 (1943).

22. Edmund Wilson, "The Mind of Justice Holmes and Mrs. Bowen's Mind," *New Yorker,* April 22, 1944, p. 75.

23. Max Lerner, "Olympian in Butter," *New Republic,* May 29, 1944, p. 742.

24. Matthew A. Fitzsimons, "Book Review," 30 *Catholic Historical Review* 501 (1944).

25. The play was Emmet Lavery's *The Magnificent Yankee* (1946); the movie, with the same title, appeared in 1950, produced by Metro-Goldwyn-Mayer.

26. For more detail on Holmes's fluctuating image from the 1960s through the 1980s, see G. Edward White, "The Rise and Fall of Justice Holmes," in White, *Patterns of American Legal Thought,* 194–226, and G. Edward White, "Looking at Holmes in the Mirror," in White, *Intervention and Detachment: Essays in Legal History and Jurisprudence,* 106–131 (1994).

27. There had been an earlier effort to characterize Supreme Court justices in ideological terms, Gustavus Myers's *History of the Supreme Court of the United States,* which appeared in 1912. But Myers's book cannot be treated as evidence that prior to the 1930s commentators were making an effort to separate the individual jurisprudential contributions of justices from their roles as members of a collective institutional body, or as evidence that commentators were attaching ideological labels to judges, because the labels Myers employed were applied uniformly to the Court and all its justices. Myers asserted that "the Supreme Court as an institution has throughout its whole existence incarnated into final law the demands of the dominant and interconnected sections of the ruling class," and then proceeded to supply information about individual judges that confirmed their class sympathies. Id., 7.

28. Louis D. Brandeis, "The Living Law," 10 *Illinois Law Review* 461 (1916).

29. Louis D. Brandeis, *Business—A Profession* (1914); Louis D. Brandeis, *Other People's Money and How the Bankers Use It* (1914).

30. See "Brandeis," *New Republic,* February 5, 1916, pp. 4–6; "Brandeis and the Shoe Machinery Company," *New Republic,* March 4, 1916, pp. 117–119; "The Close of the Brandeis Case," *New Republic,* June 10, 1916, pp. 134–135.

31. Two of those discussed Brandeis's involvement with the Zionist movement. See "Rebuilding Zion," *Independent,* August 27, 1930, p. 154; Dorothy Thompson, "The Hope of a New Palestine," *Outlook,* September 8, 1920, pp. 54, 55. The third was a pictorial essay in the *Survey* in 1920 that grouped Brandeis with

Holmes and Charles Evans Hughes (not then on the Supreme Court) and other "men and women who recently broke silence and revealed a great body of public opinion ready to uphold the liberties of the founders." "Keepers of the Faith," *Survey,* February 7, 1920, pp. 535, 536. The *Survey* essay's reference was to the group's support for freedom of speech.

32. 285 U.S. 262, 280 (1932).

33. The *Times* had suggested that Brandeis was a "radical," better suited for "the legislative hall" than for "the Bench of the Supreme Court." See A. L. Todd, *Justice on Trial,* 242 (1964).

34. See Stephen W. Baskerville, *Of Laws and Limitations: An Intellectual Portrait of Louis Dembitz Brandeis,* 305–307 (1994). The Baskerville volume is an excellent overview of Brandeis's social and political attitudes and a searching analysis of Brandeis's agenda as a judge.

35. Quoted in *New York Times,* March 22, 1932, p. 2.

36. Id.

37. For an early manifestation of this image, see Edwin W. Patterson, "Mr. Justice Brandeis—75 Years Old," *Nation,* November 11, 1931, p. 513: "Fortunate indeed is he who can live to see his earlier insights accepted among the enduring ideas of his generation. Mr. Justice Brandeis, on his seventy-fifth birthday, is thus to be congratulated . . . His insights were prophetic."

38. See Baskerville, *Of Laws and Limitations,* 153, 179–180; Philippa Strum, *Brandeis: Beyond Progressivism,* 143–147 (1993).

39. *New York Times,* November 8, 1931, sect. 3, p. 1.

40. 285 U.S. at 310.

41. *New York Times,* November 8, 1936, p. 3.

42. R. L. Duffus, "Justice Brandeis: Crusader at Eighty," *New York Times Magazine,* November 8, 1936, pp. 4, 24.

43. 79 *University of Pennsylvania Law Review* 665 (1931).

44. Id. at 668.

45. Id. at 683, 697, 705.

46. Max Lerner, "Homage to Brandeis," *Nation,* February 25, 1939, p. 222.

47. Charles Evans Hughes, quoted in *New York Times,* October 7, 1941, p. 24; Zechariah Chafee, Jr., "Unique among Judges in Modern Outlook," *Harvard Alumni Bulletin,* October 18, 1941, in Irving Dilliard, ed., *Mr. Justice Brandeis: Great American,* 67 (1941).

48. Warren H. Pierce, "Shaper of Economic Thought," *Chicago Daily Times,* October 7, 1941; Edward A. Evans, "Believed in Realities, Not Formulas," *Denver Rocky Mountain News,* October 6, 1941, in Dilliard, *Mr. Justice Brandeis,* 58, 84.

49. Pierce, "Shaper of Economic Thought," in id., 58.

50. A. A. Imberman, "Evolved a New Judicial Technique," *Des Moines Register,* October 7, 1941, in id., 75.

51. See Baskerville, *Of Laws and Limitations,* 305–332.

52. See id., 324–330.

53. Id., 326–331.

54. In addition to the works of Yosal Rogat in the 1960s, such as "Mr. Justice

Holmes: A Dissenting Opinion," 15 *Stanford Law Review* 3 (1963) and "The Judge as Spectator," 31 *University of Chicago Law Review* 213 (1964), see Irving Bernstein, "The Conservative Justice Holmes," 23 *New England Quarterly* 435 (1950). Bernstein asserted that the "cherished American myth . . . that Oliver Wendell Holmes was a 'liberal' [was as] baseless as the tale of Washington and the cherry tree." Id. at 445.

55. Alexander M. Bickel, *The Unpublished Opinions of Mr. Justice Brandeis,* 33, 158 (1957).

56. See, e.g., John P. Frank, "Book Review," 10 *Journal of Legal Education* 401, 404 (1959); Henry J. Friendly, "Book Review," 106 *University of Pennsylvania Law Review* 766 (1958). Frank did mention that he felt personally disillusioned by the information. A contemporary reader may find it interesting that commentators were more concerned with the propriety of Bickel's disclosures than with that of Brandeis's negotiations.

57. Louis L. Jaffe, "Was Brandeis an Activist? The Search for Intermediate Premises," 80 *Harvard Law Review* 986, 987 (1967).

58. See generally G. Edward White, "The Evolution of Reasoned Elaboration," 59 *Virginia Law Review* 279 (1973).

59. Jaffe, "Was Brandeis an Activist?" 989.

60. Robert Cover, "The Framing of Justice Brandeis," *New Republic,* May 5, 1982, p. 17.

61. Id., 18, 20. Cover suggested that the extraordinarily close personal relationship between Brandeis and Frankfurter—Brandeis once described Frankfurter as being his "half brother, half son"—made this interpretation plausible. Cover was referring to a letter quoted in Melvin Urofsky and David W. Levy, eds., *"Half Brother, Half Son": The Letters of Louis D. Brandeis to Felix Frankfurter,* 5 (1991).

62. Cover, "The Framing of Justice Brandeis," 17, 21. Emphasis in original.

63. See, e.g., Myron H. Bright and David T. Smorodin, "A Flawed Tale," 16 *Loyola Law Review* 205, 206 (1983); John D. French, "Book Review," 67 *Minnesota Law Review* 287, 288 (1982).

64. See Baskerville, *Of Laws and Limitations,* 273–274.

65. Brandeis set forth such a list in his separate opinion in Ashwander v. Tennessee Valley Authority, 297 U.S. 288, 347–354 (1936).

66. Samuel Krislov, "Reappraising Brandeis: Comments on Recent Works," 4 *Constitutional Commentary* 319, 319–320 (1987).

67. "The Great Pragmatist," *New York Herald Tribune,* October 6, 1941, in Dilliard, *Mr. Justice Brandeis,* 60.

68. Daniel A. Farber, "Reinventing Brandeis: Legal Pragmatism for the Twenty-First Century," 1995 *Illinois Law Review* 163, 164.

69. In a 1994 collection of biographical essays Van Devanter, McReynolds, Sutherland, and Butler were each identified as one of the "Four Horsemen," a group that was characterized, alternatively, as "the Court's conservative bloc . . . in the 1930s," a "reactionary . . . align[ment]," a "conservative" and "intransigen[t]" group of justices, and a group that "consistently opposed the economic programs of Franklin D. Roosevelt." See David J. Danelski, "Pierce Butler"; Mi-

chael Allan Wolf, "James Clark McReynolds" and "George Sutherland"; and Rebecca Shepherd Shoemaker, "Willis Van Devanter," in Melvin I. Urofsky, ed., *The Supreme Court Justices: A Biographical Dictionary*, 84, 298, 449, 487 (1994).

For a devastating critique of this characterization, see Barry Cushman, "The Secret Lives of the Four Horsemen," 83 *Virginia Law Review* 559 (1997), which demonstrates that not only were the individual decisions of Van Devanter, McReynolds, Sutherland, and Butler not invariably "conservative" by the terms of the conventional account, but the "Four Horsemen" regularly opposed one another's positions.

70. See Albert P. Blaustein and Roy M. Mersky, "Rating Supreme Court Justices," 58 *American Bar Association Journal* 1183, 1186 (1972); and Roy Mersky and Gary Hartman, "Rating the Justices," 84 *Law Library Journal* 113 (1992).

71. For a description of the editorial shift in the *New York Times*, see Richard Shepard, *The Paper's Papers: A Reporter's Journey through the Archives of the New York Times* (1996). Evidence of similar editorial shifts among urban papers in the 1930s can be seen in the *Boston Globe*, the *Philadelphia Inquirer*, the *Baltimore Sun*, the *Washington Post*, the *Cleveland Plain Dealer*, and the *St. Louis Post-Dispatch*. The *Chicago Tribune* was conspicuous in maintaining a consistently conservative editorial position from the early 1930s through the Second World War.

72. United States v. Standard Oil Co., 173 Fed. 177 (C.C.E.D. Mo. 1909).

73. *New York Times*, December 14, 1910, p. 2.

74. *New York Times*, July 27, 1914, p. 1.

75. *New York Times*, August 19, 1914, p. 9.

76. In 1925 the *Times* gave a brief report of a speech McReynolds made to the Tennessee Society of New York. *New York Times*, January 9, 1925, p. 3.

77. The *Times* reported that fact, mentioning only that "the Senate paid a compliment to ex-Senator Sutherland by confirming his nomination immediately in open session . . . The confirmation was unanimous." *New York Times*, September 6, 1922, p. 19.

78. *New York Times*, September 10, 1922, p. 2.

79. *New York World*, November 25, 1922, quoted in David J. Danelski, *A Supreme Court Justice Is Appointed*, 90 (1964). The Danelski study remains the single most illuminating work on Butler's career.

80. *New York Times*, November 25, 1922, quoted in id., 90–91.

81. "No Longer Supreme," *Nation*, December 13, 1922, p. 653 ("Mr. Harding is trying to pack the Supreme Court with friends of the railroads"); "Pierce Butler and the Rule of Reason," *New Republic*, December 20, 1922, p. 82 ("the kind of man who would assuredly use a warped or doubtful interpretation of a phrase in the Constitution to prevent needed experiments in economics and government").

82. See Danelski, *A Supreme Court Justice Is Appointed*, 137–138.

83. *New York Times*, December 23, 1922, quoted in id., 139.

84. "From Log Cabin of West to Supreme Court Bench," *New York Times*, December 3, 1922, p. 3.

85. The fact that Butler's views on political and social issues were generally un-

known at the time of his appointment did not prevent commentators on his nomination from suggesting that he would be likely to adopt an "anti-progressive" stance as a judge. Even though there had been far more evidence available to commentators about Van Devanter's judicial tendencies when he was nominated in 1910, they had not made comparable suggestions.

86. Mildred Adams, "Nine Men the Nation Watches Intently," *New York Times Magazine*, February 18, 1934, p. 4.

87. 290 U.S. 398 (1934).

88. 291 U.S. 502 (1934).

89. Adams, "Nine Men the Nation Watches Intently," p. 4.

90. Id. at 5.

91. Id.

92. R. L. Duffus, "Nine Philosophers of Our High Court," *New York Times Magazine*, April 7, 1935, p. 9.

93. Id., 17.

94. 297 U.S. 1 (1936).

95. "Court Line-Up on New Deal," *New York Times*, January 6, 1936, p. 10.

96. Arthur Krock, "Nine Judges—and Nine Men, Too," *New York Times Magazine*, March 29, 1936, p. 1.

97. Id., 1–2.

98. Drew Pearson and Robert S. Allen, *The Nine Old Men* (1936).

99. Id., 18.

100. Id., 185, 195–196.

101. Id., 230, 231, 233, 237.

102. Id., 198, 199, 200–201, 206.

103. Id., 116, 119, 127, 133, 136, 137.

104. See, respectively, West Coast Hotel v. Parrish, 300 U.S. 379 (1937); Wright v. Vinton Branch, 300 U.S. 440 (1937); National Labor Relations Board v. Jones & Laughlin Steel Corp., 301 U.S. 1 (1937); Stewart Machine Co. v. Davis, 301 U.S. 548 (1937); and Helvering v. Davis, 301 U.S. 619 (1937). The last two cases both involved the Social Security Act.

105. See Russell Porter, "Truth and Justice for All," *New York Times Magazine*, May 28, 1939, p. 6.

106. *New York Times*, May 19, 1937, pp. 1, 18.

107. "Van Devanter Dies, Ex-Justice Was 81," *New York Times*, February 9, 1941, p. 3.

108. "Justice Van Devanter," *New York Times*, February 10, 1941, p. 16.

109. Delbert Clark, "Staunch States' Righter of Our High Court," *New York Times Magazine*, May 23, 1937, p. 7.

110. "Justice McReynolds," *New York Times*, August 26, 1946, p. 22.

111. This characterization was made despite the *Times*'s own findings that Sutherland had written a majority opinion in the 1936 Term "sustaining the right of the government to finance public electric plans," and that he had also voted in that term in favor of a revised municipal bankruptcy law and a revised railroad pension act. "Sutherland Quits Supreme Court; Past 75, He Notes," *New York Times*, January 6, 1938, pp. 1, 10.

112. "George Sutherland Dies in Berkshires," *New York Times*, July 19, 1942, p. 31.

113. "Many Mentioned for High Court," *New York Times,* November 17, 1939, pp. 1, 14.

114. "Associate Justice Butler," *New York Times,* November 17, 1939, p. 20.

115. For some examples from police power/due process cases in the New Deal period in which one of the "Four Horsemen" wrote a majority opinion in which the others joined, see Mintz v. Baldwin, 289 U.S. 346 (1933) (Butler, whose opinion was joined by Van Devanter, McReynolds, and Sutherland, upholding a state statute requiring imported cattle to be certified against infectious disease); Fish Flour Co. v. Gentry, 297 U.S. 422 (1936) (Sutherland, whose opinion was joined by Van Devanter, McReynolds, and Butler, upholding a state statute regulating the processing of sardines); and National Fertilizer Association v. Bradley, 301 U.S. 178 (1937) (McReynolds, whose opinion was joined by Van Devanter, Sutherland, and Butler, upholding a state law requiring labels on products used in the fertilization of crops). For earlier examples of cases in which one of the four justices wrote an opinion, joined by the others, sustaining legislation against a Contracts Clause challenge, see Rooker v. Fidelity Trust Co., 261 U.S. 114 (1923) (Van Devanter, joined by McReynolds, Sutherland, and Butler); Columbia Railway Gas & Electric Co. v. South Carolina, 261 U.S. 236 (1923) (Sutherland, joined by Van Devanter, McReynolds, and Butler); and Millsaps College v. City of Jackson, 275 U.S. 129 (1927) (McReynolds, joined by Van Devanter, Sutherland, and Butler).

116. For examples from the New Deal period, see Guaranty Trust Co. v. Blodgett, 287 U.S. 509 (1933) (Sutherland, joined by Van Devanter, McReynolds, and Butler, dismissing a Contracts Clause challenge to a state tax); Roberts v. Richland Irrigation District, 289 U.S. 71 (1933) (McReynolds, joined by Van Devanter, Sutherland, and Butler, upholding irrigation tax assessment on taxpayer who demonstrated that his taxes exceeded the benefits he received from irrigation); and Liggett & Myers Tobacco Co. v. United States, 299 U.S. 383 (1937) (McReynolds, joined by Van Devanter, Sutherland, and Butler, upholding a federal tax on tobacco products used in state hospitals). For numerous other examples, see Cushman, "The Secret Lives of the Four Horsemen," 586–590.

117. See, e.g., Ashwander v. Tennessee Valley Authority, 297 U.S. 288 (1936), where only McReynolds dissented from an opinion holding that Congress had power to create a public authority that could sell electricity in competition with private power companies; Wright v. Vinton Branch, 300 U.S. 440 (1937), where all four justices joined an opinion upholding the constitutionality of national bankruptcy legislation; and Alabama Power Co. v. Ickes, 302 U.S. 464 (1938), where Sutherland, for McReynolds and Butler (Van Devanter having retired), denied a power company standing to challenge grants and loans made by a unit of the Public Works Administration to finance the construction of electrical distribution systems. For additional examples, see Cushman, "The Secret Lives of the Four Horsemen," 604, 624.

118. For examples of cases in which one of the Four Horsemen, joined by the others, upheld the powers of the Interstate Commerce Commission, see United States v. New River Co., 265 U.S. 533 (1924) (Butler, joined by Van Devanter,

McReynolds, and Sutherland); Standard Oil Co. v. United States, 283 U.S. 235 (1931) (Sutherland, joined by Van Devanter, McReynolds, and Butler); Louisiana Public Service Commission v. Texas & Northern Oklahoma Railroad, 284 U.S. 125 (1931) (Butler, joined by Van Devanter, McReynolds, and Sutherland); and United States v. Illinois Central Railroad, 291 U.S. 457 (1934) (Sutherland, joined by Van Devanter, McReynolds, and Butler). For examples of cases in which all of the four justices, or the three remaining justices in the group, joined opinions upholding the powers of the Federal Trade Commission to issue cease and desist orders, see FTC v. Pacific States Paper Trade Association, 273 U.S. 52 (1927) (Butler for the Court, joined by Van Devanter, McReynolds, and Sutherland); FTC v. Algoma Lumber Co., 291 U.S. 67 (1934) (all four justices join the opinion of the Court); and FTC v. Standard Education Society, 302 U.S. 112 (1937) (McReynolds, Sutherland, and Butler join the opinion of the Court; Van Devanter retired).

119. For examples of cases in which the "Horsemen" voted to invalidate criminal convictions because they believed law enforcement officials had violated the constitutional rights of defendants, see Gambino v. United States, 275 U.S. 452 (1927) (Van Devanter, McReynolds, Sutherland, and Butler join opinion of the Court finding an illegal search and seizure under the Fourth Amendment); Byars v. United States, 273 U.S. 28 (1927) (Sutherland, joined by Van Devanter, McReynolds, and Butler, overturning conviction on the basis of an illegal search and seizure); United States v. Lefkowitz, 285 U.S. 452 (1932) (Butler, joined by Van Devanter, McReynolds, and Sutherland, overturning conviction on ground that a search had not been incident to an arrest and was thus "unreasonable" under the Fourth Amendment); and Taylor v. United States, 286 U.S. 1 (1932) (McReynolds, for Van Devanter, Sutherland, and Butler, overturning conviction, based on a warrantless search of defendant's garage, on Fourth Amendment grounds). For additional examples, see Cushman, "The Secret Lives of the Four Horsemen," 639–643.

For examples of cases in which the four justices voted to invalidate statutes on the basis that they restricted preincorporated or incorporated "liberties" of expression, see Fiske v. Kansas, 274 U.S. 380 (1927) (all four justices join an opinion in which the Court overturned the conviction of a member of the International Workers of the World under a criminal syndicalist statute); Grosjean v. American Press Co., 297 U.S. 233 (1936) (all four justices join opinion in which Court strikes down a state statute imposing a tax on newspapers having more than a certain circulation on First Amendment grounds); De Jonge v. Oregon, 299 U.S. 353 (1937) (all four justices join an opinion in which the Court invalidated a conviction of a union organizer under a state criminal syndicalist statute on First and Fourteenth Amendment grounds); Meyer v. Nebraska, 262 U.S. 390 (1923), Bartels v. Iowa, 262 U.S. 404 (1923), and Farrington v. Tokusighe, 273 U.S. 284 (1925) (McReynolds, joined by Van Devanter and Butler in the first two cases and Van Devanter, Butler, and Sutherland in the third, interpreting "liberty" in the Fourteenth Amendment's Due Process Clause to include a right on the part of parents to choose the form of education for their children); and Pierce v. Society of Sisters, 268 U.S. 510 (1925) (all four justices join an opinion upholding the right of parents to send their children to parochial schools on similar grounds).

120. Compare Pearson and Allen, *The Nine Old Men*, 222 ("Some years ago, McReynolds scarcely wrote an opinion . . . Finally, however, criticism in legal circles . . . forced him to bestir himself, and he now turns out a moderate quota of work") with Fred Rodell, *Nine Men*, 219 (1955) ("McReynolds, . . . for some years a lazy judicial workman whose opinions were largely copied from lawyer's briefs, . . . became the New Deal's most vocal and violent Court opponent"). Compare Pearson and Allen, *The Nine Old Men*, 163 ("First and foremost [Brandeis] has been a crusader") with Rodell, *Nine Men*, 227 ("where Holmes was the philosopher, Brandeis was the crusader").

121. "The nine men who are the Supreme Court of the United States are at once the most powerful and the most irresponsible of all the men in the world who govern other men." Rodell, *Nine Men*, 4.

122. "[N]one of the Supreme Court's constitutional decisions . . . can be explained or analyzed or understood . . . except in terms of the justices, the *men*, who made them." Rodell, *Nine Men*, 31 (emphasis in original).

123. Id., ix.

124. Id., 256.

125. Id., 10–11.

126. Id., x.

127. The "mastiffs" description was repeated by Stone to Frankfurter in 1931. See Harlan Fiske Stone to Felix Frankfurter, June 2, 1931, in Felix Frankfurter Papers, Library of Congress. The "Battalion of Death" description was repeated by Frankfurter to Stone in 1936. See Felix Frankfurter to Harlan Fiske Stone, February 14, 1936, Harlan Fiske Stone Papers, Library of Congress. The 1931 letter is quoted by Richard D. Friedman in "Switching Time and Other Thought Experiments: The Hughes Court and Constitutional Transformation," 142 *University of Pennsylvania Law Review* 1891, 1908 (1994); the 1936 letter is quoted in M. Paul Holsinger, "Mr. Justice Van Devanter and the New Deal: A Note," 31 *The Historian* 57, 62 (1968).

128. Pearson and Allen, *The Nine Old Men*, 111. "Most Supreme Court justices," they added, "get so afraid to open their mouths lest some hint of future decision fall forth that they go around with a hermetically sealed expression on their faces. But Stone continues frank and outspoken, though, once or twice, remarks he has dropped to close friends, supposedly in confidence, have burst into print, causing him no end of embarrassment." Id.

129. See Laura Kalman, *Legal Realism at Yale, 1927–1960*, 119 (1986).

130. Rodell, *Nine Men*, x.

131. Rodell, *Nine Men*, 3.

132. G. Edward White, *The American Judicial Tradition*, 199 (2nd ed., 1988). One of the nice things about getting older is a chance to repent previous excesses.

133. The results of the survey were published in Blaustein and Mersky, "Rating Supreme Court Justices," and, in a more extended version, in Albert P. Blaustein and Roy M. Mersky, *The First One Hundred Justices*, 32–51 (1978). For a list of

the sixty-five academics who were asked to rate justices, see *The First One Hundred Justices,* 117–118.

134. Blaustein and Mersky, *The First One Hundred Justices,* 34–37, 40.

135. See Blaustein and Mersky, "Rating Supreme Court Justices," 1186, describing "many" of the participants in the survey as "'liberal' professors." See also Robert W. Langran, "Why Are Some Supreme Court Justices Rated as 'Failures'?" 1985 *Supreme Court Historical Society Yearbook* 9, 14 (1985), referring to "a liberal bias on the part of the evaluators, especially in behalf of both the New Deal and civil liberties."

136. "Many of those questioned for this study admitted frankly that they did not even recognize the names of some of the pre-Marshall Justices, much less have an opinion about them." Blaustein and Mersky, "Rating Supreme Court Justices," 1185. Of the eleven justices appointed to the Court before John Marshall, ten were classified as average. See Blaustein and Mersky, *The First One Hundred Justices,* 40. Several other justices who were likely not well known to the participants in the study, such as John Blair, Thomas Todd, Gabriel Duvall, Samuel Blatchford, and Joseph Lamar, were also rated "average." This suggests that for many of the participants "average" was a residual category into which obscure justices were swept. In contrast, the eight "failures" were all twentieth-century justices, Van Devanter, McReynolds, Butler, James F. Byrnes, Harold H. Burton, Fred M. Vinson, Sherman Minton, and Charles Whittaker. "Failures" were thus justices with whose careers the participants were tolerably familiar.

137. Burton was a member of the NAACP before being appointed to the Court and was a consistent opponent of state-enforced segregation in the years between 1947 and his retirement from the Court in 1958. Minton was an early opponent of racial desegregation, and Vinson was the author of Shelley v. Kramer, 334 U.S. 1 (1948), striking down the constitutionality of judicially enforced racial covenants on the sale of housing. Whittaker joined two 1958 Warren Court opinions finding unconstitutional the expatriation of American citizens, or the deprivation of American citizenship, as penalties for deserting the armed forces in wartime or voting in foreign elections. Participants in the survey were doubtless affected by the fact that all of those justices supported efforts on the part of the federal government in the 1950s to restrict the civil liberties of persons associated with or sympathetic to Communism. See the essays on Burton, Minton, and Vinson by Michael E. Parrish, Richard B. Bernstein, and Murray L. Schwartz in Leonard W. Levy, ed., *Encyclopedia of the American Constitution,* 184, 1262, 1968, 2060 (4 vols., 1986).

138. The only participants I could authoritatively place in that category were Jerome Hall of the University of California at Hastings, Robert A. Leflar of the University of Arkansas, and Alpheus Mason of Princeton University. Some others, such as Walter Gellhorn of Columbia University, Willard Hurst of the University of Wisconsin, and Clarence Morris of the University of Pennsylvania, were of sufficient age at the time of the survey to have been informed observers of the Court's response to redistributive legislation in the mid-1930s, but had not actually joined academic faculties at that time. Even if one were to expand the

number of survey participants who were informed contemporary observers of constitutional challenges to the New Deal in the mid-1930s to ten or eleven, they would still represent only about one-sixth of those surveyed.

139. See Pearson and Allen, *The Nine Old Men,* 325; Rodell, *Nine Men,* 8, quoting Charles Evans Hughes's address at Elmira, New York, May 3, 1907.

10. Cabining the New Deal in Time

1. Particularly since contemporaries in the New Deal period regularly expressed their sense of participating in a period of rapid, transformative change. For samples of such comments from New Deal lawyers, see Katie Louchheim, ed., *The Making of the New Deal: The Insiders Speak* (1983). For a discussion of the tendency of participants in the New Deal to see themselves as creators of a new world of modernist governance, see G. Edward White, "Recapturing New Deal Lawyers," 102 *Harvard Law Review* 489 (1988), reprinted in White, *Intervention and Detachment: Essays in Legal History and Jurisprudence,* 175–203 (1994).

Index

159–163; as symptom rather than cause of changing jurisprudential attitudes, 234–236, 237–239, 304–305
Cover, Robert, 283
Criminal Appeals Act (1907), 70
Cushman, Barry, 21–22, 30, 126, 203, 226, 230; *Rethinking the New Deal Court,* 22, 30
Cushman, Robert: *The Independent Regulatory Commission,* 121

Davis, John W., 126, 206–207
Davis, Kenneth Culp, 124; *Administrative Law,* 19
Davison, J. Forrester, 106, 107, 108
Deferential review, 163. *See also* Bifurcated review
Democracy, 131, 307; republican, 8, 78; and freedom of expression, 145–146, 147, 152–156, 158–159
Democratic Party, 13
Demonization of Supreme Court Justices, 269–273, 284–288, 292–293, 295–298, 300–301. *See also* Butler, Pierce; McReynolds, James; Sutherland, George; Van Devanter, Willis
Dewey, Thomas, 7
Dickinson, John, 105–106, 107; *Administrative Justice and the Supremacy of Law,* 105–106, 107
Discretion, administrative: and agency growth, 114–116; and objections to agency government, 116–121
Discretion, executive, 62, 76–77, 90–94, 307, 309; expanded, 47; in *United States v. Curtiss-Wright Export Co.,* 72–73; in *United States v. Pink,* 85–90
Douglas, William, 85, 87–90, 148, 151
Dowling, Noel, 256, 259–261
Due process, 3, 158, 165, 295, 364n43; substantive, 243–245, 254–261, 262–268. *See also* Due Process Clauses
Due Process Clauses, 24–25, 151, 199, 212, 249, 309, 359n65; glossing of "liberty" in, 169, 217, 219, 220, 241–246, 256–261, 278
Duffus, R. L., 280, 290–291

Economic activity, judicial response to legislation regulating, 203, 250. *See also* Legislation, redistributive
Economic liberty cases, 249, 261–265
Economic theory, described as "laissez-faire," 243, 252, 254, 261–265, 264, 268

Economy, political, 7, 8, 274; and constitutional history, 198–204
Editors, constitutional law casebook: on "rise and fall of substantive due process" narrative, 242–245, 262–265; changing treatment of due process cases by, 258–261
Einaudi, Mario: *The Roosevelt Revolution,* 19
Erie v. Tompkins, 171
Espionage Act (1918), 134, 136, 144
Expertise, as concept in administrative law jurisprudence, 99–100, 104, 115, 118

Fair Labor Standards Act (1938), 227, 228
Farnum, George, 184–187
Farrington v. Tokushige, 162
FCC. *See* Federal Communications Commission
Federal Communications Commission (FCC), 112
Federalism, 71, 96, 332n33; role of, in constitutional foreign affairs cases, 40–42, 49–53, 57, 59–60, 77–84, 89–92
Federal Power Commission, 102, 112
Federal Reserve Bank, 277
Federal Trade Commission, 102, 108, 112, 113, 277
Field v. Clark, 37–41
Fifth Amendment, 90, 153, 244, 359n65; and Due Process Clause, 255; and Just Compensation Clause, 258, 350n79
Filburn, Roscoe, 228–231
First Amendment, 153, 154, 158, 162; as modern source of free speech rights, 132–133, 139–140; as basis for incorporation doctrine, 141–143, 160; as holding preferred position in constitutional interpretation, 144–146. *See also* Constitution of the United States
First Russian Insurance Company, 86
Fiss, Owen, 21
Fitzsimons, Matthew, 275
Flag-salute cases, 146, 152
Foraker, Joseph, 101, 102
Foreign affairs, constitutional jurisprudence of, 11, 33–35, 60–61, 89, 309–310; assumptions of orthodox regime, 35–37; and constitutionality of policy-making, 37–40; federalism paradigm of, 40–42, 70; separation of powers paradigm of, 42–43, 59–60, 77–83, 84–89; role of executive agreements in, 49; effect of emerging totalitarian states on, 62–63; impact of Litvinov Agreement on, 67–69; changes in, 91–93; and free speech, 128